Fostering Independent Learning

The Guilford Practical Intervention in the Schools Series

Kenneth W. Merrell, Series Editor

Books in this series address the complex academic, behavioral, and social–emotional needs of children and youth at risk. School-based practitioners are provided with practical, research-based, and readily applicable tools to support students and team successfully with teachers, families, and administrators. Each volume is designed to be used directly and frequently in planning and delivering educational and mental health services. Features include lay-flat binding to facilitate photocopying, step-by-step instructions for assessment and intervention, and helpful, timesaving reproducibles.

Helping Students Overcome Depression and Anxiety: A Practical Guide
Kenneth W. Merrell

Emotional and Behavioral Problems of Young Children: Effective Interventions in the Preschool and Kindergarten Years
Gretchen A. Gimpel and Melissa L. Holland

Conducting School-Based Functional Behavioral Assessments: A Practitioner's Guide
T. Steuart Watson and Mark W. Steege

Executive Skills in Children and Adolescents: A Practical Guide to Assessment and Intervention
Peg Dawson and Richard Guare

Responding to Problem Behavior in Schools: The Behavior Education Program
Deanne A. Crone, Robert H. Horner, and Leanne S. Hawken

Resilient Classrooms: Creating Healthy Environments for Learning
Beth Doll, Steven Zucker, and Katherine Brehm

Helping Schoolchildren with Chronic Health Conditions: A Practical Guide
Daniel L. Clay

Interventions for Reading Problems: Designing and Evaluating Effective Strategies
Edward J. Daly III, Sandra Chafouleas, and Christopher H. Skinner

Safe and Healthy Schools: Practical Prevention Strategies
Jeffrey R. Sprague and Hill M. Walker

School-Based Crisis Intervention: Preparing All Personnel to Assist
Melissa Allen Heath and Dawn Sheen

Assessing Culturally and Linguistically Diverse Students: A Practical Guide
Robert L. Rhodes, Salvador Hector Ochoa, and Samuel O. Ortiz

Mental Health Medications for Children: A Primer
Ronald T. Brown, Laura Arnstein Carpenter, and Emily Simerly

Clinical Interviews for Children and Adolescents: Assessment to Intervention
Stephanie H. McConaughy

Response to Intervention: Principles and Strategies for Effective Practice
Rachel Brown-Chidsey and Mark W. Steege

The ABCs of CBM: A Practical Guide to Curriculum-Based Measurement
Michelle K. Hosp, John L. Hosp, and Kenneth W. Howell

Fostering Independent Learning: Practical Strategies to Promote Student Success
Virginia Smith Harvey and Louise A. Chickie-Wolfe

Fostering Independent Learning

Practical Strategies to Promote Student Success

VIRGINIA SMITH HARVEY
LOUISE A. CHICKIE-WOLFE

THE GUILFORD PRESS
New York London

A Division of Guilford Publications, Inc.
72 Spring Street, New York, NY 10012
www.guilford.com

Printed in Canada

This book is printed on acid-free paper.

Last digit is print number: 9 8 7 6 5 4 3 2 1

Library of Congress Cataloging-in-Publication Data

Harvey, Virginia Smith.
Fostering independent learning : practical strategies to promote student success / Virginia Smith Harvey and Louise A. Chickie-Wolfe.
p. cm. — (Guilford practical intervention in the schools series)
Includes bibliographical references and index.
ISBN-13: 978-1-59385-451-5 (pbk. : alk. paper)
ISBN-10: 1-59385-451-X (pbk. : alk. paper)
1. Independent study. 2. Learning, Psychology of. 3. Academic achievement.
I. Chickie-Wolfe, Louise A. II. Title.
LB2395.2.H37 2007
371.39′43—dc22

2006102860

To our husbands, Tim and Raleigh,
in gratitude for their support and forbearance

To our children and grandchildren

And to Louis Chickie,
who did not have the opportunity to graduate from high school,
yet became a strong lifelong and self-taught learner
without the benefit of a book such as this to guide him

About the Authors

Virginia Smith Harvey, PhD, is a professor and director of the School Psychology Program at the University of Massachusetts Boston, and was a school psychologist and supervisor in Indiana and New Hampshire for 18 years. Her research interests include study skills, increasing student resilience, and issues relating to the professional development of school psychologists. Dr. Harvey received her doctorate in educational/school psychology from Indiana University, is past president of the New Hampshire Association of School Psychologists, and is a fellow in Division 16 of the American Psychological Association. She frequently gives presentations and workshops at national conferences and is the author of numerous articles and book chapters, including chapters in *Best Practices in School Psychology* and *Helping Children at Home and at School*, and coauthor with J. A. Struzziero of *Effective Supervision in School Psychology*.

Louise A. Chickie-Wolfe, PhD, is currently a teacher of fifth-grade general education, special education, and gifted/talented students in Munster, Indiana. She was an educational/behavioral consultant, coordinator, and special education teacher of children with learning disabilities and/or emotional–behavioral disorders for 27 years, and twice was named Outstanding Teacher of the Year. Dr. Chickie-Wolfe has been cited as a Professionally Recognized Special Educator for Special Education Teaching by the Council for Exceptional Children. She received her doctorate in education and human development from Vanderbilt University and is the author of educational books and materials for teachers, administrators, and parents, including *Cognitive Nourishment: Life-Changing Affirmations for the Savvy Teacher.* For 30 years Dr. Chickie-Wolfe has been an adjunct faculty member at Purdue University Calumet, teaching graduate-level special education and general education courses. She is a private-practice consultant and has presented numerous workshops and seminars throughout the United States and in England.

Introduction

This book will help adults empower students to become independent learners. The topic of study skills often targets mechanics of academic learning and focuses on areas such as improving homework completion and time management. This book goes beyond these mechanics by addressing underlying psychological factors that influence learning. We expand the goals of improving study skills from simply helping students get better grades in school to helping them become independent learners who know how to learn effectively in any life situation. Adopting this expanded focus will enable adults to help students learn independently in academic and nonacademic areas throughout their school years into adulthood.

Our emphasis is on transforming the focus of learning from adult-driven efforts to student self-regulation, such that students become experts in charge of their own learning. This focus entails a shift in the adult–learner relationships: Adults working effectively with students on these skills become collaborating consultants *with* the students, rather than teachers, parents, or experts giving direction *to* the students. The adult assumes a role similar to that of a mentor who advises, guides, and supports from the sidelines. Power is transferred to learners so that they can accomplish tasks more effectively and with less frustration once they understand the methods that work best for them. This approach enables students to control their own learning experiences and even overcome detrimental environmental factors. The goal is to help each individual determine how to learn best—which varies from student to student, from subject to subject, and from situation to situation. Students are encouraged to appreciate that no strategy will be appropriate for every situation, and that they will need to adopt new strategies whenever new challenges present themselves. The adult's role is to help the learner determine what he or she needs to do to become an independent learner such that he or she can "figure out how to learn" everything from algebra to how to download music onto an iPod.

STRUCTURE OF THE BOOK

This book is intended to be a useful guide to helping readers become more proficient, knowledgeable, and successful solvers of problems related to learning in students from upper elementary school through college. In order to design and implement effective interventions that improve students' learning and study skills, readers need to understand the theoretical foundations and current research in these areas. Therefore, we have synthesized current research and data-based interventions across the disciplines of educational psychology, developmental psychology, special education, gifted/talented education, and counseling psychology. We also provide vignettes (with names and identifying details altered to preserve confidentiality) drawn from our combined seven decades of experience in the fields of education and psychology, to illustrate challenges and strengths of learners in various situations. Each chapter concludes with a discussion of moving to student-regulated strategies; materials that might be included in a student's Personal Learning Guide, or How I Like to Learn (HILL) Binder; and reproducible handouts and worksheets, including checklists that summarize the chapter content.

Learning is a complex process with many interconnecting facets. While the book is divided into chapters, this is not intended to suggest that the chapter topics are discrete entities. Indeed, there is continual overlap among topics, and often issues are presented and then revisited from other perspectives in subsequent chapters.

INTENDED AUDIENCE

This book will be a valuable resource for any adults attempting to help students acquire the ability to learn independently, including general education teachers, school psychologists, special education teachers, reading teachers, tutors, school counselors, and coaches. Moreover, other adults who are helping students learn will also find the recommended strategies useful. These might include university professors and student service personnel, therapists, and parents, particularly those who are home-schooling their children.

The strategies and methods described herein can be used in a variety of settings. Many of them can be implemented with an entire class by a general education teacher alone or with the support of a school psychologist or special education teacher. They also can be implemented with targeted small groups of at-risk students, or with individual students, by special education teachers, school psychologists, reading teachers, tutors, and school counselors. Many of the assessment techniques described can be used by educators; a few, such as individual intelligence tests, require the specialized training of a licensed/certified psychologist.

FOREWARNING

We forewarn our readers that they will be constantly thwarted in successfully implementing the ideas in this book. Frustrations will originate from at least three sources.

First of all, this approach is based on a participant model in which the student assumes increasing responsibility for self-managing behavior, controlling the environment, and planning for the future: "The goal of treatment is termination" (Kanfer & Gaelick-Buys, 1991, p. 306). Consequently, an essential first step before independent learning skills can be developed is for the students to perceive a need to change. Unless they perceive this need and desire change, students will have neither any reason to change their approach nor any motivation to overcome longstanding habits. Therefore, readers should collaborate with students to develop the *students'* ability to assess and address their learning skills. Although it may be useful for an adult to determine that a student needs to improve self-regulation of motivation, feelings, behavior, time management, organization, cognitive strategies, reading strategies, writing skills, math/science/technology skills, or test taking and performance, it is much more helpful for the *student* to determine the same. Specific strategies to address resistance and a lack of motivation are included in Chapters 1 and 4.

Second, readers will experience frustration as they collaborate and consult with other adults. Our ecological, systemic focus assumes that the most effective interventions result when families, schools, other sources of social support, and students work closely together. Familial, social, and instructional factors can be modified to support independent learning, but such modifications require collaboration. Overwhelmed, apathetic, or undertrained individuals can resist efforts to collaborate. Further, collaborators also must perceive a need before they will be able to change their approaches or overcome long-standing habits. Readers will need to address these and other negative influences within the school, home, and community. Strategies to this end are included in Chapters 1, 2, and 3.

Finally, readers implementing the ideas in this book will encounter internally derived difficulties. Just as students face obstacles in becoming independent learners, so too our readers will face obstacles as they apply these new skills; they will need to apply the very principles, and follow the very steps, that this book recommends in working with students, just as we authors have had to do in writing this book. That is, the readers will need to consider, address, monitor, and self-regulate their own motivation, emotions, behavior, time, organization, strategies, and physical functioning, and to be sensitive and responsive to the obstacles that prevent consistent implementation of the methods described. Opportunities for procrastination lurk at every turn. Time pressure to perform other tasks, unplanned events, temptations, periods of low motivation, and emergencies can disrupt the best-laid plans. Readers will need to continually resist internal as well as external pressures in order to avoid reverting back to previous, unsatisfactory practices.

To address this issue, we urge readers to self-monitor their *own* performance as well as that of students, gather data about the results, and adjust their own strategies in order to maximize success. Many readers will feel like novices as they learn these strategies, but allowing oneself to tolerate the discomfort of being a novice is a necessary part of learning. Like all novices, readers will experience anxiety and sequential, incremental skill acquisition. Novices need structure, guided learning opportunities, and concrete learning tools; they also need to allow themselves to feel the anxiety inherent in most new learning situations. To foster our readers' learning at the novice level, we include multiple illustrative vignettes and reproducible forms.

Just as students are taught to be aware of and utilize their best learning strategies, the readers of this book need to be aware of and utilize their most effective intervention strategies. It is important not only to use methods that have been proven through empirical research to be effective, but also to use methods that prove to be personally effective and to seek support when appropriate. For example, a school psychologist assigned to multiple schools may need to solicit help from another educator in order to provide daily check-ins for students, because the psychologist may not be available on a daily basis.

Finally, the reader is reminded that *no one person can do it all.* All of us struggle to accept our own limitations—both authors of this book continually struggle to face the reality that there simply isn't enough time to implement all that needs to be done or all that we know will benefit students. No one person can do *everything* that is included in this book! If an obligation to "do it all" is perceived, failure is inevitable. We therefore give official permission for our readers to use only those parts of this book that meet their immediate needs and will improve performance on a case-by-case basis.

Let the learning begin!

Acknowledgments

We would like to acknowledge our many students from whom we have learned so much about studying and learning independently. We would also like to thank Tim Dawson, Raleigh Wolfe, Erin Roberts, Anne Duncan, Peg Dawson, Craig Thomas, and Kenneth Merrell for their support, comments, editorial suggestions, and resources.

Contents

List of Figures, Handouts, Worksheets, and Tables

FIGURES

HANDOUTS

WORKSHEETS

TABLES

1

Working with Students to Promote Independent Learning

Studying is deliberate and purposeful learning that is pursued autonomously.

OVERVIEW

Each component in the definition above is extremely important. Studying is deliberate, not incidental, learning; it is purposeful, not random, learning; and it is autonomous and independent, rather than controlled by an adult. While some students seem to know instinctively how to learn independently, most need to be taught both strategies and methods to implement these strategies.

> **Ruth** has attention-deficit disorder (ADD/ADHD) and a mild learning disability in written language. Throughout her elementary and high school years, she struggled with academics and often felt inferior to her high-achieving friends. She was placed on a Section 504 plan in high school and received some assignment modifications, but the primary interventions were direct instruction in study strategies. Ruth's earlier struggles eventually paid off: The study strategies she learned as an adolescent have enabled her to self-regulate her learning at college, unlike her friends who had "never had to learn how to study." As a college student, Ruth breaks large assignments down into components, begins working on assignments early, and disciplines herself to study and complete assignments before other activities. She uses computer spell and grammar checkers, and also has a friend double-check her papers before submission. She reads assignments before class, takes notes from the readings, and then combines them with her lecture notes to facilitate reviewing for exams, because she knows she can only remember material when it is presented in context. Recently she was so inspired by reading *Emma* for her literature course that she began writing a novel in her free time. Her parents cannot believe that the fourth grader who was frustrated to tears with homework and called herself "stupid" is now a self-motivated, enthusiastic scholar.

How did Ruth learn to become a self-motivated and enthusiastic scholar? How did she learn to self-regulate her motivation, emotions, and behaviors? How did she learn to manage her time and organization? How did she learn which study strategies helped her read, write, and learn well enough that she could generalize them to the self-chosen and highly demanding task of writing a novel? How can adults empower other students to acquire similar skills? This chapter provides an overview of general student considerations relevant to the acquisition of study skills. It focuses on the relevance of self-regulation to factors that must be addressed to help students learn deliberately, purposefully, and autonomously. Concepts contained in this chapter are summarized in Worksheet 1.1, Checklist of Strategies to Promote Independent Learning.

RESEARCH FOUNDATIONS

The topic of "studying" was specifically addressed by neither educators nor research psychologists for many years, because it was presumed that students developed and generalized these skills independently (Rohwer, 1984). Unfortunately, the reality is that unless students are taught specific study strategies, they rarely develop the necessary self-monitoring skills for optimal academic performance (Harvey, 2002). In recent years considerable research has been devoted to examining skills relevant to studying. As a result, shifting from simply teaching specific study strategies to teaching students self-regulation is now recommended (Zimmerman & Martinez Pons, 1986; Zimmerman, 1998b). As indicated by Puustinen and Pulkkinen (2001), a major educational goal should be the "development of self-regulatory skills and the creation of opportunities for life-long learning. Self-regulated learners actively and autonomously guide their own learning and update their knowledge whenever necessary" (p. 283).

The Importance of Self-Regulation

When athletes use "mental training" to improve performance, they set realistic short- and long-term goals, cultivate awareness, harness motivation, deliberately relax the body and mind, experience yet manage negative emotions such as anxiety, improve attention and concentration, and visualize success (Murphy, 2005). Similar methods are used in other disciplines such as music and professional writing, both when skills are initially being developed and when they are being maintained at a professional level. Guided instruction in, and the adoption of, self-regulatory strategies when individuals are learning chess, computer programming, athletics, music, typing, and writing have been found to be more important than innate talent. By the time musicians are top-level performers, they have practiced 10,000 hours—3 hours per day, 6 days per week, for 10 years—a level of sustained practice requiring motivational, behavioral, and emotional self-management (Ericsson & Charness, 1994; Zimmerman, Bonner, & Kovach, 1996; Zimmerman, 1998a).

Similar strategies are employed when successful students learn academics independently: They self-regulate motivation, emotions, behavior, time management, cognition, and context to optimize their learning. They apply specific strategies as they learn, think about how well these strategies are working, and then modify their strategies according to their success (Peklaj, 2002; Schunk & Ertmner, 2000; Zeidner, Boekaerts, & Pintrich, 2000; Zimmerman, 2000b).

Factors and Microprocesses in Self-Regulation

Each factor involved in learning is a component of a dynamic system that continually and mutually influences other factors in the system (Bronfenbrenner, 1979; Shapiro & Schwartz, 2000), as depicted in Figure 1.1. Within each factor, many microprocesses are involved. These include holding positive beliefs about one's capabilities; experiencing and fostering positive emotions about learning; managing goal orientations; setting goals for learning; strategic planning; attending to and concentrating on instruction; using effective cognitive strategies to organize, code, and rehearse information to be remembered; employing metacognitive strategies to assess learning and the efficacy of learning strategies; monitoring performance; managing time effectively; estab-

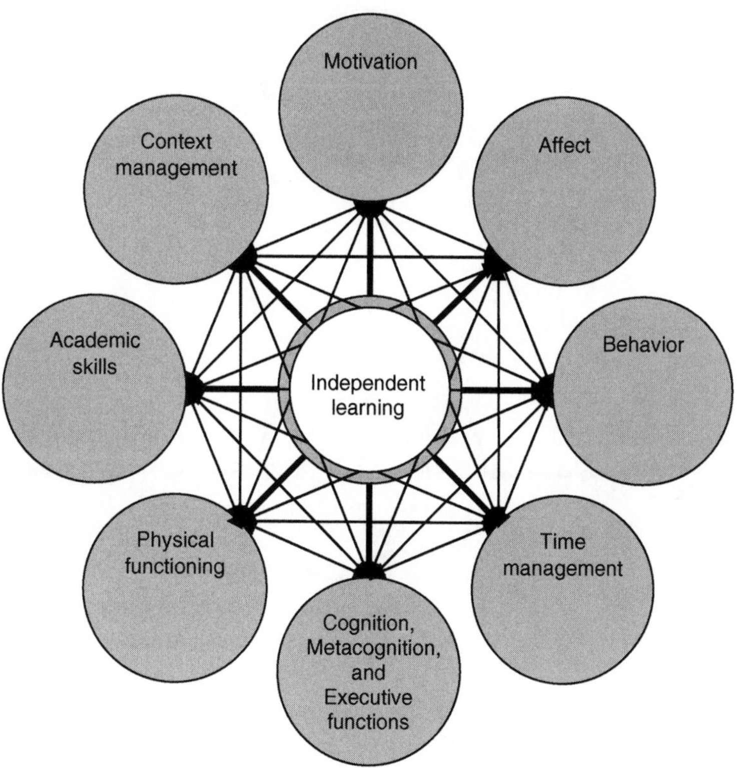

FIGURE 1.1. Student factors involved in independent learning.

lishing a congenial and productive work environment; using resources effectively; and seeking assistance when needed (Schunk & Ertmer, 2000; Zeidner et al., 2000).

While it can be daunting to realize that so many elements are involved and can potentially contribute to difficulty with independent learning, it is also encouraging, because so many elements can be addressed to improve functioning. Just as in family therapy, every component can be seen as part of the problem or, alternatively, as part of the solution (Minuchin, 1974). The use of self-regulatory strategies, particularly organization, record keeping and monitoring, record review, and environment control, predicts academic achievement level 96% of the time (Zhou, Zhang, & Fu, 2001).

Furthermore, instructional, familial, and social factors interact with student factors to form a larger dynamic system (Bronfenbrenner, 1979; Shapiro & Schwartz, 2000). This dynamic is depicted in Figure 1.2. As the figure suggests, the manner in which a student is treated influences his or her performance, and in turn a student's performance influences the manner in which he or she is treated. Highly motivated students have teachers, parents, and friends who respond to them quite differently than do disruptive students who are not highly academically motivated. Likewise, highly motivated students treat parents and teachers differently than poorly motivated students.

The Cycle of Self-Regulation

Models of self-regulation vary somewhat according to an author's theoretical orientation but all agree that self-regulation involves at least three phases (Pintrich, 2000b). Throughout this book we have chosen to refer to these phases as: (1) *preparation* (forethought, task definition, planning, goal setting, task analysis, strategy selection, selection of beliefs such as self-efficacy, outcome

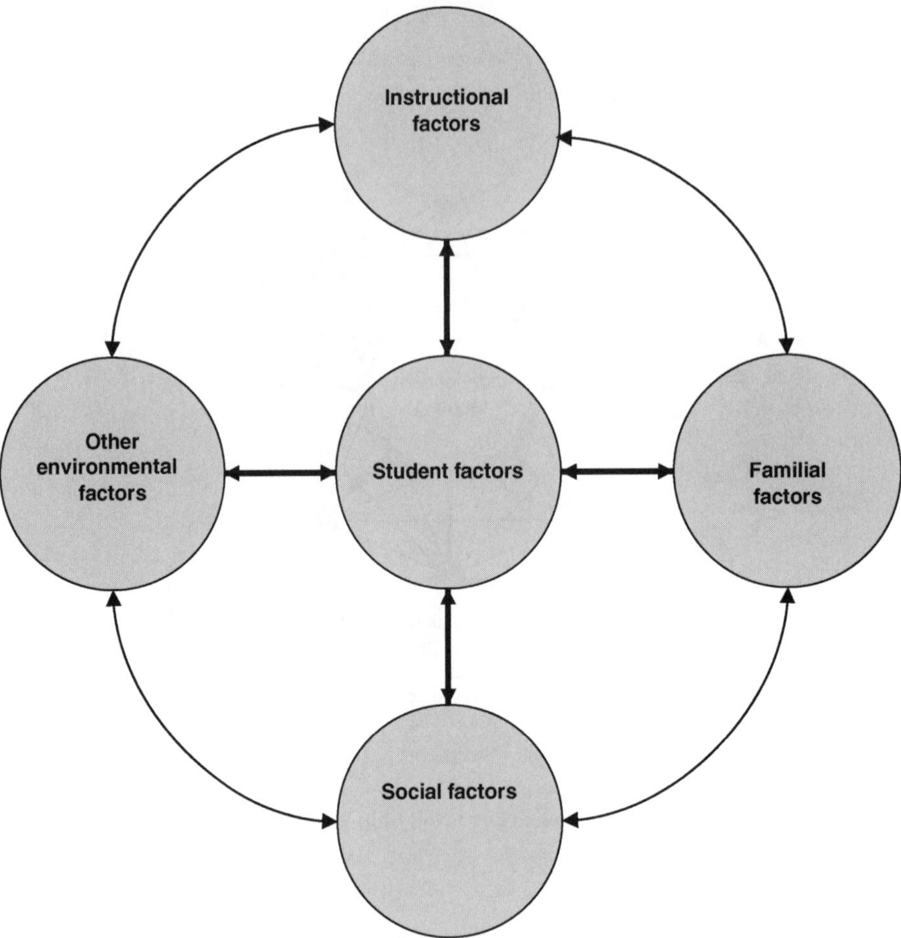

FIGURE 1.2. The interaction of student and environmental factors.

expectations, valuing, and intrinsic motivation); (2) *performance* (goal striving, strategy use, strategy monitoring and revision, self-monitoring, self-instruction, attention focus, self-recording, self-experimentation, and self-control); and (3) *appraisal* (self-reflection, self-judgment, performance evaluation, performance feedback, and self-satisfaction). The appraisal phase leads to subsequent modifications in preparation, performance, and appraisal, in a recurring cycle (see Figure 1.3) that decreases discrepancies between current and ideal performance (Pintrich, 2000b; Puustinen & Pulkkinen, 2001; Zeidner, Boekaerts, & Pintrich, 2000; Zimmerman, 1998a, 1998b, 2000a).

Unfamiliar, nonhabitual learning situations require conscious and deliberate attention to the phases of preparation, performance, and appraisal. When in familiar learning situations, learners proceed through the three phases of self-regulation automatically. However, not infrequently these automated strategies are inefficient, resulting in frustration and learning problems. Thus effective interventions—in truth, the focus of this book—encourage students to examine, evaluate, and modify their automatic and habitual strategies.

The aforementioned microprocesses involved in self-regulation can be organized by considering the domains of self-regulation across all three phases. That is, motivation, affect, behavior, time management, cognition, academic skills, and context can each be considered according to the phases of preparation, performance, and appraisal (Pintrich, 2000b).

For example, a successful self-regulating learner manages *motivation and emotions* throughout the three phases of self-regulation. In the first phase, preparation, the learner adopts effective

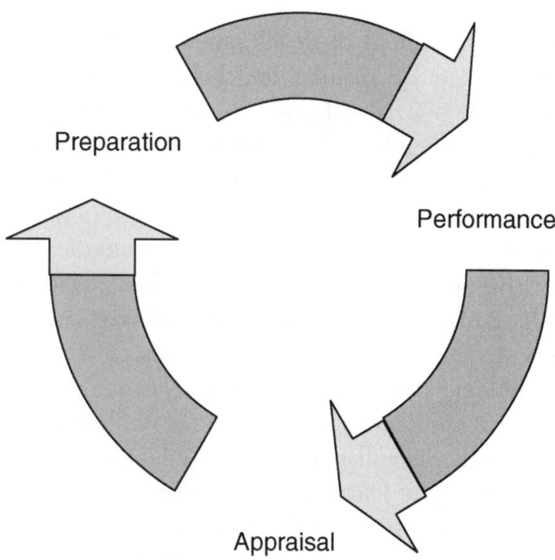

FIGURE 1.3. The self-regulation cycle.

goal orientations and attributions for success and failure, and appropriately accepts responsibility for his or her own learning. In the performance phase, the learner monitors and implements strategies to maintain motivation and regulate emotions. In the appraisal phase, the learner reflects on emotions and motivation experienced during the learning experience and uses those reflections to change future goals, attributions, and emotions.

Similarly, self-regulated learners apply methods of self-regulation to their *behavior and time management*. In the preparation phase, they set goals, plan their time, and break larger assignments into manageable components. In the performance phase, they monitor their behavior through self-observation and control the natural tendency to procrastinate. In the appraisal phase, they reflect on their performance and use those reflections to change their behavior and time self-management strategies in the future.

A self-regulating learner also manages *cognitive and metacognitive strategies* as well as *academic skills* throughout the three phases of self-regulation. In preparation, the self-regulated learner evaluates the current level of knowledge, sets appropriate goals, assesses the learning task, and selects appropriate learning strategies to code and store information. In the performance phase, a self-regulated learner strives to meet goals by implementing the strategies to complete the tasks. In the appraisal phase, a self-regulated learner self-assesses learning and uses those self-assessments to change learning strategies in the future.

Self-regulated learners also plan, monitor, reflect on, and control *contextual factors* that affect their learning (Pintrich, 2000b). In the preparation phase, they consider and adjust contextual factors such as the setting in which they study, the use of resources, partnering with a peer, or seeking help from an adult. In the performance phase, they monitor and adjust contextual factors to take into consideration success or the lack thereof. For example, they seek help when they are "stuck," even though they originally thought they could complete the task independently. Finally, in response to the appraisal phase, self-regulated learners modify contextual factors in subsequent learning experiences.

Finally, self-regulated learners also apply methods of self-regulation to their *physical and neurological well-being*, because these functions have a profound impact on the ability to study and learn independently. Clearly, all effective learning strategies are "brain-based"; the recent explosion of information resulting from new methods of analyzing brain functioning has led to the emergence of the interdisciplinary field of developmental cognitive neuroscience, addressing complex interactions at the molecular, cellular, and behavioral levels. The simplest behavioral tasks involve activity in multiple neural pathways. Because biological systems are embedded in other systems, they are significantly affected by environmental variables, and learning has been found to change brain function in fMRI images, as well as neurological structures (Johnson, 1999; Young, 1994). For example, complex neural systems are involved in the regulation of emotion and motivation. Positive emotions can be distinguished from negative emotions by neurobehavioral features; rewards and positive affect are neurologically linked, as are negative experiences and depression (Forbes & Dahl, 2005). Although the brain's primary growth spurt occurs prenatally and during the first two postnatal years, those brain regions most critical to higher cognition—including reasoning and problem solving, self-regulation, personality, and strategic functioning—have a maturational course extending into adolescence and adulthood. The fact that the portion of the brain critical to self-regulation is still under development has obvious implications for high school and college students' ability to learn independently.

Hopefully, self-regulated students apply their self-regulation to employ regular exercise, maintain general health, and optimally manage any chronic physical disease. In the preparation phase, self-regulating students ensure that they have appropriate nutrition and adequately corrected vision and hearing for the work required. They obtain adequate sleep, because inadequate sleep has a detrimental affect on the ability to focus attention, monitor behavior, and learn (sleep deprivation has been found to be equivalent to the ingestion of two to three alcoholic drinks within an hour in terms of impairing the attention, vigilance, and task performance of medical residents; Arnedt, Owens, & Crouch, 2005). If necessary, self-regulated learners address insomnia by using "good sleep hygiene" (avoiding caffeine, irregular sleep hours, or distressing activities before bedtime), because insomnia not only leads to fatigue but is also associated with depression, anxiety, and alcohol and drug abuse (Taylor, Lichstein, & Durrence, 2003). During the performance phase, self-regulated learners ensure that they are physically comfortable and have adequate lighting. They avoid physical states that are inherently detrimental to learning success, such as drinking alcohol or abusing prescribed or illicit drugs. They also deliberately ration the amount of time they spend on intense studying, because expert learners know that taking regular breaks results in more efficient learning (expert musicians practice 4 hours per day, but take a rest after each hour, since practicing while fatigued is not only ineffective but can be harmful; Ericsson & Charness, 1994). In the appraisal phase, self-regulated students consider physical factors that may have contributed to or detracted from their success, and modify them accordingly during future learning sessions.

METHODS

Preparation

Assessment of Self-Regulation

Self-regulation, like other personality traits, can be considered relatively stable and enduring over time and place, as in a trait theory such as the "Big Five" personality dimensions (openness to experience, conscientiousness, introversion, agreeableness, and neuroticism; McCrae & Costa, 2003). In contrast, self-regulation, like personality, can also be viewed as highly responsive to situational variables, as in social learning theories that emphasize contextual variations in personality (Bandura, 1986; Mischel & Shoda, 1995; Patrick & Middleton, 2002; Winne & Perry, 2000). Finally, self-regulation, like personality, can be viewed from an integrated perspective that combines trait theories with contextual factors (McAdams & Pals, 2006). Assessment of self-regulatory skills from a trait perspective includes interviews, questionnaires, and adult judgments. Assessment from a contextual/event-related perspective includes think-aloud methods, error detection tasks, trace methodologies, observations, and real-time measures. Because of its complexity, the assessment of self-regulatory skills is best conducted using an integrated approach incorporating both trait and contextual factors.

INTERVIEWS

In an unstructured interview, the student is asked to "tell me how you go about learning things for school," and the interviewer asks additional questions only as needed for clarification. As De Groot (2002) indicates, unstructured interviews can be very time-consuming, can be difficult to evaluate, and are highly dependent upon the skill of the interviewer.

In a semistructured interview, the consultant asks open-ended questions and follows up with more detailed questions as the student reveals areas of concern. One semistructured interview technique involves guiding the student in a self-assessment in six steps (Santa Rita, 1997). The consultant helps the student (1) consider goals and objectives; (2) identify barriers to success (e.g., time management, procrastination, lack of positive relationships with teachers); (3) analyze previous grades and other measures of achievement to identify patterns and trends; (4) analyze time expenditure; (5) assess study skills and habits, including note-taking, reading, and test-taking skills; and (6) reconsider goals and objectives. The reader is referred to Worksheet 1.2, Menu of Interview Questions About General Learning Skills for questions that might be used in such an interview.

In the semistructured interview approach developed by Zimmerman and Martinez Pons (1986), the student is asked, "Most teachers give tests at the end of marking periods, and these tests greatly determine report card grades. Do you have any particular method for preparing for this type of test in English or history? What if you are having difficulty? Is there any particular method you use?" (p. 617). Similar questions are asked about planning and writing a short paper outside of class, completing an assignment in class, and working when the student feels unmotivated. For each strategy mentioned, the student indicates how frequently she or he uses each strategy on a 4-point scale, ranging from "seldom" to "most of the time." Strategies are scored on Likert-type scales for the extent to which they reflect self-evaluation, organizing and transforming, goal setting and planning, seeking information, keeping records and monitoring, environmental structuring, self-consequences, rehearsing and memorizing, seeking social assistance, or reviewing records. The reader is referred to Worksheet 8.1 in Chapter 8, which can be used to score student responses to such a semistructured interview.

QUESTIONNAIRES

Questionnaires have been developed to assess students' self-regulation and study strategies. Some of these are completed by students themselves; others are completed by parents and teachers; and still others have parallel forms for students and adults. The latter are clearly the most useful for a collaborative problem solving approach. Unfortunately, the usefulness of self-report and parent/teacher report scales in assessing study skills and self-regulation is limited for several reasons. First of all, although questionnaires can provide helpful data about the use of learning strategies, motivational beliefs, and feelings about academics and school, they do not obtain the "critical information" that is available only through interviews (De Groot, 2002). Information obtained through questionnaires completed by students is also limited by the bias that affects self-reports. Even honest self-reporting is colored by individuals' inner standards if their inner standards are unique relative to the general population. For example, perfectionistic, highly organized persons might describe themselves as "unorganized" because they are comparing themselves to unreasonably high standards. Other students might declare that they "have studied" when they have simply read over the material, because they do not know what studying entails.

Although the instruments that have been developed cannot stand alone as decision-making tools, they can be useful as stimuli for information gathering. Currently there are several questionnaires that consultants may be interested in using. The Behavior Rating Inventory of Executive Function (BRIEF; Gioia, Isquith, Guy, & Kenworthy, 2000) and the Behavior Rating Inventory of Executive Function—Self-Report Version (BRIEF-SR; Guy, Isquith, & Gioia, 2004) are intended to assess the executive function and self-regulation of students ages 11–18. The first is completed by an adult familiar with a student, while the second is individually administered to a student. Both scales yield subscale scores in behavioral regulation, inhibition, behavioral and cognitive shift, emotional control, initiative, working memory, planning and organization, monitoring, metacognition, and global executive skills. Reviewers of the BRIEF-SR (Benton & Benton, in press; Martinez Pons, in press) indicate that it is of limited usefulness, whereas reviewers of the BRIEF indicate that the tool has merit (Fitzpatrick, in press; Schraw, in press).

The School Motivation and Learning Strategies Inventory (SMALSI; Stroudt & Reynolds, 2006) is a self-report inventory appropriate for use with students ages 8–18. It is intended to identify poor learning strategies that have a negative impact on academic performance; it generates scores in study strategies, note-taking/listening skills, reading comprehension strategies, writing/research skills, test-taking strategies, organizational techniques, time management, academic motivation, test anxiety, and concentration and attention.

The Learning and Study Strategies Inventory—High School Version (LASSI-HS; Weinstein & Palmer, 1990) is designed to assesses high school students' attitude, motivation, time management, anxiety, concentration, information processing, ability to select main ideas, study aids, self-testing, and test strategies. It can be administered individually or in a group. Williams (1998) indicates that the norms of the LASSI-HS are not useful, but since it has good content and construct validity, it can help obtain information useful in developing interventions.

The Self-Regulation Strategy Inventory—Self-Report (Cleary, 2006) measures high school students' use of self-regulation strategies. The two motivational beliefs of task interest and perceived instrumentality converge as a higher-order factor. The three factor-analytically derived subscales are: seeking and learning information, managing the environment and behavior, and maladaptive regulatory behaviors. This scale can reliably discriminate between high- and low-achieving ninth and tenth graders.

The Motivated Strategies for Learning Questionnaire (MSLQ; Pintrich, Smith, Garcia, & McKeachie, 1991) was developed to assess self-efficacy, values, learning anxiety, cognitive strategies, metacognitive strategies, and resource management. Although it was standardized with college students, it is appropriate for both college and high school students. It is readily available, since the student services departments of many universities offer online versions for self-appraisal (see, e.g., www.ulc.arizona.edu/quick_mslq.html), and a paper-and-pencil version of the test is available for a modest price from its senior author at the University of Michigan. However, for psychometric reasons reviewers suggest that the MSLQ be considered a screening (or research) instrument (Benson, 1998; Gable, 1998).

The Survey of Teenage Readiness and Neurodevelopmental Status (STRANDS; Levine & Hooper, 2001) provides an overview of an adolescent's perceptions of his or her functioning through a combination of a structured clinical interview and a student-completed questionnaire. This self-report examines the relationship between metacognitive knowledge and psychosocial skills; subtests cover attention, memory, sequencing, language, visual processing, motor functions, organization strategies, higher-order cognition, school skills, school life, social life, school and work preferences, and reasons.

OBSERVATIONS AND BEHAVIOR SAMPLING

Often interviews and questionnaires are not sufficient for assessing self-regulation, because self-reporting is so often poorly correlated with actual behavior (Shiffman & Hufford, 2001). Therefore, supplementing interviews and questionnaires with observations and behavior sampling can provide more accurate information. This is done by deliberately seeking opportunities for students to demonstrate self-regulatory strategies or provide evidence that they have done so in the past.

Observations can occur in classrooms or one-to-one sessions. In both settings an adult observes a student at work and notes the percentage of time the student is on task, as well as any strategies that the student engages in to monitor behavior, such as self-coaching. In *trace methodology*, observable indicators of cognitive strategies, such as highlighting, underlining, creating mnemonics, and studying notes, are collected and examined (Winne, Hadwin, Stockley, & Nesbit, as cited by Puustinen & Pulkkinen, 2001). In *think-aloud* analysis, students stop and say whatever they are thinking when they are working or reading; adults record the students' responses and then analyze the responses for patterns (Sainsbury, 2003).

Error detection task analysis requires that adults develop nonsensical items directly from curriculum materials and use them to check student comprehension. Students can be asked to detect errors such as inconsistencies in reading material, missing elements in math word problems, and inaccuracies in music performance (Koch & Eckstein, 1995; Kostka, 2000; Schmitt, 1988; Stahl & Erickson, 1986; Van Haneghan, 1990; Zabrucky & Ratner, 1992).

Because data based on retrospective recall tend to be both biased and unreliable, *real-time measures* have been developed to ameliorate these effects (Shiffman & Hufford, 2001). One very effective method is to have students monitor the focus of their attention and their studying by recording their studying behaviors in a log. Often students are not aware of the amount of time they waste while "studying" until they keep such a log (Zimmerman et al., 1996). Maintaining a log can be as simple as keeping a weekly 3" x 5" card listing each subject and marking it with a hatch mark for each half hour of sustained attention. More complex logs indicating and evaluating particular activities are included among the worksheets in Chapter 7.

Finally, self-regulation strategies can be monitored in real time by using specially designed software that requires students to log strategies and behaviors at specific times, either generated by a random time sampler or at specific time intervals (e.g., every 5 minutes on the clock). For example, electronic experience diaries (Shiffman & Hufford, 2001) are most often used in medicine, but could be used to assess study habits. Hadwin and Winne (2001) describe a software program designed to foster and monitor psychology students' self-regulation; while complex, it suggests future promise in the development of technology as a tool for assessment, intervention, and promotion of these skills.

Performance

Fostering Self-Regulation

DEVELOPMENTAL FACTORS

Self-regulation may be thought to require some degree of formal operations thinking, insofar as it requires self-reflection and the ability to make and test hypotheses about barriers to self-regulation and learning. Given that most children do not even enter the beginning stages of formal operations thinking until about the age of 11 (Piaget & Inhelder, 1969), and that even many adults exhibit formal operations thought only in areas in which they are expert (Neimark, 1979), it might be concluded that most students are not capable of self-regulatory thinking. However, research has demonstrated that this is not the case. While older individuals are clearly more proficient in formal operations thinking, such thinking is also promoted by direct instruction (Laurendeau-Bendavid, 1977). Furthermore, even students as young as second grade have been found to profit from direct instruction in self-regulatory processes in writing (Perry, 1998). As they achieve success through their selection of learning strategies, students develop positive self-efficacy and attribution, link positive emotions to learning, improve their motivational states, and progress from lower-level to higher-level cognitive skills. These experiences result in the development of self-regulation.

CONTEXTUAL FACTORS

The development of self-regulatory strategies is affected by the context experienced by the learner—including the social context provided by peers, parents, and teachers, as well as the learning environments created in the classroom, school, and home (Puustinen & Pulkkinen, 2001). Self-regulated learning is least likely in highly structured settings where goals are set by others, such as classroom settings with teacher-dictated learning experiences. Conditions that foster self-regulated learning are opportunities to learn, a student-perceived need to learn, affectively charged goals, and contexts that either foster autonomy or are natural (Boekaerts & Niemivirta, 2000; Pintrich, 2000b).

> **Jennifer** is such a gifted soccer player that as an eighth grader she already is receiving tentative offers from college soccer coaches. She began playing soccer at the age of 2, when her 8-year-old brother and father (a former soccer player) began teaching her how to dribble the soccer ball. She was always included in the neighborhood pickup games with her brother's friends, and she and her parents attended every league and school-sponsored game in which her brother played. Jennifer first played on an organized team at the age of 6, and her family has provided ongoing support for her participation in the sport. She loves the game and plays at every opportunity. Jennifer developed superior soccer skills because she had optimal learning conditions: natural physical coordination, enthusiasm, social support, and guided practice that led to her high motivation, hours of practice, and eventual self-regulation.

According to Zimmerman (2000a), the ability to self-regulate is developed primarily through social cognition (Bandura, 1986). The child first observes the self-regulation displayed by parents, siblings, peers, and teachers closely enough that he or she is able to discern important strategy features. The child then imitates these strategies under another's guidance, thereby developing the ability to control emotions, motivational state, cognitive strategies, and performance and behavior under structured conditions. When the child displays these self-regulatory strategies independently, he or she has reached the level of self-control. At the most advanced level, the child generalizes self-regulation strategies to new and diverse situations.

Such learning usually occurs incidentally without direct or deliberate instruction. When a child is exposed to positive models, this can work quite well. However, many students are regularly exposed to models with poor self-control and self-regulation (e.g., parents with poor emotional control, or siblings or peers with poor study skills). These experiences result in learning maladaptive strategies, and interventions in which the students are directly taught successful self-regulatory strategies are needed.

OTHER FACTORS

Dysfunction in self-regulation relative to study skills can also be a result of students' being reactive rather than proactive in their approach to studying, their lack of interest in a particular subject, or a trait such as a learning disability (Zimmerman, 2000a). In addition, self-regulation dysfunction often "appears" when a student moves from highly structured contexts to contexts that depend on self-regulation. For example, many graduate students who excel in structured learning contexts, such as classes with reading lists and specified writing assignments, flounder when they are required to learn and produce independently.

> **Wanda** completed her undergraduate and graduate work with distinction: She finished her undergraduate work with high honors in 3 years, and the coursework for her doctorate with a 4.0 grade point average, in another 3. Six years after she completed her doctoral coursework, however, she has still not completed her dissertation. Although her proposal was accepted, she has neither finished the comprehensive literature search nor collected preliminary data, despite many meetings with Dr. Ray, her dissertation chair. Although Dr. Ray perceives Wanda to have the potential to become an accomplished scholar, he is beginning to admit that she is highly likely to join the 50% of doctoral students who do not obtain doctorates because they never develop the high level of self-regulation needed to complete a dissertation.

Collaborative Consultation

Self-regulatory skills are best taught in a problem-solving approach in which a student, parents, teacher, and consultants collaborate. In this model, each individual has distinct areas of expertise (Kampworth, 2006; Sheridan, Kratochwill, & Bergan, 1996) and students attend school meetings as "experts on themselves." For example, traditional parent–teacher conferences can be reformulated into student-led conferences in which the student explains to adults the work that he or she has self-evaluated and collected in a portfolio (Amatea, Daniels, Bringman, & Vandiver, 2004; Austin, 1994). In the spirit of this model, this chapter on working with students addresses consultation.

Problem-solving consultation identifies general and specific consultation goals, timeframes, confidentiality limitations, and responsibilities of each participant. Meeting notes are taken; an action plan is developed; and every participant leaves each meeting with at least one concrete task to perform in order to help the student (Amatea et al., 2004). Often it is helpful to develop a contract with each person's responsibilities clearly specified (Zins & Erchul, 2002).

The steps involved in "student expert" collaborative consultation are incorporated into Worksheet 1.3, Problem Identification and Intervention Selection Tool, and Worksheet 1.4, Consultation Outcome Monitoring Tool and are summarized within Worksheet 1.1. In this type of consultation, the first step is to *establish collaborative partnerships* and include the student as a full member of the consultation team. Rapport is built with all members; particular care is taken to be sensitive and responsive to differences due to culture/ethnicity, age/generation, and time/work responsibility, and to keep all members engaged throughout all process phases. Using information from all sources, particularly the "student expert," the team then collaboratively *identifies and analyzes the problem*, defining it in specific, measurable, and behavioral terms. The team members also determine the actions that have already been taken to address the problem; gather (or have the student gather) baseline data about the frequency, duration, and severity of the problem; identify the time of day, situations, or conditions most associated with the problem *and* those most likely to alleviate the problem; identify consequences that are helping to maintain the behavior; identify consequences that could be used to reinforce improved performance; assess other environmental variables, such as expectations and attitudes of friends, peers, family members, and others; collaboratively agree upon the acceptable level of performance; and identify resources such as the student's strengths, helpful materials, and supportive individuals. After conducting this assessment, the team *develops a list of possible interventions* by asking the student, parent(s), and teacher(s) what they would like to do next to solve the problem; delineating positive and negative aspects of each possibility; and assessing the need for guided intervention instruction or modeling. The team then *selects* interventions, timeframe, responsibilities, and implementation strategies. Once these selections are made, the interventions are *implemented*, using guided instruction or modeling as necessary. Members of the team then *assess* (or have the student assess) implementation success and modify interventions; *implement* modified interventions and reevaluate success; *develop strategies to promote generalization and student self-regulation*; *implement* these strategies; *reassess* (or, preferably, have the student assess) successes and failures and appraise need for continued intervention use; and return to previous step(s) as appropriate.

Several potential barriers to successful consultation are associated with each step of the consultation process (Ingraham, 2000; Meichenbaum & Turk, 1987; Zins & Erchul, 2002). Collaborative relationships may be hindered by unsatisfactory interpersonal relationships; insufficient communication skills; inadequate interpersonal skills; insufficient involvement or participation on a member's part; dissatisfaction with one another's skills; or insensitivity about relevant cultural, racial, ethnic, gender, or other issues. Participants may also sometimes undermine the consultation process by not engaging in active problem solving, implementing recommendations, challenging unacceptable outcomes, or clarifying problems or interventions. Such disengagement is most likely when an individual's input is ignored or devalued; when follow-up strategies are not implemented; or when irrelevant, limited, or vague interventions are recommended (Slonski-Fowler & Truscott, 2004). Time constraints are often problematic as well. Parents and educators often feel overloaded and pressured for time, and teachers sometimes feel as though time spent in collaborative consultation detracts from the time they need for meeting classroom responsibilities. Finally, students sometimes perceive themselves as passive recipients rather than as active team members.

Difficulties with interpersonal relationships can be manifested by any of the team members: students, parents, and/or teachers. To ameliorate these difficulties, positive interpersonal relationships can be fostered by establishing and nurturing rapport, respect, trust, and collaborative problem solving among participants throughout the process. It is also important to encourage full participation of every member throughout all stages of the consultation process. Collaboration is fostered by the development of common vocabulary and fluency in each other's "language." Concerns about time need to be directly discussed and addressed by careful time management and ensuring that consultation results in meaningful gains. Students can be encouraged to be active members of their own team through being included in the collaborative process, being carefully listened to as "experts" about themselves, and by encouraging them to think positive affirmations such as those found in Table 1.1.

Consultation in multicultural settings requires unique sensitivity and skills. Ingraham (2000) has identified five components of multicultural school consultation: (1) consultant learning and development, (2) consultee learning and development, (3) cultural diversity in consultation con-

TABLE 1.1. Student Affirmations about Independent Learning

- I work as a team member with my teachers and parents.
- I am responsible for my own learning.
- I am a self-starter, and I persevere.
- I have good study skills, and I use them.
- I put forth the necessary effort to learn well.
- I monitor how well my strategies work, and then I change them as needed to improve my performance.

stellations, (4) contextual and power influences, and (5) methods to support consultee and client success. She points out that "it is not the race of the consultant but the attentiveness and responsiveness of the consultant to racial issues brought up in the session that determines ratings of consultant effectiveness and multicultural sensitivity" (p. 324). Cultural differences often result from differences in race or ethnicity. However, they also often result from differences in socioeconomic status, professional identity (the teaching profession might be considered a different culture from that of psychology), or generation/age (there is often a considerable cultural difference between a student and the adult members of the team!).

Addressing interpersonal difficulties stemming from cultural differences requires that adults:

- Develop an understanding of their own culture.
- Develop an understanding of the impact of their own culture on others.
- Respect and value others' cultures; seek feedback and cultural guides; and take care to value multiple perspectives when framing the problem.
- Respect individual differences within cultural groups.
- Understand the impact of multiple cultural identities on individuals.
- Acquire cross-cultural communication methods and multicultural approaches for developing and maintaining rapport, matching methods to the consultee's style.
- Understand appropriate consultation and interventions, given the cultures of students, parents, and teachers in the collaborative relationship.
- Create emotional safety, yet balance emotional support with new learning.
- Provide support in order to build confidence and feelings of self-efficacy.
- Seek systems interventions to support learning and development.
- Model bridging and other processes for cross-cultural learning.
- Continually increase knowledge, skill, objectivity, and reflective thinking.

Given that cultural differences result (as noted above) from differences in age/generation, socioeconomic status, and professional identity, as well as from race and ethnicity, the challenges are many. As Ingraham (2000) indicates, "There is always more to learn" (p. 343).

Problem identification and analysis can be hindered when a student, parent, or teacher does not believe that a problem exists. In particular, the student clearly must agree that a change needs to occur. Successful problem identification and analysis is dependent upon the participants' (1) problem-solving skills; (2) ability to clearly define and analyze attributes of the problem behavior, including its antecedents and maintenance factors; and (3) ability to take into consideration the instructional context, including the situation, tasks, and teaching methods (Rosenfield, 1995). Barriers related to problem identification can be ameliorated by careful attention to each participant's description of the problem, what they have done to solve the problem to date, and additional ideas they have to address the problem (Ortiz & Flanagan, 2002).

Students, teachers, parents, and other educators can be unmotivated or resistant to implementing interventions for a number of reasons. Participants may:

- Doubt that an intervention will be helpful.
- Doubt that they have the skills and knowledge necessary to carry out the intervention.
- Consider the intervention too complex or costly in terms of time or resources.
- Consider the intervention intrusive.
- Feel overwhelmed by an intervention of long duration.
- Find that the intervention does not result in immediate and obvious benefits.
- Have strongly habituated responses.
- Perceive the intervention as a threat to self-image.

- Perceive that there is insufficient support for appropriate implementation.
- Be experiencing personal stress from some other source.
- Experience cognitive dissonance with the concept behind the intervention (e.g., may believe that a positive reinforcement is a "bribe").

To deal with such resistance, the consultant should determine its source, reinforce collaborative and positive interpersonal relationships, and address the resistance realistically by modifying the plan or obtaining additional resources (Kampworth, 2006). Discomfort with sharing "turf" can be minimized by an "exchange of expertise," whereby general education teachers usually provide expertise in curriculum content and consultants usually provide expertise in learning and behavior management strategies. A consultant can provide direct instruction in study skills and metacognition in a classroom, while the regular education teacher acts as a support, followed by a consultants' serving a supportive role by providing extra support for at-risk students working in a small group (Goldberg, 1995).

An instrument called Outcomes: Planning, Monitoring, Evaluating (PME; Stoiber & Kratochwill, 2001) can be used to facilitate the collaborative process. As its name indicates, it provides a procedure to plan, monitor, and evaluate the outcomes of social and academic service delivery programs. This tool helps education teams identify concerns, consider context, measure baseline performance, monitor and graph student progress, evaluate intervention effectiveness, and plan next steps.

Instruction in Strategies

Throughout this book, strategies are recommended to facilitate student functioning. These include cognitive study strategies; methods to improve metacognition and executive skills; and processes to facilitate self-regulation of affect, motivation, and behavior. Many of these strategies will require direct instruction in order for students to become skilled and capable of generalizing them to multiple settings. For students to become independent in their use of strategies, educators must first model the strategies, teach the strategies, empower the students to become independent, and then foster generalization across contexts.

As Gleason, Archer, and Colvin (2002) recommend, first adults model a strategy while exaggerating critical steps, verbally describing the process, and "thinking aloud" questions and comments. Then the adults guide students in their initial attempts at using the strategy, augmenting students' questions and comments with their own. The students are then provided with at least three guided practice sessions with varied materials, decreasing guidance with each session. Finally, the adults determine whether the students can use the strategy independently; the students self-appraise their ability to use the strategy; and the students appraise the effect the strategy has had on their learning. These steps are included in Worksheet 1.1.

When a student is having particular difficulty grasping and applying a new procedure, *self-instruction* can be helpful (Alberto & Troutman, 1995). Boone (1999) investigated the effectiveness of "self-directed instruction" on students' attention, study skills, and grade averages for reading, mathematics, science, and social studies, in comparison with those of a group receiving "teacher-directed study skills instruction" and a control group receiving no instruction. Boone found that self-instruction improved study skills and reduced attention problems. In teaching self-instruction as defined by Meichenbaum and Goodman (1971), an adult follows these steps:

1. The adult ensures that the student understands the purpose of the task.
2. The adult completes the task while talking aloud, modeling problem definition, attention focusing, self-encouragement, self-evaluation, and correction (cognitive modeling).

3. The student completes the task, following the adult's verbal directions (overt external guidance).
4. The student completes the task while self-instructing aloud (overt self-guidance).
5. The student whispers self-instructions while completing the task (faded overt self-guidance).
6. The student completes the task, self-guiding with private speech (covert self-instruction).
7. The student collects data on behavior and assesses the outcome.

With increasing success, external supports are removed so that the student independently approaches learning tasks in an orderly manner (Borkowski & Burke, 1996). Steps to facilitate generalization of study strategies to new learning situations are discussing the benefit experienced by using a previously learned strategy; encouraging the student to enumerate at least three additional settings in which the strategy might be beneficial; encouraging the student to apply the strategy in at least three settings, while monitoring both strategy use and learning success; having the student self-appraise the use of the strategy in multiple settings; and having the student self-appraise learning success after using the strategy in multiple settings. These steps are also included in Worksheet 1.1.

When the school psychologist, **Mr. Jones**, received his fourth referral from the sixth-grade math and science teacher, Ms. Kinsel, he noticed that the referred students all were doing very well in language arts and social studies but failing in math and science. Their sixth-grade language arts and social studies teacher, Ms. Clavier, was extraordinarily organized. She taught her students how to follow routines, how to use assignment notebooks, how to organize notebooks, and how to take lecture notes. Every student knew what to do upon entering the class after the bell, where to place completed assignments, and what to do with free time after completing assignments. In contrast, Ms. Kinsel had a chaotic classroom. Much of each period in her class was spent in transition activities. Students did not know when or where to submit completed assignments, and they were often lost. Unit tests were composed of problems that had been assigned as homework, whether or not they had been actually completed. Little instruction occurred, and misbehavior increased as some students delighted in tormenting their absent-minded teacher. Mr. Jones observed in both classrooms and noticed that Ms. Clavier's class had many characteristics that fostered study skills, while Ms. Kinsel's had very few. He approached Ms. Kinsel with suggestions about improving organization, but she declared that being organized wasn't her style: she thought of herself as a "creative scientist" and wasn't interested in following or imposing "rules." Mr. Jones *was* able to convince Ms. Kinsel to write assignments on the board and have a bin for completed assignments. With her permission, he met with the class members and brainstormed ways they could use the same strategies in math and science that they used in language arts and social studies. The students admitted that they could take notes and use assignment books, even if doing so was not required.

Appraisal

Appraising self-regulatory strategies requires revisiting those strategies that have been employed during a learning experience and determining whether or not they have been effective. Students can be assisted in developing these skills via daily or weekly "coaching" sessions, during which the students review completed activities and apply the questions "What did I do?", "How well did it work?", and "What do I need to change?" (Dawson & Guare, 2004). In addition, many of the assessment strategies discussed above, such as guided self-evaluation, interviews, questionnaires, and trace methodology, can be useful tools in the appraisal process. Worksheets and handouts to assist in the use of these techniques are included at the end of each chapter. Although these subjective techniques are helpful to assess strengths and weaknesses in self-regulation, they should be augmented by quantitative outcome measure data (such as pre- and postintervention scores on weekly or unit tests, curriculum-based measurement scores, and grades). Adults should also help students develop Personal Learning Guides as described below.

Help Students Develop Their Personal Learning Guides (HILLs)

A Personal Learning Guide can be a very effective tool to encourage self-appraisal in regard to developing self-regulation of study skills. Each student's Personal Learning Guide is a sturdy loose-leaf binder into which the student inserts materials tailor-made for his or her personal learning. The intent is for this to be a resource that will be maintained and modified annually, throughout the student's life.

At the elementary and middle school levels, students might be encouraged to label their Personal Learning Guides their How I Like to Learn (HILL) Binders. The acronym HILL is an easily understood metaphor for the challenges (hills or obstacles) they will encounter in learning. Some challenges will be small and readily overcome; others will be more stressful; and some will require a great deal of persistence and application of study skills. Those that are small and readily overcome might be considered small bumps in a road, while the most challenging could be considered mountains—challenging but surmountable with great perseverance. Relative to self-regulation, students can include in their Personal Learning Guides forms and notes regarding strategies that they have found to be particularly effective. Materials pertinent to this topic and appropriate for inclusion in the self-regulation portion of the Personal Learning Guide includes the following:

Worksheet 1.1. Checklist of Strategies to Promote Independent Learning
Worksheet 1.2. Menu of Interview Questions about General Learning Skills
Worksheet 1.3. Problem Identification and Intervention Selection Tool
Worksheet 1.4. Consultation Outcome-Monitoring Tool
Table 1.1. Student Affirmations about Independent Learning

WORKSHEET 1.1.

Checklist of Strategies to Promote Independent Learning

Assess skills.	
	1. The student's self-regulatory traits were assessed, using semistructured interviews and questionnaire (see Worksheet 1.2 and Chapters 4–5).
	2. The student's self-regulatory behaviors and strategies were assessed, using think-aloud methods, error detection tasks, trace methodologies, observations, and/or real-time measures (see Chapter 6–12).
Establish collaborative partnerships in a team composed of the student, parent(s), teachers, and other educators.	
	3. The student is included as a full member of the consultation team.
	4. Rapport is built with all members; differences due to culture/ethnicity, age/generation, and time/work responsibility are respected.
	5. All members remain engaged throughout the process.
Collaboratively identify and analyze the problem.	
	6. The problem is defined in specific, measurable, and behavioral terms.
	7. The actions that have already been taken to address the problem are defined.
	8. Baseline data are gathered (preferably by the student) about the frequency, duration, and severity of the problem before any new intervention is implemented.
	9. The conditions most closely associated with the problem are determined.
	10. The conditions most likely to alleviate the problem are determined.
	11. The consequences that are helping to maintain the behavior are determined.
	12. The consequences that could be used to reinforce improved performance are identified.
	13. Expectations and attitudes of friends, peers, family members, and others are considered.
	14. Home variables are considered (see Chapter 2).
	15. Classroom variables are considered (see Chapter 3).
	16. The team collaboratively agrees upon the acceptable level of performance.
	17. Resources such as the student's strengths, helpful materials, and supportive individuals are identified.
List and select possible interventions.	
	18. The student, parent(s), and teacher(s) are asked what they would like to do next to solve the problem.
	19. Positive and negative aspects of each possibility are delineated.
	20. The need for guided intervention instruction or modeling is determined.
	21. One or more interventions are selected.
	22. Timeframe is determined.
	23. Implementation strategies are determined.
	24. Responsibilities for each team member are designated and written in a contract, which is signed by all team members.

(continued)

Checklist of Strategies to Promote Independent Learning *(page 2 of 2)*

<table>
<tr><td colspan="2">Implement interventions, initially through guided instruction and modeling.</td></tr>
<tr><td></td><td>25. An adult ensures that the student understands the purpose of the task.</td></tr>
<tr><td></td><td>26. The adult models the strategy while exaggerating critical steps such as problem definition, attention focusing, self-encouragement, self-evaluation, and self-correction, and while verbally describing the process and “thinking aloud” questions and comments.</td></tr>
<tr><td></td><td>27. The adult guides the student in initial attempts at using the strategy, augmenting student questions and comments with his or her own.</td></tr>
<tr><td></td><td>28. The student completes the task while self-instructing aloud.</td></tr>
<tr><td></td><td>29. The adult provides the student with at least three guided practice sessions with varied materials, decreasing guidance with each session. The student fades to whispering and self-guiding with private (silent) self-direction while completing the task.</td></tr>
<tr><td></td><td>30. The adult determines whether the student can use the strategy independently.</td></tr>
<tr><td></td><td>31. The student self-appraises his or her ability to use the strategy.</td></tr>
<tr><td></td><td>32. The student appraises the effect the strategy had on his or her learning.</td></tr>
<tr><td colspan="2">Modify interventions if the success of the implemented interventions is less than desired, using steps 1–24 above.</td></tr>
<tr><td colspan="2">Implement modified interventions and reevaluate success, using steps 25–32 above.</td></tr>
<tr><td colspan="2">Reassess (preferably have the student assess) success and appraise need for continued use.</td></tr>
<tr><td colspan="2">Return to previous step(s) as appropriate.</td></tr>
<tr><td colspan="2">Develop and implement strategies to promote generalization and student self-regulation.</td></tr>
<tr><td></td><td>33. Discuss with the student the benefit experienced from using the strategy.</td></tr>
<tr><td></td><td>34. Encourage the student to enumerate at least three additional settings in which the strategy might be beneficial.</td></tr>
<tr><td></td><td>35. Encourage the student to apply the strategy in at least three settings while monitoring both strategy use and learning success.</td></tr>
<tr><td></td><td>36. Have the student self-appraise the use of the strategy in multiple settings.</td></tr>
<tr><td></td><td>37. Have the student self-appraise learning success after using the strategy in multiple settings.</td></tr>
</table>

WORKSHEET 1.2.

Menu of Interview Questions about General Learning Skills

Student ______________________ Date ______________

1. What are five jobs you might like to have as an adult?

2. What are your learning goals for this year?

3. What do you do especially well? What are your strongest skills and abilities?

4. What do you do least well?

5. What are the barriers to your success in school? (Examples might include poor time management, procrastination, or a lack of positive relationships with your teachers.)

6. Looking at your cumulative file, previous report card grades, achievement test grades, and grades on papers and tests, what do you see in terms of patterns and trends?

(continued)

Menu of Interview Questions about General Learning Skills *(page 2 of 2)*

7. Describe how you spend your time outside of school/class.

8. Describe your study habits, including note taking, reading, and studying for tests.

9. Looking at your study aids (schedules that you make, readings that you have highlighted or underlined, mnemonics you use to help you remember, notes you have taken, and outlines/flashcards/study guides you have made), what patterns do you see? Which work best for you?

10. While completing some work, catch yourself every few minutes and identify what you are thinking about.

11. For the next day (or week), keep track of exactly how and when you study and complete homework by maintaining a Homework Log, or keeping a weekly 3" × 5" card listing each subject and marking it with a tally mark for each half hour of sustained attention. What patterns do you notice?

WORKSHEET 1.3.

Problem Identification and Intervention Selection Tool

Date ____________________

Collaboration team members: Student ______________________ Parent(s) _______________

Educators ____

1. Problem identified and analyzed:
   a. Specific, measurable, and behavioral definition of the problem:

   b. Actions that have already been taken to address the problem:

   c. Baseline data about the frequency, duration, and severity of the problem behavior:

   d. Time of day, situations, or conditions most associated with the problem behavior:

   e. Time of day, situations, or conditions most likely to alleviate the problem behavior:

   f. Consequences that are helping to maintain the behavior:

   g. Positive consequences that could be used to reinforce improved performance:

   h. Other environmental variables, such as expectations and attitudes of others:

   i. The acceptable level of behavior:

   j. Resources (such as the student's strengths, helpful materials, and supportive peers and adults) that can be used for intervention implementation:

(continued)

Problem Identification and Intervention Selection Tool *(page 2 of 2)*

2. All team members' ideas about what they would like to do next to solve the problem:

3. Possible interventions and their positive and negative aspects:

4. Selected intervention(s):	Person(s) responsible:	Implementation date(s):

WORKSHEET 1.4.

Consultation Outcome-Monitoring Tool

Date ______________________________

Collaboration team members: Student ____________________ Parent(s) __________________

Educators ____

1. Initial assessment of implementation's success, using (baseline) data measures about the frequency, duration, and severity of the problem behavior. Date: ____________

2. Modification of interventions needed:

3. Assessment of modified implementation's success, using (baseline) data measures about the frequency, duration, and severity of the problem behavior. Date: ____________

4. Strategies to promote generalization and student self-regulation:

5. Reevaluation of implementation's success, using (baseline) data measures about the frequency, duration, and severity of the problem behavior. Date: __________

6. Six-month follow-up results. Date: ________

7. One-year follow-up results. Date: ________

2

Working with Families and Friends to Promote Independent Learning

Family members' and friends' support of academic achievement is highly correlated with students' success.

OVERVIEW

Clair had an assignment to build a working model of a medieval trebuchet. As directed, she researched trebuchets on the Web and located a picture to help with her design. Her father helped her refine the design and find materials around the house to use in its construction. Clair's father supervised her as she used a drill and saw to construct the model, and then helped her use the scientific method to "test and tune" the machine until it could propel a wad of Silly Putty at least 3 feet. Clair met the assignment objectives of researching on the Internet, building a machine that worked, and testing it by using the scientific method. She also learned that she has the ability to successfully plan and execute a complicated project, and that her father believes schoolwork is important. Best of all, she and her father had fun working together.

Clair obtained home-based support that directly resulted in academic success. Her father did not build the trebuchet for her, but provided support, encouragement, and knowledge. How did Clair's father know how to be appropriately involved—when to help and when to expect independence? How did he turn what could have been a frustrating experience with unfamiliar information and challenging new tools into an experience that he and his daughter enjoyed sharing? How can family members and friends similarly support students as they learn?

This chapter reviews strategies to help families support students as they study and learn independently. The reader is referred to Worksheet 2.1, Checklist of Home Qualities that Foster Independent Learning for a concise list.

RESEARCH FOUNDATIONS

Although we think of studying and independent learning as resulting from individual goals and behaviors, they are actually socially mediated. "Self-regulation" implies that *internal* forces regulate behavior, but the ability to self-regulate is predicated upon *environmental variables* (social, physical, and economic) that are not universally available. In addition, when students self-regulate they compare their current performance with an ideal and adjust future behavior to better approximate that ideal. Yet such ideals are culturally embedded because they are developed in a "network of socially mediated factors, such as family, organizational, and group-based needs, goals, and desires" (Jackson, MacKenzie, & Hobfoll, 2000, p. 276).

Furthermore, students have difficulty succeeding in school without familial support (Hale, 2001; Christenson & Anderson, 2002), and positive peer relationships are also critical (Wentzel & Watkins, 2002). One factor that distinguishes high-achieving students from low-achieving students is that they seek help: 50% of high-achieving students seek help from peers and 35% seek help from adults, while only 23% of low-achieving student do so (Zimmerman & Martinez Pons, 1986). Thus, even though students often need help when they attempt to study and learn, many need to be encouraged to seek help (Balli, Demo, & Wedman, 1998).

The involvement of parents and parent figures (such as custodial adults) in students' education is closely tied to school attendance, higher achievement test scores, increased homework completion, more appropriate behavior, and improved high school completion rates (National Middle School Association, 1995; Northwest Regional Educational Laboratory, 1999; U.S. Department of Education, 1997). While most educators intuitively understand that parental involvement is important, they sometimes mistakenly believe that involvement is defined by attendance at school functions such as conferences and PTA meetings. In truth, the most important type of familial involvement is home-based support (Fantuzzo, McWayne, Perry, & Childs, 2004). Home-based *positive relationships*, *supportive beliefs*, and *provision of learning opportunities* are manifestations of family involvement that improve students' learning.

Relationships and Parenting Styles

Child–parent relationships and parenting styles affect students' ability to develop self-regulated learning. Children and adolescents perform best academically when raised in homes where parents or parent figures have an *authoritative* parenting style (high but reasonable demands, good communication, and mutual respect). Children and adolescents do less well when raised in homes with parents or parent figures who are overly *permissive* (too lenient, uninvolved, or with few or no expectations) or *authoritarian* (strict, unyielding, leaving no room for negotiation, and emotionally closed) (Baumrind, 1991; Steinberg, Lamborn, Dornbusch, & Darling, 1992). These differences continue through the college years (Strage, 1998).

Friends' support also affects students' ability to self-regulate. For example, the most common reason adolescents give for not exercising is a lack of support from friends (Field, Diego, & Sanders, 2001). If students do not have friends and are socially isolated or rejected, their engagement in school decreases, and their academic success diminishes correspondingly (Juvonen, Nishina, & Graham, 2000; Wentzel & Asher, 1995). If they do have friends, the social group to which students belong influences academic effort, habits, motivation, and time spent on academic work. Friends can provide one another with academic support, make learning more pleasurable, and increase one another's desire to succeed academically (Barber, Eccles, & Stone, 2001; Christenson & Anderson, 2002; Malecki & Elliott, 2002; Wentzel, 1993).

Even acquaintances, such as peers who are not friends, significantly affect students' ability to study and learn independently (Schunk, 1987). As they move into secondary school, students increasingly turn to peers for information, support, and coping strategies. Insofar as students perceive peer relationships as positive and supportive, their motivation is increased, and their academic success is positively affected (Wentzel & Watkins, 2002).

Supportive Beliefs

The attitudes toward, and beliefs regarding, learning and academic achievement held by people to whom a student is emotionally attached—family members and friends—profoundly influence academic effort and the student's own beliefs about what it takes to do well in school (Stipek & Gralinski, 1991). Parents consciously and unconsciously convey beliefs and attitudes about learning, education, and their children's potential to them, and in turn students frequently adopt an academic self-image based on their parents' beliefs (Sigel, McGillicuddy-DeLisi, & Goodnow, 1992). In fact, Phillips (1987) found that students are more likely to believe parental assessments of their academic skills than information contained in their own cumulative records!

Provision of Learning Opportunities

The provision of learning opportunities in the home is manifested by active promotion of a *learning environment* (such as ensuring that children have access to reading material they find interesting), provision of *learning activities* (such as lessons in an area of interest), *parent–child conversations* about school and school activities, the promotion of *educational experiences* (such as going to the library), and *homework supervision* (Bempechat, 2004; Bempechat, Drago-Severson, & Boulay, 2002). Students whose families support intellectual development experience more familiarity with school-like tasks (Grolnick & Slowiaczek, 1994) and are encouraged to do more homework and reading at home (Hoover-Dempsey et al., 2001).

Familial homework supervision, particularly in the elementary and middle school years, makes it much more likely that homework will be completed. Successful homework completion has several benefits. It can cause children to believe they can face challenges and achieve throughout life (Bempechat, 2004); help them develop adaptive motivational skills, including responsibility, confidence, persistence, goal setting, planning, the ability to delay gratification, and the ability to self-regulate (Epstein & Van Voorhis, 2001; Warton, 2001); reinforce classroom learning; and increase academic achievement, particularly at the secondary level (Cooper, Valentine, Nye, & Lindsey, 1999), because the amount of time devoted to homework is positively correlated with academic success (Trautwein & Köller, 2003).

However, successful homework completion at home requires considerable familial commitment and can be perceived as an infringement upon family life (Xu & Corno, 1998). It can be especially overwhelming to parents with limited time, resources, or education. Although some parents know how to provide appropriate support and a positive atmosphere, probably because their parents did so, many parents struggle with this.

Parents do understand that they can positively influence their children's academic progress and that teachers expect them to help their children with homework (Hoover-Dempsey et al., 2001). Contrary to some stereotypes, parents across socioeconomic levels and ethnic groups are willing to help their children with homework and believe that doing so is part of their job as parents. Both middle-income and low-income parents usually provide a daily structure and place for homework completion; clearly communicate expectations and standards for behavior and academic performance; monitor due dates for assignments; share personal stories to motivate their children; visit the school when possible; and help with homework, even if they have difficulty understanding it (Delgado-Gaitan, 1992). Drummond and Stipek (2004) found that low-income parents of diverse ethnic backgrounds (African American, European American, and Latino/Latina) all indicated that helping their primary-level children with their homework was a very high priority. Across ethnic groups, low-income parents care deeply about their children's intellectual development, and they employ rich and varied means to encourage both a love of learning and a deep value for education (Ogbu, 1995). Low-income parents want children to be challenged and prepared for the competitive world of work; they recognize that homework completion is an integral part of this preparation.

However, parents also indicate that they sometimes have difficulty helping with homework because they do not have sufficient knowledge—for example, of math concepts—to help appropriately (Balli et al., 1998). Parents with lower levels of education have been observed to have difficulty with the vocabulary and mathematical calculations required at the elementary level, much less at the secondary level. Further, low-income parents have indicated that they have limited time to be involved in children's education, as well as a lack of self-confidence regarding educational matters (Lareau, 1996; Shumow, 1998; Shumow & Miller, 2001). Family members of all socioeconomic levels struggle with homework supervision because of busy or conflicting schedules—whether the conflicts arise from students' extracurricular activities or from parents' work responsibilities.

Further, individual students need varied degrees of parental supervision. Children who have significant difficulty with homework require intensive parental involvement—often a structured homework completion program developed through conjoint parent–teacher–student–consultant behavioral consultation (Sheridan et al., 1996). Such programs can be highly effective at increasing the rate of homework completion even for students who were previously failing, and the effect has repeatedly been found to extend past treatment (Rhoades & Kratochwill, 1998; Weiner, Sheridan, & Jenson, 1998). After such a program, Cancio, West, and Young (2004) found that homework completion rates rose from 2% to 92%, and scores on standardized individual achievement tests rose an entire year in 4 months!

However, family members can accidentally provide support that is counterproductive to their children's learning. For example, they might overemphasize word-calling accuracy at young ages and discourage early, developmentally appropriate attempts at reading and writing (such as invented spelling). Parents have been observed offering very limited strategies for problem solving (e.g., saying "sound it out" in response to every misread word, rather than encouraging children to use contextual cues). Or adults and siblings trying to help students with homework might simply correct errors, rather than ask students how they might solve a problem and then help with solution implementation (Perry, Nordby, & VandeKamp, 2003). Furthermore, parents can increase negative emotions associated with homework. Milgram and Toubiana (1999) studied the interplay of academic anxiety, academic procrastination, and parental involvement. They found that academic anxiety and procrastination were both associated with high levels of parental criticism and an authoritarian parenting style. On the other hand, when homework is successfully supervised at home, there are several benefits. Homework:

- Provides students with opportunities to develop specific study strategies and methods, because it is difficult to learn independently in distracting classrooms.
- Provides a venue for communication between parents or parent figures and their children regarding academic matters, thereby giving daily opportunities for the adults to be involved in their children's education and day-to-day lives. Shumow and Miller (2001) found that parental involvement in monitoring homework was closely associated with adolescents' orientation toward school—the more involvement, "the more important students thought it was to learn and perform well in school" (p. 84).
- Provides parent figures an opportunity to convey positive attitudes toward academic achievement. At all grade levels, parental attitudes about homework predict children's attitudes and beliefs about homework. At the secondary level, these attitudes and beliefs are reflected in student achievement (Cooper, Lindsey, & Nye, 2000).
- Provides parents an opportunity to teach their children methods to solve problems, manage challenges, and deal with frustration.

In short, "parental involvement in homework is important, not just because it provides immediate assistance to students, but because this involvement models positive attitudes and study skills needed to succeed in school. Parents make particularly strong models because children see parents as both competent and similar to them" (Keith, Diamond-Hallam, & Fine, 2004, p. 226).

Though it may be difficult for some parents to imagine while in the midst of "the homework battles," it is actually possible for parents to engineer homework completion so it is primarily an enjoyable experience and provides a positive learning environment for their children. In fact, this is just what parents of successful students do. Xu and Corno (1998) videotaped and analyzed the homework environments of six ethnically diverse, middle-class families of high-achieving students. They found that even successful students frequently experienced negative moods when doing homework, but that their parents significantly helped minimize the effect of these emotions.

METHODS

Improving student study skills involves facing the challenge of facilitating home-based positive relationships, supportive beliefs, and provision of learning opportunities. Doing all this requires the same phases students use in self-regulation: preparation, performance, and appraisal.

Preparation

When working with families and friends to help students study and learn independently, educators develop a "student expert" collaborative consultation process, address barriers to home–school collaboration, and assess strengths and weaknesses in social supports. Developing a "student expert" collaborative consultation process has been addressed in Chapter 1, and the reader is referred to that chapter. As they develop collaborative relationships with families, educators will need to be sensitive to and address barriers to home–school relationships. These may include time constraints due to child care and work schedules, transportation constraints, cultural and language differences, expectations that educators will be unresponsive to parental needs or desires, previous negative experiences with schools, the perception that education is solely the province of schools, feelings of inadequacy, lack of experience, limited knowledge regarding or access to resources, and limited resources (Christenson, 2004; Ortiz & Flanagan, 2002).

Assessment

Assessment methods specifically germane to families and friends can include semistructured interviews, observations, and rating scales.

INTERVIEWS AND OBSERVATIONS

Interview questions that might be used to assess a student's perceptions regarding familial characteristics, parent–child relationships, and friends' attitudes toward academics are included in Worksheet 2.2, Menu of Interview Questions about Family and Friends. Parallel questions that might be used to assess a parent's perceptions regarding home variables are included in Worksheet 2.3, Menu of Interview Questions for Parents. Educators can directly assess parenting style, involvement, aspirations, and support by observing parent–child interactions, particularly when parents supervise a student completing a homework assignment. Finally, educators can assess the strengths and weaknesses of a student's social support systems by *observing* in a classroom or small-group setting while friends or peers work together to complete a collaborative assignment or study for a test.

RATING SCALES

Several rating scales provide opportunities for parents to express concerns regarding their children's self-regulatory strategies and emotional regulation. These include the Behavior Rating Inventory of Executive Function (BRIEF; Gioia et al., 2000) and the Behavior Assessment System for Children, Second Edition (BASC-2; Reynolds & Kamphaus, 2004). These are discussed in more detail in Chapters 1 and 5, respectively.

Two rating scales may assist in assessing the quality of parent–child relationships. The Parent Success Indicator (Strom & Strom, 1998) has two forms, one to be completed by parents and one to be completed by students. It was developed for students ages 10–14 and is available in English, Spanish, Japanese, and Mandarin. Designed to be used before and after a parent education program as well as for individual consultation, the scale generates six subscales: communication, use of time, teaching, frustration, satisfaction, and information needs. Solomon Scherzer (in press) and Young (in press) indicate that the instrument is technically sound and suggest using it to generate conversations in parent groups or in parent–child relationship work.

The Parent–Child Relationship Inventory (PCRI; Gerard, 1994) was developed to assess parents' attitudes toward their parenting and their child. Reviews of the PCRI (Boothroyd, 1998; Marchant & Paulson, 1998) indicate that it is psychometrically sound, although it was developed with a restricted sample. Again, the items can be helpful in generating information and discussions.

After conducting interviews and observations and using selected rating scales, educators can use the Worksheet 2.1 to integrate information and facilitate collaborative problem solving and intervention design.

Performance

Educators can enable families to support students as they study and learn by focusing on the following areas:

1. Increasing motivation.
2. Fostering positive emotions about studying and learning.
3. Helping children identify and cope with negative emotions about learning.
4. Fostering positive behavior.
5. Fostering time management and organization at home.
6. Fostering children's mastery of study skills in specific areas.
7. Helping parents support their children as they prepare to take tests.
8. Fostering home–school communication and collaboration.

Increasing Motivation

Parents can increase their children's achievement motivation by providing verbal encouragement, attempting to make the homework more interesting, and ensuring that the children have a chance to engage in preferred activities after completing homework. Motivation is improved by fostering positive parent–child relationships, fostering children's talents and interests, expressing beliefs that academic success is possible, maintaining clear academic and behavioral expectations, discussing and prioritizing goals, providing a positive learning environment, and supporting children's efforts.

FOSTERING POSITIVE PARENT–CHILD RELATIONSHIPS

Since motivation is increased by positive and respectful parent–child relationships, fostering such relationships at home is critical. At times, parents will need to find more ways to "like" their children. This is especially true when a child has a particularly difficult temperament, reminds a parent of a disliked relative or ex-spouse, or develops an "adolescent attitude" of resistance.

Educators can work with parents to improve child–parent relationships by encouraging parents to talk respectfully, listen nonjudgmentally, provide help, share mutually enjoyable activities, and make a deliberate effort to keep everyday routines and chores pleasant. Spending 15 minutes per day sharing an activity of the child's choice ("special time") can be an effective relationship-building method, as can having open conversations while driving together in the car. Some parent–child relationships will be so toxic that the educator will need to refer the family to family therapy. Less negative relationships, however, are often responsive to following the "Fish philosophy": "Be there, play, make their day, and choose your attitude" (Lundin, 2006; Lundin, Paul, & Christensen, 2000).

FOSTERING CHILDREN'S TALENTS AND INTERESTS

Because motivation is increased when children have opportunities to develop individual interests, educators can help parents become aware of and attend to their children's unique talents and interests. Parents can help children become experts at an activity or topic in which they are naturally interested (e.g., music or sports) and use this opportunity to encourage their children to read, write, look up information in the library or on the Internet, and learn about that area of interest in depth. Students can express areas of interest in responses to Worksheet 1.2 and Worksheet 4.2, as well as in other tools and assessment instruments.

EXPRESSING THE BELIEF THAT ACADEMIC SUCCESS IS BOTH POSITIVE AND DESIRABLE

As mentioned previously, parents have considerable impact on their children's understanding that they have control over academic success and that success in school is not luck or due to "good" teachers, but a result of effective studying. To help parents convey these beliefs, educators need to consider familial and student characteristics, because there is considerable variation among families (and even from child to child within one family) in this regard. The parent affirmations in Table 2.1 can help support positive beliefs and attitudes.

MAINTAINING CLEAR ACADEMIC AND BEHAVIORAL EXPECTATIONS

Parents can increase their children's motivation by maintaining high but reasonable expectations. It's best when parents provide a balance of reasonable structure (chores and expectations) and freedom, so that their children become both responsible and independent. When an adolescent develops an intense need for freedom and becomes argumentative, educators can encourage parents to "pick their battles." For example, parents can be urged to see the benefits of permitting increased autonomy in areas that are not likely to have negative lifelong consequences (such as bedroom cleanliness), while standing firm in those areas that do (such as dropping out of school).

TABLE 2.1. Parent Affirmations

- I provide a good study environment for my child.
- I make sure my child has the necessary materials to study properly.
- I keep others from interrupting my child when he or she is studying.
- I am aware of how my child is doing in school.
- I encourage my child to be an independent learner.
- I provide assistance when it is appropriate, but I do not *do* my child's work.
- Once I am sure my child knows how to do the work, I move away and allow independence.
- I praise my child for good effort and perseverance.
- I provide tutors when necessary.
- I quiz my child before a test and give specific feedback on what needs further studying.
- I am careful not to put undue pressure on my child.
- I value learning, and everyone in my household is aware of that.
- I model good study skills for my child.
- I use common sense regarding my child's schoolwork.
- I reward a job well done.
- I encourage my child to strive for his or her personal best.
- I do not overschedule or overcommit my child's time.
- I make books, newspapers, and other learning materials readily available in my home.
- We discuss interesting topics in our home each day.
- I use vocabulary terms that "stretch" my child's knowledge and relate to what is being learned.
- I encourage my child's use of new vocabulary words learned at school.
- I limit and monitor my child's use of the television and computer for non-school-related activities.
- I limit my child's use of the telephone and instant messaging.
- I keep open lines of communication with my child and his or her teachers.
- I attend school conferences and participate in school activities.
- I am flexible and change my plans to accommodate homework requirements whenever possible.
- I do not bail out my child when he or she makes an irresponsible choice.
- I provide support and encouragement to my child.
- I do not lie for my child.
- I listen carefully to my child and am not judgmental regarding his or her emotions.
- I model lifelong learning for my child.

Marc's parents allowed him to paint his bedroom walls deep purple, and, though they were honest in their distaste for multiple body piercings, refrained from making them a cause of household battles. On the other hand, they never wavered from expressing the expectation and requirement that Marc would maintain at least a B average and go on to complete college.

Effective parenting skills, including authoritative parenting styles and positive parent–child relationships, can be fostered in parent training programs. For example, Bronstein et al. (1998) developed a program entitled Aware Parenting, designed to prevent low-income students' decline in academic functioning upon their entrance to middle school. In this program, consultants provided education support groups for parents of sixth-grade students, and these sessions resulted in changed parenting strategies that persisted for a year.

DISCUSSING CHILDREN'S SHORT- AND LONG-TERM GOALS, AND HELPING THEM PRIORITIZE THESE

Children's motivation is fostered when parents collaborate in developing academic and learning goals. A long-term goal might be a certain career. A short-term goal might be learning how to compute decimals well enough to calculate sports statistics—*and* obtaining a grade of B or better on a test. The best goals address learning and obtaining "good" grades rather than avoiding failure. It is critical that these goals are shared by the children and not held solely by parents.

Educators may need to encourage parents who have not attained high educational levels themselves, or who are economically disadvantaged, to develop high yet realistic aspirations for their children. This may involve helping parents become aware of resources and opportunities, as well as of successful individuals from similar circumstances who can serve as mentors and role models for their children. Worksheet 4.3 can be used to help parents and students develop goals. At times, educators will need to help students and their families reconcile conflicting goals and priorities.

> **Ann**, a sixth grader, was seemingly compliant but did poorly in school because she did not complete homework. The school psychologist met with Ann and found that her entire family participated in church activities three evenings a week and all weekend, giving Ann no time at home to complete her assignments. When the school psychologist met with Ann and her parents, it became obvious that her parents wanted Ann to do well in school, but were unaware of the amount of schoolwork she needed to complete during the evening hours. They also wanted Ann to "be with the church family" and did not want to leave her alone at home. Being very careful to express respect for the family's faith and admiration for their values, the school psychologist helped the family realize that they were inadvertently conveying to Ann that schoolwork and academic success were unimportant. As a group, they brainstormed solutions and determined that the most satisfactory strategy was to set up a study corner for Ann in the corner of a church school room, away from other activities, where she could complete her work.

PROVIDING A POSITIVE LEARNING ENVIRONMENT

Both at home and by exposing children to community activities, parents foster a positive learning environment. Parents can model curiosity; encourage their children's curiosity; and take them to the library, museums, or other sites for learning experiences. It is obviously best when these activities are in a child's areas of interest. Even attending a motorcycle show can be a powerful learning experience when a parent encourages the child's interest, curiosity, enthusiasm, and application of academic skills.

When it is not possible for families to provide positive homework supervision, homework-away-from-home programs can be helpful. Although these homework completion programs sometimes do not have as much positive impact on grades as does homework completed at home (Keith et al., 2004), after-school homework support programs can reduce at-risk children's likelihood of starting the "failure spiral" in school (Cosden, Morrison, Gutierrez, & Brown, 2004). Regular attendance in a homework program improves study skills and provides structured opportunities for homework completion. They seem to be particularly helpful for those students whose parents do not speak English and therefore have great difficulty assisting with homework, or for those in need of increased access to adult mentors. Clark (1990) reported that high-achieving students who lived in large urban areas typically spent between 25 and 30 hours per week in constructive learning experiences in addition to time in school. During these hours, the students received critical support and guidance from mentoring adults other than their parents, such as coaches, ministers, tutors, and relatives.

Educators can help students and parents determine when such a program is necessary, and help them locate appropriate venues. Educators can also play a pivotal role in designing and providing such programs. For example, school psychologist Chuck Ott developed and ran an after-school care program located in the community room of a low-income housing project. Dr. Ott taught resident teenagers and elderly adults how to serve as effective homework tutors and mentors to younger children. The program provided supervised after-school care, homework supervision, recreational activities, and snacks; it significantly improved both the children's and adolescents' academic functioning and behavior (C. Ott, personal communication, 1991).

PRAISING AND SUPPORTING CHILDREN'S EFFORTS

To help students understand that effort is paramount, educators should encourage parents to focus on students' effort and on the quality of their work, rather than strictly on grades received. In other words, educators can help parents understand that when their children obtain a B on a challenging assignment that required perseverance, it is more commendable than obtaining an A+ without effort.

Fostering Positive Emotions about Studying and Learning

Positive emotions are fostered when parents model enthusiasm for learning and share interests, express interest in their children's learning, encourage pride, avoid criticizing, tolerate mistakes, and encourage fun.

MODELING ENTHUSIASM FOR LEARNING AND SHARING INTERESTS

Parents model enthusiasm toward learning when they talk with their children about their own interests and topics they enjoy learning about. Parents also convey enthusiasm for learning when they read, attend other learning events, and discuss what they read and learn with their children.

EXPRESSING INTEREST IN CHILDREN'S LEARNING

Parents convey an interest in their children's learning when they ask positive and supportive (yet not overly intrusive) questions about school events, activities, and assignments. Homework can be an ideal positive venue for the expression of parental interest in their children's learning.

ENCOURAGING PRIDE

Parents foster positive emotions about studying and learning when they encourage children to think of homework as an opportunity to learn, work independently, be responsible, and demonstrate ("show off") knowledge and skills. Parents can also encourage children to feel proud by praising and publicly acknowledging success.

> **Yolanda** would never have let on, but she was thrilled when she overheard her mother "bragging" to her grandmother about Yolanda's success in learning the multiplication tables.

AVOIDING CRITICISM AND TOLERATING MISTAKES

Educators can help parents learn to "correct kids' behaviors instead of the kids" when they are unhappy with something their children have done. That is, it is more effective for parents to address specific problem behaviors than to criticize the children or give them pejorative labels such as "lazy." In addition, even when addressing specific behaviors, parents should take care not to humiliate their children publicly. It is much more effective to correct a child's behavior privately. Finally, when parents tolerate mistakes, they help children think of mistakes as temporary setbacks rather than failures; this encourages the children to try again.

ENCOURAGING FUN

When parents encourage their children to *have fun and laugh* as they are learning, they foster positive emotions. Parents can also help by making homework more relevant to their children's interests, such as helping with a topic selection.

> When **Caterina** had to select a topic for her physics class project, she thought that as a theater buff she had no possible interest in any physics topic. However, as she and her mother looked through her textbook for ideas, they found acoustics discussed in the chapter on sound. Caterina selected "theater acoustics" as her topic. Although the project was challenging and never her favorite, it interested her enough that she was able to be successful.

Helping Children Identify and Cope with Negative Emotions about Learning

As discussed earlier, even highly successful students experience boredom, frustration, and anxiety when they study, particularly in those subjects they find most difficult. Parents can help children minimize the effect of these inevitable negative emotions in several ways. First, they can *normalize negative emotions* by explaining that negative feelings are common and expected, yet do not preclude completing assignments. Parents can also help their children *plan strategically*. Many students find it helpful to complete their more challenging work first, when they are less likely to be tired. Similarly, almost everyone finds it helpful to break down assignments into smaller parts.

When successful students become frustrated, parents *teach strategies to cope with frustration* by reassuring them, teaching them to work on a less frustrating task for a period, and encouraging them to take a short break. Many students find it helpful to alternate 30 minutes of studying with 15 minutes of a favorite activity, to set small goals and then take a short break after achieving each one, or to make sure that they have a favorite activity waiting for them after they have completed assignments—essentially, *building in rewards*. Finally, parents can encourage their children to *obtain help* when their work is too difficult.

> When **Ruth**, whom we met at the beginning of this chapter, was a fourth grader, she had a daily math assignment to copy and solve 30 arithmetic problems. Because she had difficulties with focusing her attention, just copying the problems took her more than an hour and was extremely frustrating. After copying the problems, she was too tired to accurately compute them, much less complete other homework. Her mother decided to copy the problems while her daughter completed other assignments, and then gave them to Ruth to compute and check. After a week or two, her mother had Ruth accurately copy the problems herself, using a timer to record time spent, and striving to improve her speed each day.

Since excessive anxiety interferes with performance, it can be important for educators to help parents find ways to help their children reduce anxiety. Perfectionist parents will need to reduce the academic pressure they place on their children. Other parents will find that their children will become less anxious as they develop time management and organizational strategies, study skills, or use strategies such as exercise or progressive relaxation for anxiety management.

> **Jason**, a sixth grader, began to have difficulty falling asleep every night before he was to have a test in school. His mother recognized that Jason was suffering from test anxiety, because she had suffered from the same problem. After she and Jason consulted with the school psychologist, she helped him implement several strategies. First, as soon as Jason knew a test was scheduled, they developed a plan that included a short period of daily review to prevent procrastination. Jason's mother also helped him use the teacher-prepared study guide, which

lowered his anxiety, since he knew exactly what to expect on the exam. Finally, the evening before each test, he stopped studying at least 1 hour before bedtime to relax and watch TV.

Fostering Positive Behavior

Most parents find that a natural, positive event after homework completion fosters positive study habits, just as a favorite dessert following a meal fosters eating vegetables. For most children, natural, semistructured, and inexpensive reinforcers after completing homework are sufficient. These might be any of the following:

- Time, attention, and affection—a half hour of "special time" with a chosen family member, making something like a dessert with a parent, working on a puzzle together, or playing a child-selected game with family members.
- Fun—the chance to participate in a preferred activity, watch TV, play a computer game, learn something new such as a dance, or learn how to make something.
- Freedom—the chance to select tomorrow night's dinner or choose an activity.
- Privilege—a sleepover, a small treat, or points toward a larger special object.

However, some students require highly structured behavior management plans, and developing and monitoring such plans are well-established methods to improve academic achievement. For example, after five parent training sessions in which parents were taught interventions such as providing a structured homework time, fourth- and sixth-grade students significantly increased their homework completion (Rhoades & Kratochwill, 1998). Eighth- and ninth-grade students similarly benefitted from a structured math homework program and maintained or improved their gains for some time after the intervention (Weiner et al., 1998). Very often parents will need help when they first develop and monitor structured behavior plans. The reader is referred to methods of effective problem definition and collaboration described in Chapter 1, and methods for developing effective behavior management programs described in Chapter 6, for detailed information. Effective home–school behavior management programs often include the following components:

1. *Parent training* focused on implementing a structured homework completion schedule, rewards for homework completion and accuracy, and home–school communication.
2. *Supporting written material*, including homework checklists, instruction sheets, answer keys, a homework performance log, points records, and a reinforcement menu.
3. *Ongoing (daily) home–school communication* via notebooks or checklists.
4. *Clearly designated responsibilities for students, family members, and educators* (i.e., students' completing assignments at specified levels of accuracy, parents' checking that homework is completed and accurate, teachers' correcting and returning homework within a specified time table, consultants' meeting with the student daily for a coaching session).
5. *Both oral and written commitment* on the part of parents, students, and educators to participate in the program, verified by signed contracts.
6. *Reinforcement* for satisfactory performance.

Occasionally educators will need to help some parents understand that rewards are not bribes.

When a consultant suggested that **Zed Lee** and his father participate in a homework program that would reward assignment completion with something Zed would choose from a "menu"

> of tangible rewards, Mr. Lee immediately interrupted by saying, "Oh, no! I will not *bribe* my son. I don't believe in that sort of stuff." The consultant then explained the difference between a "bribe" (giving someone something they value for doing the *wrong* thing), and a "reward" (giving someone something they value for doing the *right* thing).

Infrequently, rather than a positive reinforcement, it is necessary to impose a restriction when academic assignments are not completed.

> **Carlos** frustrated his parents and teachers by not completing homework. Whenever his grades were based entirely on test scores, he received high honors. Whenever his grades reflected homework completion, he failed. When his teachers and parents attempted to implement homework monitoring and reinforcement programs, they failed because either Carlos was not interested in the reinforcements offered or he partook of them on his own (for example, waking up to play his "reward" computer game in the middle of the night). This year Carlos's parents finally hit upon a successful strategy that was tied to his allowance. Carlos received an allowance of $10 per week. On Friday, each of Carlos's five teachers emailed his parents and indicated whether he had submitted that week's homework. He was "docked" $2 for any subject in which he was missing any assignment. The consultant would have preferred a "positive" reward—but she had to admit that this intervention finally worked!

MOVING TO STUDENT-REGULATED STRATEGIES

While it is important for parents to foster appropriate study behaviors, eventually students must be able to learn independently and self-regulate their behavior. Whenever parents use a program with external reinforcers to promote homework completion, after a period of success they should fade adult monitoring and begin making the transition to a student-regulated program. Often educators need to help parents and students engineer this transition successfully. The reader is referred to Chapter 6 for more information.

Fostering Time Management and Organization at Home

Families initially help students develop skills in time management and organization by modeling these skills. Children learn basic strategies when families provide an organized home with flexible yet regular schedules. Most parents find it helpful to keep a family calendar; have a designated place for school-bound materials; and have routines for meals, chore completion, bedtime, and homework. Parents of successful students also structure the physical and psychological environment prior to the homework period by clearing table space, minimizing distractions, and remaining accessible for supervision and attention.

Parents directly teach time management strategies when they help children budget time to meet deadlines (including designating a specific time for homework completion), keep track of assignments, and plan long-term projects. Parents also teach time management as they help their children prioritize schoolwork and extracurricular activities; determine how long it takes to complete tasks, and use that knowledge in scheduling; and track studying time and results by monitoring time spent and grades subsequently received.

As their children get older, parents can help them determine which organization and time management strategies are most effective for them as individuals. It is also important for parents to encourage students to modify their environment to provide optimal learning experiences. For example, if a student normally completes homework at the kitchen table, but finds that setting too noisy and distracting when studying for an exam, parents can help him or her to recognize that fact and take corrective steps—probably by finding a quieter location or time to study.

Forstering Children's Mastery of Study Skills in Specific Areas

Parents provide essential support in the development of study skills and independent learning by fostering children's mastery of study skills in specific areas (reading, spelling, writing, math, and other content areas) as they supervise homework. When parents are not sure how to supervise homework effectively, they can be taught specific strategies in educator-led workshops. These workshops typically teach parents the difference between assisting with homework and giving answers, provide directions on how to model strategies for children, and give parents the opportunity to complete sample assignments. They often are supplemented by resource materials such as games to use at home; enrichment activities; lists of books; and information regarding community resources such as tutors, libraries, clubs, after-school care or community centers that provide homework support. Workshops also provide educators with the opportunity to ask parents what supports they need as they help their children acquire study skills and develop independent learning strategies (Balli et al., 1998; Drummond & Stipek, 2004; Keller, 2004). During such workshops, parents can also be taught to use guided strategy statements, think-aloud strategies, elaborating explanations, and reciprocal questioning. These strategies are summarized in Handout 2.1, Tutoring Guide.

READING

Specific strategies that parents can use to foster *reading* skills are to:

- Demonstrate that reading is pleasurable and important by reading in front of their children often.
- Regularly and collaboratively read aloud with their children to foster comprehension and vocabulary development. Very young children can read the words they recognize, and even high school students and their parents can enjoy reading assigned books (such as *A Tale of Two Cities*) aloud to each other.
- Keep interesting reading material in the house for family members of all ages.
- Nonjudgmentally encourage children to select their own books and magazines for pleasure reading, and encourage their children to read for pleasure every day.
- Associate reading with affection (encourage children to read aloud or silently, in the company of loving family members and/or friends).
- Associate reading with extra privileges (e.g., staying up a half hour later).
- Associate function with reading by having children read signs, labels, recipes, menus, phone book entries, and notes.
- Associate pleasure with reading (e.g., read with a child while the child is enjoying a treat).
- Find materials that support children's reading assignments, such as online textbooks (which resolve the "I left my book at school" problem) and publisher-provided activities (e.g., practice tests).
- Associate success with reading (encourage children to read familiar words, and ensure that they have reading materials at appropriate difficulty levels).

Young children often have homework assignments to read aloud at home. Family members should be careful not to be too quick to correct children's attempts to read unknown words.

Regardless of age, "sounding it out" is only one strategy to use with unknown words; other important strategies include using contextual cues, prefixes, suffixes, and base words.

Pleasure reading material should be easily read by students and should contain few if any unknown words. Instructional material should be of moderate difficulty, meaning that students should know 9 out of 10 words. When reading material is too difficult and the student misses more than 10% of the words, alternative materials should be obtained.

> **Emma**, a seventh-grade student with a learning disability, was assigned to read the first chapter of a novel about World War I. This book was written at a reading level far beyond her capabilities. Emma thought she could "handle" this assignment if she worked really hard, so she did not discuss this assignment with either her parents or the resource room teacher who helped her modify assignments from the general education classes. Though Emma devoted hours to "reading" this chapter, all of her energy was spent trying to decode the unknown words. Using the dictionary added to her confusion, and using context cues was not helpful because she had such limited prior knowledge about this war. Emma's "reading" was so dysfluent that her comprehension suffered significantly, and even after devoting a great deal of time and effort, Emma was unable to pass the teacher's pop quiz the next day.

In this situation, parents and educators could have collaborated to find materials that would have considerably reduced Emma's frustration, such as a novel about the same topic at a lower reading level, or a movie about the same topic. Another alternative is to obtain textbooks, workbooks, recreational reading materials, magazines, and reading materials in Talking Books format, used with the Talking Books machines available from public libraries. These materials allow students to listen through headphones as the materials are read orally, while the students read along. In this way, the students hear new vocabulary words that are pronounced properly; fluency is achieved; and comprehension is enhanced. The machine can be slowed down or passages repeated to allow the students to grasp the material or find the answers they seek. This Talking Books opportunity has "saved" many students with reading disabilities at all grade levels, and continues to be available through college and adulthood. Many successful adults with learning disabilities or visual difficulties receive a daily version of *The Wall Street Journal* through Talking Books and attribute much of their success to this helpful technology.

SPELLING

Parents can foster the development of early spelling skills by encouraging their young children to write at home, including birthday cards, thank-you notes, telephone messages, grocery lists, letters, and stories. Parents can support inventive spelling while respecting their own need for correct spelling and math. For example, they can say, "That's a good try. You spelled it the same way it sounds. I spell it . . . " instead of saying, "That's wrong" (Anderson & Gunderson, 1997).

Most students have weekly lists of spelling and vocabulary words to learn throughout their elementary, middle school, and high school years, and parents are frequently called upon to help with these tasks. Strategies that are particularly helpful include the following:

- Have the child use multiple modalities while studying the words (listen, speak, look, write, remember in context).
- Space and repeat learning through short study sessions every day.
- Encourage the child to use memory tricks (mnemonic devices) such as "The princi*pal* is my *pal*" and "*i* before *e* except after *c*."
- Encourage the child to link the current words with previously learned words.
- Quiz the child on words and definitions.

WRITING

Even parents with little formal schooling can provide significant support to their children during all stages of the writing process. During the *prewriting* stage, parents can encourage their children to discuss, talk through, and plan the assignment by using their parents as sounding boards. Parents can also provide valuable experiences (e.g., trips or movies) that will help children develop ideas about which to write. After the children select a topic, parents can provide guidance as their children locate necessary information, using books, maps, graphics, newspapers, dictionaries, libraries, the Internet, and other reference tools.

During the *drafting* stage, parents can encourage their children to use outlines, visual maps, or other advance organizers (see Handout 3.1) to arrange their information before beginning to write. Parents or friends can help students review drafts and give feedback during the *revising* stage.

During the *editing* stage, parents can encourage their children to check for proper grammar, spelling, punctuation, and appearance. If they are knowledgeable themselves, parents and other family members can also help children become skilled in keyboarding and effective word-processing skills such as cutting and pasting; using spelling and grammar checkers; and using electronic dictionaries, thesauruses, and encyclopedias. With some of these skills, students need to determine which of the suggestions generated by the computer (such as spelling alternatives) are correct. Finally, parents can serve as an audience for the finished writing during the *publishing* stage.

CONTENT AREA KNOWLEDGE

To foster skills in science, math, and social studies, one of the most helpful things that parents can do is help their children understand how useful it is to know and understand concepts in these areas. For example, parents and children might do the following together:

- Use science knowledge to predict changes in the weather.
- Use math skills to count change, work with fractions in recipes, estimate quantities, budget and shop for school clothes, and calculate time.
- Use science and math concepts when helping with relevant household repairs.
- Use social studies knowledge to understand the news, write letters to obtain information, or develop travel plans for an upcoming family vacation.
- Link content area learning to long-term goals, such as success in a desired occupation or the ability to deal with personal finances.
- Play games and engage in activities that reinforce math, science, and social studies information.

FINDING AND USING ADDITIONAL RESOURCES

It is useful and advantageous for multiple family members (including siblings) to be involved in homework completion, because it reduces the stress on the primarily involved parent, conveys the message to the child that multiple family members consider schooling important, and takes advantage of the expertise of more than one person. One parent might be better at math, while the other prefers to help with reading. Older siblings can also help, as long as their own homework is completed first. Balli et al. (1998) found that when families were encouraged to become involved with homework, most students (87%) worked with someone other than a parent for at least one assignment.

> Only when his mother was sick did **Charlie** discover how helpful his father could be with homework. Whereas his mother always "multitasked" other duties while helping him, his father gave Charlie his complete attention. He explained things so clearly and calmly that Charlie's work was done in half the time. This positive experience led his dad to change his schedule so he could provide homework assistance often, even after Charlie's mother recovered.

When family members do not know how to help with a particular subject, students can turn to outside supports. Many schools and libraries have tutoring programs and lists of tutors, including volunteers such as National Honor Society members.

Helping Parents Support Their Children as They Prepare to Take Tests

When their children are studying for quizzes and tests, parental support in the development and use of study guides can be invaluable. Parents can also encourage children to review corrected math and science homework, and check whether they understand their errors.

ENCOURAGING CHILDREN TO WORK WITH STUDY BUDDIES

The value of studying with a partner is not always understood by parents. In advanced math and science, "study buddies" and study groups are particularly helpful and can play a critical role in academic success. Parents can help their children work with study buddies by encouraging their children to phone study buddies, or invite them to their home to work together. Studying with a partner works best, at least initially until routines are established, when parents provide supervision and the studying takes place in a somewhat public area; these precautions make it less likely that study hours become social hours. It is also helpful for parents to encourage their children to associate with peers who value academic success. Students who have friends who value academic achievement, and whose parents value education, are much more likely to be academically successful. Although some students obtain social approval for academic achievement from family or high-achieving friends, too often the social environment does not support academic success, and high achievement can be difficult for students who are motivated to maintain the approval of low-achieving friends (Urdan & Maehr, 1995). Given that the impact of peers (particularly in adolescence) is profound, parents are well advised to encourage association in terms of studying and project collaboration with those students who are relatively academically inclined and motivated. "Best friends" are not necessarily "best study buddies."

Fostering Home–School Collaboration

As discussed previously, a number of barriers commonly interfere with home–school collaboration. Since positive home–school relationships have very beneficial effects on student learning, it is important for both parents and educators to make deliberate efforts to foster positive collaboration. School personnel can do this by supplementing traditional methods of in-person communication. For example, educators can:

- Provide parent training sessions to foster authoritative approaches to parenting (high but reasonable demands, good communication, and mutual respect).
- Provide workshops in which parents are taught appropriate methods to help their children study or prepare for high-stakes testing.
- Convert an unused classroom into a parent/educator drop-in center (as is found at the Burke School in Boston), stocking it with coffee, snacks, and books.

- Hold sessions in which family members and educators openly communicate about cultural differences regarding discipline, education, homework, and morals.
- Encourage parents to support learning in culturally meaningful ways—for example, encouraging memorization when this is culturally important (Anderson & Gunderson, 1997).
- Check that written assignments are clear enough for parents and students to understand their purposes and requirements.
- *Send group newsletters* to communicate what children are learning and describe how parents can help children master material, relate information to new contexts, or practice skills (Drummond & Stipek, 2004).
- Communicate about individual students by *writing comments* on assignments or in "homework planners." This works best when teachers specifically invite families to write comments on and sign the homework planners (Balli et al., 1998).
- Use *contingency contracts*, collaboratively developed, to foster homework completion.
- Use *communication notebooks* to send daily messages between parents and educators.
- Have children complete *homework completion graphs and share them with their parents* (green for when homework was handed in on time, yellow if a day late, and red if not submitted; Bryan & Sullivan-Burstein, 1997).
- Judiciously use electronic communication methods, such as *email and Internet virtual communities.* Some parents, particularly those with limited English proficiency, prefer asynchronous methods because they give extra time to reflect and gather thoughts; this can reduce the intimidation they often feel when speaking directly with educators (Beghetto, 2001).

Parents can foster positive home–school communication by:

- Fostering positive attitudes toward, and trusting relationships with, teachers.
- Taking advantage of opportunities to communicate, both in writing and electronically.
- Participating in school activities such as open houses and parent training sessions.
- Telling teachers about learning experiences provided at home that teachers can support.
- Giving feedback to educators regarding what they would like their children to learn.
- Telling teachers strategies that they find most successful when helping their children.
- Telling teachers when excessive time is being spent on homework, so that assignments can be appropriately modified.

Missy was spending more than twice the amount of time on homework that her classmates typically spent getting the same amount of work done. With her mother's encouragement, she summoned the courage to tell her teacher that she thought she had too much homework. When the teacher called home, Missy's mother told of the many hours that were spent doing homework as Missy tried to do her work "perfectly." Missy, her parents, the teacher, and a consultant worked together to minimize Missy's notion that her work had to be perfect. It took several months of everyone working together to enable Missy to relax and say, "It's OK. Nobody's perfect."

Appraisal

Appraising implemented strategies requires determining whether or not they have been effective. As described in Chapter 1, appraisal often results in modifying interventions. After interventions are designed and implemented, members of the team follow these steps: (1) assess (or have the student assess) implementation success, (2) modify the interventions, (3) implement the modified interventions, (4) reevaluate success, (5) develop strategies to promote generalization and student self-regulation, (6) implement strategies to promote generalization and student self-regulation, (7) reassess (or, preferably, have the student assess) successes and failures, (8) appraise the need for continued intervention use, and (9) return to previous step(s) as appropriate.

Assessment strategies, discussed in the beginning of the chapter and used to define and explore the problem, can be appropriately readministered to generate outcomes data and appraise the success of the intervention. For example, Sayger, Horne, Walker, and Passmore (1988) used behavior rating scales, parent daily reports, and family environment scales as pre- and post-measures to determine that their 10-week parent training course significantly changed the family environment, parental problem-solving strategies, and student behavior. They also used the same measures 9 to 12 months after the end of the intervention to determine whether or not lasting effects had been accomplished.

On the other hand, often the simplest appraisal methods are the most appropriate because they are most likely to be used. For example, if a student is referred because homework is not completed accurately, a fitting appraisal question after the implementation of interventions is obvious: whether or not the homework is now completed accurately. The basic questions are: "What did we do?" "How well did it work?" and "What do we need to change?"

Help Students Develop Their Personal Learning Guides (HILLs)

In their Personal Learning Guides or HILLs, students can insert notes on strategies they have found to be effective regarding family and friends. The students might also include copies of recently filled out and blank versions of the following materials related to this topic:

Worksheet 2.1. Checklist of Home Qualities That Foster Independent Learning
Worksheet 2.2. Menu of Interview Questions about Family and Friends
Worksheet 2.3. Menu of Interview Questions for Parents
Handout 2.1. Tutoring Guide
Table 2.1. Parent Affirmations

WORKSHEET 2.1.

Checklist of Home Qualities That Foster Independent Learning

Family members foster student motivation.	
	Parents foster positive relationships with children by listening, providing help, and sharing activities.
	Children are treated as individuals and encouraged to meet varied needs and develop unique talents.
	Parents express the belief that their children's academic success is both positive and desirable.
	Parental academic and behavioral expectations and standards are clear.
	Family members talk with children about short- and long-term goals and help prioritize them.
	A positive learning environment is provided in the home and by encouraging learning experiences.
	Family members frequently praise and support children's efforts.
Positive emotions are fostered and negative emotions are actively managed.	
	Enthusiasm for learning is modeled by family members; homework is positively regarded.
	Fun, laughter, and opportunities to experience pride and joy when learning are provided.
	Children are not publicly humiliated or criticized, and mistakes are tolerated.
	Negative emotions such as boredom, frustration, anxiety, and anger are identified and addressed.
	Family members encourage children to brainstorm alternatives when setbacks are experienced.
Appropriate behavior is fostered.	
	Children collaborate with family members in developing clear behavioral expectations.
	Appropriate behavior is publicly acknowledged, and it has positive (internally) rewarding consequences.
	Inappropriate behavior has appropriate consequences that are consistently applied.
	Children are encouraged to monitor and evaluate their own behavior.
Time is managed well, organization is encouraged, and routines are established.	
	The home is organized (calendar, place for school-bound materials) and well structured.
	Parents encourage children to consciously develop their own organization methods for school work.
	Parents help their children plan and prioritize school work and extracurricular activities.
	Parents encourage their children not to overschedule activities.
	Children determine how long it takes to complete tasks and use that knowledge to make schedules.
	Children regularly complete homework in a quiet place with minimal distractions.

(continued)

Checklist of Home Qualities That Foster Independent Learning *(page 2 of 2)*

Physical functioning is monitored.	
	Children's hearing and vision have been checked and are monitored.
	Parents help their children monitor their own nutrition and physical fitness.
	Parents help their children manage fatigue, including taking study breaks and getting enough sleep.
Skill development is encouraged.	
	Families encourage children's development in individual areas of interest and talent.
	Families encourage reading by providing reading materials that are interesting to the child.
	Parents help children connect reading, writing, math, and science knowledge to "real-life" skills.
	Parents help their children use the writing process (prewriting, drafting, revising, editing, publishing).
	Homework is effectively supervised, and supporting resources are tapped.
	Parents encourage children to evaluate and appraise their own learning success and study strategies.
Test taking is facilitated.	
	Parents help their children develop and use study guides.
	Parents encourage their children to work with "study buddies."
Family members foster positive home–school partnerships.	
	Family members respect educators and do not speak negatively about school to children.
	Regular two-way communication between home and school is maintained.
	Parents participate in solution-oriented, conjoint consultation with educators to address problems.
Families foster positive social relationships.	
	The family climate promotes helping, sharing, cooperating, and collaborative problem solving.
	Family members help children identify methods to obtain help from classmates and friends.
	Parents encourage socialization with friends who value academic success.

WORKSHEET 2.2.

Menu of Interview Questions about Family and Friends

Student ______________________________ Date ______________________

1. What are your parents' long-term goals for you? What do they expect from you in terms of studying and learning? What happens when you do not meet their expectations? Do you have adults besides your parents who encourage you and support your doing well in school?

2. Do you have a regular schedule for studying? If so, what is it? Where do you usually study or do homework? Is this an atmosphere that promotes your best work? How could you improve it?

3. What do you do when you need help with studying? Who do you ask for help? Do you have different people for different subjects? Do you have access to good tools for learning—the library, books, and the Internet?

4. How do your parents help you study or do homework? Is there anything your parents do that cause you problems in terms of studying? How could you improve that?

5. How do your brothers or sisters help you study or do homework? Is there anything they do that cause you problems in terms of studying? How could you improve that?

(continued)

6. At home, what rules do you have? Who makes these rules? What happens when they are not followed? If you wanted a rule to change, how would you go about getting it changed?

7. At home, what chores do you have? How are your chores decided? What happens when you don't do them? If you wanted a chore to change, how would you go about getting it changed?

8. Do you think that your classmates want you to do well in school? Do you ask classmates for help? Do your classmates help you study?

9. Which of your friends believe that doing well in school is important? Which of them believe that participating in school activities is important? Do your friends help you study? Are there things that your friends do that cause you problems in terms of studying? How could you improve that?

10. Do you ever study with a friend or classmate? What works well when you study together? What doesn't work well? How could you improve that?

WORKSHEET 2.3.

Menu of Interview Questions for Parents

Student ______________________ Parent ______________________ Date ______________

1. What are your long-term goals for your child? What do you expect in terms of studying and learning? What grades do you expect your child to achieve? What happens when your child does not meet your expectations?

2. When your child does well in school, to what does he or she attribute this success? When your child does *not* do well in school, what does he or she blame?

3. Does your child have a regular schedule for studying? If so, what is it? Where does your child usually do homework? Does this atmosphere promote good work? How could it be improved?

4. What does your child do when he or she needs help with studying? How do you or other family members help your child study or do homework? How could that be improved?

5. Does your child keep track of assignments? Does your child keep his or her work organized?

6. Do you help your child manage and budget time to meet deadlines, keep track of assignments, and plan long-term projects? How could that be improved?

(continued)

Menu of Interview Questions for Parents *(page 2 of 3)*

7. Do you see your child's studying and doing homework at home as an opportunity for you to be part of your child's educational experience? Do you see it as an opportunity for your child to learn, work independently, and be responsible?

8. Do you try to improve your child's motivation (encouraging, attempting to make the homework more interesting, and ensuring that your child has a chance to engage in a preferred activity after completing homework)?

9. What does your child enjoy learning about? Have you ever found that when your child was learning, he or she became excited to the point of forgetting to do something (such as watch a favorite TV show)? If so, describe this.

10. What does your child get nervous or anxious about when learning? What does your child do when nervous or anxious? What do you do or say when your child is nervous or anxious?

11. What does your child find most boring to learn? What does your child do when bored? What do you do or say?

12. Is there anything that makes your child angry or mad when doing schoolwork? What does your child do when angry or mad? What do you do or say?

(continued)

Menu of Interview Questions for Parents *(page 3 of 3)*

13. What does your child do when he or she doesn't feel like doing an assignment? What do you say or do?

14. When your child is frustrated, do you help him or her monitor emotions by reassuring, calming, redirecting, turning to another person for help, and giving space?

15. If your child has a problem with learning, do you contact anyone at the school? If so, who and how? Some parents have trouble communicating with educators, because they have little time or they don't feel comfortable. Do you find that to be true? If so, why?

16. Do you think that there are things your child's teacher could do differently that could help your child have more success with homework and studying? What are they?

17. What are some fun things your child likes to do with you? What learning experiences do you share?

18. At home, what rules are there? What happens when they are not followed? What chores does your child have? How are rules and chores decided? What happens when they aren't done?

19. Do you think your child's friends believe that doing well in school is important? Do they help your child study?

HANDOUT 2.1.

Tutoring Guide

Rephrase!

Restate ideas and feelings in your own words.

Be positive!

Make positive comments about ideas and work.

No put-downs!

Encourage thinking even if an idea seems silly or wrong.

Guide!

Teach to guide, not dominate. Describe a plan for solving a problem.

Think aloud!

Convey the reasons behind your thinking.

Elaborate!

Give clear, step-by-step explanations and answers.

Question!

Ask a series of step-by-step questions.

3

General Classroom Considerations

Good teaching includes teaching students how to learn, how to remember, how to think, and how to motivate themselves.

—WEINSTEIN AND MAYER (1985, p. 315)

OVERVIEW

Mary, Theresa, Donella, and Joanne, all age 23, meet periodically to refresh the friendship they began in elementary school. At their most recent reunion they reminisced about their sixth-grade teacher, Ms. Clavier, and her creative strategies to help them learn. They laughed as they remembered her "rainbow chalk." Ms. Clavier used various colors when she wrote lecture notes on the blackboard. Yellow was reserved for important information that would be on the test. Other colors conveyed "just for fun" information—red for information that made her angry, pink for material that made her laugh, purple for extra questions that made her think. She had the students use ink to write the essential (yellow chalk) information in their notebooks, and pencil to write the additional information—teacher- and student-generated questions, comments, and jokes. With this approach, Ms. Clavier taught her students how to take notes and capture essential information; increased their ability to differentiate essential information from less important details; fostered idea elaboration; and encouraged positive emotions—having fun—while learning. A simple strategy, yet one that still impressed all four women years later.

This entire book addresses methods that teachers can use to empower students to learn independently and regulate motivation, emotions, behavior, time, organization, cognitive strategies, metacognition, and executive functions. This separate chapter, focusing on strategies that are applicable only to classrooms, is included for several reasons.

First, this chapter addresses *general classroom characteristics* that either foster students' ability to learn independently or are serious barriers to the same. Many classroom characteristics—such as providing standards and expectations, structure, opportunities to learn, and positive climate—profoundly affect students' ability to learn independently (Christenson & Anderson, 2002). For example, one very important strategy is accurately tracking assignments, and students should be taught to keep assignment books and calendars. However, if a classroom teacher does not clearly articulate assignments, it is very difficult for students to track them. Similarly, an important method for students to use as they study for tests is to review previously corrected tests, quizzes, and papers. However, to do so, they obviously must have those corrected materials.

In addition, *general classroom climate* has a significant effect on students' ability to study and learn independently. Classrooms in which students are individually and collectively perceived as collaborators in the learning process induce self-regulated learning. As Dawson and Guare (2004) describe, implementing whole-class strategies such as clear classroom rules, classroom routines, organization systems, integrating executive skill development into daily instruction, and integrating coaching into the classroom foster all students' executive skills.

Finally, while specific methods to help students regulate motivation, emotions, behavior, time, organization, cognition, and metacognition described throughout this book can be used by consultants as they work individually and in small groups with students, they also can and should be taught within the *classroom context*. Consultants need to consider and address global classroom characteristics regarding *how* material is taught whenever they design interventions for students. If taught in isolation, study skills are unlikely to be maintained or transferred from one setting to another. Best practice involves collaborating with general education teachers to teach study skills in conjunction with established curricula (Langer & Neal, 1987; Slate, Jones, & Dawson, 1993). Such collaboration can result in dramatic improvement in student learning. For example, when consultants taught students study skills in conjunction with the social studies curriculum and simultaneously provided teachers workshops on study skill improvement, students' exam scores rose from the failing range to the honor roll range (Leland-Jones, 1997). Similarly, consultants who taught study skills in general education classrooms at the same time that they provided teachers in-service workshops on study skills, and met with students to review cumulative files and develop individual learning goals, found that in one academic year students improved their standardized test scores by a three-grade equivalent (Carns & Carns, 1991).

The reader should note that this chapter provides a menu of strategies. It is neither possible nor desirable for any teacher or consultant to incorporate every strategy simultaneously. For a concise list of methods discussed in this chapter, the reader is referred to Worksheet 3.1, Checklist of Classroom Qualities That Foster Independent Learning.

RESEARCH FOUNDATIONS

Effective schools have a school climate conducive to learning, are free of disciplinary problems and vandalism, have schedules that emphasize basic skills instruction and high levels of student time on task, incorporate a system of clear instructional objectives for monitoring and assessing student performance, and have effective school principals who are strong leaders, set school goals, maintain student discipline, frequently observe classrooms, and expect every teacher to believe all students can achieve. Effective classrooms and teachers mirror these qualities: They maintain high expectations for students; provide routines and opportunities to learn; foster a safe and positive climate; develop emotionally supportive relationships; provide positive models; and provide academic and social help, advice, and instruction (Christenson & Anderson, 2002; Wentzel & Watkins, 2002).

Doll, Zucker, and Brehm (2004) describe such positive classrooms as *resilient*, "where all children can be successful emotionally, academically, and socially" (p. 7). Resilient classrooms foster students' academic self-determination, behavioral self-control, and feelings of academic competence. They also promote positive in-school and home–school relationships.

Classrooms that foster study skills and independent learning extend these characteristics and foster student self-regulation of motivation, emotions, and behavior, as well as knowledge of learning strategies, metacognition, self-appraisal, and information synthesis. Zimmerman et al. (1996) recommend that teachers conceptualize classrooms as "academies" where, in addition to academic content, self-regulatory learning processes are explicitly taught—similar to the manner that music academies teach musicianship as well as music content.

This conceptualization articulates the fact that classroom teachers have two types of goals: those related to the *products* of learning, and those related to the *process* of learning. The product goals focus on *content*, such as the skills and factual information assessed via high-stakes testing. The *process goals* focus on *strategies* students use as they learn. Both types of goals are better met when teachers apply constructivist approaches (Piaget, 1970). These approaches assume that learning is an internal experience influenced by the learner who actively processes information rather than passively receives it. For example, students who complete a project and presentation on a self-selected topic are likely to remember more than students who hear a lecture on the same material, because they actively process the information. In traditional classrooms, learning tends to be fragmented, based on indirect experiences, and steered by teacher-set goals (Boekaerts & Niemivirta, 2000). In constructivist classrooms, learning tends to be integrated, based on direct experiences, and steered by teacher–student goals.

A constructivist approach also facilitates student knowledge about the *process* of learning—that is, knowledge of study skills and independent learning strategies. In the constructivist approach, teachers allow students to choose their own learning strategies and as much as possible decide when, where, and how they learn, while simultaneously fostering social relationships and personal responsibility (Boekaerts, de Koning, & Vedder, 2006). Infusing the curriculum with these methods helps students become strategic, motivated, and independent learners who deliberately use self-regulatory strategies in reading, writing, task engagement, time planning and management, text summarization, test preparation, and self-appraisal (Paris & Paris, 2001; Randi & Corno, 2000).

METHODS

As is true of effective interventions with individual students, effective classroom interventions incorporate the phases of *preparation*, *performance*, and *appraisal* (Doll et al., 2004). During the preparation phase, the consultant and teacher assess classroom elements that foster study skills and independent learning; develop specific, observable, and measurable descriptions of missing elements; gather baseline data; set specific and measurable goals for improvement; consider factors that reinforce the absence of the missing elements; and develop plans for intervention strategies, including a timeline and the persons responsible. During the performance phase, the teacher, consultant, and students implement the plan and collect data regarding the integrity of the implementation. During the appraisal phase, the teacher, consultant, and students collect and analyze postintervention data, then modify future plans and strategies.

Preparation

Assessment of Classroom Characteristics

Methods to assess self-regulation, family–school partnerships, motivation, affect, behavior, learning strategies, metacognition, reading, writing, and content knowledge are described in the respective chapters on these topics. Methods specifically germane to the classroom assess classroom climate, teacher–student relationships, and relationships among peers. These methods can include semistructured interviews, observations, checklists, and questionnaires.

SEMISTRUCTURED INTERVIEWS, OBSERVATIONS, AND CHECKLISTS

Interview questions that might be used to assess a student's perceptions regarding classroom characteristics, teacher–student relationships, and relationships among peers are found in

Worksheet 3.2, Menu of Interview Questions about School. Teachers and consultants can use those results in conjunction with observations and Worksheet 3.1 to hypothesize areas of need.

QUESTIONNAIRES

Doll et al. (2004) describe the classroom assessment and intervention methodology *Class Maps*, which involves surveying students with a questionnaire that taps feelings of academic efficacy, academic self-determination, behavior self-control, teacher–student relationships, peer relationships, and home–school relationships. The results are graphed and used to generate whole-class discussions and develop problem-solving strategies.

Ysseldyke and Christenson (1993) created The Instructional Environment System–II: A System to Identify a Student's Instructional Needs (Second Edition) (TIES-II) to help analyze a student's instructional environment. The instrument was designed to increase communication, so it uses multiple informants (teacher, support personnel, administrators, and parents). The TIES-II avoids blaming teachers for instructional deficits by focusing on factors associated with positive learning outcomes and high levels of student academic performance: instruction matched to student needs and goals; realistic yet high teacher expectations; effective classroom management techniques; effective instructional presentation; emphasis on thinking skills and learning strategies; deliberate use of motivational strategies; opportunities for student practice; informed, immediate, specific, and corrective feedback on student performance; a high level of academic engaged time; using adaptive instruction to accommodate a specific student's needs; direct and frequent assessment; and clear student understanding of what to do and how to do it (Tindal, 2002; Ysseldyke & Christenson, 1993).

The Classroom Environment Scale, Second Edition (CES; Moos & Trickett, 1987) is a psychometrically strong instrument (Smith, 1989) that assesses the social climate of secondary classrooms. It addresses three dimensions: relationships (involvement, affiliation, teacher support); personal growth and goal orientation (task orientation, competition); and system maintenance and change (order, organization, rule clarity, control, and innovation).

After conducting interviews and observations, and using selected questionnaires, consultants can use the Worksheet 3.1 to integrate the information, generate collaborative conversations, and facilitate brainstorming problem-solving interventions. The consultant, teacher, and students can then collaborate to develop observable and measurable descriptions of missing elements, gather baseline data, set goals, and develop intervention strategies (Doll et al., 2004).

Performance

To help students acquire and generalize study skills, teachers need to foster students' overall self-regulation and positive home–school–student–peer collaboration. They also need to develop students' motivation; emotional self-regulation; behavioral self-control; time management and organization; cognitive and metacognitive strategies; and independent skills in reading, writing, content area knowledge, and test taking. Finally, they need to develop their own personal executive skills to manage the conflicting (and probably impossible) expectations placed on teachers.

Fostering Students' Self-Regulation

Self-regulatory skills are best taught in an atmosphere in which teachers *consider students collaborators in the learning process*, and, as much as possible, jointly select goals, determine timeframes, delegate responsibilities, and select assessment measures. Students are encouraged to meet their varied needs and develop their unique talents, and (again, whenever possible) are encouraged to select their own learning topics.

Furthermore, teachers who encourage student self-regulation teach them to *self-evaluate their learning success*. For example, teachers can have students keep a folder of their "personal best" work and use those samples as standards against which they can compare completed assignments before submission. Students can also maintain performance records, such as graphs of curriculum-based measurement tasks, graphs of homework completion rates, and corrected tests and assignments with process notes.

Teachers that encourage student self-regulation also encourage students to *self-appraise their learning strategies*. Material contained throughout this book suggests specific methods to this end. For example, teachers might encourage students to include teacher-developed materials, as well as many of the worksheets and handouts included in this book, in their Personal Learning Guides (HILLs).

Fostering Positive Home–School–Student–Peer Collaboration

To foster independent learning, it is important for educators to maintain the attitude that parents know their own children well, are experts regarding their children, are coteachers (along with educators), and are equal partners in their children's education. It is also important to foster solution-oriented family–educator collaboration and family-centered practices that respect culture (Esler, Godber, & Christenson, 2002). For example, teachers might explicitly include family members in homework assignments, or ask family members about their educational priorities.

FACILITATE COMMUNICATION

Teachers also need to develop, maintain, and publicize proactive, and persistent regular formal and informal two-way communication methods in a variety of modalities: in person, in writing, and electronically. Home–school communication methods should be as user-friendly as possible, so that both teachers and parents can easily convey both concerns and commendations. Teachers should share positive information routinely with parents, both to maintain parental connections with children's learning and to provide foundations for positive, collaborative home–school partnerships. Table 3.1 lists the components of successful school-to-home communications.

> **Mrs. Baker**, a fifth-grade teacher, usually enjoyed a warm and positive relationship with her students and their parents. Because she had minimal time for routine communications with the parents, she relied on their attendance at school functions to develop parent–teacher relationships. However, Fred's parents never attended any school functions, and she had not met them. When a serious behavior problem arose in April, she telephoned them. Unfortunately, Fred's parents had long before concluded that this teacher was the cause of their son's difficulties. Their negative suspicions had grown and festered over time, and when Mrs. Baker called, the conversation exploded with tension on both sides. Mrs. Baker found herself defensively trying

TABLE 3.1. School-to-Home Communication Components

School-to-home communications should include:

1. Sufficient information so that parents can support learning.
2. Information regarding the individual student's performance.
3. More positive than critical comments.
4. An emphasis on the shared responsibilities of family members and school personnel.
5. Specific suggestions regarding techniques to support learning at home.
6. Specific invitations for family participation.

to establish that she was indeed a caring teacher and not the cause of their son's problems. Finding herself in this unpleasant "lose–lose" situation immediately changed Mrs. Baker's mind about the importance of routine communications with parents of her students. She now contacts each child's parent(s) at least monthly, and uses a checklist to track which parents are due to receive a 2-minute "positive comment call" or a "congratulatory email."

DESIGNING HOMEWORK ASSIGNMENTS AS POSITIVE EXPERIENCES THAT FOSTER FAMILY–STUDENT–SCHOOL COLLABORATION

A number of variables have been identified as important for homework success (Olympia, Sheridan, & Jenson, 1994; Rosenberg, 1989). Teachers make it more likely that all students will complete and actually enjoy their homework when they:

- Make the homework purpose and objectives clear to the students.
- Match the homework to the ability level of the students so they can complete it with at least 80% accuracy in a reasonable period of time.
- Ensure that instructions are clear.
- Give assignments in a variety of formats.
- Use homework assignments to review and reprocess material already taught, rather than to introduce new material.
- Ensure that assignments result in a specific product.
- Provide prompt and specific feedback.

Students with learning difficulties need additional support and are most likely to be successful with homework when teachers:

- Have students complete homework assignment sheets, self-graph homework completion, and set short-term goals (Trammel, Schloss, & Alper, 1994).
- Involve parents (Salend & Schliff, 1989; Salend & Gajria, 1995).
- Use peer supports and tutors (Salend & Gajria, 1995).
- Use an assignment completion routine (Rademacher, Schumaker, & Deshler, 1996).

HELPING STUDENTS IDENTIFY SOURCES OF SUPPORT FOR HOMEWORK COMPLETION

Many parents are well equipped, both educationally and temperamentally, to help students with homework. Many are not. When parents are not able to support homework completion, teachers can help parents and students identify other sources of support, such as supervised after-school day care programs, after-school teacher support, email communication with teachers, telephone hotlines, Internet websites, and community- and library-based tutorial services.

USING CONJOINT CONSULTATION TO ADDRESS PROBLEM SITUATIONS

As described by Sheridan et al. (1996), conjoint behavioral consultation effectively addresses problematic situations. In this approach, students, educators, and family members collaborate to develop specific goals and find effective methods to monitor and change student behavior.

FOSTERING POSITIVE PEER RELATIONSHIPS

In school, learning is often a social endeavor. The quality of peer relationships in a classroom has considerable impact on student learning. Negative social relationships detract from student learning, while positive social relationships promote learning and positive feelings toward school and academics. Teachers can foster these learning-friendly peer relationships by promoting prosocial behaviors, such as helping, sharing, cooperating, and collaborative problem solving (Doll et al., 2004; Pianta, 1999). Positive peer relationships are also fostered through emphasizing learning rather than competition, and by assigning well-designed and interesting cooperative learning projects to which all students must contribute.

ENLISTING THE SUPPORT OF PEERS

Teachers should be aware that students are likely to turn to peers for academic assistance—often more than they will turn to teachers (Watkins, 2002). Teachers can take advantage of this tendency and encourage students to identify appropriate "study buddies" for each subject—peers or friends who share telephone numbers, get together at home, and work together during class. Teachers will need to remind students that (as noted in Chapter 2) "best study buddies" are unlikely to be "best friends." Study buddies need to be able to *work* together to:

- "Talk through" assignments.
- Quiz one another in preparation for tests.
- Remind each other to self-monitor strategy use.
- Provide specific yet positive performance feedback.

Teachers can promote effective "study buddying" by allowing study buddies to begin their collaboration in school, where teachers can monitor strategies and provide feedback.

We suggest that teachers directly teach students how to give one another positive performance feedback by (1) providing a list of possible conversation starters (e.g., a time when you were injured, a family vacation, how your family celebrates your favorite holiday, your most embarrassing moment, or a future job you would love to have and why); (2) writing each role (speaker, listener, and observer) on the board and giving students a copy of Table 3.2; (3) demon-

TABLE 3.2. Positive Performance Feedback Roles

Speaker:	Talk about a topic for approximately 3 minutes.
	Thank the listener and observer for their feedback.
Listener:	Look at the speaker, and lean forward slightly to show interest.
	Keep hands quiet, and do not interrupt.
	Think about what the speaker is saying (content).
	Ask questions to clarify the message.
	Make comments that indicate you are thinking about what has been said.
	Thank the observer for his or her feedback.
Observer:	Keep a record of the listener's performance.
	Give specific comments to the speaker, such as "You did a good job because . . . "
	Give specific comments to the listener, such as "You did a good job because . . . "
	Give helpful suggestions that are truthful.
	Begin with something positive.
	Avoid the word "should."
	Avoid following "That was good" with "But . . . " because "But . . ." negates the compliment, but do say, "Next time you might try . . . " or "I suggest you . . . "
	End with a positive comment.

strating the roles of speaker, listener, and observer to the entire class; and (4) grouping the class into triads to give each student a chance to practice each role.

TRAINING STUDENTS TO TUTOR ONE ANOTHER

After students have mastered methods to provide positive feedback, they can be taught methods to tutor each other. Peer tutoring has been found to effectively increase the learning of children with learning disabilities and attention-deficit disorders (Fuchs et al., 1997; Wentzel & Watkins, 2002). Effective strategies, summarized in Handout 2.1, include:

- Attending to and engaging the peer.
- Elaborating and contextualizing explanations.
- Permitting the peer to apply new information in a constructivist manner.
- Using think-aloud strategies.
- Using reciprocal questioning.
- Using guided strategy statements.
- Focusing on process more than product.

Fostering Motivation

CLARIFYING EXPECTATIONS

To foster motivation, it is very important that teachers clearly state expectations, establish learning goals, and set clear standards for performance. Motivation is also increased when teachers ensure that students know the goals and objectives for lessons and assignments, and know in advance what to expect in learning activities. Teachers cannot assume that most students will understand assignment and worksheet directions. Miller (1990) found that only 78% of high-achieving elementary students and only 33% of low-achieving students understood "difficult" worksheet directions. Even "easy" directions were only understood by 80% of the low-achieving students. Thus it is essential for teachers to ensure that assignment directions are understood by all students. One way is to have students circle action words in directions and cross them off upon completion (Kuepper, 1990). Also, a teacher can check whether students comprehend directions by having them retell what needs to be done in their own words.

FOSTERING POSITIVE AND RESPECTFUL TEACHER–STUDENT RELATIONSHIPS

Students' motivation is closely connected to positive, caring relationships with their teachers. Teachers convey that they care about students by mentoring and nurturing them, getting to know them as individuals, talking with them in a supportive manner, listening to them nonjudgmentally, providing help with work, and demonstrating fairness (Doll et al., 2004; Pianta, 1999). Some teachers schedule one-to-one conversations after students fill out a "request for a 5-minute appointment" card. Others devise a way to regularly spend 5–15 minutes with a difficult-to-reach student, such as working together to collate papers every morning before class. Many secondary teachers use after-school hours as a time to connect with students, while others use student journals or reaction papers as methods to foster communication. Some high schools are reducing transitions so that "functional" teacher–student ratios are minimized (Pianta, 1999), by adopting block schedules (90 minutes daily per subject for one semester rather than 45 minutes daily the entire year). This results in three major classes each day per semester rather than six, which is more manageable for students and teachers. It provides opportunities for in-depth projects, reduces transition times between classes, and increases opportunities for teacher–student communication and relationship building.

Frequently students with poor academic motivation have a long history of negative interactions with teachers and tend to anticipate similarly negative interactions in the future. Although clearly student behavior and attitudes contribute to student–teacher relationships, teachers have considerable power to change negative relationships into positive ones. To reverse negative patterns, teachers must deliberately, repeatedly, and *genuinely* communicate appreciation for the students. Because it takes time to develop negative patterns, it also takes time to reverse them (Brown, 2004), but such effort is worthwhile. It is our experience that positive teacher–student rapport is essential before learning can take place, just as positive rapport is essential before effective counseling can occur (Rogers, 1951). Therefore, it is critical for teachers to find something to like about each student.

FOSTERING A POSITIVE CLASSROOM ATMOSPHERE

Students' motivation is increased by feeling academically competent. Academic competency is encouraged by regular, publicly acknowledged academic success. An absence of the threat of teacher belittlement or harshness enables students to feel safe, relaxed, and free to take the risks required to answer a difficult question or complete an assignment in a creative fashion.

CONNECTING ACADEMIC SUCCESS TO REAL-WORLD SUCCESS

Students often need help seeing how math, science, and social studies are important in their lives, and teachers can encourage students to perceive these skills as relevant (Shernoff, Csikszentmihalyi, Schneider, & Shernoff, 2003).

> **Mr. Norton's** eighth-grade students struggled to see the relevance of the math they were asked to study. One day he asked which students had seen their parents use a math book as they paid bills, did taxes, or purchased an automobile. The students laughed, and no hand was raised. "Well, then," Mr. Norton said, "it seems that this textbook isn't useful in the 'real world.' "
>
> Ben raised his hand and said, "But my dad uses what's *in* my math book when he does those things. Like he looks for the best interest rates when he takes out a car loan."
>
> Mr. Norton replied, "Well, you have a point. If you don't master basic math skills while you're in school, you'll be at a distinct disadvantage when it comes to handling money matters and making decisions as adults. Most of you will be out in that 'real world' in 5 years. Will you be ripped off by credit card companies because you don't understand interest rates? Will you be able to manage a household budget, or negotiate for the best salary when you land a great job?" With this discussion, Mr. Norton's students began to understand that learning their math—even fractions and decimals—would enable them to better manage their money and their lives.

Fostering Positive Emotions and Managing Negative Emotions

Classroom teachers can use several strategies to help students foster positive, and manage negative, emotions as they learn. One fundamental strategy is to *be sensitive and responsive to students' emotional states*. Because public experiences intensify emotions, teachers should take care as they give students feedback. In general, praise for success can be given in public, as it can increase positive emotions such as pride. In contrast, criticism should generally be given in private, because criticism can increase negative feelings such as anxiety. A pivotal experience enabling students to manage negative emotions and foster positive emotions is for them to observe adults doing the same. Teachers can model enthusiastic learning by sharing their own learning experiences—including their frustrations and triumphs—with their students.

> At the beginning of the year, **Ms. Garcia** shared with her high school math students that she too was in school—working toward her master's degree at a local university. On occasion, she shared some of her homework problems with her students and showed them how she had worked through the challenge of solving them, even enlisting their thinking and suggestions. She also shared her studying experiences with her students. They were surprised to find out that she attended class and did homework in the evenings and during weekends, after finishing her class preparations and correcting their papers. Since many of her students in that urban high school had difficulty imagining how they would ever go to college, much less on to graduate school, she took them on a field trip to see the university and meet some of her professors. Her openness regarding the frustrations, challenges, and successes of her educational experience made a profound impression on her students. They were thrilled to see her diploma.

Teachers are in an ideal position to help students develop *pride* in learning by focusing on the improvement of individual skills and using competency-based measures rather than group norms. Teachers can foster *joy* in learning by using a number of methods. They can help students identify a topic they like to learn about, such as lives of celebrities, a hobby, or an academic subject, and then help them link learning about their favorite topic with standard academic work. Or teachers can allow students to indulge their natural curiosity regarding a subject about which they are already passionate. Since positive emotions such as joy in learning are much more likely to occur in *active learning,* it is helpful for teachers to emphasize assignments that enable students to be active participants rather than passive learners listening to lectures, watching videos, or taking exams. Finally, whenever students become deeply involved with an activity, as much as possible adults should ensure they have time to *finish the activity* without interruption to foster persistence and "flow" (Carlton, 2004; Shernoff et al., 2003).

Positive emotions can also be increased with well-designed assignments. Teachers can encourage students to have fun as they learn with creative assignments that don't involve paper-and-pencil tasks—such as building a model, painting a mural, writing a song, choreographing a dance, interviewing a well-known person, conducting an experiment, conducting debates, discovering alternative problem-solving strategies, completing projects, analyzing case studies, taking part in role plays, or taking a trip. *Complex* assignments are also helpful. In a series of studies, student motivation was increased when teachers modified reading and language arts assignments to increase the number of opportunities students had to write multiple paragraphs, collaborate with peers, and monitor progress over extended time periods. In classrooms where the teachers implemented these modifications, the students were less focused on teacher approval and normative standards of evaluation. Low-achieving students reported considerably less work avoidance and considerably higher achievement. Over a 3-year period, retentions were decreased by 81% and special education referrals by 47% (Miller, 2003; Meece & Miller, 1999).

Teachers can help students manage negative emotions by teaching them to name emotions such as boredom, frustration, anxiety, and anger, and helping them understand that these emotions are normal but do not preclude completing assignments. Teachers can also remind students to utilize anxiety-reducing strategies such as physical exercise, progressive relaxation exercises, controlled and slow breathing exercises, positive thinking, and meditation before tests. In addition, teachers can help students reduce negative emotions such as academic anxiety in open class discussions, in which students are helped to understand that they are not alone in their fear of tests or a particular subject such as math, and during which students are provided emotional support from peers and adults. Classroom discussions can employ bibliotherapy to stimulate meaningful classroom conversations, with books such as *Defeating Math Anxiety* by Kitchens (Hebert & Furner, 1997). Teachers can reduce frustration by reframing failure as setbacks, and helping students brainstorm alternatives when setbacks are experienced.

Most importantly, teachers can minimize negative emotions experienced by students when assignments are at an appropriate level of difficulty—stimulating, challenging, and manageable—within each student's Zone of Proximal Development (Vygotsky, 1978). Assignments that are too easy result in boredom, and assignments that are too difficult result in frustration and anxiety. Therefore, teachers should carefully choose and monitor the difficulty level of assignments. Teachers should also ensure that the challenge of assigned tasks and the self-efficacy of students are both high and in balance by directly asking the students for feedback about the assignment difficulty, the time expended, and their personal experiences and expectations for success (Shernoff et al., 2003).

If assignments are too difficult for a particular student, they will need to be appropriately modified. Common strategies include:

- Shortening the assignment (assigning every other problem or those "down the left side" of a page, or reducing the number of spelling words required).
- Lessening the difficulty level of the task.
- Providing choice as to the method of evaluating the student's knowledge (oral tests, demonstrations, or projects instead of paper-and-pencil tests; having the student draw what happened in a science experiment instead of writing about it).
- Providing additional opportunities for rehearsal and review.
- Providing a sample of the expected work product.
- Encouraging social support, such as collaborating with a study buddy.
- Allowing the use of assistive tools such as a multiplication grid, calculator, tape recorder, or the computer spelling and grammar checkers.

It must be said, however, that the ideal of every task falling within each student's Zone of Proximal Development is very difficult to implement in any group learning situation, and is becoming even more difficult as classrooms are becoming increasingly diverse. Most teachers compromise by assigning some assignments to *all* students, providing enrichment opportunities for advanced students, and seeking supplemental support for students whose skills need remediation.

Ms. Roberts was a 10th-grade American history teacher whose students exhibited a wide range of talents and abilities. Anna read historical novels, enthusiastically visited historical sites with her family, and vividly remembered the American history learned in earlier grades. Liza found history excruciatingly boring and had so little memory of the earlier curriculum that she thought Abe Lincoln wrote the Declaration of Independence. Because she understood the importance of mastering state curriculum frameworks and passing relevant tests, Ms. Roberts used the standard curriculum and gave unit tests to every student. However, she supplemented the standard curriculum with student- and teacher-designed projects to meet individual needs. Anna's project was a complex paper on the influence of Freud on the American culture. Liza's project involved teaching younger children history facts, using a computer game that provided instant information correction.

Interestingly, using a comprehensive, multiweek series of lessons to develop *effective study skills* is a powerful method for teachers to help students manage negative emotions, because improved study skills have been found to reduce anxiety, anger, and frustration (Beidel, Turner, & Taylor-Ferreira, 1999; Hattie, Biggs, & Purdie, 1996).

Fostering Appropriate Behavior

Appropriate student behavior is an essential component of a positive learning environment. Teachers can foster appropriate student behavior by proactive classroom management, consistent monitoring and supervision, clear directives for behavior, appropriate consequences for both compliance and non-compliance, and tying natural consequences to compliance. Classrooms are most likely to foster appropriate self-regulated behavior when students collaborate in developing the behavioral expectations, help analyze inappropriate behavior for its function, determine more appropriate behaviors that serve the same function, and monitor and evaluate their own behavior. For example, students can help develop class rules, sign contracts agreeing to the rules, and monitor compliance. Detailed information regarding appropriate strategies is included in Chapter 6.

Fostering Time Management and Organization

Time management and organization involve planning and prioritizing activities; scheduling events, including components of long-term projects; writing down assignments and their components in an assignment book; keeping notebooks, desks, and lockers organized; and having regular routines for transitions, submitting assignments, and organizing materials.

When teachers empower their students to be good time managers, they model good time management and share their own time management strategies. They maintain a highly visible calendar with significant dates and assignments, and employ other visual reminders such as posters, schedules, calendars, bulletin boards, and charts. To help students transition to student-regulated time management, teachers can lead discussions in which they help students plan, schedule, and prioritize their tasks and activities. Students should be responsible for scheduling study time each day, making daily lists of tasks to complete, carrying an appointment book, writing reminder notes, keeping a daily log, carrying a notebook, scheduling weekly events, keeping records, using lists, preparing for the next day the night before, organizing paperwork, and leaving a clean workspace.

Writing assignments on the board, preferably in the same location each day when the assignment is given orally, helps *teach students to track assignments.* Assignment books should be required of all students who are expected to complete work independently. Until students are able to maintain assignment books on their own, they will need teachers to monitor their use daily. A calendar is also essential for older students who have many long-term assignments from different teachers. These materials can be checked (and signed) by the teacher (and parent) until their use is automatic. Teachers should encourage students to break assignments down into manageable chunks and write each part down separately in their scheduler. Students often need specific guidance in learning how to break long-term assignments into small components, even in postsecondary education. They also need to be taught to carry over any components that were not completed into the next day's or week's schedule. Classroom teachers can facilitate students' breaking down larger assignments and completing the components in a timely fashion by:

- Having students turn in each smaller task as completed for an initial project.
- Having students turn in a weekly "progress report" on which they note what tasks they have completed toward the larger assignment for a midlevel project.
- Having students develop a plan and keep a weekly "progress report" for their own records for an advanced project.

HELPING STUDENTS GAIN CONTROL OVER TIME

In order to feel a sense of control over time, students must avoid becoming overly involved in small details or unimportant tasks, taking on too many tasks, underestimating the time needed to complete a task, socializing too often, or procrastinating. Teachers can help students acquire a sense of control over time by holding open classroom discussions on these issues and having students brainstorm problem-solving strategies.

Often students can learn to manage their time more efficiently by using various devices to clock their activities—kitchen timers, hourglasses/sand timers, stopwatches, or battery-operated silent timers that show the amount of time remaining on the clock face. Such devices enable students to track how long it takes them to do a task, such as read a page of social studies or complete a math problem. They can then use that information to budget their time more accurately.

FOSTERING ORGANIZATION

Classrooms should also be organized and free of clutter, so that students can easily find materials they need and have areas in which to work. Teachers should establish procedures within the classroom concerning such things as how, when, and where to turn in homework assignments, late work, corrected papers, and completed projects; how to check out classroom library books; and where to keep materials.

Teachers can encourage students to organize their own materials by various strategies. For example, students might keep a pocket folder for assignments with "work to do" in the left pocket and "work to turn in" in the right pocket. Or, students might keep class notes, handouts, and returned assignments arranged chronologically in a loose-leaf notebook, separated by subject. Teachers can also help students keep desks, cubbies, and lockers neat enough to locate required materials by designating times for the entire class (possibly in "study buddy" partnerships) to organize desks, lockers, and/or notebooks.

> **Trey** was a fourth grader with Asperger's Disorder. One problem that challenged his teacher was his disorganization; he was always losing his homework, misplacing his books, and shoving things into his desk. An easy solution was to provide a large plastic crate on the floor beside his desk for storage of books and additional materials. This method kept the inside of Trey's desk relatively empty to be used for daily work folders and notebooks, and reduced stress for his teacher and himself. Trey's fifth grade teacher chose to assign him two desks placed side by side, and taped, to the corner of the desks, charts showing the items that belonged in each.

When teachers take time management and organization to the next step and empower students to become self-regulating, they help students become aware of these strategies and of methods to generalize organization to other settings. Teachers can accomplish this by leading classroom discussions about the *reasons* for organization and how students can maintain these strategies even in less organized situations. They can also encourage students to consciously develop their own organization methods for notebooks, lockers, and desks. Methods to accomplish these goals are discussed in more detail in Chapter 7.

Fostering Cognitive and Metacognitive Strategies

As discussed throughout this book, to become efficient independent learners, students need to develop cognitive and metacognitive strategies. Teachers can foster (or detract from), the acquisition of these skills by several methods. Some of these methods have been discussed earlier in this chapter, including explicitly discussing learning goals and methodology, having students set their own learning goals and develop strategic plans to meet these goals, and returning corrected assignments in a timely fashion. Teachers also foster students' cognitive and metacognitive growth when they use strategies to help students focus attention and benefit from lectures. These strategies include using attention cuing words, providing advance organizers such as definitions of unfamiliar vocabulary words or lecture outlines, using visual aids, distinguishing important information from less important information, frequently checking for students' understanding and rephrasing when appropriate, and attaching personal meaning to lecture material by relating the material to students' lives and prior learning.

Effective teachers foster the ability of students to focus and sustain their attention by controlling environmental factors such as classroom noise and activity level during periods when students are attempting to complete independent work. Students can be empowered to politely request reductions in distractions, such as the ability to change their seat or work in the library, when necessary. Effective teachers also gain students' attention before speaking. They can do this by speaking succinctly and prefacing important statements with cue words such as "Listen up," "This is important," "You don't want to miss this," "Here comes a million-dollar fact," "Yes, this *will* be on the test," or "I will begin when everyone is ready."

Before beginning a lecture, it is helpful to present *advance organizers* to prepare students for the material to be covered. These can include a list of the topics to be covered, definitions of new vocabulary words, or a graphic organizer that depicts the relationship of the new information to previously learned material. Many students benefit from having an outline, study guide, vocabulary word list, or a teacher's notes to follow in advance of a lecture, experiment, or activity. Teachers can hand out outlines from their notes to help students follow the flow of the material before presenting a lecture. Or teachers can encourage students to preread related materials before the lecture on the same material. As teachers lecture, it is important for them to use organizers to facilitate understanding, and for students to take notes to facilitate memory. (See "Note-Taking Skills," below.)

Graphic organizers help students see relationships between topics, main ideas, supporting details, and abstract concepts. These are useful to help students understand orally presented material. They are also useful to help students understand reading material (see Chapter 9) and to organize their own writing (see Chapter 10). Therefore, it is important for teachers to use graphic organizers themselves, and also to teach students how to develop them on their own.

As shown in Handout 3.1, graphic organizers can take many forms. The appropriate type to use varies according to the content of material and the underlying questions necessary to understand a topic (Baxendell, 2003; Jones, Pierce, & Hunter, 1988; Sebranek, Meyer, & Kemper, 1998). The steps in constructing a graphic organizer are as follows:

1. Scan the text (including the initial summary, headings, subheadings, and illustrations) to determine whether the information is structured hierarchically, in a timeline, in a compare-and-contrast format, or as an explanation.
2. Hypothesize which type of graphic organizer will best fit the structure of the information.
3. Sketch the graphic organizer.
4. Read the material to fill in gaps and additional important information.
5. Compare information in the passage with the graphic organizer.
6. Reflect on understanding and revise and correct the graphic organizer.
7. Summarize the material contained in the graphic organizer.

When teaching students to develop graphic organizers themselves, teachers should:

1. Present a good example of the graphic organizer.
2. Model how to construct each type of organizer, including thinking aloud and making and correcting errors.

3. Discuss why students should use the graphic organizers and how they might use them in other subjects.
4. Noncritically coach the students in their first attempts to make graphic organizers.
5. Provide multiple opportunities for practice (Jones et al., 1988).

Note-taking skills. When simply listening to lectures, students tend to miss 50% or more of the main ideas, and they forget even more material shortly after the lecture. Consequently, students who take and review notes score higher on tests than students who do not (Baker & Lombardi, 1985). As Zimmerman et al. (1996) relate, learning to take notes well is an essential study skill that involves listening, analyzing, selecting, and writing. Note taking has three vital operations: recording, revision, and reviewing.

Recording facilitates information retrieval for later review. Teachers should assess students' abilities to record orderly notes by evaluating students' notes at the beginning of the school year. For students with inadequate note-taking skills, supervised practice should be provided and eventually faded. Initially, note-taking skills can taught by providing "flexible skeletons"—that is, outlines of lectures with some material missing, which students can complete as the lecture progresses. As students become more independent in note taking, teachers should periodically check that their notes contain all key words and supporting details.

Revision facilitates memorization by having students rewrite the information, reorganize it into a more meaningful order, and assimilate the material into their cognitive schemata. *Reviewing* notes is clearly necessary for students to retain information well enough to be able to recall it. The more often notes are reviewed, the better the retention. Having students mark a tally each time they review their notes encourages spaced reviews and therefore aids learning (Lazarus, 1996).

In summary, the following are components of high-quality note taking:

1. *Recorded* notes should be labeled, legible, and contain key words and supporting details.
2. *Revised* notes are rewritten and reorganized. They include not only key words and supporting details, but additional questions and thoughts from the student's perspectives.
3. *Review tallies* are recorded to indicate the number of times the student reviewed the notes.

A variation on these steps, the Cornell Method (Pauk, 2000), recommends five note-taking steps: (1) *Record* notes during the lectures; (2) *reduce* those notes within 24 hours to as few key words as possible; (3) *recite* information by looking at the key words and attempting to recall the lecture; (4) *reflect* about the main ideas and any poorly understood concepts; and (5) *review* notes periodically.

Students with learning disabilities are often encouraged to use laptop computers for in-class note taking. The use of an outlining function in a word-processing program can be an effective tool for this purpose, and some computer programs have the additional capacity to move from an outline function to a graphic organizer function (Anderson-Inman, Knox-Quinn, & Horney, 1996; Tenny, 1992). Computers can act as an intermediary between print and understanding by enabling a student to insert, delete, and reorganize information. Computers also facilitate moving from one source to another and enable the student to view information from multiple perspectives. One system, the CoNoteS2 (Hadwin & Winne, 2001), is an electronic notebook that guides students in note taking and studying. It encourages students to integrate, organize, and synthesize information from multiple sources.

Finally, students' ability to understand lectures is greatly facilitated by tying lecture material to previously learned information. Students can understand new material better when they can associate it with concepts they already know. Teachers are encouraged to remind students how new material relates to their past learning, and to encourage information processing in the classroom. For example, the Connected Learning Assures Student Success (CLASS) program (B.

Pederson, personal communication, 2006) recommends using the strategy "Say it, play it, relay it, weigh it" to help students process information. After listening to a lecture, students:

1. *Say it* by pairing up and telling each other the main ideas just presented.
2. *Play it* by doing something with the new knowledge, such as playing a game, writing a poem, creating a poster, or building a model;
3. *Relay it* by teaching the new concept to one another.
4. *Weigh it* by assessing their knowledge of the topic.

Similarly, comprehensive approaches such as a *feedback lecture*—in which the teacher distributes study guides before the lecture, and follows the lecture with discussion components relevant to students' lives—effectively engage students with differing learning styles (Ogden, 2003).

Fostering Independent Skills in Science, Math, Reading, Writing, Test-Taking, and Performance

Ways to promote independent reading skills are addressed in Chapter 9; strategies to foster independent writing skills are covered in Chapter 10; strategies to foster independent science, math, and technology skills are presented in Chapter 11; and methods to foster successful test taking and performance are addressed in Chapter 12.

Fostering Personal Metacognition

Finally, teachers are encouraged to nourish their own executive skills, because they are currently expected to manage extraordinarily challenging and often seemingly impossible jobs. They typically are expected to plan lessons, gather materials, develop student materials and activities, teach concepts required by state standards, provide individualized instruction, guide practice opportunities, assess student performance, reteach lessons to students who need extra help, manage classroom behavior, grade papers, maintain clerical records, fill out report cards, communicate regularly with parents, meet with student development teams, and serve on school committees. The degree of stress requires a high level of executive functioning to avoid overload and burnout. Several strategies can help.

- Teachers can foster their own executive strategies in terms of organization, time management, and other strategies (Dawson & Guare, 2004).
- Teachers can learn to recognize situations that call for "adaptive metacognition" (Lin, Schwartz, & Hatano, 2005). These are common situations (such as students' not completing homework) that result from very diverse sources. Although they appear routine, they are variable and require individualized responses.
- To develop adaptive metacognition, teachers can use "critical event instruction" (Lin et al., 2005): They can consider a "routine" problem situation, individually generate questions regarding additional information they would like in order to solve the problem, listen to each other's perspectives, generate possible solutions from various perspectives, reflect on the possible effectiveness of these solutions, and share their thinking with each other.
- Teachers are encouraged to adopt an approach that stresses a positive outlook and having fun. For example, many teachers and some entire schools have adopted the "Fish philosophy." Originally developed as a motivational tool for business, this approach focuses on building relationships, mindfulness, and positive thinking through the four cornerstones: "Be there, play, make their day, and choose your attitude" (Lundin, 2006; Lundin et al., 2000).

TABLE 3.3. Teacher Affirmations

- I make a difference in my students' lives.
- I create a safe and friendly atmosphere in my classroom.
- I smile a lot and am very positive in my work.
- I say exactly what I mean and mean exactly what I say.
- I realize that teaching is a profession of utmost importance.
- I am organized and plan ahead.
- I am not the same teacher I was yesterday, because each day I learn and experience more.
- I help my students find academic and personal success.
- I seek and find peace in my workplace as I help build a better world.

Note. From Chickie-Wolfe (2005a). Copyright 2005 by Corwin Press. Reprinted by permission.

- Teachers can use affirmations to foster feelings of empowerment (see Table 3.3). Additional positive affirmations for teachers are presented in *Cognitive Nourishment: Life-Changing Affirmations for the Savvy Teacher* (Chickie-Wolfe, 2005a).

Appraisal

Appraising the classroom strategies implemented to foster study skills and independent learning again requires determining whether or not they have been effective by asking "What did we do?" "How well did it work?" and "What do we need to change?" After interventions are designed and implemented, teachers and consultants assess how well the interventions were implemented and how well they succeeded at changing the target behaviors and outcomes. Often, appraisal results in modification of interventions, as when a teacher finds that insufficient time makes the originally selected implementation impossible. After modified interventions have been implemented successfully, strategies to promote generalization and student self-regulation are designed and implemented.

Assessment strategies used to explore and define the problem, discussed in the beginning of this chapter, can be appropriately readministered to generate outcomes data and appraise the success of the intervention. Doll, Zucker, and Brehm (2004), for example, recommend reassessing a classroom's climate by completing another Class Map. Less formal appraisal methods are also appropriate. For example, a teacher who initiated monthly Parent–Teacher Coffees to encourage parental involvement and improved homework completion can appraise her success by tracking parent attendance and student homework completion.

Help Students Develop Their Personal Learning Guides (HILLs)

In their Personal Learning Guides or HILLs, students can insert notes on classroom strategies they have found to be effective. The students might also include copies of recently completed and blank versions of the following materials related to this topic:

Worksheet 3.1. Checklist of Classroom Qualities That Foster Independent Learning
Worksheet 3.2. Menu of Interview Questions about School
Handout 3.1. Graphic Organizers

WORKSHEET 3.1.

Checklist of Classroom Qualities That Foster Independent Learning

The classroom atmosphere encourages student self-regulation.	
	Students are treated as individuals and encouraged to meet varied needs and develop unique talents; as often as possible, students select learning topics.
	Students are treated as collaborators in the learning process.
	Students are taught to evaluate and appraise their own learning success.
	Students are encouraged to evaluate their own learning and study strategies, and to maintain Personal Learning Guides (HILLs).
School personnel foster positive home–school–student–peer collaboration.	
	Family members are treated as coteachers and equal partners in students' education, are encouraged to hold high expectations for students, and are explicitly included in homework assignments.
	Family input is gathered regarding academic priorities; culture-respecting and family-centered practices are employed.
	Proactive, persistent, and regular formal and informal two-way communication between home and school is maintained in person, in writing, and electronically.
	Homework assignments reinforce successful classroom experiences and are well designed.
	Student self-regulation of homework completion is encouraged by goal setting, graphing, and tracking.
	Teachers help students identify methods to obtain help from family members, hotlines, and websites.
	Solution-oriented, conjoint consultation is fostered to address problem situations.
	The classroom climate promotes prosocial behaviors such as helping, sharing, cooperating, and collaborative problem solving with peers.
	Teachers model respect and courtesy toward students; they communicate that respect and kindness toward both peers and adults are expected and required.
	More popular students are encouraged to accept and "sponsor" new and rejected children.
	Teachers help students identify methods to obtain help from peers, including the identification of "study buddies" and study groups for each subject.
	Students are taught how to give specific and positive feedback on academic work and how to tutor.
Classroom procedures foster student motivation.	
	Teachers convey that they care about students by nurturing and getting to know them as individuals.
	Assignments evoke curiosity and positive emotional responses.
	Students are given challenging yet manageable tasks, and enough help so they can make progress.

(continued)

Classroom Qualities That Foster Independent Learning *(page 2 of 3)*

	Students are given some control over assignments and projects; content is personalized.
	Academic and behavioral directions, expectations, and standards are clear to students.
	Teachers frequently provide verbal praise and support, and write positive comments on papers.
	Feelings of academic competency are encouraged by regular, publicly acknowledged success.
	Each student's short- and long-term learning goals are collaboratively developed.
	Work is collected, corrected with specific and qualitative feedback, and returned promptly.
	Effort and accuracy are emphasized when students complete tasks.
	Students are encouraged to attribute success to increasing competence and sustained effort.
	Academic success is tied to real-world success.
Positive emotions are fostered, and negative emotions are actively managed.	
	Enthusiasm for learning is modeled by educators.
	Positive emotions are encouraged by incorporating fun and laughter, as well as opportunities to experience pride, joy, and "flow" (concentrated work on enjoyable learning activities).
	Students are not subjected to public humiliation or criticism; mistakes are used as teaching tools.
	Negative emotions such as boredom, frustration, anxiety, and anger are identified and addressed.
	Teachers encourage students to brainstorm alternatives when setbacks are experienced.
	Assignments are stimulating and challenging but manageable (at an appropriate level of difficulty).
Appropriate behavior is fostered.	
	Students collaborate with teachers in developing clear behavioral expectations.
	Appropriate behavior has positive and preferably internally rewarding consequences.
	Inappropriate behavior has appropriate consequences that are consistently applied.
	The function of inappropriate behaviors is assessed, and more appropriate behaviors are substituted.
	Students are encouraged to monitor and evaluate their own behavior.
Time is managed well, and organization is encouraged.	
	The teacher uses time management strategies and shares those strategies with students.
	The teacher leads discussions encouraging students in planning and prioritizing their activities.
	The teacher gives assignments both orally and in writing that are clear and provide work models.
	The teacher encourages students to write assignments in an assignment book.
	For large projects, students submit weekly progress reports or smaller parts as completed.
	Students use their knowledge of the time it takes to complete tasks to schedule appropriately.
	The teacher models organization and encourages students to consciously develop methods for organizing their work.

(continued)

Classroom Qualities That Foster Independent Learning *(page 3 of 3)*

Cognitive and metacognitive strategies are taught and encouraged.	
	The classroom has minimal distractions and is quiet for independent work.
	The teacher directly and specifically teaches memory strategies.
	Lectures are effectively structured.
	Students are taught effective note-taking skills and required to add details and review.
	Students are encouraged to develop metacognitive skills in assessing their own learning.
Math and science skills are developed.	
	Math and science instruction is guided and is tied to real-life skills.
	Math and science skills are assessed through trace methodology and think-aloud procedures.
	Teachers strike an appropriate balance between comprehension and memorization.
	When calculators are used, students are skilled in application, but also estimate answers.
	Cross-disciplinary collaboration is fostered.
Reading skills are developed.	
	Teachers provide varied reading materials, and varied approaches to reading are taught.
	Students are taught methods to increase concentration and comprehension as they read.
	Teachers check for students' ability to understand textbooks and provide appropriate alternatives.
Writing skills are developed.	
	Students have opportunities to observe effective writing, and writing is connected to real-life skills.
	Effective methods in spelling are used.
	The writing process (prewriting, drafting, revising, editing, publishing) is fostered.
	Student self-regulation of writing is assessed through trace methodology and interviewing.
Test-taking skills are developed.	
	Material to be covered on tests is clear; study guides are provided or developed by students.
	Students are reminded to use corrected work as study guides.
	Students know test question formats and are given sample test questions.
	Grading criteria and rubrics are shared with students.
	Students collaborate in developing assessment measures or help develop test questions.
	Students monitor their own learning and plan their studying, using previously successful strategies.
	Tests are administered in a low-anxiety atmosphere.
	Students are encouraged to use tests as opportunities to demonstrate knowledge.
Teachers develop their own metacognitive skills.	
	Teachers respond to seemingly identical circumstances, such as lack of homework completion, with strategies responsive to individual circumstances.

WORKSHEET 3.2.

Menu of Interview Questions about School

Student ______________________________ Date ______________

1. How do your teachers help you learn? Is there anything your teachers do that cause you problems in terms of learning? What would you like to be different?

2. Which of your assignments are "just right"? Which are too hard? Which are too easy?

3. What are some examples of projects or assignments you were able to choose or design yourself? Would you like to have more chances to choose or design assignments?

4. What are some times that your teachers or classmates made being in class fun? Do you think your teachers should make being in class more fun?

5. What are some times that your teachers or your classmates made you upset, mad, or nervous? How would you like that to be different?

6. What do you think are your teachers' goals for you? What do they expect from you in terms of learning? What happens when you do not meet those expectations?

(continued)

Menu of Interview Questions about School *(page 2 of 2)*

7. What rules do you have in school? How are these rules determined? What happens when they are not followed? If you wanted to change a rule, how would you go about getting it changed?

8. Who do you ask for help when you need help with an assignment? Do you have different people for different subjects? What adults encourage you to do well in school?

9. Do you think that your classmates want you to do well in school? Do you feel able to ask classmates for help? Do your classmates help you study? Is there anything they do that cause you problems in terms of studying? Do you ever study with a classmate? What works well when you study together? What doesn't work well?

10. Is your class well organized and predictable? Do you know where to turn in work, how to find out assignments, and when different events will take place?

11. How do your teachers help you prepare for weekly or unit tests? How do your teachers help you prepare for the state tests? What could they do differently to help you more?

HANDOUT 3.1.

Graphic Organizers

Name of organizer	Sample
Concept map Shows a central idea with its characteristics.	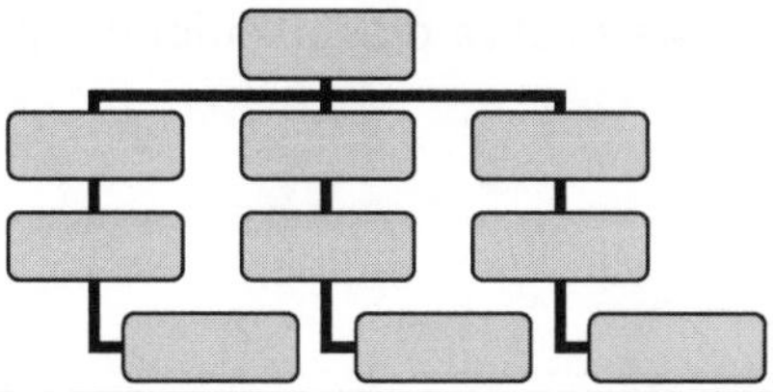
Contrast-and-compare matrix Shows similarities and differences between two or more ideas, things, or people.	Name 1 / Name 2; Attribute 1; Attribute 2; Attribute 3
Cycle Shows a process with a continual cycle or a series of events that produce a set of results repeatedly.	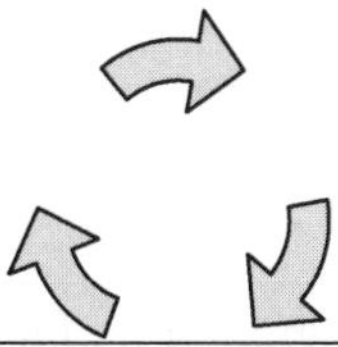
Flow diagram or sequence chart Shows the steps in a linear sequence of events, the stages of something, or the goals and actions of a person.	Initiating event → Event 2 → Final outcome
Family tree Shows how multiple factors, people, ideas, or events coalesce to one outcome.	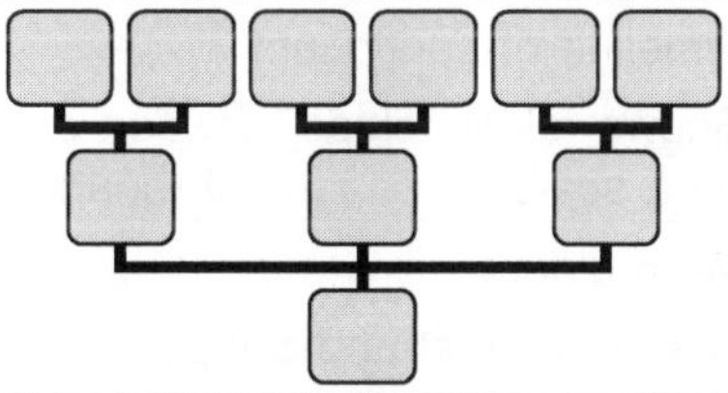
Network tree or organization chart Shows hierarchy of relationships, causal information, or branching procedures.	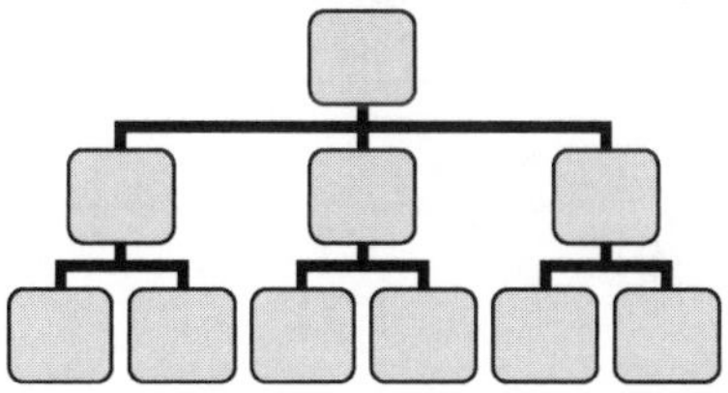

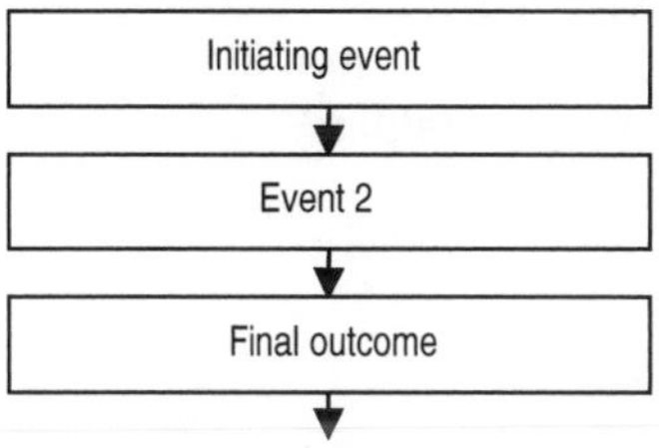

(continued)

Graphic Organizers *(page 2 of 2)*

Name of organizer	Sample
Pie chart Shows relative proportion of components.	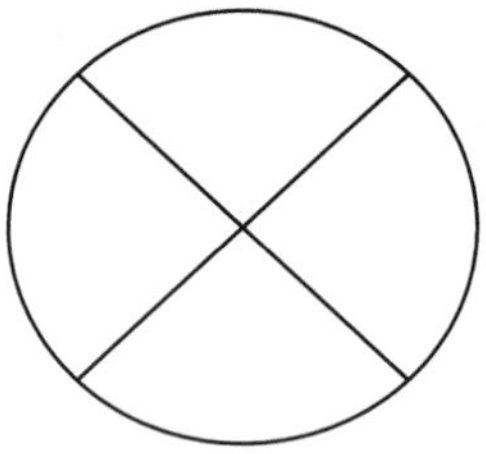
Problem-and-solution outline Represents a problem, the solutions attempted, the results of each attempt, and the final outcome.	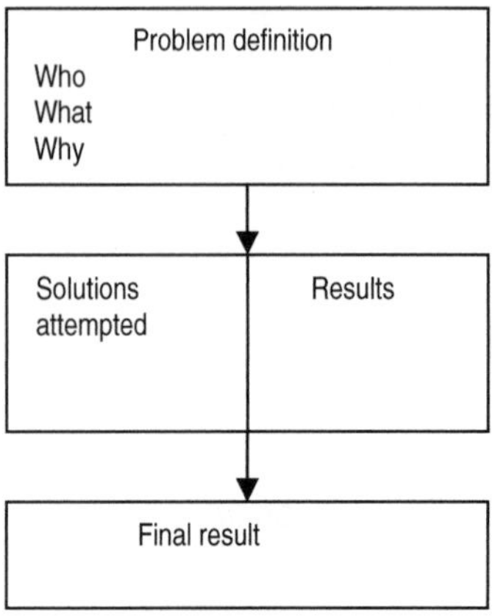 Problem definition Who What Why Solutions attempted / Results Final result
Map of main idea and supporting details Describes a central idea, concept, or process and its supporting details.	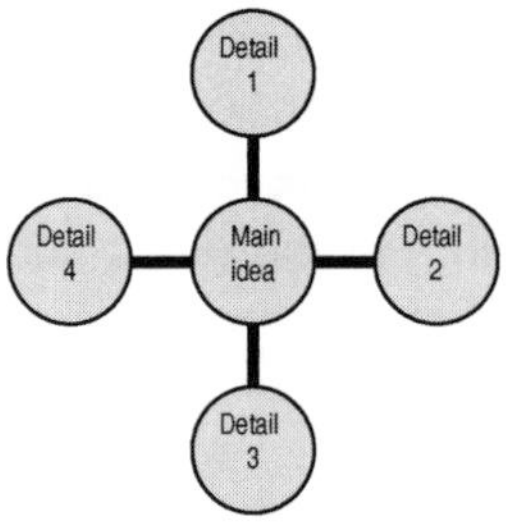 Detail 1 Detail 4 — Main idea — Detail 2 Detail 3
Timeline or continuum Shows relationships between events, ages, degrees or ratings on a scale, or shades of meaning.	Low/beginning — High/end point
Venn diagram Like a contrast-and-compare matrix, shows similarities and differences between two or more ideas, things, or people.	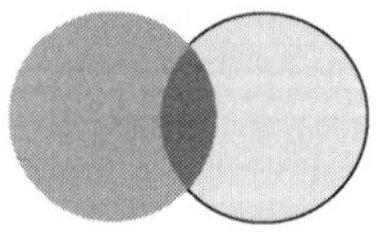

4

Empowering Students to Self-Regulate Motivation to Study and Learn

Motivation is best considered a set of beliefs and behaviors rather than a personality trait. Every student is "motivated"—just not necessarily to do what adults would like!

OVERVIEW

Ms. Coe teaches in a very impoverished inner-city school, with students who believe they are destined to the same hopeless, unemployed, periodically incarcerated lives they observe in neighborhood adults. To counteract this belief, in September Ms. Coe has each student select a positive affirmation and make a poster about it. She tacks these posters up and refers to them throughout the year. She also supplements the standard sixth-grade curriculum with biographies about individuals who have "made it" out of grinding poverty—not through glamorous professional sports or show business, but through science, politics, medicine, and education. She invites local business owners and employees in as guest speakers, and also shares her own story as a first-generation college graduate. "This could be you," she tells them—and even has them sing, "This could be me! I can make it too!" The kids know it's corny—but they still love it.

As discussed in previous chapters, environmental variables are critical when considering study skills and independent learning. However, it is also important to address individual student factors such as motivation, because the ability to self-motivate is essential for independent learning. Regardless of family, friends, and classroom variables, at some point students need to know how to manage their own motivation across contexts. This chapter focuses on methods to address motivation directly; additional chapters, such as Chapters 7 and 8, describe interventions that affect motivation indirectly. Strategies discussed in this chapter are appropriate for students who are referred because they do not have academic goals, seem not to care, believe that success is more closely tied to ability than to effort, or are pessimistic. The tools discussed in this chapter are concisely summarized in Worksheet 4.1, Checklist of Strategies to Promote Motivation.

RESEARCH FOUNDATIONS

Student motivation and self-discipline have an obvious and profound impact on academic achievement. As Duckworth and Seligman (2005) note, self-discipline predicts grades, attendance, course selection, and homework completion better than either intelligence or achievement test scores do. Motivation clearly matters.

Theories and research addressing why individuals are "motivated" (i.e., direct their energy toward achieving certain goals) permeate psychology and are extremely diverse. A comprehensive review of these theories, and the research that supports or refutes them, is beyond the scope of this book; the reader is referred to Pintrich and Schunk (2002) and Stipek (2002) for detailed reviews. However, we will briefly review relevant theories because we have found that integrating these diverse theories is helpful. Reasons for academic motivation, or lack thereof, vary enormously.

For all students, academic motivation varies according to the subject matter, assignments, classroom climate, teacher–student relationships, peer relationships, and other situational factors ranging from health to environmental stressors. Successful students can be extrinsically (externally) motivated to achieve an end result, intrinsically (internally) motivated to participate in an activity for its own sake, or *both* extrinsically motivated to do well and intrinsically motivated by an interest in the material (Pintrich & Schunk, 2002). To help students increase their academic motivation, it can be appropriate to tap one or more of the following perspectives:

- Students are motivated by a drive for personal growth, which is fostered by positive relationships with parents, teachers, and mentors. (Person-centered: Rogers, 1951.)
- Students are motivated when they are reinforced (rewarded) or when they observe others receiving reinforcements. (Behaviorism: Skinner, 1953; Bandura, 1986.)
- Students are motivated to meet deficiency needs, such as survival, safety, belonging, and self-esteem, first. Then they can turn to meeting growth needs, such as intellectual achievement, aesthetics, and self-actualization. (Humanism: Maslow, 1970.)
- Everyone chooses methods to meet basic needs for fun, safety, love/belonging, freedom, and power/control. Any given activity can meet multiple needs, or can meet one need while conflicting with another. (Choice theory: Glasser, 1998.)
- Students are internally motivated to be competent, control their environment, and relate to others. (Psychosocial development: Erikson, 1963; self-determination: Deci & Ryan, 1985.)
- Students are motivated by their cognitions, including their belief in self-efficacy, attributions for success and failure, locus of control, and goals. (Cognitive theory: See below.)

Of the theories described above, cognitive theory has generated the most research relevant to study skills. This research has found that *positive self-efficacy* regarding academic tasks results in academic success, because it is associated with greater persistence, decreased procrastination, increased use of self-regulatory strategies, and higher grade attainment—to the point that self-efficacy has been described as "the key to improving the motivation of struggling learners" (Margolis & McCabe, 2003, p. 162). However, feelings of self-efficacy are task specific and vary for each subject and even for each task and assignment (Bandura, 1997; Wolters, 2003).

A considerable body of research has differentiated goal orientations into four types: those related to *mastery, performance approach, performance avoidance,* and *work avoidance*. Each orientation type has been associated with particular settings and academic outcomes (Ames, 1992; Elliot, 1999; Harackiewicz, Barron, Pintrich, Elliot, & Thrash, 2002; Meece & Miller, 1999; Pintrich, 2000a; Urdan, 1997; Wolters, 2002, 2003).

Students with *mastery goal orientations* are intrinsically oriented and focus on improving their knowledge, skills, and understanding of the material. These orientations are most prevalent in settings with competency-based or criterion-referenced standards. Students with these orientations tend to value learning as an end in itself, use more effective cognitive learning strategies, prefer more challenging tasks, and display greater persistence in learning.

Students with *performance goal orientations* focus on external assessments by others. These orientations are most prevalent in competitive settings with norm-referenced standards. Students with performance *approach* goal orientations express interest in pleasing others, impressing others by "looking good," receiving high grades, bringing honor to their families, maintaining friendships with high-achieving friends, or obtaining rewards. These students obtain higher grades than those with only mastery goal orientations, but they may tend to learn superficially, and to prefer less challenging assignments and surface-level processing. Students with performance *avoidance* goal orientations focus on not "looking bad" or appearing incompetent. They frequently suffer from test and performance anxiety, fear of success, or fear of failure. Performance avoidance goal orientations are associated with poor academic outcomes, superficial learning, and a preference for less challenging assignments and surface-level processing.

Students who have *work avoidance goal orientations* focus on minimizing the amount of time and effort they expend. These students have the poorest academic outcomes and are likely to procrastinate, use poor cognitive study strategies, have insufficient metacognitive awareness, have poor test performance, withdraw from courses, and drop out of school. Students who have difficulty in school can have motivational impairments. For example, Carlson, Booth, Shin, and Canu (2002) found that relative to nondisabled children, those with ADHD preferred easier work, enjoyed learning less, had less persistence, and relied more on external than on internal standards to appraise their own performance.

Students usually develop their belief systems by adopting the belief systems of their parents and teachers. Thus educators' and parental expectations, conveyed overtly and covertly, have a profound influence on the development of students' beliefs about their ability to do well in school and have a direct impact on academic performance. When educators or parents convey low expectations, students respond with lower achievement and have lower self-assessments of their ability. High expectations for student achievement are a hallmark of educational excellence, because students respond with higher achievement and improved academic self-efficacy (Bempechat, 2004; Stipek & Gralinski, 1991). One way that teachers convey expectations is by the difficulty level of assigned work. Miller and Meece (1999) found students who had opportunities to complete high-challenge tasks preferred them because they felt creative, experienced positive emotions, and worked hard. Those not exposed to high-challenge tasks questioned whether they had the ability to complete them and were bored with the low-challenge tasks.

Further, *adults' reactions* affect students' self-assessments of their ability. When an adult responds with concern in response to low achievement, students understand that the adult believes that they did not expend enough effort and can respond with increased effort in the future. On the other hand, sympathy regarding a low grade causes students to understand that adults believe they have low ability, and consequently lowers future achievement (Weiner, 1994).

Self-Regulation and Motivation

Self-regulated students actually deliberately regulate their motivation level. Wolters (1998) found that successful students used a variety of cognitive, social, volitional, and extrinsic and intrinsic motivational strategies, and that they varied these strategies according to context. Cognitive strategies described included summarizing readings, making flashcards, and taking and reviewing notes (22% of the strategies). Social strategies included seeking help from a professor, teaching assistant, or friend (11%). Volition strategies involved using methods to regulate learning environments (14%), maintaining or increasing concentration (3%), intensifying willpower (7%), and regulating emotions (1%). Strategies tied to extrinsic regulation included reminding themselves that they wanted to do well (15%) and giving themselves a reward after completing work (5%). Strategies tied to intrinsic regulation included focusing on mastery goals such as learning for the sake of learning (1%), increasing task value by focusing on relevance and utility to their own lives (9%), increasing interest by making the task more enjoyable or interesting (8%), and making the task seem easier (1%). Students who used intrinsic strategies were more likely to have learning goal orientations and to use cognitive strategies. In contrast, students using extrinsic regulation strategies were likely to use neither intrinsic regulation strategies nor cognitive study strategies. Successful students invoked different strategies according to the task at hand—cognitive strategies with difficult tasks, and volitional strategies with boring tasks.

METHODS

Preparation

Assessing Motivation

Assessing a student's motivation is complex and requires an ecological approach. First, it is useful to review the *cumulative academic file* to determine any pattern of academic difficulties, noting fluctuations by subject area, age, school, and so forth. Often collaboratively reviewing the file with the student can be quite illuminating. It can also be helpful to assess social factors, as discussed in Chapter 2, and classroom factors, as discussed in Chapter 3.

Adults can informally assess variables that affect motivation and are internal to the student by using the menu of questions contained in Worksheet 4.2, Menu of Interview Questions about Motivation. They can use Worksheet 4.3, Goal Setting and Prioritization Work Sheet and Worksheet 4.4, Visualization Exercise to help students develop goals and priorities. Finally, Worksheet 4.1, Checklist of Strategies to Promote Motivation can be used to assess which motivation strategies a student already employs.

For example, in the *visualization exercise* (Chickie-Wolfe & Harvey, 2006b; see Worksheet 4.4) students are asked to envision "the best student in the world" and imagine what that student does after school, while studying, and when completing homework. Students are asked to compare the "best student's" behavior with their own and adopt some of the strategies used by the "best student."

> When **Corey's** fifth-grade teacher asked him to visualize "the best student in the world," he imagined that this student would complete homework before watching television, turn in assignments on time, and study for at least three evenings before a test. Corey also visualized that the "best student" would be "curious about everything" and would "do crazy things like read the encyclopedia for fun instead of playing hockey." Corey wasn't interested in being the best student in the world, so he decided to forgo reading the encyclopedia. However, he did adopt three of the strategies he described: completing homework before watching television, turning in assignments on time, and studying three evenings before every test. He was very pleased to find that these simple strategies made a significant difference in his report card grades.

Another method to help students determine their goals is to conduct a relaxed brainstorming session in which the student discusses desired accomplishments. As in all brainstorming sessions, no value judgments should occur until the end of the session, when questions regarding feasibility are addressed. Possible questions are included in the interview form in Worksheet 4.3 and are expanded upon below.

1. "Take 3 minutes to quickly write down your long-term academic, career, and personal goals. Would you like to graduate from high school? Attend college? If so, which college(s)? What are three jobs you might like to have as an adult? As an adult, would you like to have a family? Do you know where you might like to live? Now put stars by your most important long-term goals."

2. "Take 3 minutes to quickly write down your short-term academic, career, and personal goals. What would you like to accomplish in the next year? What would you like to learn? What grades would you like to get? How would you like to spend your free time? In what activities would you like to participate? When you look at your long-term goals, what are additional short-term goals to add to this list? What short-term goals are necessary to make your long-term goals possible? Now put stars by your most important short-term goals." (Note that students usually need help developing the list of short-term goals that are necessary for them to achieve their long-term goals.)

3. "What things that you spend time on now will help you achieve your important long- and short-term goals? What things that you spend time on now will not help you achieve these goals?" (Examples: Helpful activities might include doing homework, going to school, playing basketball every day. Unhelpful activities might include watching TV or listening to music, unless these are tied to a goal such as spending some time relaxing.)

4. "What people or things in your life will help you achieve each important long- and short-term goal? Which of your friends and family members support each goal? What are your habits and talents that make each goal more possible?" (Examples: Parents who are saving money toward college, or an athletic talent that, with practice, could result in making a team or obtaining a scholarship.)

5. "What people or things in your life will make it difficult to achieve each important long- and short-term goal? Which family members or friends do not support each goal? What are your habits and nontalents that make the goal less possible?" (Examples: Friends who want to text-message instead of doing homework, or the habit of forgetting books.)

6. "Let's brainstorm several specific actions you could take to overcome each difficulty." (Examples: To avoid text-messaging with friends instead of doing homework, a person could tell friends to text-message him or her only after 8 P.M., or could turn off the cell phone.)

7. "Select specific activities from that list that you plan to do, and set a deadline for each." (Examples: Decide, starting today, to turn off the cell phone during study time and tell friends at lunch to text-message only after 8 P.M.)

8. "What additional help do you need to achieve each important long- and short-term goal?" (Examples: Parental help in math homework, or teachers' writing homework assignments on the board.)

9. "What are some ways that you can increase the time you spend on the goals and activities you feel are most important? How can you reduce the time you spend on those you feel are less important? What are some ways that you can focus your attention on your important activities and avoid interruptions as you work on them?"

10. What do you consider "doing well enough" in school? What do your parents consider "doing well enough?" (Example: Parents want the student to maintain a B average, but the student feels quite comfortable with grades of C.)

11. What goals do you set for yourself when completing homework or studying for a test? Tell me about them. (Example: One student wants to "get it done" without consideration for accuracy, whereas another student strives for 100% accuracy.)

12. Let's look at your goals compared to how you spend your time. What do you think? (Example: Some individuals' goals and time expenditures are diametrically opposed to one another, resulting in considerable frustration.)

Published assessment tools can be used to assess motivation as well. DiPerna and Elliott (2000) developed the Academic Competence Evaluation Scales (ACES) to measure academic skills (reading/language arts, mathematics, and critical thinking) and academic "enablers" (motivation, study skills, engagement, and interpersonal skills) for students from kindergarten through college. The ACES has a teacher form (grades K–12) and a student form (grade 6–college) that can be administered to groups or individuals. Reviews of the ACES indicate that it has psychometric validity and the accompanying computer scoring software can be helpful in designing and tracking interventions over time (Hambleton, in press; Sabers & Bonner, in press).

The Children's Academic Intrinsic Motivation Inventory (CAIMI; Gottfried, 1986) assesses the intrinsic motivation of students to learn, as shown by curiosity, persistence, and the desire to master challenging tasks. The CAMI is designed for use with children in grades 4–8 and assesses academic motivation by subject area (reading, math, social studies, science, and general learning). Results are positively correlated with achievement, negatively correlated with anxiety, and not correlated with intelligence.

The Achievement Motivation Profile (AMP; Friedland, Mandel, & Marcus, 1996) was developed to measure adolescents' motivation for academic achievement. Subscales cover motivation for achievement, response style, inner resources, interpersonal strengths, and work habits. The AMP can be administered to groups or individuals. The limited normative sample suggests that this instrument is useful only in the context of a broader assessment, however (Owen, 2001).

The Assessment of Core Goals (ACG; Nichols, 1991) is a nonstandardized instrument that can be used to help adolescents determine their primary goals and delineate activities to meet these goals. A student lists up to 25 satisfying activities and experiences, examines 15 of these experiences in depth, groups the experiences according to associated feelings, identifies core goals, and considers positive and negative aspects of goals.

After interviewing a student, reviewing the student's records, and employing selected assessment tools, the student's team members can develop an intervention plan. Worksheets 4.1 and 4.3 can be used to facilitate this process, then used as monitoring tools, and finally used to appraise intervention outcomes.

Performance

To increase students' academic motivation, adults can focus on developing positive relationships, ensure that they are reinforced for expending effort and producing accurate work, help them develop positive belief systems regarding their potential, help them develop and prioritize short- and long-term learning goals, encourage them to foster constructive attributions and an internal locus of control, foster optimism, help them connect academic success to real-world success, foster strategy differentiation, and help them learn to self-regulate motivation.

Helping Students Develop Positive Belief Systems Regarding Their Academic Potential

It is critical for adults to convey to students that they believe the students can succeed and that this success is desirable. As discussed previously, the belief systems and academic expectations conveyed by parents and teachers are often adopted by students, but even one adult who believes in a student can make a pivotal difference. Neighbors, relatives, athletic coaches, school personnel, and many other adults can all take the role of mentor and facilitate a student's developing a positive belief system. Remarkably, many autobiographies of highly successful or resilient adults attest to one adult's having told them, at a critical moment, "I know you can do it."

Adults can develop positive mentoring relationships with students and thereby increase academic motivation by getting to know the students as individuals, listening to their concerns attentively, and helping them strategize methods to cope with personal and academic challenges. Adults can also foster motivation by encouraging students to develop unique talents, by taking an interest in their assignments, and by encouraging curiosity and positive emotions about academic assignments.

In particular, adults can strategize with students to help them meet personal needs, or postpone attending to them, in order to attend to academic requirements sufficiently that personal goals are met. For example, when a teenager falls in love and experiences pleasurable sexuality in conjunction with intense feelings of love and affiliation, gratifying these needs often takes priority over schoolwork. An adult can help a student find ways to apply problem-solving strategies so that both affiliative needs and academic goals can be met.

> **Alice**, a high school senior, was living alone with her father; her mother had died 6 months earlier. Although she had previously been an honor student, this spring semester Alice was failing every class because she was not submitting major assignments. She was referred to the school psychologist a month before she was to graduate from high school, when she was in danger of not graduating *and* of having her college grant revoked. Alice indicated that she was aware of the implications of this lack of work completion, yet seemed unable to change her behavior. Alice had many friends who were high achievers and on their way to college, but her boyfriend of the past year was planning to take time off before going to college. The school psychologist helped Alice become aware that she was hesitant to "lose" her boyfriend and father in addition to having lost her mother, and was experiencing a conflict between her needs for affiliation and achievement. They brainstormed alternatives, and Alice decided to attend a nearby college for the time being.

Ensuring That Students Are Reinforced for Expending Effort and Producing Accurate Work

Teachers, parents, and consultants can collaborate to ensure that students are assigned challenging yet manageable tasks, are evaluated with competency-based rather than criterion-referenced measures, and are reinforced for both effort and accuracy at home and in school. Adults can personally attend to and praise students' effort and high-quality work production, and express concern (rather than sympathy) when students have low achievement. Teachers can also increase academic motivation by providing frequent feedback (e.g., giving frequent quizzes).

Helping Students Develop and Prioritize Short- and Long-Term Learning Goals

An important component of motivation is defining short- and long-term goals that are both general (e.g., "go to college and become an engineer") and specific (e.g., "obtain a score of at least 85% on tomorrow's math test"). Long-term goals should be personally meaningful and achievable. Short-term goals should be tied to long-term goals; they should also be specific, moderately difficult, achievable, and capable of being easily and frequently measured (Bandura, 1997; Margolis & McCabe, 2003; Schunk, 1999).

Any adult expectation for a student contains implied goals (e.g., "This student could go to college and become an engineer," "This student is capable of being on the honor roll and therefore should achieve grades of 85% or better on any test"). Further, any referral question has at least one implied goal. For example, a referral of a student because she does not complete homework has the implied goal that homework will be completed. A referral of a student because of poor test scores has the implied goal that test scores will improve. These implied goals are the foundations for preintervention and outcomes-based assessment. In the first of the two examples above, pre- and postintervention assessments would include an assessment of the frequency and accuracy of homework completion. In the second, pre- and postintervention assessments would include test results. Although these goals are most often set by adults, researchers have found that student achievement is higher when students develop their own goals rather than strive to meet adult expectations (Mithaug & Mithaug, 2003). Given that the best academic outcomes are achieved by students with mastery and performance approach goal orientations, adults should encourage students to move away from performance and work avoidance orientations. This can be accomplished by:

- Interviewing students regarding their personally meaningful, achievable long-term personal goals (Mithaug & Mithaug, 2003).
- Helping students write specific, moderately difficult, and achievable short-term goals that can be easily and frequently monitored (Bandura, 1997; Margolis & McCabe, 2003; Schunk, 1999).
- Openly discussing the benefits of mastery and performance approach goal orientations, and helping students rewrite and reframe their performance and work avoidance goals as mastery and performance approach goals (Wolters, 2003).
- Advocating for criterion-based, performance-based assessments rather than normative based standards that compare one student with another (Meece & Miller, 1999).
- Emphasizing collaborative rather than competitive assignments (Glasser, 1990).
- Helping students convert short- and long-term goals into weekly plans that include study strategies (Seon & King, 1997).
- Increasing student control of goals and assignments (Deci & Ryan, 1985).

At times the goals that adults have in mind for student performance can be very different from the goals that students themselves have in mind. In such cases, students, parents, consultants, and teachers can work collaboratively to reconcile goals and objectives. Sometimes this requires both adults and students to modify their expectations. For example, adults may need to accept that, at least for the time being, particular students will do just enough to "get by"; they will even have to strive to help these students not to "close doors."

> Every year, 11th-grade English teacher **Mr. Schmuckler** asked the principal for the lowest-level English class because he loved the challenge. Every September, he gave his "not closing doors" speech. Pointing to a poster of a partially opened door, he told the students, "This poster is for this class. Even though your parents think you're taking English, you aren't. You are really taking a class called "Not Closing Doors." This picture of an open door is to remind you that *this* class is about *not closing doors*. I know that you don't want to be here. I know that many of you are much more interested in other things—having a good time with your girlfriend or boyfriend and your music—than this class. I know that many of you *hate* English. But this class is about *not closing doors*, not English. It's about doing well enough, and learning enough, so that when you are older you won't have closed the door on going to college. You might not want to go through that door now, and that is your choice. But if you *don't close* the door now, you can always change your mind later. I will help you keep all of your doors, all your options, at least a little open."

Fostering Constructive Attributions and an Internal Locus of Control

Success in school is not simply luck, nor does it depend entirely on having "good" teachers—it is closely tied to effective studying. Adults can help students understand that success in school is a direct result of sustained effort, appropriate strategies, and increasing competence, and that academic difficulties result from inadequate strategies or insufficient effort.

Not uncommonly, students will spend much time doing what they think is studying, only to fail a test afterward. This happens when they study the wrong things or in the wrong way. It doesn't take too many of these experiences for students to conclude that they are not smart, and that studying does not produce school success and is a waste of time. For this reason, it is important to help students revisit the notion that effort does relate to the outcome, but only when the studying is done properly. Adults should investigate students' study strategies by asking them to describe exactly what they do when they study and examining their studying materials. With this approach, they can identify what is and is not working, and can determine whether the students *studied the right things wisely and efficiently*. Otherwise, students will not even try to "study" again, believing that they are unable to learn.

Students with an external locus of control can be helped to foster an internal locus of control by being led through successful experiences. Such experiences help them understand that the effort they expend relates to the outcome they experience, that their success in school is not simply an effect of innate ability or luck, and that their difficulties are due either to a lack of appropriate effort or support. This understanding often results in their adopting more positive ways of dealing with academics, such as asking for help and taking time to check their work (Diener & Dweck, 1978). Students can also be helped to develop an internal locus of control through "attribution retraining" (Brophy, 1986). That is, an adult employs cognitive-behavioral therapy to:

- Increase a student's ability to concentrate and pay attention.
- Reduce thoughts of failure.
- Retrace steps to find errors or an alternative approach.
- Help the student attribute failure to insufficient information, insufficient effort, or ineffective strategies, while avoiding attributing failure to insufficient ability.
- Encourage the student to think of effort as an investment, not as a risk.
- Develop a view of skill development as incremental and subject-specific.
- Help the student focus on attaining mastery.

Fostering Optimism

Optimism is critical to student success and can be more important than skill level. For example, optimism can be more highly correlated with college success than SAT scores are (Goleman, 1995; Seligman, 1991; Snyder, 1991). Adults can foster students' positive thinking by teaching them to tell themselves, "I can do it if I try," "One step at a time," and by helping them perceive disappointments as temporary setbacks. Additional positive affirmations are contained in Table 4.1. The vignette about Ms. Coe that opens this chapter describes one teacher's methods to foster students' optimism.

Positive belief systems can be developed by fostering such optimism and the belief that "a setback is a comeback waiting to happen." Students sometimes have the impression that if they do not find immediate success, they have failed. When such experiences are reframed as setbacks, the student begins to understand that three steps forward and one back (a setback), repeated over time, still result in moving forward and in ultimate goal attainment.

TABLE 4.1. Student Affirmations about Motivation

- I am responsible for my own learning.
- I strive to achieve my personal best.
- I work well with others when we study together.
- I am a self-starter.
- I can do this!

> **Babe Ruth** is remembered for having a record number of home runs—but he also had a record number of strikeouts. Babe Ruth considered each strikeout as merely a setback, not a failure, and kept putting forth effort that culminated in his incredible accomplishments.

At times it will be necessary to address a profound lack of optimism that results from highly stressful environmental factors. For example, it is not possible for students to employ self-regulation of study skills if they believe "I'll be shot by the time I'm 20," rather than "If I complete homework, I will receive good grades and get a job" (Hayes, Gifford, & Ruckstuhl, 1996). Adults can counteract this belief system by sympathetically expressing the hope that getting shot by age 20 won't be the case—and that preparing to live past 20 is a good idea no matter what happens.

Helping Students Connect Academic Success to Real-World Success

For many students to be motivated, they must understand the purpose of their learning the material and see how the material relates to their world. Specific strategies to accomplish this are included in Chapters 2 and 3. This is particularly critical for students who feel disenfranchised or marginalized, such as inner-city or minority students (Kramer-Schlosser, 1992).

Some students need to obtain real-world experience before they can understand the need to exert effort in schoolwork.

> **Marvin** couldn't understand why his parents kept "on his back" about "buckling down" so that he could make good enough grades to go to college. He insisted that he could work in construction just like his father and earn a good living. One summer his father said, "All right, come with me," and Marvin was hired as a laborer on his father's construction team. He loved the money he made toward buying a car, but by the end of the summer Marvin was bored out of his mind with the tedium of carrying construction materials for the team. When he complained, his father nodded in agreement. "It bores me, too. I've been bored constantly for 25 years, but it's all I can do. That's why I want you to go to college, so you have the choice of getting a job where you use your brain. You can always do construction, but it's better to have a choice."

> Many students need to be encouraged to perceive school success and learning as their "jobs."

> We have already met **Carlos,** whose parents docked his allowance for missed assignments. They told him that doing his schoolwork and getting grades of at least a C was his job, and that his allowance was his pay. His parents reminded Carlos of Captain John Smith's threatening Virginia colonists with "If you don't work, you won't eat." They said, "Before you go out on your own, we want you to understand that this is the way life is. If docking your allowance doesn't work, we will stop buying your soda and snacks."

Appraisal

Interventions are appraised by reviewing whether collaboratively set goals have been met successfully. If not, the goals should be revised and strategies revisited. After successful adult-guided interventions to improve students' motivation, strategies to foster student-regulated motivation should be employed.

Moving to Student-Regulated Motivation Strategies

When helping students learn to self-regulate motivation, adults must first help students understand that they can actually accomplish this. Not all students understand that they can monitor and actually change their motivation, often because they believe that being "motivated" is a personality trait rather than a function of beliefs and behaviors. To self-regulate motivation, therefore, it is important for students themselves to address their belief systems and behavior. Once students understand that they can self-regulate motivation, the adults can help them move through the phases of preparation, performance, and appraisal relative to motivation. For example, the adults might take the following steps:

1. Help students self-assess motivation, using Worksheet 4.2 and 4.3.
2. Collaborate with students in developing plans for using appropriate motivation strategies for each task.
3. Coach students as they implement motivational strategies.
4. Help students appraise the effectiveness of motivational strategies.
5. Help students modify plans for future motivational strategy use.

Motivation self-regulation is fostered when students maintain an idea of their desired level of work. One method to accomplish this is for students to keep a folder of their "personal best" work for comparison purposes to assess their present level of performance. In this way, students rather than adults decide that assignments need to be redone.

Since self-regulating students invoke different strategies according to the task at hand, adults can teach students to differentiate motivational strategies appropriately. Worksheet 4.1 lists a number of such strategies, separated by type. The adult can use this menu to collaborate with the student to select appropriate strategies for the task at hand.

Fundamental methods to self-regulate motivation include students' reminding themselves that they want to do well, giving themselves a reward after completing work, focusing on mastery goals such as learning for the sake of learning, increasing the value of a task by focusing on its relevance and utility to their own lives, increasing interest by making the task more enjoyable or interesting, and finding ways to make the task seem easier. Information-processing strategies (such as summarizing readings, making flashcards, taking and reviewing notes, rehearsal, organization, elaboration, critical thinking, and metacognition) and social strategies (seeking help) are most useful with difficult tasks. Volitional strategies, such as regulating environment, focusing attention, intensifying willpower, and regulating emotions, are most effective with boring tasks.

Help Students Develop Their Personal Learning Guides (HILLs)

The strategies that students select to self-regulate motivation will need modification as their academic requirements change. Therefore, students should be encouraged to keep both completed and unused copies of assessment and intervention sheets, so that they can continually reflect upon and readjust their strategies. Relevant materials include the following:

Worksheet 1.1. Checklist of Strategies to Promote Independent Learning
Worksheet 1.2. Menu of Interview Questions about General Learning Skills
Worksheet 1.3. Problem Identification and Intervention Selection Tool
Worksheet 1.4. Consultation Outcome-Monitoring Tool
Worksheet 4.1. Checklist of Strategies to Promote Motivation
Worksheet 4.2. Menu of Interview Questions about Motivation
Worksheet 4.3. Goal-Setting and Prioritizing Worksheet
Worksheet 4.4. Visualization Exercise
Table 4.1. Student Affirmations about Motivation

WORKSHEET 4.1.

Checklist of Strategies to Promote Motivation

Students foster academic motivation by:	
	Collaborating in the assessment of their strengths and challenges through interviews, cumulative file review, visualization exercises, goal-setting exercises, or assessment tools.
	Setting and prioritizing positive short- and long-term goals that focus on mastery.
	Selecting and practicing positive affirmations about learning and motivation.
	Using learning strategies such as summarizing information, taking and reviewing notes, rehearsing information, organizing and elaborating information, and critical thinking skills.
	Recognizing that learning success results from expending effort.
	Fostering optimism.
	Using effective time management and organizational strategies.
	Comparing current work with their "personal best."
	Seeking help when needed from teachers, other adults (such as parents), friends, or other peers.
	Working with a "study buddy."
	Regulating the learning environment (such as moving to a quieter location).
	Deliberately focusing attention and intensifying willpower.
	Accepting and working through negative emotions such as boredom and frustration.
	Fostering positive emotions such as having fun while learning.
	Focusing on wanting to do well.
	Having a treat after completing work.
	Thinking of tasks as useful and relevant, and connecting learning to real-world success.
	Not "closing doors" to future accomplishments.
	Making tasks more enjoyable, interesting, or easier.
Parents foster academic motivation by:	
	Fostering positive relationships through listening, providing help, and sharing activities.
	Treating their children as individuals with varied needs and unique talents.
	Expressing the belief that their children's academic success is desirable and possible with effort.
	Making academic and behavioral expectations and standards clear.
	Talking about short- and long-term goals, and helping to prioritize them.
	Providing a positive learning environment by encouraging learning experiences.
	Frequently praising and supporting their children's efforts.

(continued)

Checklist of Strategies to Promote Motivation *(page 2 of 2)*

Teachers foster academic motivation by:	
	Conveying that they care about students through getting to know them as individuals.
	Conveying to students that they believe in them and their ability to succeed.
	Assigning work that evokes curiosity and positive emotional responses.
	Assigning work that is challenging yet manageable.
	Providing just enough help so that students make progress.
	Giving students some control over assignments and projects and personalizing content.
	Making academic and behavioral directions, expectations, and standards clear.
	Frequently providing verbal praise, support, and positive comments on papers.
	Encouraging feelings of academic competency through regular, public success experiences.
	Collaboratively developing each student's short- and long-term learning goals.
	Collecting and returning assigned work promptly, corrected with specific feedback.
	Emphasizing effort and accuracy when students complete tasks.
	Encouraging students to attribute success to increasing competence and sustained effort.
	Tying academic success to real-world success.

WORKSHEET 4.2.

Menu of Interview Questions about Motivation

Student ______________________________ Date ______________

1. What are some reasons you study? What do you say to yourself or do when you do *well* in school? And when you *don't* do well in school? What grades do you think you should get?

2. What do your parents say or do when you do *well* in school? What do your parents say or do when you *don't* do well in school? What grades do your parents think you should get? How do your brothers/sisters do in school? What do your parents say or do about that?

3. What do your teachers say or do when you do *well* in school? What do your teachers say or do when you *don't* do well in school? What grades do your teachers think you should get?

4. What do your friends say when you do *well* in school? When you *don't* do well? What grades do your friends think you should get?

5. Everybody has a need to have fun. What are some things you like to do for fun when you aren't in school? When you are in school? With your parents? Brothers and sisters? Friends? By yourself?

(continued)

Menu of Interview Questions about Motivation *(page 2 of 3)*

6. Everybody has a need to feel loved, cared about, and as though they belong. What things or people make you feel as though you are loved or cared about? At home? At school? Is there anyone that makes you feel not loved, or as though you don't belong? If so, describe that.

7. Everybody has a need to feel as though they have power and control over what happens. What are some activities, things, or people that make you feel as though you are powerful or have control? Is there anything or anyone that makes you feel that you don't have much power or control? If so, describe that.

8. Everybody has a need to feel free to make choices. What are some activities, things, or people that make you feel as though you have freedom to make choices? Is there anything or anyone that makes you feel that you don't have much freedom to choose? If so, describe that.

9. Everybody has a need to feel safe and secure. What are some activities, things, or people that make you feel safe and secure? What are some activities, things, or people that make you feel *not* safe?

10. Do you have enough ways to have fun? If not, what are some ways to have fun that you would like to add to your life?

(continued)

Menu of Interview Questions about Motivation *(page 3 of 3)*

11. Do you have enough ways to feel cared about? If not, what would you like to be different?

12. Do you have enough (appropriate) ways to feel powerful and in control? If not, what are some ways to feel powerful and in control that you would like to add to your life?

13. Do you have enough (appropriate) ways to feel free to choose? If not, what are some ways to feel free to choose that you would like to add to your life?

14. Do you have enough (appropriate) ways to feel safe and secure? If not, what are some ways to feel safe and secure that you would like to add to your life?

15. What do you like to learn about? How are studying, learning, and doing well in school fun? How are they *not* fun? What are some good things that happen when you study and learn? How could you increase them?

WORKSHEET 4.3.

Goal-Setting and Prioritizing Worksheet

Student ____ Grade ________ Date ________________

1. Take 3 minutes to quickly write down your long-term academic, career, and personal goals.

2. Take 3 minutes to quickly write down your short-term academic, career, and personal goals.

3. What things that you spend time on now will help you achieve your important long- and short-term goals? What things that you spend time on now will not help you achieve these goals?

4. What people or things in your life will help you achieve each important long- and short-term goal?

5. What people or things in your life will make it difficult to achieve each important long- and short-term goal?

6. Let's brainstorm several specific actions you could take to overcome each difficulty.

(continued)

Goal-Setting and Prioritizing Worksheet *(page 2 of 2)*

7. Select specific activities from that list that you plan to do, and set a deadline for each.

8. What additional help do you need to achieve each important long- and short-term goal?

9. What are some ways that you can increase the time you spend on the goals and activities you feel are most important? How can you reduce the time spent on those you feel are less important?

10. What do you consider "doing well enough" in school? What do your parents consider "doing well enough"?

11. What goals do you set for yourself when completing homework or studying for a test? Tell me about them.

12. Let's look at your goals compared to how you spend your time. What do you think?

WORKSHEET 4.4.

Visualization Exercise

Student ____________________________________ Date ________________

Describe the very best student in the world.

What does that student do after school?

What does that student do when completing homework?

What does that student do while studying?

How does that compare to what you do after school?

When completing homework?

While studying?

What is holding you back from being the best student in the world?

Which of the "best student's" habits and behaviors could you adopt as your own?

5

Empowering Students to Self-Regulate Emotional Reactions to Learning

Effective independent learners regulate their own emotional states. They minimize and cope with negative emotions such as frustration and anxiety, and foster positive emotions such as pride and joy in learning. Adults can help guide students as they learn strategies to manage their emotions and then mature into emotion self-regulators.

OVERVIEW

> As a ninth grader, **Clair** (whom we have already met in Chapter 2) completes all of her assignments with enthusiasm and high quality, even those in subjects she finds relatively uninteresting. Her weakest area is spelling, and that is indeed a weak area. Although she is in honors classes and achieves above grade level in her academic subjects, her spelling skills are so far below those of her peers that her friends tease her about misspellings in notes she passes. Her spelling errors do not faze her, however: She just laughs when she makes comical errors, automatically uses spell checkers for her academic work, and asks parents and friends to help her proofread assignments for spelling errors. She finds joy in learning almost anything and often completes "challenge" math assignments for fun. Clair compensates beautifully for her significant weakness, and is proud of her accomplishments.

Clair knows how to self-regulate her emotional states as she learns. She manages the negative feelings of boredom in the subjects she finds uninteresting. In the subject she finds most challenging, spelling, she manages anxiety and frustration constructively. Her coping strategies work so well that she experiences positive emotions such as pride and joy in learning.

How does Clair know how to do this? What strategies does she use to regulate her emotional state, and how did she learn these strategies? How can adults help other students regulate negative emotions and acquire positive emotions about learning?

This chapter addresses methods to assess and address students' negative and positive emotions as they relate to studying and independent learning. Again, the focus is on helping students eventually become independent self-regulators in the use of these strategies as they study and learn. Suggestions in this chapter are appropriate for students who are referred because of problems related to emotional issues. These students may be anxious, frustrated, defiant, or bored. Although this chapter addresses emotional states separately, for best success they are addressed simultaneously with students' belief systems, motivation, and behavior. Addressing these issues via collaborative, solution-focused, result-oriented "coaching" from both the cognitive and behavioral perspectives has been shown to increase learning; improve academic self-concept; and reduce test anxiety, non-study-related anxiety, and depression on a long-term basis (Grant, 2003). Worksheet 5.1, Checklist of Strategies to Foster Positive and Manage Negative Emotions contains a concise summary of methods discussed in this chapter.

RESEARCH FOUNDATIONS

Although emotions might be considered the antitheses of self-control, in fact they are essential components. High-level cognition can be enhanced by emotional states, because emotions can modulate the neural mechanisms that support cognitive control (Gray, 2004). There are two important things to teach students about the relationship between emotions and learning: They need to understand both that emotions play a huge part in success, and that to a large part they themselves can control their emotions rather than be controlled by them.

Emotional intelligence is defined as essential to academic and professional success—the "master aptitude"—by Goleman (1995). As Goleman indicates, because negative emotions can overwhelm cognitive functioning, students who are anxious, angry, or depressed don't learn. "People who are caught in these states do not take in information efficiently or deal with it well" (p. 78). In contrast, the ability to foster positive emotional states is one of the hallmarks of successful individuals. In addition to fostering optimism, self-efficacy, impulse control, and management of their behavior, individuals with high levels of emotional intelligence minimize anxiety and "bad moods," and even foster positive emotions as they work.

Emotional health is also reflected in the theory of William Glasser (1998). Because humans have an intrinsic need to learn, learning can be fun. When academic success results in the approval of peers and adults, it helps meet students' need for love/belonging. Educators can take the need for fun, love, and belonging into consideration as they develop interventions to help students learn. For example, students' needs for love/belonging can be met by encouraging collaborative work with peers, or positive experiences can be routinely built into academic activities to help meet students' need for fun.

As Schutz and Lanehart (2002) indicate, "emotions are intimately involved in virtually every aspect of the teaching and learning process . . . [and] an understanding of the nature of emotions within the school context is essential" (p. 67). Students experience a wide variety of emotions while learning. These can be *negative activating* emotions (anger, anxiety, shame); *negative deactivating* emotions (hopelessness and boredom); *positive activating* emotions (enjoyment of learning, hope for success, pride); or *positive deactivating* emotions (contentment, relief, relaxation after success). These emotions affect, and are affected by, students' academic achievement, cognitive resources, learning strategies, motivation, self-regulation, and ability to set and meet mastery goals (Linnenbrink & Pintrich, 2002; Pekrun, Goetz, Titz, & Perry, 2002).

Negative Activating Emotions

Negative activating emotions such as *academic anxiety*, *anger*, and *shame* can have different effects on different students, depending upon each person, each situation, and the strength of each emotion. A mild level of these emotions is actually beneficial, in that anticipatory anxiety, anger, and fear of shame can provide the motivation necessary to overcome procrastination (Gregor, 2005). On the other hand, strong negative emotions can be considerably disabling, in that they distract attention away from tasks, reduce working memory, and have a severe impact on difficult tasks that require complex processing. These negative emotions are positively correlated with the tendency to rely on extrinsic motivators and relatively simple learning strategies such as rote memorization (Pekrun et al., 2002).

Academic anxiety is the most common negative emotion experienced in conjunction with learning (Pekrun et al., 2002). Students affected by it report experiencing it when in class and when studying at home, as well as when taking tests. Academic anxiety is heightened with achievement pressure and fear of failure. Excessive academic anxiety results in poor grades, presentations, and test performance (Beidel et al., 1999; Seipp, 1991). It is also correlated with increased procrastination, particularly in paper writing and test preparation (Milgram & Toubiana, 1999). Studies have found that test anxiety affects one-third to one-half of intermediate-level students, and is particularly prevalent in certain subjects (such as math) even among gifted students (Betz, 1978; Chiu & Henry, 1990). Since excessive anxiety depresses performance, debilitating academic anxiety can be particularly problematic for this gifted population, since these students' self-image is so closely tied to academic success (Hebert & Furner, 1997).

Negative feelings toward teachers can sometimes affect students' studying. However, students need to understand that their primary job as students is to glean needed information and knowledge from every single teacher they have, regardless of their personal feelings.

> **Marisa** was a middle school student whose recent report card surprised her parents: She had all A's except for a D in social studies. They first praised her good grades, but then felt compelled to ask, "What's with this social studies grade?" Immediately Marisa replied, "I don't like my social studies teacher."

Even good students can incorrectly conclude that if they don't like a particular teacher, they don't need to work as hard for him or her as they work for a teacher they admire. Students sometimes need help understanding that *all* teachers have knowledge they must acquire. While liking a teacher helps make learning more enjoyable, it is not a requirement for learning!

Additional negative emotions, such as *frustration* and *anger*, are often associated with assignments that are beyond a student's independent work level. When assignments are at the appropriate level, a student's anger and frustration regarding studying are greatly reduced. Thus it is extremely important that assignments be scaffolded, and that homework be within the student's independent level. This means that students should be able to read with 90–95% accuracy any readings assigned for math, science, and history, as well as language arts homework.

While often the adult's job is to modify assignment difficulty, at other times the adult's job is to help the student acquire appropriate realistic expectations and develop strategies that foster perseverance. For example, athletes and musicians must put in hours of practice before attaining a minimal skill level. Persevering through these hours, whether repeatedly throwing free throws or practicing études, takes determination and the ability to cope with considerable frustration.

> **David**, a high school junior, had two friends who started a band with others who also had been playing instruments since fifth grade. David wanted to be able to join the band by playing the bass guitar, an instrument he had always admired. He bought a guitar and taught himself basic chords, but quickly became extremely frustrated with the discrepancy between his skills and those of the others. After 2 months of desultory attempts, David gave up, feeling like a failure. He didn't recognize that his friends had practiced 1,000 hours apiece, in comparison to his 10 hours.

Negative Deactivating Emotions

Negative deactivating emotions, such as *boredom* and *hopelessness*, can be a severe detriment to motivation. They consistently have a strong negative correlation with academic achievement, and a positive correlation with course withdrawal and dropping out of school altogether. These negative deactivating emotions also lead to superficial processing of information, increased irrelevant thoughts, and reduced attention to tasks. Interestingly, students report feelings of boredom both when they perceive academic tasks as too easy and when they perceive academic tasks as too difficult (Pekrun et al., 2002). Many students need to be made aware that they "have to" complete tasks even when they "don't feel like it."

> Although **Keith's** Full Scale IQ of 71 and severely impaired adaptive behavior made him eligible for identification as mentally handicapped and placement in a self-contained special education class, he spent part of his school day in a general education inclusive fifth-grade classroom. It was obvious that Keith enjoyed and benefited from class discussions, debates, group oral reading, and his teacher's storytelling. Though he was practically a nonreader and hated math, he responded with great excitement when the class discussed topics that were actually happening throughout the world during social studies. He didn't often have much homework, and his teacher differentiated instruction to make his assignment one he could easily manage at home with minimal assistance. His teacher was surprised and disappointed when he came to school one day empty-handed. When she asked why he didn't get his homework finished, he instantly answered, "I didn't feel like doing it."
>
> After taking a minute to think, Keith's teacher realized that he was not trying to be rude, flippant, or indifferent. He was telling the actual reason why he did not do his homework, for he sincerely believed that he (and others) would only do homework when they felt like it.
>
> This was a revelation. His teacher asked the other students to raise their hands if they hadn't felt like doing their homework the night before. Many students raised their hands. She directed Keith's attention to his classmates' response. Then she asked how many of those who hadn't felt like doing their homework did it anyway. They all kept their hands up. Keith looked perplexed. He said to them, "But you said you didn't feel like doing it. I don't get it."
>
> His teacher explained that she never felt like scrubbing toilets in her house, but she still did it, because otherwise her family would not have a clean house in which to live. Keith looked suspicious as he tried to grasp this new and mysterious concept. Finally, after other examples from his friends, he began to understand. His teacher helped him get started on the homework in class, though he initially resisted. She praised him profusely for his efforts, explaining that everyone just has to do things others expect them to do, regardless of whether they feel like doing them or not. At the end of the school year, when students shared the most important thing they had learned in fifth grade, Keith proudly announced, "Learning that you have to do things, even when you don't feel like it, made me smarter." The spontaneous applause of his classmates reinforced Keith's momentous conclusion.

Positive Activating Emotions

Positive activating emotions, such as *enjoyment of learning*, *pride*, and *hope for success*, enhance academic motivation and achievement. These positive emotions also facilitate students' ability to think more flexibly and to use sophisticated learning strategies such as critical evaluation, elaboration, organization, and metacognitive monitoring. Furthermore, they are correlated with intrinsic motivation and self-regulation strategies (Pekrun et al., 2002).

In a deficit-based model, reducing negative emotions tends to be the goal of consultation strategies. However, consultants, students, teachers, and parents should deliberately seek methods to foster positive emotions associated with independent learning, because only when students enjoy learning and anticipate and take pride in their success will they become truly self-regulated learners.

In addition to regulating negative emotions, strong independent learners deliberately induce and foster positive emotional states as they learn. When these positive emotions are successfully aligned with intense focus, students experience "flow" (Csikszentmihalyi, 1990). Flow results in feelings of joy combined with highly skilled performance. When experiencing flow, individuals are so absorbed in the task at hand that they forget themselves, disregard preoccupations of daily life, and become oblivious to the world around them. The state of flow is most likely to occur during work on a task that is somewhat difficult—neither boringly easy nor frustratingly difficult. The experience of flow is highly positive and gratifying, even at young ages (Miller & Meece, 1999; Turner, 1995). High-achieving students have been found to experience flow a fair amount of time as they study, whereas low-achieving and disengaged students are more likely to experience academic anxiety as they study and positive emotions in non-study-related situations (Nakurma, as cited by Csikszentmihalyi, 1990; Shernoff et al., 2003). Although it may seem that students lose self-regulatory habits while in the state of flow because they are so deeply involved in activities that they lose track of time and self-consciousness, actually self-regulation is an antecedent to flow. Flow can actually be deliberately induced through applying self-regulation strategies to attention, context, and task selection (Reed, Schallert, & Deithloff, 2002).

METHODS

Interventions regarding emotions can be initiated by adults. However, their ongoing maintenance should be transferred to students as soon as possible to foster independent learning.

Preparation

Helping Students Identify and Assess Emotional States

The ability to perceive and differentiate emotions is a necessary precursor to self-regulation of emotion, but many students have difficulty identifying their emotional states. Therefore, students might first need to learn to be able to identify when they feel angry, anxious, shameful, hopeless, bored, joyful, hopeful, proud, content, relieved, or relaxed. Adults can assess students' ability to perceive and identify these emotions by asking them to describe situations in which they feel each of the emotions. Tools such as the poster "Feelings—How Are You Feeling Today?" (Creative Therapy, 2005) and The Talking, Feeling, Doing Game may be helpful.

Adults can identify the emotional states experienced by students as they study through interviews, observations, self-report questionnaires, and teacher–parent reports. Academic anxiety, anger, frustration, hopelessness, boredom, enjoyment of learning, pride, and hope for success are often identified by students during *individual interviews*. Such an in-depth interview has been found to produce quite accurate qualitative information (Pekrun et al., 2002). A menu of possible questions to ask students regarding their emotions when they learn independently is included in Worksheet 5.2, Menu of Student Interview Questions about Feelings.

Direct observations and parent–teacher interviews should be used to supplement information obtained in the student interviews. Parents, teachers, and consultants can easily observe signs of frustration such as frowns, complaints, giving up easily, becoming angry, scribbling on work, or wadding up/ripping up papers. Academic anxiety can be evident behaviorally when students perform significantly worse on actual tests than on practice tests or other independent work. Worksheet 5.3, Menu of Interview Questions about a Student's Feelings contains questions designed to elicit parents' and teachers' observations of students' emotional states.

Structured and unstructured self-report methods can also be used by trained psychologists to illuminate emotional states. The Behavior Assessment System for Children, Second Edition

(BASC-2; Reynolds & Kamphaus, 2004) and the Achenbach System of Empirically Based Assessment (ASEBA; Achenbach et al., 2003) are global systems that utilize information from parents, teachers, and students regarding students' emotional functioning.

If a student's ability to learn independently is compromised by depression or anxiety, it is appropriate for psychologists to consider whether or not the depression or anxiety is of clinical proportions. This can be determined through unidimensional instruments such as the Children's Depression Rating Scale, Revised (CDRS-R; Poznanski & Mokros, 1996); the Beck Depression Inventory-II (BDI-II; Beck, Steer, & Brown, 1996); the Multiscore Depression Inventory for Children MDI-C; Berndt & Kaiser, 1996); the Beck Anxiety Inventory (BAI; Beck & Steer, 1996); or the Multidimensional Anxiety Scale for Children (March, 1997).

Psychologists can assess global personality factors with the Personality Inventory for Children, Second Edition (PIC-2; Lachar & Gruber, 2001); the Personality Inventory for Youth (PIY; Lachar & Gruber, 1995); the 16PF Adolescent Personality Questionnaire (APQ; Schuerger, 2001); and the Minnesota Multiphasic Personality Inventory—Adolescent (MMPI-A; Butcher et al., 1992). In addition, some instruments that directly assess emotions related to learning and studying have been developed. These include the Academic Emotions Questionnaire (Pekrun et al., 2002), as well as the Motivated Strategies for Learning Questionnaire (MSLQ; Pintrich et al., 1991), described in Chapter 1.

Helping Students Understand the Costs of Negative Emotions and Benefits of Positive Emotions

When the above-described assessment strategies reveal that a student's performance is compromised by anxiety, boredom, frustration, or anger, adults will need to take several steps before initiating interventions:

1. Raise the student's awareness of negative emotions and their costs.
2. Help the student become aware that it is possible and desirable to moderate and/or tolerate negative emotions and to foster positive emotions.
3. Identify the student's motivation to regulate emotions.
4. Obtain a commitment to implement chosen interventions.

Through interview questions, observing students while they complete work, and analyzing portfolios and cumulative files, adults can help students determine what types of academic work they like and dislike. Many students assume that they dislike all types of homework when they actually do like some types (projects, perhaps). Adults can then have students use their knowledge of preferences as they develop their study schedules. For example, some students prefer to get the disliked homework done first, while others prefer to start with easier work to "prime the pump." Adults can also help students analyze what they like or dislike about the way they *handle* homework; brainstorm alternative strategies; and then select, try, and evaluate one of the brainstormed solutions. For example, students may dislike their habit of procrastinating, and may decide to self-reward by text-messaging a friend or playing pool after finishing their work.

Performance

Training Students to Cope with Anxiety

The most effective strategy to alleviate debilitating anxiety is to *prepare sufficiently* for the task at hand. For example, elite musicians and actors overlearn their material, so that they can be on "automatic pilot" when performing and can devote their energy and attention to style and expression. Similarly, when students know the material for a test extremely well, the likelihood of their becoming so anxious that their minds "go blank" is greatly reduced. The reader is referred to Chapter 8 for strategies to help students assess their learning to determine whether they have learned the material sufficiently.

However, some students still experience debilitating anxiety even when they have mastered the material. To counteract such anxiety, students can be trained to employ physiologically and/or mentally incompatible *alternative responses*. Some, such as abdominal breathing, progressive muscle relaxation, grounding, and cognitive restructuring, can be taught outside of class but can be unobtrusively employed in any setting, including the classroom. Others, such as meditation, regular physical exercise, and systematic desensitization, are employed outside of school but have benefits that extend throughout the day. Handout 5.1, Methods to Calm Anxious Behaviors, can be duplicated and given to students for reference.

Abdominal breathing is an excellent tool to immediately reduce anxiety and can be of enormous help to students who are overcome by test anxiety, performance anxiety, or stage fright. The students take the following steps:

1. Slowly and deeply breathe in while silently counting to 4 (or 8).
2. Hold in that breath while silently counting to 4 (or 8).
3. Slowly breathe out while silently counting to 4 (or 8).
4. Pause without breathing while silently counting to 4 (or 8).
5. Repeat until the anxiety is alleviated.

Progressive muscle relaxation is another excellent tool to control anxiety and, like abdominal breathing, can be applied unobtrusively before a test, performance, or other anxiety-producing event. The students sequentially tighten (while counting to 10) and then relax muscle groups in this order: feet, legs, buttocks, fists, arms, shoulders, jaw, and face.

Grounding involves taking a few minutes to become consciously aware of immediate and current physical sensations, such as the feeling of one's feet on the floor, buttocks on the chair, arms on the desk, the texture of one's clothing, the temperature of the air, the feeling of one's hair, the moisture in one's mouth, and so forth.

Daily *meditation* has been shown to significantly reduce global anxiety, depression, stress, and hypertension. To meditate, students do the following (Benson, 1975):

1. Set aside time to spend in a quiet, calm environment with as few distractions as possible, preferably more than 2 hours after a meal.
2. Sit comfortably, progressively relax all muscles, and keep them relaxed.
3. Select a focus point—something to which to return attention when distracting thoughts occur. The focus point can be an object to gaze at, a soothing word or phrase to repeat silently, or simply the breath.
4. Adopt a passive attitude; when distracting thoughts occur, bring attention back to the focus point, while refraining from judging oneself for getting distracted.
5. Meditate for 10–20 minutes, without an alarm. Afterward, sit quietly for a few minutes.

Regular physical exercise, pursued moderately for 30–60 minutes a day, decreases anxiety and depression; it also contributes to physical health by positively affecting neurotransmitters in the brain, in addition to the muscular and cardiovascular systems. While many students obtain physical exercise by participating in competitive sports, many other students do not enjoy those activities. However, many middle schools, junior highs, high schools, and Boys and Girls Clubs have intramural or informal sports. Some students enjoy dancing, walking, hiking, snowboarding, yoga, or biking. The most important consideration is to find a physical activity that a student enjoys enough to participate in it willingly and regularly. Particularly for adolescents, it is helpful when friends enjoy the same activity.

School psychologists and counselors can use *systematic desensitization* in individual sessions with students whose anxiety is not controllable through the methods described above. To conduct systematic desensitization:

1. Help a student develop a list of anxiety-provoking situations in hierarchical order, from least to most anxiety-provoking. For example, a list might include (a) doing math homework, (b) thinking about studying for a math test, (c) studying for a math test, (d) seeing the teacher handing out the math test, (e) looking at the math test, (f) starting to complete the math test, (g) being handed the graded paper by the teacher, (h) being asked "What did you get?" by friends, and (i) telling parents the grade received.
2. Have the student use progressive muscle relaxation to relax.
3. Guide the student as he or she systematically thinks about each anxiety-provoking situation while maintaining a relaxed state. If the thought of a situation results in any muscle tenseness or anxiety, have the student again progressively relax all muscles.
4. Gradually expose the student to all of the concepts that previously caused feelings of anxiety, until he or she is able to think about them without an anxious response.

Cognitive-behavioral therapy has been found to reduce negative emotions associated with studying and independent learning, and to be significantly more effective than general, nonfocused counseling (Bauer, Sapp, & Johnson, 1999). School psychologists and counselors can conduct individual or group cognitive-behavioral therapy sessions that focus on identifying academic and behavioral goals, selecting methods to reach these goals, contracting, obtaining feedback, awarding positive reinforcements for success, and cognitive restructuring. As Meichenbaum (1977) describes it, cognitive restructuring requires the following steps:

1. Encourage a student to observe his or her feelings, thoughts, and behaviors.
2. Help the student develop positive thoughts and behaviors that are incompatible with those that are negative and maladaptive.
3. Help the student produce these thoughts and behaviors in everyday life, and assess the outcome.

The reader is referred to Chapter 6 for fuller descriptions of goal setting, contracting, and reinforcements relative to studying and independent learning.

Merrell (2001) provides practical cognitive therapy techniques in a four-step approach, together with a series of lessons appropriate for psychologists and counselors to use with intellectually bright and insightful yet depressed students ages 9 and above. After a therapeutic alliance is established, the intervention goals and techniques are to:

1. Develop an awareness of emotional variability (using tools such as the "emotional thermometer" and the "emotional pie").
2. Detect automatic thoughts and identify beliefs (using tools such as thought charts, the cognitive replay technique, thought forecasting, hypothesizing/guessing, and the downward-arrow technique).
3. Evaluate automatic thoughts and beliefs (by identifying cognitive distortions or thinking errors, examining the evidence, asking the "three questions," and evaluating positives and negatives).
4. Change negative automatic thoughts and maladaptive beliefs (using tools such as a daily

record of thoughts, the triple-column technique, reframing and relabeling, cognitive rehearsal, and increasing positive self-statements).

Fostering Strategies to Deal with Anger, Frustration, Boredom, and Hopelessness

Anger and frustration are often tied to problems with the difficulty level of the work, as well as to students' internal states and reactions. There are two methods that adults can employ to diminish students' anger and frustration. First, the adults can help students structure short-term goals to minimize frustration. For example, students can be encouraged to set a goal of doing five math problems and then taking a 3-minute break. Second, the adults can work with the students' teachers to ensure that assignments are at the appropriate level of difficulty. These strategies are described more fully in Chapter 3.

Boredom is most often associated with assignments that are either too difficult or too easy. To ameliorate boredom, adults can help students develop and utilize strategies described in Chapters 4 and 6. Again, collaborating with teachers to modify assignments appropriately is also helpful. Students feel the negative emotion of hopelessness when they experience a pervasively negative belief system and poor feelings of self-efficacy. Students can deal with these through positive affirmations (see Table 5.1) and strategies described in Chapter 4.

Fostering Strategies to Increase Pride, Joy in Learning, Hope for Success, and Flow

Learning is intrinsically motivating—fun—to human beings (Erikson, 1963; Maslow, 1970; Glasser, 1990). Most children, adolescents, and adults can identify a hobby, sport, or subject they like to learn about. Adults can help children recognize that they enjoy learning, and parents can help children link learning about their favorite topic to their schoolwork. Although students may dislike some of the practice exercises of their homework, many students enjoy related games, projects, and activities that help them use what they are learning. Consultants can help students, parents, and teachers locate these materials. In addition, using positive affirmations can increase students' experience of positive emotions. The reader is again referred to Table 5.1, which contains examples of such affirmations.

As previously described, "flow" is most often experienced when a student deliberately focuses intense concentration on an assignment that is moderately difficult. Therefore, once again, it is important to assess and correct assignment difficulty. In addition, whenever possible it is important for parents and teachers not to interrupt students who have become involved with an activity until they have reached a stopping point on their own. Reed et al. (2002) indicate that the

TABLE 5.1. Student Affirmations about Feelings

- I love learning.
- I am a capable student.
- I happily invest the time necessary to master new learning.
- Learning is fun.
- I monitor and celebrate my results.
- I am proud of my work and my effort.
- When my results are less than I expected, I know it is just a setback and not a failure.
- When I get off track, I regroup, restart, and reward myself.

following strategies are useful in generating positive readiness to begin a writing task so that a student can experience flow:

1. Discuss the task with the anticipated audience before beginning.
2. Minimize distractions and interference from other tasks.
3. Ensure physical and psychological readiness.
4. Plan and draft ideas before actually beginning to write.
5. Write freely.
6. Revise and rewrite.

Considering Generalized Anxiety, Depression, and Other Psychological Disorders

As described above, negative activating emotions such as anxiety and anger can have a considerable negative impact on students' ability to study and learn independently. Psychological disorders in which such emotions play key roles—such as generalized anxiety, depression, posttraumatic stress disorder, bipolar disorders, and schizophrenia—clearly have a seriously detrimental effect on students' ability to focus their attention on academic matters. Several of the interventions described above, including cognitive restructuring, progressive muscle relaxation techniques, deep breathing, meditation, and physical exercise, are beneficial for individuals with these disorders. However, while it is certainly appropriate to directly address issues relevant to study skills and independent learning, adults should also acknowledge that students with these conditions will often need additional treatment beyond interventions directed at fostering independent learning.

Appraisal

Appraising the interventions designed to help students manage negative and foster positive emotions requires determining whether or not they have been effective. After designing, implementing, modifying, and reimplementing interventions, members of the team assess success. Again, the fundamental questions are: "What did we do?" "How well did it work?" and "What do we need to change?"

It is most effective when the student assesses implementation success, particularly for those strategies that are targeting internal states such as anxiety. The assessment strategies discussed in the beginning of this chapter can be appropriately readministered to generate outcomes data and appraise the success of the intervention; that is, depression inventories and anxiety scales can be used to appraise the success of interventions designed to ameliorate these conditions. On the other hand, many of the interventions described in this chapter require regular and recursive application. For example, meditation is effective in reducing anxiety but only when regularly employed. One attempt will not result in meaningful gains. Therefore, it is important to monitor treatment integrity as well as outcome, which requires moving to student-regulated strategies.

Moving to Student-Regulated Strategies

Because studying and independent learning are, by definition, conducted independently by students, any implemented strategy must be designed so that students can take over and monitor its use. Self-monitoring is required for short-term interventions because the student must determine when they are necessary; it is required for long-term interventions to ensure their ongoing use.

Short-term interventions include activities such as deep breathing and progressive relaxation to control anxiety, deliberately focusing attention to induce flow, taking short breaks to reduce boredom, or breaking a task down into small bits to reduce frustration. These interventions require that students learn to recognize emotional states on their own, determine that they need to employ a learned intervention, and actually use that intervention. For example, if a student learns to use deep breathing to regulate anxiety, he or she needs to (1) notice a decrease in performance, (2) recognize that anxiety is contributing to that decrease, and (3) practice deep breathing until the anxiety dissipates.

Long-term interventions, such as meditation or regular exercise, require ongoing planning to reduce anxiety and frustration. These interventions require regular use without the cue of discomfort to be effective, much like taking multivitamins without the cue of physical illness. To employ these measures on a preventative basis, students typically will need to monitor their implementation until a habit is established. Chapter 6 describes methods to use in helping students record their efforts in behavior changes.

Once a strategy has been found to be effective during guided practice, an adult can check with a student to ascertain whether and how well the strategy continues to be practiced. Often it is helpful for students to log their use of various strategies on a calendar or in their assignment book, to facilitate remembering to use them. Initially check-ins will need to be frequent, but as the students become autonomous, the frequency of the check-ins should be diminished. It can be very helpful for an adult to schedule a semiannual preventative check-in, similar to a semiannual dental appointment, to ensure that a student has transferred necessary skills to new situations.

Help Students Develop Their Personal Learning Guides (HILLs)

Relative to emotions, students can include in their Personal Learning Guides forms and notes regarding strategies that they have found to be particularly effective in helping them manage negative emotions and foster positive emotions. Appropriate materials to include are the following:

Worksheet 5.1. Checklist of Strategies to Foster Positive and Manage Negative Emotions

Worksheet 5.2. Menu of Student Interview Questions about Feelings

Handout 5.1. Methods to Calm Anxious Emotions

Table 5.1. Student Affirmations about Feelings

WORKSHEET 5.1.

Checklist of Strategies to Foster Positive and Manage Negative Emotions

	The student can perceive, differentiate, and identify emotions.
	The range of emotions experienced by the student during learning experiences is assessed via interviews, observations, self-report questionnaires, and teacher–parent reports.
	The student understands the cost of negative and the benefits of positive emotions.
	The student is aware that it is possible to moderate and/or tolerate negative emotions and to foster positive emotions.
	The student is motivated and has made a commitment to self-regulate emotions.
	The student knows and uses effective methods to manage academic anxiety, including thorough preparation and alternative responses (abdominal breathing, progressive relaxation, grounding, cognitive restructuring, meditation, physical exercise, systematic desensitization).
	The student knows and uses strategies to deal with anger, frustration, boredom, and hopelessness, such as short-term goals, self-rewards, and positive affirmations.
	The student fosters positive emotions such as pride, joy in learning, hope for success, and flow by identifying topics and learning experiences he or she enjoys; using positive affirmations; deliberately focusing intense concentration; selecting activities that are challenging but achievable; and attending to the preparation, performance, and appraisal phases of learning.
	The student can recognize emotional states, determine the need to employ a short-term intervention, and use that intervention independently.
	The student has mastered and can independently monitor a long-term intervention to manage negative and foster positive emotions.
Parents foster positive emotions and teach students to manage negative emotions by:	
	Modeling enthusiasm for learning and a positive regard for homework.
	Providing fun, laughter, and opportunities to experience pride and joy when learning.
	Refraining from publicly humiliating or criticizing their children, and tolerating mistakes.
	Helping their children identify, address, and manage negative emotions such as boredom, frustration, anxiety, and anger.
	Encouraging their children to brainstorm alternatives when setbacks are experienced.
Teachers foster positive emotions and teach students to manage negative emotions by:	
	Modeling enthusiasm for learning.
	Encouraging positive emotions by incorporating fun and laughter, as well as opportunities to experience pride, joy, and flow (concentrated work on enjoyable learning activities), in the classroom.
	Refraining from publicly humiliating or criticizing students, and encouraging them to use mistakes as teaching tools.
	Helping students identify, address, and manage negative emotions.
	Encouraging students to brainstorm alternatives when setbacks are experienced.
	Assigning work that is stimulating and challenging but manageable.

WORKSHEET 5.2.

Menu of Student Interview Questions about Feelings

Student ______________________________ Date ______________

1. What do you like to do best in school? At home?

2. What do you like to do least in school? At home?

3. What do you like most about school? Dislike?

4. What do you find most interesting to learn in school? At home?

5. What do you find most fun to learn—in school, at home, or someplace else?

6. What do you find most frustrating to learn? What do you do when you get frustrated? Do you have a way to get over it?

(continued)

Menu of Student Interview Questions about Feelings *(page 2 of 2)*

7. Is there anything about school or learning that makes you feel very nervous or anxious, like taking tests? If so, do you think this nervousness helps you or hurts your performance? What do you do when you get nervous or anxious?

8. Is there anything you have to learn that you find boring? If so, do you have a way to get over it?

9. Is there anything about school that makes you angry or mad? If so, how do you get over it?

10. What do you do when you don't feel like studying or doing homework, but it is due soon? How do you get over wanting to put studying off?

11. Have you ever gotten so excited about a learning activity that you forgot to do something, such as watch a favorite TV show? If so, describe it.

WORKSHEET 5.3.

Menu of Interview Questions about a Student's Feelings

Student ____________________ Adult ____________________ Date ____________

1. What does the student like to do best in school? At home?

2. What does the student like to do least in school? At home?

3. What does the student like most about school? Dislike?

4. What does the student find most interesting to learn in school? At home?

5. What does the student find most fun to learn—in school, at home, or someplace else?

6. What does the student find most frustrating to learn? What does the student do when frustrated? Does the student have a way to get over it?

(continued)

Menu of Interview Questions about a Student's Feelings *(page 2 of 2)*

7. Is there anything about school or learning that makes the student feel very nervous or anxious, like taking tests? If so, do you think this nervousness helps or hurts the student's performance? What does the student do when nervous or anxious?

8. Is the student bored with any learning assignments? If so, how does the student get over it?

9. Is there anything about school that makes the student angry or mad? If so, does the student have a way to get over it?

10. What does the student do when he or she doesn't feel like studying or doing homework that is due soon? How does the student get over wanting to put studying off?

11. Have you ever noticed the student getting so excited over a learning activity that he or she forgot to do something, such as watch a favorite TV show? If so, tell me about it.

HANDOUT 5.1.

Methods to Calm Anxious Emotions

Abdominal breathing

1. Slowly and deeply breathe in while silently counting to 4 (or 8).
2. Hold in that breath while silently counting to 4 (or 8).
3. Slowly breathe out while silently counting to 4 (or 8).
4. Pause without breathing while silently counting to 4 (or 8).
5. Repeat until the anxiety is alleviated.

Progressive muscle relaxation

Sequentially tighten (while counting to 10) and then relax muscle groups in this order: feet, legs, buttocks, fists, arms, shoulders, jaw, and face.

Grounding

Take a few minutes to become consciously aware of your current physical sensations, such as the feeling of your feet on the floor, buttocks on the chair, arms on the desk, the texture of your clothing, the temperature of the air, the feeling of your hair, the moisture in your mouth, and so forth.

Meditation

1. Set aside time to spend in a quiet, calm environment with as few distractions as possible, preferably more than 2 hours after a meal.
2. Sit comfortably, progressively relax all muscles, and keep them relaxed.
3. Select a focus point—something to which to return your attention when you are experiencing distracting thoughts. The focus point can be an object to gaze at, a soothing word or phrase to repeat silently, or simply your breath.
4. Adopt a passive attitude; when distracting thoughts occur, bring your attention back to the focus point, while refraining from judging yourself for getting distracted.
5. Meditate for 10–20 minutes, without an alarm. Afterward, sit quietly for a few minutes.

6

Empowering Students to Self-Regulate Behavior

Skills in managing one's behavior and performance are essential for academic—and personal—success. Many students need the support of adult-regulated behavior management programs before they can monitor their own behavior and become self-regulating.

OVERVIEW

In previous chapters we have met **Clair,** who self-regulates her academic behavior to a remarkable degree. She completes her homework on her own every afternoon as soon as she comes home from school. When her English teacher assigned a long-term project requiring writing a paper and delivering a presentation on Greek gods, Clair started her Internet research the same day the assignment was given. She completes assignments with high quality, and she keeps up with readings so well that she needs to spend little additional time studying for exams.

How can adults help students modify and self-regulate their behavior so they can study as effectively as Clair? How can students independently maintain such strategies? This chapter addresses students' abilities to assess and manage their behavior as it relates to studying and independent learning. It addresses strategies to facilitate the maintenance and generalization of positive behavior change, both when monitored by others and when self-monitored. Suggestions in this chapter are appropriate for students who do not complete assignments or complete them poorly, do not turn in homework, cannot work independently, or need immediate reinforcement. Worksheet 6.1, Checklist of Strategies to Foster Appropriate Behavior, summarizes the methods discussed in this chapter.

RESEARCH FOUNDATIONS

Studying and learning are manifested in both unobservable and observable behaviors. The unobservable behaviors, such as remembering, thinking, and calculating, are essential components of studying and learning but can be measured only indirectly through observable and measurable behaviors (e.g., the number of assignments completed or test questions answered correctly). Thus improving observable behaviors, or performance, is a necessary but not sufficient step toward improving study skills and independent learning. Furthermore, although parents and teachers tend to monitor the behavior of young students very closely, students are expected to increasingly manage their own behavior as they get older.

Classroom teachers, knowingly and unknowingly, employ contingency behavior management systems. An almost universal explicit behavior contract is the grading system, and many teachers, particularly at the elementary school level, use additional reward systems such as points leading to prizes. Many classroom behavior systems are at the "independent group-oriented level," where each student in a group has access to external rewards based upon his or her own achievement. For example, each student has the independent opportunity to obtain an A or earn a place on the honor roll (Skinner, Skinner, & Sterling-Turner, 2002). The problems with contingencies applied universally across groups are the wide differences among individuals in learning rates, capabilities, and what they find reinforcing and punishing. Using the same criteria makes it highly unlikely that less capable students can earn the reward, and what one student finds reinforcing (e.g., being on the honor roll) may not be at all reinforcing for another.

More explicit and carefully designed behavior contracts are effective methods to reduce undesirable behaviors and substitute desirable student performance, because they (1) provide positive reinforcements for desired behaviors; (2) serve as cues to change performance; (3) allow the use of a wide range of reinforcers, including those that are delayed; and (4) encourage compliance as a result of public commitments (Olympia, Petterson, & Christiansen, 2005). Numerous research studies have established that educators and parents can implement behavior contracts and successfully increase students' homework completion, organization, study skills, and academic success (Dunlap et al., 1993; Gable & Hendrickson, 2000; Rhode, Morgan, & Young, 1983). These programs can be used to initiate and shape successful academic performance, even in the face of extreme performance deficiencies. As discussed previously, the most effective programs are those designed and implemented collaboratively by educators, parents, and students.

Ideally, behavior management programs involve several transitions. They progress from being adult-directed to being student-monitored; from being continuously reinforced (most use-

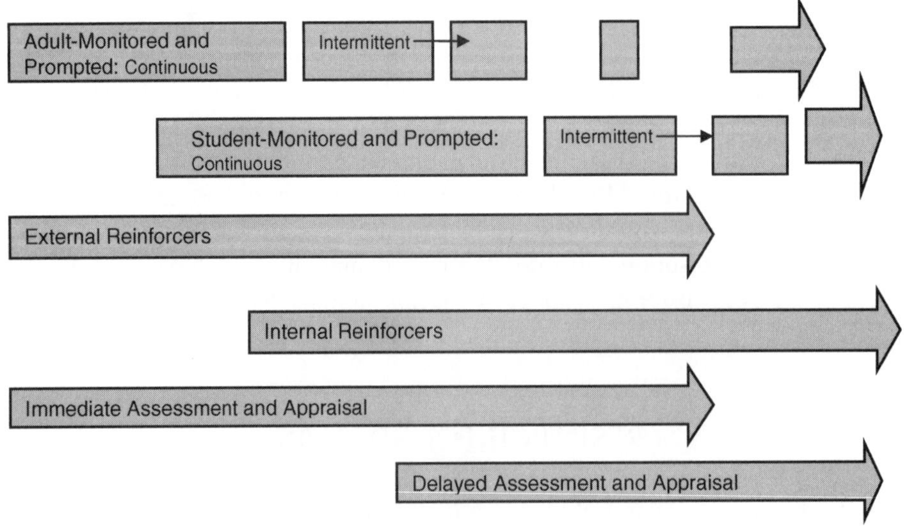

FIGURE 6.1. Behavior management program transitions.

ful in establishing new behaviors) to intermittently reinforced (most useful in maintaining behaviors); from using external reinforcers to internal reinforcers; from overt prompts (i.e., adult-cued) to covert prompts (i.e., student self-talk); and from immediate assessments (e.g., placing a star on a chart with each completed assignment) to time-delayed assessments (e.g., reviewing at the end of a week). These transitions are illustrated in Figure 6.1.

METHODS

Preparation

Assessment

DETERMINE BEHAVIOR FUNCTION

A functional behavior assessment—that is, an assessment of the underlying function(s) of a problem behavior, and a subsequent reframing of the behavior—can be very helpful in developing interventions (Center for Effective Collaboration and Practice, 1999; Watson & Steege, 2003). The need for this assessment stems from the reality that identical misbehaviors can result from many different sources. For example, not completing homework can serve the functions of alleviating frustration, alleviating boredom, gaining adult attention, freeing up time for other activities, reducing anxiety, and/or many other possibilities. In a functional behavior analysis, adults consider the emotional, biological, environmental, and social factors that initiate, sustain, or end the misbehavior, and thereby determine the benefits that the student obtains by this misbehavior. It is important to remember that the *behavior* may be judged, but that the *function* is not. The function of a behavior is rarely in and of itself inappropriate. "Getting high grades and acting-out may serve the same purpose (i.e., getting attention from adults), yet the behaviors that lead to good grades are judged to be more appropriate than those that make up acting-out behaviors" (Center for Effective Collaboration and Practice, 1999, p. 3).

Information from interviews and data from observations are combined to determine the antecedents and consequences for misbehavior and generate hypotheses regarding its functions. Often misbehavior serves more than one function, in which case all of the functions must be identified and addressed in the intervention design (Watson & Steege, 2003). The following questions are explored:

- How do adults perceive the misbehavior?
- In what settings does the misbehavior occur?
- In what similar settings does the misbehavior *not* occur?
- How do these two settings differ (assignment, seating arrangement, time of day, etc.)?
- Who is present when this misbehavior occurs?
- What activities occur just prior to this misbehavior?
- What usually happens immediately following the behavior?
- What does the student believe causes the problem?
- What does he or she feel or think about when the misbehavior occurs?
- What does the student believe is expected of him or her?
- What does the student perceive typically happens as a result of this misbehavior?

OBTAIN BASELINE

A baseline of the behavior is obtained through direct and objective observations or the examination of permanent products (e.g., papers, test scores). It is most helpful if the observations occur across different situations and times, and generate both qualitative and quantitative data. No deliberate intervention is applied during the collection of the baseline data.

IDENTIFY APPROPRIATE ALTERNATIVES

After identifying the function(s) of the misbehavior, the student, parent, teacher, and consultant collaborate to determine more appropriate behaviors for the student to obtain the same benefit, and decrease the need for the inappropriate behavior. For example, if a student misbehaves to avoid completing homework that is too difficult, he or she might be taught to approach adults and politely say that the work is too difficult, which should then result in adjustments to the difficulty level.

SET GOALS

As described in Chapter 4, an essential element of a study skills improvement program is delineating clear and mutually agreed-upon goals. This is particularly crucial for behavior contracts, because student and adult goals must be aligned.

> **Gus** was in his first year in middle school. He did not complete his homework, and he received failing grades in social studies, science, and language arts because of this. His best academic grades were in math, where he still did not complete homework but did so well on tests that he received passing grades. Whereas Gus's parents and teacher were concerned that he did not complete his homework, Gus was concerned that he was often in trouble and didn't get enough time to "relax" and play computer games. A behavior contract was initially developed to meet the goals of all concerned. When Gus completed his homework with at least 80% accuracy, he earned the opportunity to play video games.

Performance

Implement, Monitor, and Revise Individualized Behavior Contracts

Again, the phases of *preparation, performance*, and *appraisal* across multiple cycles must be maintained. During the first preparation phase, adults designing the program determine the target behavior, collect data on rate of current performance, negotiate specific goals and rewards with the student, and develop a contract that includes (1) the desired behavior, goal, and rewards; (2) consequence for not meeting goal and a bonus for exceeding the goal; (3) names of those monitoring the contract; (4) the timeline and anticipated date for revision; and (5) the signature of student, teacher, parent, and consultant. During the first performance phase, the program is implemented. During the first appraisal phase, progress is frequently checked and graphed. During the second preparation phase, the contract is revised, the rewards and consequences are revised so that they are more natural, and self-monitoring is introduced. During the second performance phase, the revised program is implemented and again, progress is checked and graphed during the appraisal phase. During the third preparation phase, the program is revised to require total self-monitoring and it is implemented during the performance phase. During the appraisal phases, periodic postintervention assessments of the target behavior are taken, the results graphed, and modifications made as necessary. For easy duplication and ready reference, these steps are summarized in Handout 6.1, Steps to Establish a Behavior Management Program. To facilitate selecting appropriate reinforcers, Worksheet 6.2 contains a menu of rewards. Figure 6.2 is a playful sample behavioral contract, and a blank version of such a contract can be found in Worksheet 6.2.

To maximize the effectiveness of behavior contracts in improving study skills and independent learning, the steps delineated in Handout 6.1 should be followed. The following strategies can be employed:

Name: *Joe* Date: *7/7/07*

Goal: *On the Firefighter Exam I will receive a passing score.*

These are my rewards when I meet this goal:

1. *Liz agrees to pay me $50 on the day the exam scores are posted.*
2. *Liz agrees to restain my deck within 1 week of the exam. (I will provide the stain and equipment.)*

These are my consequences should I not meet my goal:

1. *I agree to pay Liz $50 on the day the exam scores are posted.*
2. *I agree to pull all the weeds in Liz's flower garden within 1 week of the exam. (Liz will provide the weeds and equipment.)*

Signatures: Date:

____________________________ __________________

FIGURE 6.2. Sample self-regulated behavioral contract.

1. Use reward systems to initiate behaviors, then scaffold to foster increasing competence, and fade as soon as possible.
2. Select relevant *target behaviors* that are likely to be naturally and predictably reinforced. A behavior should be easy to measure, clearly defined in observable and objective terms, and practical for eventual self-monitoring by the student.
3. Select attainable goals. If the baseline behavior is extremely low, an attainable starting goal would be 70%. Otherwise, a performance level of 80–85% should be initially rewarded, and this level should be increased with continued success to 90–95%. Rarely is 100% an appropriate goal.
4. Select goals that give students frequent opportunities to engage in and be reinforced for appropriate behavior—so that they will come to recognize that the desired behavior is more effective, more efficient, and more relevant than the problem behavior.
5. When possible, select goals that are cumulative, to prevent discouragement.
6. Include study strategies and processes within expectations as well as products, and attach these expectations to specific outcomes.

Springfield Junior High School's music department has a policy that grades for band and orchestra are based upon the amount of time each student practices. For each quarter, every student is given a practice card with a row of spaces for each week. The back of the card has a list of practice expectations (e.g., learning C and F# scales in two octaves, memorizing the marching band song "Seventy-Six Trombones"). The student writes down the amount of time on each activity; the parent signs the card the end of each week; and the teacher checks the card weekly.

7. Base rewards on the quality of work whenever possible.
8. Encourage students to personally choose their rewards. Again, a menu of possible rewards is included in Worksheet 6.2.
9. Include "mystery motivators," such as an unknown reinforcer in a sealed envelope (Madaus, Kehle, Madaus, & Bray, 2003).

Mr. Grimwald, a fourth-grade teacher, has a "reward box" from which students can select their rewards when they have completed a specified number of homework assignments with a specified level of accuracy. There are a few concrete objects in the box (such as a rubber ball for recess), but most of the rewards are cards stating privileges such as "Be line leader for a week," "Get 10 extra minutes of recess," "Take a free long drink of water," and "Have lunch with Mr. Grimwald on Tuesday."

10. Vary rewards according to the skill level and learning rate of individual students.

Mrs. Ring believes that every student should leave her sixth-grade classroom able to accurately complete a page of 100 multiplication facts in 1 minute. However, her student Suzy entered sixth grade able to complete only 10 problems, in comparison to the typical 50 of other students. Mrs. Ring consulted with the school psychologist; in reviewing Suzy's file, they realized that although she is very intelligent, Suzy has extreme difficulty with sequential memory and therefore finds tasks such as memorizing spelling words and multiplication tables quite difficult. Mrs. Ring changed her practice of posting "number correct" on her 1-minute-timed-test "Brag Chart" to "percent improved." In that way Suzy could be just as proud of her "50% improvement" (indicating a movement from 10 to 15 correct) as her classmate who moved from 50 to 75 correct.

11. Modify rewards when necessary—such as when a student's interest in a reward declines; the timeframe is too long; the reward is too far removed from the target behavior; or the transition to student-monitored behavior management (wherein the rewards need to be increasingly natural and/or student-controlled—see below) is being made.
12. When possible, use interdependent group contracts, whereby an entire group is given an award "contingent upon the group's academic behavior meeting specified group-oriented criteria such as a class average" (Skinner, Williams, & Neddenriep, 2004, p. 387). This fosters collaborative work and individual achievement, increases student engagement, enhances learning, and decreases inappropriate behavior.

Mr. Smith's eighth-grade class will earn a field trip to the *USS Constitution* and Bunker Hill Multimedia Museum when the total class average on a history unit test is 80%. The students are assigned to study groups for the test, and each group has developed strategies to help members review and memorize information. Next door, **Miss Young's** class earns one letter of the word "homework" each day that *all* students turn in homework assignments on time. When the class members successfully spell the word "homework," they enjoy a class celebration.

13. Plan to fade the program gradually by extending the timeline and reducing the external reinforcers until the student demonstrates the target behaviors independently.

Appraisal

As described earlier, appraisal is an essential component of effective behavior management systems. Within each recursive cycle, effectiveness is evaluated and the program is modified accordingly.

Moving to Student-Regulated Strategies

Although it is often necessary to start with adult-monitored behavior modification programs to establish desirable behaviors, making the transition to self-monitored programs is essential for students to become independent learners. Self-monitoring, composed of observing and recording behaviors, can effectively address both behavioral and academic problems (Chickie-Wolfe, 1995; Shapiro, Durnan, Post, & Levinson, 2002). As long as students are relying upon adult-regulated behavior management programs, they are not *independently* learning. Instructing students in self-management strategies promotes maintenance and generalization of positive behavior changes, helps students move away from artificial external controls to control by natural consequences, promotes student responsibility, and enables students to become truly self-regulated independent learners.

Both general education and special education students can be taught to monitor and regulate their own behavior through the use of data recording, evaluation of their behavior, and self-reinforcement. These strategies can be used to increase academic productivity, improve on-task and attentive behaviors, increase academic accuracy, improve written expression, and improve behaviors. Often internal rewards, such as satisfaction or relaxation/play after having completed a homework assignment, are relied upon more in self-management procedures than external rewards such as concrete objects are (Hughes & Lloyd, 1993).

> In **Mrs. Foster's** class, students not only changed their behavior through a management system, they also graphed their progress and posted their charts around the room. Rarely could visitors come into the room without students' wanting them to look at their graphs and see their improvement. The system not only improved students' behavior, but fostered great pride.

Teachers should routinely give students the opportunity to calculate and monitor their own grades, both on individual assignments and across time. Graphing academic data is especially useful to students. Using self-reporting and self-evaluating in this way helps students become motivated to put forth the kind of consistent effort that thwarts school failure. Teachers should provide time for students to maintain and evaluate their own performance records.

> For a portfolio on the Civil War, **Ms. Washington** asked her students to produce two self-assessments. The first was assigned after the first week of the project. Students were asked to evaluate their levels of effort, cooperation with others, and performance thus far, and to project what they planned to do in the future to complete the project. Their second self-assessment was due 3 weeks later. This assignment helped students reach their projected goals, because they knew that if they did not reach their goals, they were accountable to explain why.

When adults are collaborating with students to design a self-monitoring program, it is important to follow specific steps, just as is done when developing an adult-monitored behavior management program. These steps are depicted in Table 6.1.

> **Dr. Chickie-Wolfe** once courageously used an Applied Behavioral Analysis (ABA) approach to teach an entire classroom of general education students to simultaneously work on behavior change projects. First, she taught them the basic principles of behavior and then explained the process of ABA, pointing out that people follow these same steps to bring about a behavior change of any kind (increasing, decreasing, eliminating, or maintaining a behavior). She was pleased at the high level of interest shown by the students as they followed her step-by-step approach and as each identified a specific behavior they wanted to change. The behaviors they selected varied greatly. A student with ADHD targeted decreasing talking in class, while a shy and quiet student targeted increasing talking and volunteering in class; a disorganized student targeted turning in homework on time; an unmotivated student targeted increasing study time at home, while a student who rushed through work decided to try to work more carefully, and a perfectionist student decided to work more quickly yet not

TABLE 6.1. Establishing Student Self-Monitoring of Behavior

1. Preparation
   a. Assist the student in attending to and assessing his or her behavior, determining the function(s) of inappropriate behaviors, and committing to control behavior.
   b. Concretely and explicitly define the desired behavior.
   c. Select an easy-to-use method for the student to record the behavior.
   d. Select a prompting method (i.e., teach cuing or a recorded tone) and schedule.
   e. Train the student to use the recording and prompting methods.
2. Performance
   a. Implement the self-monitoring program; initially use continuous adult monitoring, continuous prompting, external reinforcers if necessary.
   b. Fade to intermittent monitoring and prompting.
   c. Pair external reinforcers with social praise and internal reinforcers.
3. Appraisal
   a. With the student, collaboratively appraise the success of the self-monitoring procedure.
   b. With the student, collaboratively appraise learning success.
   c. Modify the self-monitoring program appropriately.
   d. Move to covert cuing and delayed assessment and appraisal.

lower accuracy. The students collected baseline data, laid out their Behavior Change Plans (which were carefully stated, observable, measurable, and included a reward system), and began implementing their plans while collecting raw data. After a week on the projects, students graphed their raw data to visually "see" their progress, and modifications were made when necessary. Students routinely encouraged one another while praising noticeable behavior changes, and parents expressed both an interest in the project and amazement at the changes they saw in their children. The students were astonished to realize that these principles could be useful not only in regard to schoolwork, but also in their personal lives, now and in the future.

Although this was an ambitious endeavor, the high levels of self-monitoring, self-evaluating, and self-esteem evidenced by the students brought about significant behavioral and academic improvements as well as increased levels of independence for these students. Affirmations regarding their behavior, such as those found in Table 6.2, encourage students to employ such self-regulatory behavior strategies. Eventually students should be able to assess their own behavior, determine its function, and apply appropriate interventions independently.

Lucy found herself putting off writing her master's thesis for so long that she had to ask for four extensions. Often the very time slots she set aside for working on her thesis ended up being spent doing something completely different—going out for a walk with her neighbor or

TABLE 6.2. Student Affirmations about Behavior

- I do not play until my work is finished.
- I have good study skills, and I use them.
- I persevere.
- I choose "right" over "easy."
- I think before I act.
- My actions are responsible.
- I put forth the necessary effort to get the job done well.

shopping with friends. When she forced herself to stay at her desk, she found herself answering email and making telephone calls. After conducting a functional behavior assessment on herself, she realized that many factors were contributing to her problem. With a stressful job, she had too many demands on her time and very little time to connect with family and friends. In addition, she felt overwhelmed by the magnitude of her thesis and feared that she would not be successful. To address her feelings of being overwhelmed, she separated the project into manageable chunks. To reduce her anxiety, she scheduled regular meetings for encouraging pep talks with her advisor. However, the most important intervention Lucy developed was finding a more efficient way to spend time with family and friends. She instituted a "Sunday Supper," a potluck dinner at her home every Sunday evening. She didn't do the cooking herself, but looked forward to ending her intense work-filled weekend by having fun with family and friends.

Help Students Develop Their Personal Learning Guides (HILLs)

Students should be encouraged to keep both completed and unused copies of behavioral assessment and intervention sheets in their binders, so they can continually reflect upon and readjust their strategies. Materials pertinent to this topic include the following:

Worksheet 1.2. Menu of Interview Questions about General Learning Skills
Worksheet 1.3. Problem Identification and Intervention Selection Tool
Worksheet 1.4. Consultation Outcome-Monitoring Tool
Worksheet 2.2. Menu of Interview Questions about Family and Friends
Worksheet 4.3. Goal-Setting and Prioritizing Worksheet
Worksheet 4.4. Visualization Exercise
Worksheet 6.1. Checklist of Strategies to Foster Appropriate Behavior
Worksheet 6.2. Menu of Rewards
Worksheet 6.3. Student Contract
Worksheet 8.3. Study Plan Strategy Tool
Handout 6.1. Steps to Establish a Behavior Management Program
Table 6.2. Student Affirmations about Behavior

WORKSHEET 6.1.

Checklist of Strategies to Foster Appropriate Behavior

	Function(s) of inappropriate behavior(s) are determined, including antecedents and consequences.
	A baseline is obtained prior to the implementation of a deliberate intervention.
	Appropriate alternative *target* behaviors are identified that are likely to be naturally and predictably reinforced, easy to measure, clearly defined in observable and objective terms, and practical for eventual self-monitoring by the student.
	Goals are selected that are attainable and give students frequent opportunities to engage in and be reinforced for appropriate behavior; when possible, they are cumulative.
	Reward systems are used to initiate behaviors, scaffolded, and faded as soon as possible.
	Study strategies and processes are included in expectations as well as products.
	Rewards are based on the quality of work whenever possible.
	Rewards are motivating and personalized—chosen by students and varied according to the skill level and learning rate of individual students.
	Rewards are modified when appropriate.
	When possible, interdependent group contracts are used.
	Behavior management programs are gradually faded by extending the timeline and reducing the external reinforcers until a student demonstrates the target behaviors independently.
	Adults collaborate with students to design a self-monitoring program in which the students monitor and regulate behavior through data recording, evaluation, and self-reinforcement.
	Students are given the opportunity to calculate, monitor, and graph their own grades.
	Individualized behavior contracts are implemented, monitored, and revised.
Parents foster positive behavior by:	
	Collaborating with children to develop clear behavioral expectations.
	Publicly acknowledging appropriate behavior with natural, rewarding consequences.
	Consistently applying appropriate consequences for inappropriate behavior.
	Children are encouraged to monitor and evaluate their own behavior.
Teachers foster positive behavior by:	
	Collaborating with students in developing clear behavioral expectations.
	Providing routines and structures that positively and naturally reward positive behavior.
	Consistently applying appropriate consequences for inappropriate behavior.
	Assessing an inappropriate behavior's function(s) and substituting more appropriate behavior.
	Encouraging students to monitor and evaluate their own behavior.

WORKSHEET 6.2.

Menu of Rewards

The student chooses one reinforcer from the list, which is provided when the goal is met. Status jobs are preferred over concrete objects (such as candy).

Academic:

A no-homework coupon

Classroom helper for __ days

Spelling test giver this week

TV anchor on the morning announcements for __ days

Work in bookstore this week

Extra __ minutes of computer time

Activities:

Place words on school marquee

Library Helper for __ days

Extra __ minutes of recess

Extra __ minutes in the gym

Listen to music for __ minutes

__ minutes working on puzzle

Teacher Helper (straighten up book shelves, pass out papers, run errands, etc.)

A long, free drink of water

Peer attention:

Sit with a friend

Math Expert (help classmates with assignments for the day)

Read a book to a kindergarten buddy

Create a bulletin board with a friend

Help out in special education classroom

Play a game with a friend

Tangibles:

Earn __ tokens (__ tokens are exchanged for __ [privilege/prize])

Ice cream bar at lunch

$1 gift certificate to __ (fast-food restaurant)

Take one reward from the Reward Box

After consistent successes, adult's monitoring of the contract and reward is faded. These duties are then transferred to the student, who sets goals, self-monitors performance, makes necessary adjustments following appraisal, and then gives him- or herself the appropriate rewards.

WORKSHEET 6.3.

Student Contract

Name: Date:

Goal:

These are my rewards when I meet this goal:

1.

2.

These are my consequences should I not meet my goal:

1.

2.

Signatures: Date:

_______________________________________ _______________________

HANDOUT 6.1.

Steps to Establish a Behavior Management Program

Preparation I

1. Define target behavior.
2. Collect data on rate of current performance.
3. Negotiate specific behavior, goal, and reward menu with student.
4 Develop contract that includes the following:
    a. Desired behavior, goal, and rewards.
    b. Consequence for not meeting goal/bonus for exceeding goal.
    c. Names of those monitoring contract.
    d. Timeline and anticipated date for revision.
    e. Signatures of student, teacher, parent, and consultant.

Performance I

5. Implement the program.

Appraisal I

6. Check and graph progress frequently.

Preparation II

7. Revise contract (introduce self-monitoring).
8. Revise rewards and consequences (more natural).

Performance II

9. Implement revised program.

Appraisal II

10. Frequently check progress.

Preparation III

11. Re-revise program (total self-monitoring).

Performance III

12. Implement the re-revised program.

Appraisal III

13. Conduct periodic postintervention assessment of target behavior and graph results. Modify as necessary.

7

Empowering Students to Manage Time and Organization

Skills in managing time often distinguish high from low achievers.

OVERVIEW

As an eighth grader, **Gayle Jones** is an exasperation to her parents. The combination of junior high school and puberty has overtaxed her meager organizational skills so severely that she seems to lose everything—her math book, library books, locker key, sneakers, even her pet gerbil. She consistently forgets materials needed for homework assignments, and almost every evening she and her mother must drive back to the school to pick up necessary books. At a school meeting, Mrs. Jones indicates that she finds Gayle's completed homework papers in the laundry, under the couch, or crammed in the bottom of Gayle's backpack.

In contrast, **Nicky** is a nontraditional college student who also holds down a demanding full-time job. To get things done and still have time to spend with her family, she daily updates her "To-Do" list. She designates certain times for specified activities (e.g., Saturdays and two evenings a week are devoted to studying, but Sundays and other evenings are spent with her family). She incorporates home, work, and school activities into one appointment book, and in it she blocks out time for course assignment completion. She also keeps her desk and briefcase organized, so that when she sits down to work, she wastes little time searching for materials. Nicky was not raised to be this organized; to some extent, her fastidious organization seems to be a reaction to a chaotic childhood home. She is thankful for learning these skills from her first supervisor at work.

Nicky knows how to manage time. She doesn't procrastinate and is a truly independent learner. How does Nicky discipline herself to work when she has other attractive alternatives? How can adults help students determine which time management and organizational strategies work best for them, adopt these strategies, and maintain them independently?

This chapter addresses students' abilities to manage time and organization as they relate to studying and independent learning. Suggestions in this chapter are appropriate for students who avoid assignments and responsibilities, do not make good use of time, do not record assignments, have difficulty focusing attention, or are disorganized. For a concise summary of concepts presented in this chapter, see Worksheet 7.1, Checklist of Strategies Fostering Time Management and Organization.

As is the case for all of the chapters in this book, this chapter provides a menu of strategies. It is neither possible nor desirable for any student to use every strategy described. In implementing strategies to improve time management, it is important to recognize that there is no one correct method. Effective strategies for one person may not work for another. Furthermore, adults and students alike should understand that time management and organizational strategies are tools for studying, not ends in and of themselves. That is, students obviously should not devote so much time and energy to using these tools that they have little time left for learning. A moderate amount of effort in this area can yield remarkable results.

RESEARCH FOUNDATIONS

Many students have difficulty managing time and keeping organized, and some populations are particularly prone to such difficulties. For example, students diagnosed with Attention Deficit Disorder (ADD/ADHD) have been found to have significant difficulty with estimating time, and thus are lacking a fundamental skill required for time management (Zentall, Harper, & Stormont-Spurgin, 1993). Students diagnosed as having a specific learning disability frequently have characteristics that interfere with their ability to manage time including poor organizational skills, listening and memory deficits, difficulty accurately estimating and allocating time, difficulty self-monitoring, and a disinclination to persevere (Gleason et al., 2002; Hughes, Ruhl, Schumaker, & Deshler, 1989; Salend & Gajria, 1995).

However, difficulties with time management are not limited to students with identified educational disabilities. Such problems are almost universal for students and even for adults; indeed, they seem to be worsening with the increased availability of technology such as email and cell phones (Garhammer, 2002). It is inevitable that the readers, as well as the writers, of this book struggle with time management themselves.

Widespread difficulties notwithstanding, managing time is an essential strategy for independent learning. As Zimmerman et al. (1996) indicate, without effective study time management, students make learning decisions based on expediency because they do not have the time to implement self-regulation strategies. Thus, time management must be mastered so that students *actually have the time to implement the study skills and independent learning strategies described throughout this book*. In addition to providing time to complete assignments and employ self-regulation strategies essential to independent learning, good time management results in a greater feeling of control, reduced feelings of stress, and increased life and job satisfaction (Macan, Shahani, Dipboye, & Phillips, 1990; Peeters & Rutte, 2005). Furthermore, time management enables students to spend more time in preferred activities such as relaxing or spending time with friends, which in turn increases motivation.

Components of Time Management

By conducting a factor analysis of strategies used by college students, Macan et al. (1990) found that time management has four dimensions:

1. *Setting and prioritizing short- and long-term goals* (e.g., setting and keeping long- and short-term goals, breaking down tasks, reviewing goals and activities, setting priorities and deadlines, increasing efficiency, evaluating daily schedules, completing high-priority tasks, using wait time, avoiding interruptions).
2. *Planning and scheduling* (e.g., making daily lists of tasks to complete, making schedules, carrying an appointment book, writing reminder notes and lists, keeping daily logs, keep-

ing records, preparing for the next day the night before, organizing paperwork, leaving a clean workspace).

3. *Preferring organization* (e.g., not being disorganized, not preferring messy workplaces, preplanning and prioritizing tasks).
4. *Perceiving and gaining control over time* (e.g., not feeling overwhelmed by tasks, not fixating on small details, not agreeing to too many tasks, accurately estimating time, keeping a schedule, being able to say no, refraining from excessive socializing, thinking before acting, being unlikely to procrastinate, delegating, keeping sight of goals).

These dimensions can be independent of one another—individuals who set and prioritize goals do not necessarily make schedules, keep organized, or feel in control of time. The most important dimension is feeling in control of time. Setting and prioritizing tasks, planning and scheduling, and organizing are actually *methods* to increase time control. For example, improved organization can increase control over time because less time is wasted. On the other hand, organization is not essential to time management, for some individuals can be disorganized yet still manage time effectively (for example, the person who has piles of paper all over an office yet still knows exactly where to find a single item). Furthermore, these dimensions are effective in increasing control over time only when they are actually implemented. That is, making a schedule facilitates a sense of control over time only when the schedule is followed.

METHODS

Fortunately, it is possible to help students improve time management skills (Macan, 1996; Van Eerde, 2003). Even students with learning disabilities or attention-deficit disorder can be taught to improve these skills enough that they can independently maintain the strategies (Hughes et al., 1989; Trammel et al., 1994; Stevenson, Whitmont, & Bornholt, 2002). As is true for all components of study skills, self-regulation of time management requires *preparation*, *performance*, and *appraisal*.

Preparation

Assessment

Time management difficulties may result from (1) a lack of understanding of basic time concepts, (2) a need to set and prioritize goals, (3) a need to improve scheduling and task monitoring, (4) insufficient organization, or (5) a need to increase control over time and decrease procrastination. The source of the difficulty can be determined by interviewing the student and augmenting this interview with collaborative sessions including the student, parent, and teacher(s). These collaborative sessions provide opportunities to obtain more complete information and to clarify misunderstandings that frequently occur between students, parents, and teachers regarding goals, priorities, and expectations.

This chapter provides a variety of materials that can be used as assessment tools to determine the causes of difficulties managing time, including Worksheet 7.1, Checklist of Strategies Fostering Time Management; Worksheet 7.2, Study Time Analysis Sheet; Worksheet 7.3, Menu of Interview Questions about Time Management; Worksheet 7.4, Monthly Planner; Worksheet 7.5, Weekly Schedule; Worksheet 7.6, Daily Schedule; Worksheet 7.7, Daily Time Control Review; and Worksheet 7.8, "T" Chart for Time Management of Activities. These are intended to be modified to fit individual needs. After outcome measures are determined, preintervention data are collected, and an intervention is selected, the same worksheets can be used on a continuing basis to monitor the effectiveness of the intervention and modify it appropriately. Eventually the data gathered with these tools can be used for appraising effectiveness of strategies by comparing results with the baseline data. Initially, these worksheets would be appropriately used by consultants, students, teachers, and parents working together collaboratively to develop and implement an intervention. As students progress, the completion of forms and data monitoring should be increasingly turned over to them, and eventually the students should take full responsibility for using and modifying strategies.

Performance

Fostering the Development of Time Concepts

The ability to manage time efficiently is predicated upon the acquisition of cognitive constructs about time. Students need to be able to discriminate past, present, and future; be aware of the passage of time; recall how much time similar activities have taken in the past; roughly predict the amount of time needed to complete an upcoming task; and monitor time during task completion. Effective time management also requires being aware of the elements that fill time and the adoption of positive work habits such as motivation, self-discipline, and using time management strategies such as scheduling, organizing, and prioritizing (Kelly, 2002).

Before teaching students to develop daily and weekly schedules, it is important to determine that they are able to locate a given date on a calendar, determine when an assignment is due, use appropriate abbreviations, and record the assignments (Gleason et al., 2002). Educators need to check for these skills and also to check that the students have time to complete schoolwork every evening, understand that studying takes time in addition to completing homework assignments, and are capable of breaking down a major project into parts. Furthermore, students need to understand that time is a limited resource and that efficient time management and organization improves their learning because it enables them to observe their own learning experiences and modify their studying according to what works best for them. It is also helpful for students to understand that they gain personal and social benefits through effective time management, because it enables them to have more time to spend on activities they enjoy.

Helping Students Set, Prioritize, and Work toward Goals

When educators are attempting to address issues of time management, it can be tempting to simply help the students set up daily and weekly time schedules. However, unless students have clearly defined goals and priorities, they are unlikely to maintain such schedules. As students determine their priorities, their motivation and potential to implement and maintain time management strategies will increase. Helping students set goals has been described in detail in Chapter 4, and the reader is referred to that chapter and Worksheet 4.3. After a student develops and prioritizes goals and determines activities necessary to attain these goals, they should be written down and prioritized, possibly using Worksheet 7.8.

> To help him prioritize, **Chase's** counselor had him construct a version of Worksheet 7.8. That is, she asked Chase to write a large "T" on a blank sheet of paper with "Most Important Goals" on the left and "Most Important To-Do Activities" on the right. The next two instructions she gave made an immediate impact on Chase's awareness and success. First, all *small* tasks that seemed urgent to Chase, but that were not in fact important to his academic goals, were eliminated from this chart. Second, any activity on the "To-Do" side that was not directly related to one of the "Important Goals" listed on the left was eliminated. This process enabled Chase to focus on his most important goals and to see that he had only a few important activities needing immediate attention.

Helping Students Develop Skills in Planning and Scheduling

Adults can help students improve their sense of time by having them assess how they already spend their time (Zimmerman et al., 1996). Students can complete selected worksheets in this chapter in order to determine how much time they spend in activities such as household chores, exercising, getting to and from school, grooming, listening to music, participating in athletics, playing games, practicing instruments or attending music lessons, reading, relaxing, sleeping, spending time with family members, talking and spending time with friends, in extracurricular activities, studying, watching TV, working, or attending religious services. After maintaining a log for a period of time, students can then analyze how they spend their time and collaborate with adults to modify their time allocation. A lofty example would be a student who would like to spend less time watching TV and more time studying, and therefore develops a self-monitored behavior management system.

RECORDING TASKS AND SCHEDULES

It is critical that every student develop an effective method to write down assignments, because it is simply too difficult to remember them in detail. From the time students begin to receive homework assignments, teachers and parents should encourage them to write down all assignments correctly and completely in a planner and check them off when completed. Many different methods are available:

- A small notebook designated as an assignment book.
- Daily, weekly, or monthly planners (see Worksheets 7.4, 7.5, and 7.6).
- Keeping a running "To-Do" list.
- Devoting a 3" × 5" card to each task and taking notes regarding work sessions.
- Writing reminder notes or "stickies" that are discarded when completed.
- Writing assignments on the inside covers of textbooks they own.
- Using personal digital assistants (e.g., Palm Pilots).
- Using computer programs such as Microsoft Outlook's Tasks and Calendar.

Which type of planner is used does not matter, as long as it does the following:

1. Enables the student to include sufficient information to complete the assignment.
2. Specifies the assignment deadline.
3. Permits the student to designate when he or she will work on assignments.
4. Is comfortable and accessible enough that the student actually uses it.
5. Enables the student to record and have an overview of "big-picture" long-term assignments and their components, as well as to record short-term assignments.

Many students find it helpful to include in their planners not only homework assignments, but also commitments such as jobs, extracurricular activities, social events, and even dates permission slips are due. Teachers can help students maintain their planners by keeping a highly visible calendar with assignments shared by the entire class. However, individual students will need to incorporate whole-class assignments into their own planners to include idiosyncratic obligations.

Since many students have difficulty tracking assignments, it is important for teachers to initially monitor students' planners for accuracy and completeness. Some students have so much difficulty writing down complete assignments that a "study buddy" is enlisted to check their planners for assignment accuracy. With time, monitoring and checking should be made less frequent and predictable, so that such students become independent.

Mr. Wood created an Agenda Club for students in his fifth-grade class who did not use their assignment notebooks properly or consistently. After teaching them how to enter homework assignments, he required the students to bring their completed agendas to him at the end of each day to be checked and initialed. He asked each student's parents to check the agendas every night, look for Mr. Wood's initials, make sure that each assignment was completed and checked off by the student, and then sign the entry. Each morning every student showed the agenda to Mr. Wood, who wrote an OK in a circle beside the parent's signature while praising the student for organization and responsibility. Within 4 weeks, all the students except one were proficient enough with using their assignment notebooks to "graduate" from the Agenda Club, with only periodic checks by the teacher. Parents were encouraged to fade daily checking of the assignment notebook and spot-check until it was apparent that their child could manage this critical study skill independently.

BREAKING TASKS DOWN INTO MANAGEABLE COMPONENTS

As soon as students start to receive long-term assignments, teachers and parents should encourage them to break those assignments down into manageable chunks and write each part separately into their schedulers. Students often need guidance in how to break down long-term assignments, and they also need to be reminded to carry over components that were not completed during a planned time slot into the next section of the schedule.

MAKING DAYS MORE PREDICTABLE

Efficient students often make their days more predictable by setting aside regular times of day for certain activities. Helping parents and students agree upon a designated, regular, quiet "study time" is an extremely effective intervention. The amount of time needed varies according to the individual student and the curriculum in which he or she is enrolled. Some students need less time because they have time to complete homework in school, but others need more than the standard "10 minutes per grade" when they are in honors classes or when they have a learning disability. Furthermore, it is important for students to understand that the point is to complete the assignments with effort and high quality, not to accumulate "seat time." Therefore, the amount of designated "study time" will need frequent adjustment.

A student's ability to concentrate at different times of the day should be considered in establishing a study time. Most students focus better in the daylight hours—in the early morning or shortly after school—and many elementary school students are too tired after dinner to be able to concentrate efficiently. Some older students, however, are "night owls" who get a burst of energy in the evening. Gettinger and Nicaise (1997) recommend that students complete the most difficult work when they are most alert; this time slot must be individually determined.

Regardless of the amount of time needed, finding adequate time to study can be challenging in busy households. Many parents indicate that they have difficulty helping their children establish homework routines because of busy family schedules (Reetz, 1991). The establishment of a daily study time must take into account already scheduled extracurricular activities, chores, and recreation. It can be very illuminating—for students, parents, and educators—to have students use their schedules to block out activities such as athletics, practicing music, time with friends, favorite television shows, medical/dental appointments, and religious activities, in order to determine when students actually have time to study. Ideally, the family agrees upon a study time; the television and other distractions are turned off; phone calls are not taken; and the entire family studies, reads, or completes paperwork. Generally, students need less supervision as they get older, and by junior high they often make and keep their own homework schedules, but some adolescents continue to need considerable parental involvement.

Helping Students Develop Skills to Organize Materials

Both at home and at school, students benefit from general organization skills. Students can be encouraged to develop these habits:

1. Returning frequently-used objects to designated locations so they can be easily found.
2. Having a designated location for papers and materials that need to be moved from one location to another (for example, a backpack into which homework materials are immediately placed as soon as they are distributed in class, or a table near their home's front door on which objects to take to school are placed every night).
3. Maintaining a checklist of materials to bring to school daily (e.g., "textbooks, gym clothes, lunch money, library books, calculator") in a highly visible location.
4. Developing and using a method to organize papers and other academic materials.

Regardless of the method selected to organize papers, adults must demonstrate its use, integrate use into daily classroom and home routines, and monitor implementation until students have mastered the system and maintain it independently. Students need help in determining which papers must be kept (where and for how long), thrown out, or given to parents.

Some students successfully use *pocket folders*, perhaps a different color for each subject (even matching the color of their textbooks!), to help organize papers. These are particularly helpful for young students who receive assignments one sheet at a time and who do not take unit tests covering multiple weeks. It can be helpful to instruct students to keep new work on one side and completed work, in chronological order, on the other. Gleason et al. (2002) recommend one folder to transport materials and an additional folder for each subject in school.

When students use *organized three-ring binders*, they obtain higher grades (Lobay, 1993, as cited by Gleason et al., 2002). Requiring students to maintain organized three-ring binders is a primary intervention for some students with learning disabilities. At the Landmark Schools, all students are required to develop and maintain "working notebooks," which are regularly graded according to completeness, correct filing, and overall neatness (Sedita, 2001). The following are useful components of organized three-ring binders:

1. A checklist of materials to bring to school daily.
2. A zippered pouch for small supplies (pens, pencils, correction fluid, highlighters, paper clips, stapler, portable hole punch, protractor, and calculator).
3. Time organizers (e.g., schedules, planners, calendars, assignment book).
4. A subject divider for each subject (some students do well with arranging all classroom notes and returned assignments in chronological order; others need three to five subdividers for each subject, separating notes, homework, handouts, and study guides).
5. Reference materials (e.g., a portable spell checker).
6. Blank paper.

Some students do best with one large working notebook for all subjects. Others prefer multiple notebooks—perhaps one for each subject, or one for morning and one for afternoon classes.

Depending on the number of handouts distributed in their classes, students may or may not be able to maintain all materials in one notebook for the entire semester. If there are many handouts, students need to extract outdated material regularly at the end of each unit and file the materials on which they have already been tested in an *archive file*, for use when studying for final exams. For this purpose, Sedita (2001) recommends placing outdated materials into accordion files.

Helping Students Select Study Space

Most students benefit from a designated place in which they regularly study. It should have good lighting, a workspace such as a desk or table, minimal distractions, and moderately comfortable seating. It is helpful when home studying supplies are kept in one place, preferably adjacent to the location where studying takes place. Helpful supplies include a calculator, calendar, computer, dictionaries, erasers, glue, paper hole punch, notebooks, paper, pencils, pens, highlighters, reference books, ruler, tape, and so forth. Selecting this space needs to take into account several variables: the student's learning style, level of distractibility, and need for adult support (Hong & Milgram, 2000). For many, the ideal location is a quiet bedroom with a desk. Others find working in a bedroom difficult because they are tempted by distractions, or because they are lonely and study better at the kitchen table. Still others prefer working in the public library. The location seems to make little difference, as long as they are not distracted so much that they cannot concentrate (Stevens, 1996).

Listening to music while completing homework seems to have little impact, but watching TV seems to slow down homework completion. On the other hand, some teenagers indicated in one study that they preferred spending 2 hours completing homework in front of the television to spending 1 hour on homework without it (Bryan & Sullivan-Burstein, 1997). However, the combination of watching TV and attempting to complete tasks that require intense concentration is not appropriate.

Together, educators, parents, and each student can discuss and informally assess the student's learning style and plan methods to take advantage of this style both at home and in school. Sometimes parents may be unaware of how their children learn most effectively and may encourage them to study in a conflicting manner. For example, parents may encourage a student to complete homework at a secluded desk in his or her room, but that student may study better lying on the living room floor while listening to music (Martin & Potter, 1998). Careful observation of outcomes can determine whether the selected location is appropriate for a particular student.

> **Kyle**'s mother insisted that he do his homework at the kitchen table so she could help him while preparing dinner. Unfortunately, he was so distracted by the noise and movement in the kitchen that he found it nearly impossible to focus his attention. Kyle's older sister Karen noticed him covering his ears with his hands as he tried to study. Though studying in the kitchen had worked well for her, she recognized that this arrangement was not working for him. Karen helped him set up a new place to complete homework that was quieter than the kitchen and allowed him to concentrate with much better results. A fringe benefit was that he soon became more autonomous in completing his homework, as it was often easier to stay put and figure it out than to get help in the kitchen. Previously, Kyle had incorrectly concluded that he hated doing homework. What he actually hated was trying to do homework when he was severely distracted.

Many learners appropriately vary where they choose to study, based on circumstances, the topic, and environmental conditions. These variations should be expected, accepted, and encouraged.

> **Wendy** was a graduate student who normally liked to study at home. She usually did her work in silence at her desk on her porch. However, in winter Wendy preferred curling up under a quilt in her easy chair in the living room. During times when she needed frequent access to books and journals, she studied in the library. When studying advanced statistics, she participated in a study group at the local coffee shop, which had welcoming overstuffed sofas.

Helping Students Gain Control over Time and Decrease Procrastination

Gaining control over time is dependent on prioritizing, planning/scheduling, and organizing as described above. Gaining control over time is also dependent upon the individual's ability to control impulses and avoid procrastination, which are closely linked traits.

"Procrastination" is defined as avoiding or not completing a task even though the person believes the task is of high priority. Procrastination stems from a conflict between knowing what should be done and not wanting to do it. The ability to control procrastination and delay immediate gratification depends upon responding to "cool" cognition rather than "hot" emotions. Controlling procrastination is thus predicated upon a certain level of cognitive development and the ability to employ strategies of self-control (Metcalfe & Mischel, 1999).

Procrastination is extremely common, particularly when students are in situations requiring high levels of self-regulation. Studies have found that up to 70% of college undergraduates suffer from procrastination (Ferrari, Johnson, & McKown, 1995). It can have a serious impact on an individual's ability to set and achieve academic, career, and personal goals (Tuckman, 2003). Although procrastination provides a short-term and powerful negative reinforcer, because it temporarily reduces anxiety or discomfort associated with completing an avoided task, it eventually increases stress and anxiety as deadlines become imminent. Furthermore, because it results in insufficient time for creative, flexible, and complex thought, procrastination also results in students' completing assignments superficially and being unable to use self-regulatory independent learning strategies.

> When discussing their own study skills, **a group of graduate students** agreed that by this point in their academic career they had mastered most strategies and had learned which worked best for each of them. However, almost all indicated that they still struggled with procrastination. As one student mentioned, "It is amazing how good cleaning the bathroom can look when I should be studying." Typically, they used fear of missing deadlines and receiving unacceptable grades as tools to cope with procrastination, but they admitted that they almost inevitably ran into difficulties because they misjudged the amount of time an assignment would take. They felt they did not gain as much from their education as they might if they could manage procrastination effectively.

Several factors can increase procrastination. To a certain extent, procrastination is environmentally influenced. It increases when assignments are difficult, and when teachers and classmates focus on performance goals and competition rather than learning (Urdan, Midgely, & Anderman, 1998). Procrastination can also result when an individual is overwhelmed by environmental stressors that take large amounts of time, such as an ill family member who needs nursing care. Sometimes when assignments are boring, easy, or routine, students procrastinate until deadlines loom to present a challenge and increase motivation (Van Eerde, 2003).

At the individual level, procrastination is associated with work avoidance goal orientations and/or students' questioning their self-efficacy. Procrastinating can result from being unable to ward off the impulse to participate in a preferred activity, such as talking with friends. It also can result from fear of some aspect of completing the assigned activity (Lakein, 1973), such as fear of failing, being judged, succeeding (and thus raising others' expectations), or receiving negative social judgments from lower-achieving peers. Procrastination is most likely to be employed when the individual is overwhelmed by a task or finds it onerous, unpleasant, or boring. In particular, students are much more likely to procrastinate when they are working on relatively difficult tasks (e.g., studying for exams, reading difficult assignments, or writing papers) than when they are completing routine homework assignments or attending class. Students with poor study skills are likely to procrastinate as well (Bembenutty, 1999; Wolters, 2003).

Procrastination is associated with the inability to delay immediate gratification, which in turn is increased by temporary or chronic cognitive dysfunction and/or temporary or chronic stress. That is, when people are under either acute or chronic stress, their emotional "hot system" takes over and they are more likely to demonstrate emotionally based behaviors such as irritability, overeating, drug abuse, and procrastination (Baumeister & Heatherton, 1996; Metcalfe & Mischel, 1999). Furthermore, because the ability to delay immediate gratification normally increases with chronological age and more advanced cognitive development, older students are generally more adept at managing procrastination. Managing procrastination and delaying immediate gratification are also affected by the ability to control the environment, remove temptation, and avoid thinking about the temptation. Parents typically help elementary school children delay immediate gratification (and reduce procrastination) by controlling the study environment. With adolescence these external controls are reduced, and students are expected to monitor themselves. Consequently, procrastination often increases as parents become less involved in monitoring homework when their children become adolescents, and yet again as students move on to the freedom of college (Milgram & Toubiana, 1999). This latter transition can be particularly problematic for students who are accustomed to close monitoring in high school, as is typically true for students with identified disabilities. It is essential to wean such students from close monitoring before they encounter situations in which they are required to be autonomous.

> **Fran** failed several courses her first year in college and was not advanced to sophomore standing when she returned to college the fall of her second year. Placed on academic probation, she again failed courses—so many that she was asked not to return in the spring. The reason she failed was that she did not submit assignments on time, if at all. Fran had been identified as having a learning disability at an early age, and had received support services throughout her elementary and secondary school career. In high school these services primarily consisted of going to the resource room instead of study hall, where she received help with organization and tracking assignment completion. Fran finished high school with an excellent academic (A–) average. She was eligible for learning disability services in college, but did not avail herself of those services. Fran had been successful when she used teacher-directed organization and time management strategies in high school. Unfortunately, she had never learned to use these strategies independently, resulting in her current failures and expulsion from college.

REDUCING THE TENDENCY TO TAKE ON TOO MANY TASKS

The tendency to take on too many tasks results from the fact that students often have far more options for extracurricular activities than they have time. In addition, each of these opportunities has evolved into increasingly time consuming endeavors. For example, it is not uncommon for even an 8-year-old child to be on more than one soccer team and to spend the entire weekend playing multiple games. The desire to be admitted into competitive colleges leads some high school students to take on so many activities that their schedule precludes any time to study, much less time to relax or spend with friends and family members.

> **Dorie,** a high school senior, was discovered one lunch period working by herself in her English classroom. When her teacher asked her what she was doing, she explained that she was working on her term paper. As an editor on the school newspaper; a tutor for the National Honor Society; a contributor to the school yearbook; a weekend employee of the local bakery; and a member of the tennis team, school orchestra, and mixed glee club, Dorie had no time to complete assignments after school. Therefore, she completed her homework during school (Latin during math class, math during English, etc.). Although she was able to com-

plete routine assignments while simultaneously "listening" in class, she was not able to complete complex tasks such as term papers or studying for exams, resulting in her skipping lunch.

Similar struggles with trying to "do it all" can be seen at every age. A student struggling with the tendency to take on too many tasks is very likely to have parents and teachers struggling to juggle careers with meeting the needs of family members. Understanding that time and energy are finite, and that *one has to make hard choices on how to spend the finite resources of time and energy*, is a lesson that does not come easily. The following steps can be helpful:

1. Revisit and reprioritize long- and short-term goals and their associated activities.
2. Determine and eliminate current activities that do not support top-priority goals.
3. Continually ask, "Is this the best use of my time?" (Lakein, 1973).
4. Refuse to add a new obligation until an old obligation is eliminated.

IMPROVING THE ABILITY TO SAY NO, AND REDUCING INAPPROPRIATE SOCIALIZATION

Very often, taking on too many tasks is a result of not saying no to others' requests or suggestions. This can be a result of being relatively directionless or of being overanxious to please others. In the former case, the student can contrast the requested activity with her or his goals, choose to spend time on the requested activity when it is goal-compatible, or gracefully say, "No, thank you" when it is not. If not saying no is a result of trying to please others, the student needs to consider both the importance of the relationship and the importance of the request to the other person. If the relationship is highly valued and the request is highly important to the other person, then the student probably needs to find time for that activity. However, often the needs of others can be met by creating alternative, less time-consuming solutions. For example, a student might agree to go to the mall on the weekend with friends instead of during designated study time on a weekday, or visit by phone for an hour rather than getting together for the evening.

When **Dorie**'s English teacher learned that she was completing all of her schoolwork during the school day because of being overloaded with extracurricular activities, he asked her how she came to be involved in each of those activities and how much she enjoyed them. He found that she had become involved in the yearbook, newspaper, and orchestra because friends were involved in them, but she did not particularly enjoy them. She was a geometry tutor for the National Honor Society simply because she had been asked. She was a member of the tennis team because she enjoyed the exercise and thought it would look good on her college application. She was a weekend employee of the local bakery to earn spending money. The one activity she enjoyed for itself was mixed glee club. After discussing her long-term goals with her teacher, Dorie decided to stay involved in the school newspaper in order to stay in contact with friends, to continue working at the bakery, to stay on the tennis team, and to remain in the glee club. She resigned from the yearbook, orchestra, and tutoring.

DECREASING THE TENDENCY TO UNDERESTIMATE TIME REQUIREMENTS

Students often have unrealistic ideas of the length of time it takes to complete given tasks (Zimmerman et al., 1996). It can be very helpful for students to time themselves while they complete a portion of an assignment, to assess how long that and similar assignments will take altogether. For example, a student might find that in 1 hour he or she can read 20 pages of history, read 50 pages of a novel, or complete 15 algebra problems. With this information, the student can better estimate how long assignments will take and then block out time accordingly.

MANAGING NEGATIVE EMOTIONS THAT LEAD TO PROCRASTINATION

When procrastination is a result of feeling overwhelmed by an assignment, it can be helpful to break the ice by spending a few minutes on the avoided task daily or by completing small related tasks. Most importantly, students need to learn how to break complex, difficult assignments into manageable tasks.

> **Annie Lamott's** (1995) brother, as an elementary school student, was completely overwhelmed by a project in which he was required to identify a large number of birds. His father advised him to proceed "bird by bird," and by thus breaking down the assignment, he succeeded. Annie used these words to help her professional writing throughout her adulthood, and both authors of this book have signs that say "Bird by Bird" perched on their computers.

When procrastination results from anxiety, adults can teach stress reduction strategies such as meditation or cognitive-behavioral therapy, or help foster positive emotions as described in Chapter 5. When procrastination is a result of fear of success or failure, psychologists can help the student explore and then reduce fears, irrational thinking, and feelings of powerlessness and negative self-worth through counseling and cognitive mediation strategies (Walker, 2004).

INCREASING THE ABILITY TO DELAY IMMEDIATE GRATIFICATION

When procrastination results from the inability to delay immediate gratification, it is important to help students find ways to control their attention. For example, they might *reduce distractions* in their environment, or *reward themselves* by participating in the preferred activity after they have completed work.

Students can also foster their ability to manage time by using positive affirmations. For example, they may tell themselves, "This is not the time to make phone calls. The time to make phone calls is when I am done studying." Additional affirmations regarding time and organization are included in Table 7.1. Such affirmations are important components of cognitive remediation programs that effectively improve organizational skills, increase attention and focus, and develop impulse control for individuals with Attention Deficit/Hyperactivity Disorder. With these programs, positive effects have been found to persist for a year following 8 weeks of 2-hour cognitive remediation sessions, bolstered by weekly meetings with supportive coaches and by homework exercises (Stevenson, Whitmont, & Bornholt, 2002).

Finally, adults can help students avoid developing the habit of procrastination by directly talking about it as an issue and giving students methods and reasons to avoid it. It also helps for students to understand that adults similarly struggle but cope with procrastination.

TABLE 7.1. Student Affirmations about Time and Organization

- I keep my mind focused on my work so I won't waste my time.
- I plan ahead and stick to a schedule.
- I use my time wisely.
- I study each day and don't wait until the last minute to prepare.
- I keep my materials organized and readily available.
- I break down large tasks into small chunks.
- I begin working on an assignment once it is given; I do not procrastinate.
- I look for and find "down time" to get in extra studying each day.

The principal of Eads Elementary School invites members of the local chamber of commerce into classrooms to talk with students. They focus on the effects of using "Lifeskills" and "Life-Long Guidelines" (Kovalik with Olsen, 1994) in their businesses. In addition to this discussion, the community leaders read a selected story to the students that highlights a Lifeskill. Often when community leaders discuss Perseverance, Effort, Organization, or Responsibility, they describe actual situations in which those skills made a significant difference in their success. The topic of procrastination arises frequently, and it has been helpful to have these community leaders explain how they avert putting off tasks in their various jobs. Having these topics reinforced by individuals other than their teachers and parents offers an opportunity for students to appreciate the importance of these skills. The question-and-answer period that follows often becomes a helpful problem-solving time for students to gain suggestions about ways to get their work completed more efficiently.

Appraisal

As described earlier, the same tools that are used in the assessment of time management and organization can be used to appraise the effectiveness of interventions designed to improve them. Appraisal requires that students reflect upon the tools they used, determine how well they worked, and decide what they might do to improve their strategies in the future.

Help Students Develop Their Personal Learning Guides (HILLs)

The time management and organization strategies that students select will rarely work the first time they are implemented. In addition, as students advance in school, their needs for such strategies will change with different demands. Therefore, students should be encouraged to keep both completed and unused copies of helpful materials in their binders so that they can continually readjust their strategies. These materials might include the following:

Worksheet 7.1. Checklist of Strategies Fostering Time Management and Organization
Worksheet 7.2. Study Time Analysis Sheet
Worksheet 7.3. Menu of Time Management Interview Questions
Worksheet 7.4. Monthly Planner
Worksheet 7.5. Weekly Schedule
Worksheet 7.6. Daily Schedule
Worksheet 7.7. Daily Time Control Review
Worksheet 7.8. "T" Chart for Time Management of Activities
Table 7.1. Student Affirmations about Time and Organization

WORKSHEET 7.1.

Checklist of Strategies Fostering Time Management and Organization

Students prioritize by:	
	Working on important priorities first.
	Completing activities that help meet important long-term and short-term goals.
	Focusing on having a high-quality study time.
	Avoiding getting distracted by others.
	Avoiding self-distraction (with TV, daydreaming, or getting frequent snacks).
	Studying at a desk or table in a quiet place free of distractions.
Students schedule and plan by:	
	Updating a To-Do list.
	Updating weekly planner and monthly calendars.
	Scheduling enough study time.
	Leaving some time unscheduled.
	Breaking assignments into smaller parts and scheduling each part.
	Writing assignments accurately and completely in an assignment book.
	Starting to work on time.
	Following a schedule.
Students keep organized by:	
	Keeping necessary materials, books, and supplies nearby.
	Bringing home, and taking to school, everything needed.
	Organizing papers and materials in folders, binders, and files.
	Organizing desk, locker, and backpack.
	Gathering "back-to-school" books and papers in one place.
	Turning in assignments on time.
	Reviewing notes and assignment requirements before beginning each assignment.
Students control time and focus by:	
	Scheduling study time for a time of day when not too tired.
	Working on harder assignments before easier assignments.
	Working on one assignment at a time.
	Taking short (10-minute) planned breaks between assignments.
	Taking time for self-care (sufficient exercise, diet, and sleep).
	Seeking help from a family member, study buddy, or homework hotline as needed.
	Writing down questions to ask teachers.
	Having a reward (such as doing something for fun) after finishing work.

(continued)

Strategies Fostering Time Management and Organization *(page 2 of 2)*

Students evaluate studying by:	
	Keeping track of the time spent on studying each subject.
	Checking whether the strategies used worked well.
Parents foster time management and organization by:	
	Providing an organized home (calendar, place for school-bound materials).
	Encouraging children to consciously develop organization methods for schoolwork.
	Helping their children plan and prioritize schoolwork and extracurricular activities.
	Helping their children determine how long it takes to complete tasks and use that knowledge to make schedules.
	Encouraging their children not to overschedule activities.
	Ensuring that children regularly complete homework in a quiet place with few distractions.
Teachers foster time management and organization by:	
	Using time management strategies and sharing those strategies with students.
	Leading discussions encouraging students in planning and prioritizing their activities.
	Giving assignments both orally and in writing that are clear and include work models.
	Encouraging students to write assignments in an assignment book.
	Requiring that students submit weekly progress reports for large projects, or smaller parts as completed.
	Modeling organization and encouraging students to consciously develop organization methods.

WORKSHEET 7.2.

Study Time Analysis Sheet

Date ________________ Student ____

Date	Subject	Assignment	Time started	Time spent	Where completed	With whom	Any distractions?	Grade expected	Grade received

Appraisal: What did I do that worked well? That didn't work well? What should I change?

WORKSHEET 7.3.

Menu of Time Management Interview Questions

Student ______________________________ Grade __________ Date ______________

Setting goals (see Worksheet 4.3)

Recording and organizing assignments

1. Where do you write down your assignments? May I see how you do it?

2. Do you ever find that you forget to write down important information about an assignment, such as the problems to do on a math page?

3. Do you ever find that you are confused about when an assignment is due?

Setting and adhering to schedules

1. What time of day do you find it easiest to concentrate on homework?

2. Do you have a regular, quiet time to study at home? Is it enough time to finish your homework and also to study for tests? What does the rest of the family do while you are studying?

3. Can you tell me how long it takes you to read/compute/write a paper?

4. Do you write assignments into your assignment book?

5. Give me an example of how you would break long-term assignments into smaller parts.

6. Can you show me how you write these components into your assignment book?

(continued)

Menu of Time Management Interview Questions *(page 2 of 3)*

Other aspects of time management and organization

1. How do you spend your time? What else do you do besides go to school, sleep, and eat?

2. What is your schedule?

3. Are you generally a person who is on time? If not, why not?

4. Are you easily distracted? If so, why?

5. Are you generally aware of time passing? Do you guess the time easily?

6. Are you neat or messy?

7. Do you set yourself a schedule, such as doing your homework from 4 to 6 P.M.? Do you keep it?

8. Do you find that others keep you from working? If so, how?

9. Do you promise others that you will do things that you don't have time for?

(continued)

Menu of Time Management Interview Questions *(page 3 of 3)*

Procrastination

1. Do you begin assignments later than you had planned? If so, why?

2. Do you put off starting working on important things? If so, why?

3. Do you feel as though you can only complete an assignment when you are under pressure because it is due?

4. Do you find yourself getting something to eat or drink or being otherwise distracted when you are about to begin, or when you should stay focused, on an assignment?

5. Do you usually do something easy rather than start with a difficult assignment?

6. Do you make plans that you know are not possible?

7. Do you let time go by without getting any work done on an important assignment, or start working on assignments as soon as you get them?

8. Do you convince yourself that other things need to be done before you work on an important assignment?

Appraisal

What do you do that works well? That doesn't work well? What do you think you should change?

WORKSHEET 7.4.

Monthly Planner

Month of ____________ Student ________________________________

Sunday	Monday	Tuesday	Wednesday	Thursday	Friday	Saturday

Appraisal: What did I do that worked well? That didn't work well? What should I change?

WORKSHEET 7.5.

Weekly Schedule

Week of ______________ Student ____

Time	Sunday	Monday	Tuesday	Wednesday	Thursday	Friday	Saturday
8:00–8:30							
8:30–9:00							
9:00–9:30							
9:30–10:00							
10:00–10:30							
10:30–11:00							
11:00–11:30							
11:30–12:00							
12:00–12:30							
12:30–1:00							
1:00–1:30							
1:30–2:00							
2:00–2:30							
2:30–3:00							
3:00–3:30							
3:30–4:00							
4:00–4:30							
4:30–5:00							
5:00–5:30							
5:30–6:00							
6:00–6:30							
6:30–7:00							
7:00–7:30							
7:30–8:00							
8:00–8:30							
8:30–9:00							
9:00–9:30							
9:30–10:00							
10:00–10:30							
10:30–11:00							
Things to do:							

Appraisal: What did I do that worked well? That didn't work well? What should I change?

WORKSHEET 7.6.

Daily Schedule

Date ______________ Student ____

Time	What I scheduled	What I actually did	Comments and plans
8:00–8:30			
8:30–9:00			
9:00–9:30			
9:30–10:00			
10:00–10:30			
10:30–11:00			
11:00–11:30			
11:30–12:00			
12:00–12:30			
12:30–1:00			
1:00–1:30			
1:30–2:00			
2:00–2:30			
2:30–3:00			
3:00–3:30			
3:30–4:00			
4:00–4:30			
4:30–5:00			
5:00–5:30			
5:30–6:00			
6:00–6:30			
6:30–7:00			
7:00–7:30			
7:30–8:00			
8:00–8:30			
8:30–9:00			
9:00–9:30			
9:30–10:00			
10:00–10:30			
10:30–11:00			
Things to do:			
Appraisal: What did I do that worked well? That didn't work well? What should I change?			

WORKSHEET 7.7.

Daily Time Control Review

Date ______________ Student ____

4 = Done very well 3 = Done well 2 = Done badly 1 = Done very badly or not done

I prioritized.

I worked on top priorities first. ______

I did activities that will help me meet my top long-term and short-term goals. ______

I focused on having a high-quality study time. ______

I avoided getting distracted by others (did not try to work where others were talking, talk on the phone, do email, or instant-message friends during my study time). ______

I avoided distracting myself (with TV, daydreaming, or getting frequent snacks). ______

I studied at a desk or table in a quiet place free of distractions. ______

I scheduled and planned.

I updated my list of things to do. ______

I updated my weekly planner and monthly calendar. ______

I scheduled enough study time for the work I have to do. ______

I left at least 1 hour unscheduled. ______

I broke assignments into smaller parts and scheduled each part. ______

I wrote my assignments accurately and completely in my assignment book. ______

I started working on time. ______

I followed my schedule. ______

I kept organized.

I studied with necessary materials, books, and supplies nearby. ______

I brought home, and took to school, everything I needed. ______

I organized my papers and materials in folders, binders, and files. ______

I organized my desk, locker, and backpack. ______

I gathered my "back-to-school" books and papers in one place. ______

I turned in assignments on time. ______

I reviewed my notes and assignment requirements before beginning each assignment. ______

(continued)

Daily Time Control Review *(page 2 of 2)*

I controlled my time and focus.

I scheduled my study time for a time of day when I was not too tired. ____

I worked on harder assignments before easier assignments. ____

I worked on one assignment at a time. ____

I took short (10-minute) planned breaks between assignments. ____

I took time to take care of myself (exercised, ate well, and slept well). ____

I sought help from a family member, study buddy, or homework hotline as needed. ____

I wrote down questions to ask my teacher. ____

I gave myself a reward (such as doing something for fun) after I finished studying. ____

I evaluated my studying.

I kept track of the time I studied each subject. ____

I checked whether the strategies I used worked well for me. ____

I spent __ minutes studying today. That was just right (4) or far too little time (1). ____

Today's total ____

Personal best score ____

Date of personal best score ____

Appraisal: What did I do that worked well? That didn't work well? What should I change?

WORKSHEET 7.8.

"T" Chart for Time Management of Activities

Date ______________ Student ______________________________

Most Important Goals	Important To-Do Activities

List goals that represent most important academic requirements on the left side of this "T" chart. On the right side, list *only* those activities that directly relate to the goals listed on the left.

Be careful *not* to include those activities that seem only "urgent" in terms of time constraints, but that are *not* "important" to your academic goals. You can make another To-Do list to include these lesser activities, but only devote time to those items when you have completed one or more of the "important" activities listed on the left side.

8

Helping Students Self-Regulate Cognition, Metacognition, and Executive Functions

Effective students know, use, and self-evaluate their own cognitive and metacognitive strategies. However, most students need direct instruction to become proficient in these areas.

OVERVIEW

Tina was a successful high school student but "tested poorly." This was not because she did not study; often she spent hours reviewing homemade flashcards and rereading assigned materials and lecture notes. Nonetheless, her grades on tests were usually far below her other grades, and it was common for her to receive D's or even F's on major exams. In college, Tina compensated by primarily selecting courses that required term papers rather than exams. Finally it dawned on her to observe and modify her own learning strategies. She noticed that she most easily remembered material when she wrote it down and when it was presented in a global context rather than in isolation (as on flashcards). With this in mind, she developed a study plan that provided repeated and spaced trials, enabled her to review material in context, and required her to write and rewrite material. Much to Tina's amazement, she received A's on exams when she used this system. She later wondered how her life would have been different if she had felt free to take whatever courses interested her without worrying about whether they required exams, and if she had not wasted so much time making or flipping flashcards that were useless to her.

Tina finally discovered how to learn efficiently after suffering many painful years of ineffective "studying." It is remarkable that she persevered and did not capitulate to her feelings of frustration long before she realized that it was possible to change her learning strategies.

How can adults help students avoid the years of frustration Tina experienced? How can they empower students to be savvy, self-reflective, efficient, and effective learners? This chapter will help the reader guide students as they develop study plans for effective independent learning. Strategies discussed in this chapter are appropriate for students who have general academic difficulties, experience processing problems, do not work up to their potential, or have limited memory skills. For a concise summary of concepts presented in this chapter, the reader is referred to Worksheet 8.1, Checklist of Cognitive and Metacognitive Strategies and Executive Functions.

RESEARCH FOUNDATIONS

Good students control their learning, approach it purposefully, know various learning strategies, and monitor the effectiveness of these strategies (Puntambekar, 1995). In contrast, students who have difficulty learning independently often do not attend to their learning processes. Students who receive training in study strategies, as well as in methods to select *and* assess them, significantly outperform other groups (Graham & Harris, 1996; Greiner & Karoly, 1976).

Research in memory and cognition is often confusing because various researchers use the same terms for different constructs, or different terms for the same construct. In this book, we follow the model of Butterfield and Albertson (1995) and Borkowski and Burke (1996): We use the term "cognitive strategies" (also called "learning strategies" or "study skills") for specific strategies that students can employ to focus attention, organize material, and memorize; the term "metacognition" to describe "knowing about knowing"—knowledge about the self as a learner, about the task at hand, and about the successes and failures of specific cognitive strategies for similar tasks; and the term "executive functions" to describe the selection, implementation, monitoring, coordinating, and management of cognitive strategies and metacognition through progress monitoring, problem solving, reflecting on performance, and strategy modification.

Cognitive strategies, metacognition, and executive functions are developed sequentially. Students first learn specific cognitive learning strategies. As they use these strategies in various contexts, students become more aware of when, how, and where to use each strategy, and thus develop metacognitive skills. Eventually, as students develop the ability to select strategies and monitor their effectiveness, executive functions emerge; the self-regulation of cognitive strategies and metacognition then becomes possible.

As is true for domains discussed in previous chapters, effective cognitive functioning is dependent upon the recurring phases of preparation, performance, and appraisal. In the *preparation* phase, the student plans for learning and focuses attention. In the *performance* phase, the student uses cognitive and metacognitive strategies to foster learning and remembering. In the *appraisal* phase, the student analyzes his or her performance and revises the learning plan to improve learning. Throughout, the student uses executive functions to regulate cognitive and metacognitive strategies.

Cognitive Strategies

Students who excel in school know a variety of learning strategies; understand where, when, and why to use such strategies; select these strategies wisely; plan and monitor the use of strategies and reflect upon their use; maintain the belief that knowledge is incremental; carefully deploy effort; maintain mastery goals and intrinsic motivation; are task-oriented; recognize failure as essential to success and do not fear it; perceive tests as learning activities rather than sources of anxiety; maintain multiple, concrete visions of near- and distant-future "possible selves" (both positive and feared); have a great deal of, and easy access to, knowledge regarding many topics; and are supported in these traits by parents, schools, peers, and the larger community (Borkowski & Burke, 1996; Dawson & Guare, 2004). When students employ effective study skills, they coordinate a large number of complex cognitive processes, including acquiring, recording, organizing, analyzing, synthesizing, remembering, and applying information. Students who have learning difficulties not only have weak application of study skill strategies, but are often not even familiar with the cognitive strategies used by more successful students (Gettinger & Seibert, 2002). Effective strategies incorporate several fundamental principles of learning: deliberately attending to important information, using effective methods to improve memory, spacing and repeating learning trials, and integrating knowledge.

Deliberately Attending to Important Information

Attending involves both cognitive and physical variables and has four components: (1) selecting a stimulus and focusing attention; (2) sustaining and stabilizing attention over time; (3) deliberately shifting attention from one focal point to another; and (4) encoding stimuli. Selective attention is limited by working (short-term) memory, but learning to selectively attend can help overcome working memory limitations. Sustained attention is a function of executive functions (Sergent, 1996). These components develop along different timetables. The ability to select and focus attention is normally developed by the age of 7, while the ability to sustain attention develops throughout childhood and adolescence (Halperin, 1996).

For students to learn independently, each component of attention must be tapped. First, the student must select and focus attention on an appropriate stimulus. This ability is affected by:

- *Antecedent variables*: The complexity, duration, intensity, and modality of stimulation both internal to the student and in the environment.
- *Behavioral variables*: The type, latency, force, and duration of the student's listening, thinking, and talking.
- *Consequence variables*: The type, magnitude, and schedule of reinforcers and consequences.
- *Students' traits*: Age, sex, clinical diagnosis, genetic disorders, prenatal exposures to teratogens, metabolic disorders, health history, nutrition history, previous head trauma, developmental disorders, and behavioral history.
- *Students' temporary states*, such as acute disease or intoxication (McIlvane, Dube, & Callahan, 1996; Mirsky, 1996).

As this list suggests, many attention difficulties can be *prevented* through public policies that promote optimal neurological development or prevent injuries (e.g., universal prenatal care, proper nutrition, seatbelts, and required helmet use when bicycling and motorcycling). Moreover, established attention difficulties can be addressed through multiple avenues. One of the most common forms of intervention, prescription of stimulant drugs such as Ritalin, addresses the neurological basis of inattention. However, while stimulant medication can be successful at improving attention, this improvement does not carry into nonmedicated states or improve long-term outcomes (Halperin, 1996). In contrast, behavioral treatments have been demonstrated to be effective both in laboratory studies and in classrooms (McIlvane et al., 1996).

Memory

Memory is obviously an essential component of studying. Research in the mid-20th century identified three components of the memory system (see Figure 8.1): the *sensory memory* or *register*; the *short-term memory* (thought at that time to be limited to five to seven items); and *long-term memory* (Shiffrin & Atkinson, 1969). Since then this model has evolved.

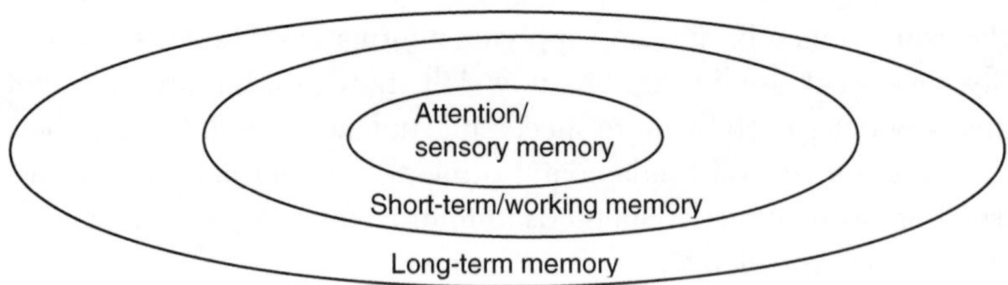

FIGURE 8.1. The memory system. Based on Wagner (1996) and Cowan (1993).

SENSORY MEMORY

Sensory memory, or sensory register, is the extremely brief registry of information recorded by sensory organs such as the eyes and ears. Sensory memory is obviously compromised by any sensory impairment, such as an unmet need for prescription glasses or an intermittent hearing loss due to ear infections. It is also adversely affected by inattention due to any of the other variables described previously.

SHORT-TERM MEMORY

Short-term memory, or working memory, is the ability to maintain and manipulate information long enough to complete a specific task such as comprehending, learning, or reasoning (Baddeley, 1992). Whereas previous researchers thought that short-term memory was stored separately from long-term memory, more recent research indicates that short-term memory is "best conceptualized as that portion of long-term memory that is temporarily at a heightened state of activation at a particular moment of time" (Wagner, 1996, p. 148). Short-term memory therefore contains the information on which the individual is currently focusing attention, as well as some items that are not in conscious awareness but are nevertheless activated. *Deliberate memory*, or *explicit memory*, requires focusing attention on an item in order to learn it. *Implicit memory*, or *incidental learning*, occurs without deliberate intent or focused attention (Bachevalier, Malkova, & Beauregard, 1996).

Examples of working memory are remembering reading material long enough to comprehend it, or remembering numbers and processes long enough to complete a math problem. Short-term/working memory is thought to be limited to four items (Baddeley, 2003; Cowan, 2005). When an individual is able to remember more than four items, it is because the material has been combined into "chunks." For example, the telephone number 1-215-555-7874 might be chunked into "long-distance area code for Philadelphia" (1-215), "exchange" (555), and "number" (7874). Even extraordinary feats of working memory have been found to result from very efficient chunking of vast amounts of information (Ericsson, Delaney, & Weaver, 2004).

Working memory has at least three distinct components. The *phonological loop* temporarily stores auditorily sensed material. The *visuospatial sketchpad* temporarily stores visual information. The *central executive* serves as a response selection control system. Information can enter long-term memory from any component of working memory, and a student may have strengths or deficiencies in one or more components (Baddeley, 2003; Boller, 1996).

Short-term memory is essential for complex cognitive processes such as language comprehension, listening, reading comprehension, and arithmetic computations, because to be successful a student must simultaneously store a record of current information, retrieve items from long-term memory, and apply higher-order comprehension processes. For example, as students compute long-division problems, they must simultaneously maintain discrete calculations in their working memory, retrieve multiplication facts and processes from long-term memory, and engage in the process of division (Baddeley, 2003; Ericsson & Kintsch, 1995; Wagner, 1996).

> **Louis** had been an avid crossword puzzle expert his entire adult life, successfully completing *The New York Times* crossword puzzle daily. After suffering a minor, localized stroke affecting his working memory, he was still able to retrieve answers from his long-term memory, but was unable to hold them in his working memory long enough to find their location in the puzzle. This loss of working memory made it impossible for Louis to continue his beloved hobby.

LONG-TERM MEMORY

When material in short-term memory, or working memory, is *encoded* so that it can be retrieved at a later time, it is considered to be in long-term memory. The retrieval can be in the form of recognition (as is assessed in multiple-choice questions) or recall (as is the case in a short-answer or essay test). Material is best encoded into long-term memory, and subsequently available to memory, when a student integrates new information with previous knowledge in order to understand the material, and later retrieves the information by reconstructing that understanding (Kuhn, 2000). This link between understanding and long-term memory is the reason why memorization through repetition alone is inefficient. When information is presented in an organized network of connected facts and concepts ("schemata"), it is more easily learned and retrieved. Learning improves even further when students form these schemata on their own (Gettinger & Seibert, 2002).

Spacing and Repeating Learning Trials

The advantages of spacing and repeating learning trials were discovered by Ebbinghaus in 1885. Nonetheless, many students of all ages do not space their learning trials, but instead rely on "cramming." This is a result of two factors (Son, 2004, 2005): Memory is subject to the *recency effect* (i.e., material most recently presented is the easiest remembered); and knowledge is acquired at a slower rate with spaced trials than with massed trials. Thus the material students review rapidly, immediately before a test, is temporarily remembered better than material previously learned, particularly if the previously learned material was insufficiently understood or encoded. This results in students' perceiving cramming as effective. However, research consistently demonstrates that spacing and repeating learning trials are advantageous over the long term, and students should be encouraged to space learning trials for maximum learning. This can be accomplished by having students keep track of their learning outcomes over the long term.

> **Tommy** was skeptical when he heard his teacher's suggestion that he study each night, Monday through Thursday, for 20 minutes rather than study 2 hours on Thursday night for Friday's math test. He always crammed for tests, but because he wasn't happy with his grades, he decided to give her suggestion a try. To his amazement, he did better on this Friday's test, even though he had studied for fewer total minutes. Even better was the fact that instead of feeling stressed and pressured, Tommy realized he knew the material and felt confident before and after the test.

Metacognition

No one cognitive study strategy is consistently superior to others. Students with effective study habits use a variety of techniques and are able to articulate their reasons for choosing particular tactics for particular assignments (Wade, Trathen, & Schraw, 1990). The number of study skill strategies used has *not* been found to correlate with achievement (Foley & Epstein, 1992); furthermore, students are very unlikely to use every type of study skill (Slate et al., 1993; Stanley, Slate, & Jones, 1999). Therefore, students need to know how to monitor the success of a given strategy and to modify their strategy use according to their success. Strategies should vary according to each student's style of learning and personal habits, the subject matter, and the teacher's approaches. Deciding upon the appropriate learning methods requires the student to employ metacognitive strategies.

> **Felicity** studies for her social studies test by making up a study sheet with possible test questions on one side and correct answers on the other. Then she reviews those questions until she knows the answers to all of the questions without looking at the opposite side. In contrast, she prepares for her flute recital by playing the music until she feels confident with the notes and has no sense of surprise when she encounters a phrase. After she has reached that point, she focuses on dynamics, musicality, and expression rather than on the memorization of notes. In social studies Felicity learns to the point that she can freely recall the answers, but in music she is learning for recognition. Her differential strategies reveal a successful "master learning plan."

The Development of Metacognition

Metacognitive skills require the ability to think objectively about one's learning and to form and test hypotheses about strategy success. It has been thought that metacognition is not possible until students develop Formal Operations thinking (Piaget & Inhelder, 1969), because the cognitive capacity for children in Concrete Operations results in less effective study habits, more difficulty focusing attention and avoiding distractions, and the inability to develop and test hypotheses (Hoover-Dempsey et al., 2001). To some extent, this perception has been confirmed in research studies. For example, Lockl (2002) found that students in third and fourth grades are more capable than students in first grade of assessing their own levels of knowledge and determining how much time to devote to a learning task. Similarly, Zimmerman and Martinez Pons (1990) found that self-regulation of learning strategies increases with age—8th graders surpassing 5th graders, and 11th graders surpassing 8th graders.

However, this phenomenon may be a result of younger students' relative lack of experience, for it appears that skills in metacognition develop as students internalize external feedback. Perry (1998) found that even children in second and third grades could be taught to improve their learning strategies over a period of 6 months through the use of writing portfolios. Horn (2004) found that many students in honors classes entered high school with self-regulatory skills and were able to apply them without adult guidance, yet still made significant improvements in these skills after a classroom intervention during which self-regulatory strategies were taught. Students assigned to standard classes did not enter high school with self-regulatory skills; they were able to learn these skills through instruction, yet had greater difficulty applying them independently.

Self-Assessment of Learning Preferences

One component of metacognition is an understanding of how one best learns. Over the past 50 years, research attempting to identify preferred learning styles has proliferated in the fields of education, psychology, health care, management, industry, and vocational training.

Multiple models of learning preferences have been proposed, ranging from the "learning styles" of Dunn and Dunn (1978) to the "multiple intelligences" of Howard Gardner (1983/1993). The field is so confusing that "road maps" have been developed to make sense of the literature

(Cassidy, 2004; Desmedt & Valcke, 2004), and Kozloff (2005) includes learning styles in a list of harmful educational fads. Contradictory research findings abound. Loo (2004) found weak linkages between teaching style and learning preferences; however, other meta-analyses found increased achievement after instruction based on learning-style preferences (Lovelace, 2005). According to Levine (2002), individual learning styles result from varied learning profiles of each child's attention control systems, memory and language, and spatial and sequential ordering system. He recommends that teachers and parents encourage students' strengths and bypass weaknesses. However, specialists in learning disabilities recommend that most learning take place via the strongest modality, while weak areas continue to be developed (Lerner, 1997).

A comprehensive and definitive overview of this literature is beyond the scope of this book, and we believe that "the jury is still out" on this topic. Although the research does not conclusively support one paradigm, intuitively it is obvious that individual students learn differently and that these differences need to be considered. It also appears that it is possible to reach almost all students, and to appeal to multidimensional learning aptitudes in each student, by using multifaceted teaching methods and permitting a variety of methods for students to demonstrate knowledge. It also seems logical that a variety of teaching methods should be used, rather than rigidly linking specific methods to specific learning styles, and that students should be encouraged to be receptive to learning through different modalities.

> At age 7, **Sean** was correctly diagnosed with a learning disability. His unusually weak visuospatial sketchpad resulted in very poor visual memory and difficulty with reading. Throughout elementary and secondary school, his Individual Education Plan required auditorily presented material, and he was provided with tape-recorded versions of all textbooks and reading material. Although this provided him with successful experiences through high school, the complete neglect of his weakest learning modality further widened the discrepancy between his ability to read print and his ability to understand verbal material. When he arrived at college, he was profoundly limited in his choice of classes, majors, and future professional opportunities.

Executive Functions

Executive functions enable students to organize many diverse cognitive and emotional processes into adaptive and intelligent behaviors that benefit themselves, their families, and society. According to Eslinger (1996), "executive functions are considered by many scientists to be the crowning achievements of human development" (p. 369). These functions include the ability to think about, plan for, and delay gratification for future benefits. They differentiate childish from adult behavior (Denckla, 1996). Executive functions appear to be primarily housed in the prefrontal cortex and its extended neurological networks, which continue to develop into adolescence and early adulthood (Eslinger, 1996).

Executive functions applied to studying include planning, controlling, thinking, inquiring, reflecting, and self-evaluation (Dawson & Guare, 2004; Gettinger & Nicaise, 1997). Executive control processes require that a student know what he or she is learning, be aware of how he or she is learning it, and appropriately decide to modify strategies. The student plans and monitors what is done, and selects, organizes, manipulates, and interprets information. Executive functions are also called into play when students transfer or generalize learning and learning processes (Borkowski & Burke, 1996).

Impairments in executive functions seriously compromise study skills and the ability to learn independently, particularly at the secondary level. However, age is not the only variable affecting the development of executive functions; they also depend upon attention, memory, and the understanding of "rules" that lead to behavioral regulation. They can be compromised by many factors, such as genetic mutations, neurodevelopmental disorders, environmental or nutritional deprivation, inadequate socialization, or lack of learning experiences.

METHODS

Preparation

General Assessment

A number of methods, including semistructured interviews, thinking aloud, trace methodology, self-report measures, and "study pies," can be used to determine which cognitive strategies, metacognitive strategies, and executive functions a student already uses. Worksheet 8.1 can be used to analyze, integrate, and interpret information from these multiple sources in order to develop an intervention plan.

The *semistructured interview* described by Zimmerman and Martinez Pons (1986), and described in Chapter 1, discriminates between high-functioning and low-functioning students when analyzed according to components of self-regulation. In a semi-structured interview, the interview states:

> "Most teachers give tests at the end of marking periods, and these tests greatly determine report card grades. Do you have any particular method for preparing for this type of test in English or history? What if you are having difficulty? Is there any particular method you use?" (p. 617)

Similar questions are asked about planning and writing papers, completing in-class assignments, and working when feeling unmotivated. For each strategy, the student is asked how frequently she or he uses each strategy on a four-point scale ranging from "seldom" to "most of the time." An analysis of the strategies the students report using determines which strategies have not yet been mastered.

In using the *think-aloud* method, the adult asks the student to express his or her thoughts while learning in a one-to-one setting. The student's responses are recorded and analyzed according to the types of cognitive processes used in studying, reading, or planning to study. This approach has been most often used to analyze a student's approaches to reading (Pressley & Afflerbach, 1995; Sainsbury, 2003), but it can also be used to analyze a student's approach to problem solving in math, science, or any other subject.

In *trace methodology*, an adult and student collaboratively examine observable indicators of cognitive strategies, such as highlighting, underlining, creating mnemonics, and taking notes when studying (Winne, Hadwin, Stockley, & Nesbit, as cited by Puustinen & Pulkkinen, 2001). This method is often used in conjunction with a semistructured interview to determine strategies the student actually implements, in contrast to those that are only reported.

Several *self-report measures* of study skills have been developed that elicit information regarding how often students use particular strategies. One self-report scale is the Learning and Study Strategies Inventory—High School Version (LASSI-HS; Weinstein & Palmer, 1990), which assesses such cognitive strategies as the ability to select main ideas, study aids, self-testing, and test-taking techniques. The Motivated Strategies for Learning Questionnaire (MSLQ; Pintrich et al., 1991) also assesses cognitive and metacognitive strategies. Both the LASSI-HS and the MSLQ are described in Chapter 1. Finally, the Metacognitive Awareness of Reading Strategies Inventory (MARSI; Mokhtari & Reichard, 2002) assesses a number of cognitive and metacognitive strategies related to reading. The MARSI and its scoring guide are included in Chapter 9 (see Worksheet 9.2).

Study Pies (Chickie-Wolfe & Harvey, 2006a) are informal self-report methods to elicit students' cognitive strategies. After completing a major learning experience, such as finishing a project or studying for a unit test, students list all the strategies used and complete a study pie indicating the approximate proportion of time devoted to each strategy. A reproducible form for constructing a Study Pie is found in Worksheet 8.2.

When **Dr. Chickie-Wolfe's** students were asked how they prepared for a test, they said, "I finished reading the chapter," or "I did my homework." She drew a large circle on the board, explained to the students that this was a *Study Pie,* and "cut" the pie into several pieces. She then wrote "Homework" on one piece and told her students that homework was only one piece of the Study Pie; there were many other things they needed to do in order to study well. She labeled various-sized pieces as follows: "Spaced practice," "Chunk," "Think," "Make personal meaning," "Reread," "Take notes," "Review notes," "Rehearse," "Make up test questions with answers," "Have someone quiz me," "Make and review flashcards," "Play games," and "Use memory tricks." Next she explained that each student learns differently, so everyone's Study Pie would look different, depending on which strategies worked best for them. The students developed personal Study Pies for language arts, and in comparing their pies found that their classmates used a wide variety of strategies. They also realized that their own Study Pies would change, depending upon the subject and the particular assignment.

Assessment of Attention

Assessing attention is difficult, because attention is fundamental to early-stage information processing but is expressed through later-stage information processing. Therefore, many measures of "attention" also measure other cognitive processes. Furthermore, using measures that vary only attention (without involving other cognitive processes) results in students' being asked to perform actions to which they are unaccustomed, or that conflict with well-established behaviors, in one-to-one settings. These activities yield results so far removed from real-world situations that they have limited generalizability (Halperin, 1996).

That said, to a certain extent, attention can be assessed through behavior rating scales, direct observations of attending behaviors in natural settings, continuous performance or vigilance tests, information-processing paradigms, maze completion tests, reaction time tasks, and subtests from individualized test batteries (Barkley, 1996; Halperin, 1996). Each method has strengths and weaknesses, making it necessary to use multiple measures and methods to obtain accurate and meaningful results.

Impressions of a student's ability to select, sustain, and appropriately shift attention can be assessed via behavior rating scales completed by parents and teachers, such as the Social Skills Rating System (SSRS; Gresham & Elliott, 1990); the BASC Monitor for ADHD (Kamphaus & Reynolds, 1998); and the Attention Deficit Disorders Evaluation Scale (McCarney & Bauer, 1990). Unfortunately, the usefulness of behavior rating scales is compromised by poor interrater reliability and by the fact that inattention is often confounded by disruptive behavior. That is, disruptive students are rated by teachers as inattentive, even though observers find the students "off target" no more often than their peers (Abikoff, Courtney, Pelham, & Koplewicz, 1993; Halperin, 1996).

Psychologists can assess students' ability to select and focus attention directly with the Working Memory and Processing Speed subscales of the Wechsler Intelligence Scale for Children—Fourth Edition (WISC-IV; Wechsler, 2003); ability to deliberately shift attention with the Wisconsin Card Sorting Test (WCST; Heaton, Chelune, Talley, Kay, & Curtiss, 1993); and ability to sustain attention with the Conners' Continuous Performance Test II (Conners & MHS Staff, 2000).

The ability to sustain attention can also be assessed through *behavioral observations* of attending behaviors in natural settings. Initially, on-task behaviors can be tallied by an adult observer. Students can also be taught to self-monitor their attending behaviors, and this self-monitoring can in turn serve as an intervention and appraisal tool.

Assessment of Memory

Whether sensory memory is intact can be determined by reviewing medical records and requesting updated hearing evaluations and near- and far-vision exams. Psychologists can assess short-term/working memory through individual measures such as the Wide Range Assessment of Memory and Learning, Second Edition (WRAML2; Sheslow & Adams, 2003); the Working Memory Test Battery for Children (WMTB-C; Pickering & Gathercole, 2001); the Woodcock–Johnson III (WJ III) Diagnostic Supplement to the Tests of Cognitive Abilities (Woodcock, McGrew, & Mather, 2003); or the Test of Memory and Learning (TOMAL; Reynolds & Bigler, 1994). It is particularly helpful to examine these results in terms of strengths and weaknesses in auditory versus visual–spatial abilities and nonmeaningful versus meaningful information.

Long-term memory can be assessed through a review of records to discern patterns and discontinuities across subject areas and modalities (e.g., projects vs. test scores). Long-term memory is also tapped by individual and group tests of achievement and intelligence, such as unit tests in given curriculum areas; Curriculum-Based Measurement applied to curriculum materials; the Verbal Comprehension subscales of the WISC-IV (Wechsler, 2003); the Wechsler Individual Achievement Test—Second Edition (WIAT-II; Wechsler, 2001); the Das–Naglieri Cognitive Assessment System (CAS; Naglieri & Das, 1997); the WJ III (Woodcock, McGrew, & Mather, 2001); the Comprehensive Test of Basic Skills (CTB/McGraw-Hill, 1990); and the California Achievement Tests (CTB/McGraw-Hill, 1993).

Self-Assessment of Knowledge

To appropriately employ cognitive strategies, students need to be able to accurately assess their own level of knowledge. Learning to estimate one's level of knowledge is positively correlated with reading and math achievement, self-monitoring, and strategic help-seeking (Tobias, Everson, & Laitusis, 1999). On the whole, high-achieving individuals often have a good understanding of what material they do or do not know (Son & Metcalfe, 2000), but students with learning difficulties are less skilled in such self-assessment. Furthermore, students sometimes confuse familiarity with knowledge. For example, relatively weak students often believe that they "know" material when they have heard about it, but are still unable to reprocess it in order to apply it. This results in their allocating less study time than they need for a particular assignment (Son & Metcalfe, 2000). Student self-assessment of knowledge serves as an intervention as well as an assessment strategy, so methods to foster this skill are discussed later in this chapter.

Assessment of Learning Preferences

As previously mentioned, the concept of "learning styles" has been beset with controversy and inconclusive findings. To some extent, psychologists can assess a student's learning style through *interpretation of well-established instruments* such as the WJ III. Another effective method to assess learning styles is to conduct a *collaborative review with the student* of data included in the student's portfolio and/or cumulative record, including attendance, grades, and test scores, to ascertain patterns of strengths and weaknesses (Carns & Carns, 1991).

Yet another helpful strategy to determine learning preferences is to examine *which modalities students choose* to learn or demonstrate proficiency when given alternative choices. When students are given instructional (input) choices, they might select watching videos, reading books, taking study trips, or participating in a group discussion or a project instead of the usual lecture format. When students are given knowledge demonstration (output) choices, they might choose building a model, making a diorama, painting a mural, giving a speech, participating in debates, conducting interviews, doing research, making graphs, or writing reports or term papers.

Performance

Improving Cognitive Strategies

As described earlier in this chapter, effective cognitive strategies incorporate the basic learning principles of focusing attention on important information, using strategies to improve memory, spacing and repeating learning trials, and incorporating corrective feedback. This chapter addresses ways to improve *general* cognitive strategies. Additional, more specific, cognitive strategies are described in the chapters addressing note taking and graphic organizers (Chapter 3), time managing (Chapter 7), reading strategies (Chapter 9), writing processes (Chapter 10), strategies to use in math and science (Chapter 11), and test-taking strategies (Chapter 12).

Whenever a consultant or teacher instructs a student on how to use a new cognitive strategy, the collaboration and coaching steps described in Worksheets 1.3 and 1.4 (Chapter 1) are employed. These steps ensure that the strategy is learned correctly, practiced, self-monitored, maintained, and generalized across learning situations (Dawson & Guare, 2004).

IMPROVING ATTENTION

Selective and sustained attention can be increased by assigning *working memory tasks* of gradually increasing difficulty over a period of several weeks. Such training has been found to decrease inattention and to maintain this decrease over time (Klineberg et al., 2005). Selective and sustained attention can also be improved through *behavior reinforcement programs that focus attention,* which have been found to be effective both in classrooms and in nonclassroom settings (McIlvane et al., 1996). The reader is referred to considerations in implementing such programs, described in Chapter 6.

A more targeted program, *Self-Monitoring Attention* (SMA), improves selective and sustained attention by having the student assess, evaluate, and record attentive behaviors and focus on increasing on-task behaviors. This approach is particularly effective for students with ADHD and has been found to increase both attentiveness and academic success (Harris, Friedlander, Saddler, Frizzelle, & Graham, 2005). Based upon the work of Hallahan, Lloyd, Kauffman, and Looper (1983), this method can be implemented by following the steps in Table 8.1.

TABLE 8.1. Self-Monitored Attention

1. A baseline of attending behaviors is taken by an adult.
2. One or more adults discuss the importance and meaning of paying attention with the student.
3. The student agrees to use a procedure to help improve attention.
4. A mellow tone is recorded at random intervals, ranging from 10 to 90 seconds.
5. The student is taught to ask him- or herself, "Was I paying attention?", upon hearing the tone through an earpiece connected to a tape player or CD player.
6. The student is taught to tally, "Yes, I was paying attention," or "No, I was not paying attention," whenever the tone sounds.
7. The student wears an earpiece and plays the recording during a specified time (e.g., during daily independent seatwork on spelling).
8. The student graphs the number of "Yes" and "No" items checked daily.
9. The student graphs the daily results, initially with adult help and then independently.

IMPROVING MEMORY

Teaching cognitive memory-enhancing strategies, also known as "mnemonics" or "memory tricks," is the first step in improving memory. However, such instruction should be accompanied by instruction in metamemory (metacognition) and self-appraisal (executive function), because the newly learned behavior quickly disappears if metacognition is not engaged (Bjorklund, Miller, & Coyle, 1997; Kuhn, 2000; Schneider & Pressley, 1997).

According to a factor analysis (van Ede & Coetzee, 1996), memory-enhancing strategies fall into four types: rehearsal, organization/association, imagery, and verbal elaboration. Regardless of the type of strategy used, memory is increased by spacing and repeating learning trials and by association with vivid emotions. *Spacing and repeating trials* can be achieved when students review the same material multiple times. For example, they might complete assigned readings before class, take notes during class, elaborate their notes after class, and study over a period of days rather than cram. *Association with vivid emotions* can be accomplished through the use of humor and emotions to "hook" students. A story about a family who experiences a hurricane can be used as a powerful way to introduce a science unit on weather. Or students can be encouraged to include humorous activities in their study plan to involve positive emotions.

Rehearsal involves repeating information multiple times, either verbally or through the use of tools such as flashcards. Rehearsal is often taught in early grades, and students are encouraged to use it to learn math facts, spelling, vocabulary, and other information by rote. It is most effective for storing short bits of information for a short time period or when the information will be used frequently (Gettinger & Seibert, 2002).

One method to increase the success of rehearsal is to *sandwich* new information within previously mastered information (Shapiro, 1996). The student intersperses unknown questions, words, or facts within a group of known items, keeping the percentage of known items between 70% and 85%. As the student self-quizzes and masters unknown items, additional items are added until mastery of the entire group is attained.

The reader should keep in mind that rehearsal relies on short-term and rote memory, so it is subject to the recency effect and gives a premature impression of mastery. Furthermore, since rehearsal alone neither processes information nor links it to previously learned material, for the most part it is not an effective study strategy. Students need to discern when rote memorization is appropriate. Most often, understanding is essential before meaningful and long-term learning can occur.

> To illustrate the importance of understanding in order to remember, **Mrs. Nagy** told her class to pay very close attention to what she was going to tell them, because she would be asking them to repeat what she was about to say when she was finished. Then she recited a Hungarian poem she had learned as a child and asked each child to repeat it. Everyone laughed, and a few could remember one or two syllables—but, of course, no one had "learned" the lesson despite paying very close attention.

Organization/association learning strategies are used when a student groups units of information. Examples of organization strategies are *making hierarchical classifications* and *sorting material into categories*. At least initially, students benefit from adult directions in selecting organization and sorting criteria, because they do not know the material well enough to be able to determine meaningful criteria (DeMarie, Miller, Ferron, & Cunningham, 2004). For example, a child may sort spelling words by length or initial letter, whereas more effective sorting criteria would be by word meanings or word families.

Examples of association strategies are *making up a story* that includes information to be remembered, and *using associative cues* (e.g., "The princi*pal* is my *pal*"). Older students can be encouraged to make up their own associations. Whenever possible, associations should be funny, involve action, and be easy to remember.

A common association strategy is to compose an *acrostic* by composing a sentence, rhyme, or saying from the first letters of key words in sequence (e.g., using the sentence "Every Good Boy Deserves Fun" to help young musicians remember that the lines of the treble staff represent the notes E-G-B-D-F). Acrostics can be very effective memory tools, but their usefulness is limited because so little retrieval information is conveyed by single letters (Levin, 1993; Carlson, Glover, & Zimmer, 1981).

Yet another association strategy, *peg words*, can be used to remember sequential or chronological order. Peg words that rhyme with numbers (e.g., "one = bun, two = shoe, three = tree, four = door, five = hive, six = sticks, seven = heaven, eight = gate, nine = vine, and ten = hen") are memorized and then associated with items on a list. For example, when attempting to remember the U.S. presidents in order, students might use a visual image of George Washington eating a gigantic bun, because "one = bun."

When using *imagery,* the student creates a mental image of an object or event (e.g., the word "frantic" could be remembered by the visual image of a girl wearing a name tag that says "Fran" with a giant tick on her arm, screaming with her hair standing up, and the word "frantic" written beneath the picture). Few students spontaneously use this strategy, but it can be taught (Pressley, Cariglia-Bull, & Deane, 1987) and is effective in learning text material, ideas expressed as sayings, social studies material, technical term distinctions, and second-language vocabulary (van Ede & Coetzee, 1996). This strategy is most effective when the mnemonic device is specially designed for the specific content (Levin, 1993). However, the learning of complex and lengthy material does not lend itself to association or imagery strategies.

Verbal elaboration involves relating new information to previously learned information, creating logical relationships, drawing inferences, and processing information deeply. As previously mentioned, information presented in a network of connected facts and concepts (schemata) is more easily learned and retrieved. Therefore, teaching students to form such schemata on their own through verbal elaboration is an extremely effective strategy to improve independent learning (Gettinger & Seibert, 2002). Verbal elaboration fosters associations with prior knowledge, and prior knowledge strongly affects learning regardless of the learning strategy used (Woloshyn, Pressley, & Schneider, 1992).

A very effective verbal elaboration method is *generative summarization.* In this process, a student summarizes the information to be learned in his or her own words, connects the new concepts, and ties the new information to previously learned material (Wittrock, 1990). Additional verbal elaboration methods include using and developing *graphic organizers*, described in Chapter 3; recording and revising *notes*, described in Chapters 3 and 10; and employing methods to *foster reading comprehension*, described in Chapter 9. These strategies often must be explicitly taught to students so that they will apply them and generalize their use. For example, most students have been exposed to *timelines* as graphic organizers in social studies texts, so they are familiar with the concept. Yet they are likely to need instruction in generating timelines independently as study aids, or using them in other settings such as when reading a novel.

Improving Metacognition

Metacognitive skills can be taught at the individual, small-group, or whole-class level (Butler, 1998; Horn, 2004; Paris & Paris, 2001; Quintana, Zhang, & Krajcik, 2005; Zimmerman et al., 1996). Strategies include planning, fostering positive attitudes, incorporating corrective feedback, and fostering self-assessment.

PLANNING

As discussed in previous chapters, setting goals and planning are essential metacognitive study strategies. The goals need to be specific and attainable. Although self-exploration and expressing positive expectations about the coming year can promote good feelings (e.g., "I may not be doing well in school this year, but I will next year"), those that promote self-regulation (e.g., "I may not be doing well in school this year, but to make sure I do better next year, I have signed up for summer tutoring") are most likely to change behavior and improve academic outcomes (Oyserman, Bybee, & Terry, 2004). For more detailed information regarding goal setting and prioritization, the reader is referred to Chapter 4.

FOSTERING POSITIVE ATTITUDES

Students can use affirmations regarding cognition and memory to foster positive attitudes about their proficiency. Possibilities are included in Table 8.2.

INCORPORATING CORRECTIVE FEEDBACK

Teachers frequently return homework, quizzes, tests, and papers to students, complete with corrections and comments. Often students simply check their grades and neglect to use or benefit from corrections and comments. To benefit from teacher feedback and master problematic concepts, students need to maintain corrected papers in an orderly manner, review errors for patterns, and use these discerned patterns to develop and implement a study plan.

> When **Mr. Hood** returned his students' persuasive writing assignments without red marks or comments, his students took notice. Mr. Hood instructed his students to "be the teacher," and mark in red all the errors they could find in their own writing. He reminded them to look for the types of errors he usually corrected on their papers. "If I usually comment that you have run-on sentences, you should look for that type of error and mark it the way I would," he said. "If you usually misspell, double-check for spelling errors and correct them." The stu-

TABLE 8.2. Student Affirmations about Cognition, Metacognition, and Executive Functions

- I enjoy learning about new things and connecting new information to what I already understand.
- I involve as many of my senses as possible as I learn new information.
- I know many "memory tricks" to help me remember new information.
- I THINK about what I'm learning and strive to make sense of things.
- I practice and use what I've learned to make my life better.
- I read and study carefully, and if I don't understand something, I go back until I do.
- I spread my learning sessions out over time.
- I try to use humor as I study.
- To help me memorize, I mix up new information with information I already know.
- I organize material I learn by sorting it, making hierarchies, or constructing organizational charts.
- To help me memorize, I make up a story or use cues, acrostics, or peg words.
- I use visual images to help me remember.
- To help me learn, I summarize material in my own words.
- I use graphic organizers to help me understand what I am studying.
- I set and prioritize my learning goals.
- I plan my studying ahead.
- When I study, I control distractions.
- I manage my time well.
- As I study, I test myself and change my strategies when necessary.
- I appraise my study strategy success.
- I reward myself for success and give myself consequences for setbacks.

dents were impressed with how time-consuming this process was, and only those students who had saved their previous writing papers were able to zero in on their customary errors. After the students finished grading their papers, the class discussed reasons why teachers correct tests, papers, and homework. After this exercise, Mr. Hood saw an immediate improvement in students' attention to his feedback, as well as increased effort to correct repetitive errors in their assignments.

FOSTERING SELF-ASSESSMENT OF KNOWLEDGE

As previously mentioned, students need to know methods to assess and monitor their own knowledge, and to take corrective action when they do not understand material. For example, good students move back and forth in their textbooks to help themselves process information; weaker students often read straight through material, without addressing gaps in comprehension by referring back to previously presented material.

Students can assess their knowledge by *testing themselves during studying* using self-monitoring strategies. For example, at specified intervals (at the end of each page of reading, or after completing a math problem), a student can check for "clicks" (understanding) and "clunks" (nonunderstanding). When the student notices that he or she is having difficulty understanding, remedial steps can be taken.

Students can also assess their own knowledge by using *sample tests* made available by teachers or testing companies. Many teachers make previous years' tests and quizzes (with answer keys) available for students to use for this purpose. Similarly, teachers assist students in their ability to self-assess their knowledge by providing them with *grading rubrics or guidelines* they can use to grade or correct their own work. Handout 10.3 in Chapter 10 is an example of a rubric developed to help students appraise their writing.

Another method is for students to develop a *personal study guide* by writing down a list of possible test questions along with their correct answers, and then quiz themselves, or enlist the help of a family member or friend to quiz them on the material. This and other strategies to improve test-taking strategies are discussed in Chapter 12.

Students can also self-assess their learning by using and comparing their work in *portfolios*, defined as "purposeful collection[s] of student work and records of progress and achievement assembled over time . . . used to examine learning and to plan for instruction" (Valencia & Calfee, 1991, p. 335). Portfolios can include not only work samples and completed assignments, but also reflective papers in which students analyze their own learning and their thinking about their learning. For example, students might conduct an error analysis of their work, analyze their academic success relative to their study strategies, analyze the appropriateness of task difficulty, or describe how their thinking changed as they worked on a project. Such assignments foster both the development of metacognitive strategies and the acquisition of academic skills (Henning-Stout, 1994).

A computer program to foster metacognitive inquiry has been designed to help students successfully deal with task understanding and planning, self-monitoring and regulation, and reflection as they acquire information online. This software helps students determine whether the material they have obtained is appropriate, monitor their success, and track future tasks by making metacognition more explicit (Quintana et al., 2005).

Improving Executive Functioning

Many students know, but neglect to use, cognitive and metacognitive strategies. Rauch and Fillenworth (1995) asked students what motivated them to use, or discouraged them from using, new study strategies. They found that students often did not know how to apply strategies to particular classes, felt strategies would take too much time, and/or had difficulty integrating the new strategies into their study habits. Knowing but not using cognitive strategies is a utilization error and is addressed, depending upon the circumstances, by increasing motivation (see Chapter 4), addressing affect (see Chapter 5), implementing a behavior management program (see Chapter 6), or improving executive functions.

When students use effective executive functions in studying, they (1) analyze the task; (2) select a learning strategy that has been previously successful with similar tasks; (3) modify the strategy to meet the demands of the new task; (4) monitor the effectiveness of the strategy; (5) remodify the strategy when appropriate; and (6) assess whether the task has been satisfactorily completed (Dawson & Guare, 2004). Completing these steps requires self-assessment in the continuous, recursive process described in Chapter 1.

Often self-assessment involves keeping detailed logs of study time and obtaining feedback from teachers, peers, or parents as well as ultimate grades (Zimmerman et al., 1996). Good planning that improves grades and increases homework completion not only includes planning for studying, but also monitoring the results of studying in order to plan better in the future (Bryan & Sullivan-Burstein, 1997; as cited in Bryan, Burstein, & Bryan, 2001; Borkowski & Burke, 1996). Students can follow the steps described in Worksheet 8.3, Study Plan Strategy Tool to develop effective study plans.

Self-Regulated Strategy Development (SRSD) is described by Graham and Harris (1996) as a method to increase self-regulation. The recursive steps of SRSD are listed in Table 8.3. A variation on SRSD, *Self-Monitoring Performance*, has been found to improve academic performance, particularly for students with learning disabilities (Harris, 1986; Harris et al., 2005). The steps of this latter process are indicated in Table 8.4.

Taylor was a slow, methodical perfectionist who usually got good grades but spent inordinate amounts of time doing her work in school and at home. Her teacher suggested that Taylor write the number of minutes it took for her to complete each page of her spelling workbook at the top of each page. After Taylor and her teacher analyzed and graphed her time and accuracy data for 2 weeks, Taylor was challenged to reduce the average number of minutes she spent on her spelling workbook while remaining accurate. Over a period of several weeks, Taylor dramatically reduced the time she spent doing her workbook.

TABLE 8.3. Self-Regulated Strategy Development (SRSD)

1. The adult helps students assess and develop any missing preskills necessary in using a new cognitive strategy.
2. The adult and students discuss strategies the students typically use to learn similar material, and their effectiveness vis-à-vis prior performance.
3. The adult and students discuss the new strategy, its benefits, its purpose, how to use it, and when to use it.
4. The students make a commitment to learn the new strategy and participate as collaborative instructors.
5. The adult (or a trained peer) models how to use the new strategy, along with verbal self-instruction (including problem definition, planning, strategy use, self-evaluation, and error correction) and statements of self-reinforcement.
6. The adult and students discuss methods to change the strategy to increase effectiveness or efficiency.
7. Each student develops personal statements to use in self-instruction and self-reinforcement.
8. Students memorize the strategy steps and their mnemonics, if any.
9. Under the supervision of the adult, students practice using the strategy, with self-instruction and self-reinforcement statements as necessary.
10. The students and adult evaluate the strategy's effectiveness and revise as appropriate.
11. Self-assessment and goal setting are introduced.
12. Students are encouraged to use the strategy independently and covertly.

TABLE 8.4. Self-Monitoring Performance

1. An adult and the student discuss the importance of completing work accurately.
2. The student agrees to use a procedure to help improve accurate work completion.
3. The student is taught to tally the number of times that work is completed accurately.
4. The student graphs the number of correct items daily.
5. Tally sheets are completed daily.

Note. Based on Reid & Harris (1989).

When using *study strategy portfolios,* students outline and commit to personal study plans, noting where, when, and with what strategies they will study. Sweidel (1996) suggests that students ask themselves the following questions: "How do I know when I have studied enough? How do I monitor my studying? How do I keep myself motivated? How many hours do I plan to study? How do I go about reading the material? Did I follow my plan? Did I make modifications? How prepared do I feel? How many hours did I actually study? Do I plan to make changes to my study plan in the future? What grade do I expect to get?" After students receive graded tests and assignments, they compare their study plans and activities to their academic achievement, indicate their satisfaction, and determine which strategies were most and least successful. The students then modify their plans as necessary, using self-reflection to assess and change their performance.

Finally, Dawson and Guare (2004) describe multiple methods to improve students' executive functions, both at the individual level through regular coaching and at the classroom level through group interventions. The reader is referred to their book for more in-depth descriptions of recommended strategies.

Appraisal

The appraisal of the effectiveness of interventions designed to improve cognitive and metacognitive strategies and executive functions should reflect the initial assessment and diagnosis of areas of difficulties as well as the goal(s) of the interventions. Again, semistructured interviews, thinking aloud, trace methodology, self-report measures, and "Study Pies" can be used to determine whether interventions have been successful. In addition, student grades on unit tests, papers, and report cards can be important indicators.

Help Students Develop Their Personal Learning Guides (HILLs)

Personal Learning Guides, updated yearly, can be very effective tools to encourage self-appraisal in terms of cognition, metacognition, and executive functions, as well as all of the other topics in this book. The intent is for these guides to be resources that will be maintained and modified over time. In regard to the present topics, the students might include the following materials:

Worksheet 8.1. Checklist of Cognitive and Metacognitive Strategies and Executive Functions

Worksheet 8.2. Study Pie

Worksheet 8.3. Study Plan Strategy Tool

Table 8.2. Student Affirmations about Cognition, Metacognition, and Executive Functions

WORKSHEET 8.1.

Checklist of Cognitive and Metacognitive Strategies and Executive Functions

The student uses good learning (cognitive) strategies by:	
	Spacing learning sessions.
	Using vivid emotions and humor.
	Rehearsing and repeating information.
	Sandwiching new information within known information.
	Sorting information into categories.
	Making hierarchies or organizational charts.
	Using association strategies (a story, cues, acrostics, peg words).
	Using visual imagery (mental images).
	Summarizing in own words and relating new to previously learned information.
	Using graphic organizers.
	Taking and reviewing notes.
	Using methods to foster reading comprehension (see Chapter 9).
	Incorporating corrected work (see Chapter 12).
The student strategizes about learning (uses metacognitive strategies) by:	
	Setting and prioritizing goals.
	Planning ahead.
	Structuring study environment and controlling distractions.
	Fostering positive attitudes and using affirmations.
	Managing time and organization.
	Assessing knowledge (testing self, using sample tests, study guides, portfolios).
	Changing strategies when necessary.
The student plans and appraises learning (uses executive skills) by:	
	Developing a study plan.
	Self-regulating strategy development.
	Conducting performance self-monitoring.
	Maintaining study strategy portfolios.
	Assessing the success of study strategies.
	Self-assigning rewards (for goal completion) and consequences (for not meeting goal).
Classroom practices foster cognitive and metacognitive strategies and executive skills by:	
	Providing minimal distractions and quiet setting for independent work.
	Giving direct and specific instruction in memory strategies.
	Effectively structuring lectures.
	Providing effective note-taking instruction, including the addition of details and review.
	Encouraging students to develop metacognitive skills by assessing their own learning.

WORKSHEET 8.2.

Study Pie

Student ______________________ Date __________ Subject ______________

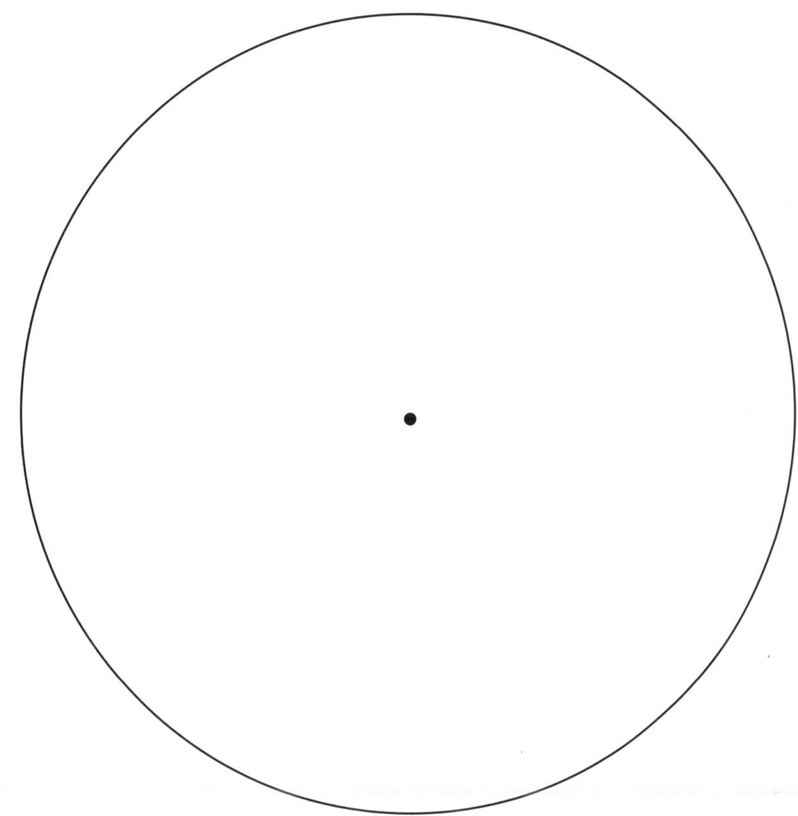

Anticipated grade:

Grade received:

Reflection:

Plan:

WORKSHEET 8.3.

Study Plan Strategy Tool

Student ______________________ Date ____________ Subject ________________

1. Before studying ask:

a. What should I try to remember?

b. How is this like anything I have learned before?

c. How have I studied material like this in the past?

d. How should I study this time?

e. Where and when do I plan to study?

f. How long do I plan to study?

g. How do I plan to focus on important information?

h. How do I plan to space learning sessions?

i. How will I include corrected work?

j. What are the methods I will use to increase comprehension and memory?

(continued)

Study Plan Strategy Tool *(page 2 of 2)*

k. How will I know when I've studied enough?

l. How will I keep myself motivated? How will I reward myself for meeting my goal? What consequence will I give myself for not meeting my goal?

2. **After studying, ask:**
   a. How did I know I had studied enough?

   b. How did I check my studying?

   c. How did I keep myself motivated? How did I reward myself for meeting my goal? What consequence did I give myself for not meeting my goal?

   d. How much time did I really spend studying?

   e. Do I feel prepared?

   f. What grade do I expect?

   g. Did I follow my study plan? If not, how did I change my plan?

3. **After receiving feedback or a grade,** review the "Before studying" and "After studying" sections above.
   a. Which strategies were most and least successful?

   b. How should the next study plan be changed?

9

Empowering Students to Self-Regulate Reading

Effective independent learners regulate their reading rate and use strategies to improve their reading comprehension.

OVERVIEW

> **Harry** conscientiously prepared the night before his social studies test. He skipped soccer practice, lowered the TV volume, and stayed up until midnight going through the portion of the textbook chapter that had not been read aloud in class. Despite his careful preparation, when taking the test he was stunned that he was unable to remember much of the material. He was frustrated because he could "almost see" the material in his mind's eye, yet was still unable to remember it. When his teacher returned his corrected paper, she made a caustic remark that he "could have at least read the book." Stung and angry, Harry snapped, "I *did* read it."

Though Harry did "read" the material, his deficient reading strategies caused him to do poorly. Reading is much more than recognizing or decoding words in a passage. Unfortunately, many students are like Harry and do not intuit how to read properly in preparation for a test or a big project; unless someone teaches them those skills, they will struggle or fail miserably.

Reading well improves vocabulary, critical thinking, spelling skills, and overall knowledge. It opens doors to endless opportunities and insights, provides leisure enjoyment, and makes the difference between success and failure both in school and in life. Conversely, difficulty with reading has a profound impact on all aspects of a student's academic functioning, because *all* other subjects (even math) rely on reading skills. Therefore, basic reading skills must be developed early in a student's academic career. Furthermore, in order for students to become *independent learners*, they must go beyond basic reading skills and approach reading constructively, purposefully, and with a repertoire of self-regulatory strategies that enable them to make sensible choices as they read.

This chapter describes methods to apply reading strategies to studying and independent learning, such as adjusting the approach according to the purpose of the task and using strategies to increase comprehension. Suggestions in this chapter are appropriate for use with students who are struggling with the application of reading in their learning. This might include students who are unable to comprehend assigned readings, who struggle to understand directions, who do not vary reading methods, or do not know how to approach complex reading assignments. A concise summary of concepts presented in this chapter can be found in Worksheet 9.1, Student Self-Regulated Reading Checklist.

RESEARCH FOUNDATIONS

During the past 30 years, research in reading comprehension has increasingly concluded that metacognitive processes in reading, or the cognitive and self-regulatory strategies one uses when reading, are critical components of skilled reading (Pressley, 2000; Pressley & Afflerbach, 1995; Wade et al., 1990). These processes include clarifying the purpose of reading, understanding the demands of the task, identifying important aspects of the reading task, focusing and recovering attention following disruptions, monitoring comprehension, and taking corrective steps to increase understanding (Brown, 1980). There are striking differences between skilled and less skilled readers (Kinnunen & Vauras, 1995), in that skilled readers employ one or more metacognitive strategies before, during, and after reading (Swanson & De La Paz, 1998), whereas unskilled readers do not.

During the *preparation* phase, before beginning to read, skilled readers approach the task with an awareness of what they are reading, an understanding of why they are reading, a strategy for monitoring comprehension, a tentative plan for handling potential problems, and a plan for the use of knowledge that they will obtain. They think about the topic, assess the demands of the assignment, and select a reading approach accordingly.

During the *performance* phase, skilled readers strategically coordinate their cognitive strategies. They find effective methods to focus their attention on important ideas and constantly monitor their reading comprehension through self-questioning and review. They adjust their reading rate according to the task—reading more slowly when studying or reading difficult material, and more quickly when reading for pleasure. They recognize when they are having difficulty understanding what they are reading, and take remedial steps such as slowing down, rereading, referring back, looking up information in reference material, reading about the same topic in an easier source, asking for help, or making a visual map. Skilled readers use and refer to supplemental materials within the text, such as maps, charts, graphs, and picture captions. They also draw upon their general knowledge to help them understand the reading material, draw inferences, and take steps to understand vocabulary in a passage. Finally, skilled readers constructively respond as they read. They search for and attend to the most important information, and actively relate to this information. Skilled readers draw upon their prior knowledge to understand material and attempt to infer information that is not explicitly stated by the author. They predict what the author will say, mentally carry on a conversation with the author and themselves, and hypothesize about the meaning of the material.

During the *appraisal* phase, and after completing the reading task, skilled readers continue to constructively respond and mentally interact with the material. They take into consideration the newly read information, consider alternative interpretations, and decide between them. They then revise their previously held knowledge and opinions as necessary. They use tools to process the material such as evaluating, interpreting, questioning, reviewing, and summarizing to determine whether they have sufficiently understood the material and, if not, seek additional resources. Finally, they reflect upon the strategies they used while reading, determine whether they were successful, and use that information as they approach future reading tasks.

In contrast, less skilled readers use limited metacognitive reading strategies and are often unaware that other strategies exist (Garner, 1994; Paris & Jacobs, 1984; Paris & Winograd, 1990). Before starting to read, they do not plan their reading, think about the topic, or look ahead. They neglect to modify their approach according to the task and may have the false notion that there is one way to read—word by word and at the same speed, regardless of the material or purpose for reading.

During the reading process, less skilled readers focus on reading as decoding rather than attempting to make sense of the material (Baker & Brown, 1984), and may not even notice or care when they do not understand what they are reading (Garner & Reis, 1981). Although students with word recognition difficulties can accurately describe their difficulties, they are not able to determine why the remedial steps they attempted did not work, or when it might have been appropriate to try another method. Even worse, students with word comprehension difficulties often are not even aware of these problems, much less how to remediate them (Miller & Yochum, 1991). Less skilled readers neither monitor their reading comprehension nor control their reading processes by attending to meaning or by relating the reading material to previous knowledge (Bos & Vaughan, 1994; Flavell, 1979; Markman, 1979). They do not know how, and therefore neglect, to use supplemental materials that increase understanding, such as indexes, dictionaries, graphs, maps, or headings (Leland-Jones, 1997). As a result, less skilled readers have difficulty detecting contradictions, integrating information, or resolving inconsistencies as they read (Oakhill & Patel, 1991; Snow, Burns, & Griffin, 1998).

Like Harry, less skilled readers may believe that they "have studied" after they finish reading, even when they have not determined whether they understood the material or isolated the main ideas. They do not reflect upon the strategies used while reading, and therefore cannot appraise their success or use such an appraisal to modify their approach to future assignments.

For students with special education needs, learning to become skilled readers can be particularly difficult. Fortunately, students both with and without disabilities can increase awareness of their own reading processes and learn appropriate strategies through systematic, direct, and carefully devised instruction (Brown, Armbruster, & Baker, 1986; Paris & Winograd, 1990). After learning various strategies, students can be taught how to determine when, where, and how to use them in order to become independent readers and learners (Garner, 1994; Paris, Lipson, & Wixson, 1983; Zimmerman et al., 1996).

METHODS

Critical reading strategies are best taught by using "real" assignments. Programs to improve these skills should involve changes in the structure, not necessarily the content, of assignments (Barton-Arwood, Wehby, & Falk, 2005). They can be taught in one-to-one sessions with consultants, in classroom settings by teachers, or at home by parents, siblings, or friends.

In the classroom, strategies such as LETME (Link, Extract, Transform, Monitor, Extend) (Shenkman, 1986) can be used to help students read more effectively and learn from text. These programs facilitate understanding, selection, organization, retention, and analysis of information through teaching students decision making, self-regulation of learning, awareness of metacognitive strategies, and training in study strategies.

Peers can also be taught to help one another implement reading strategies. Peer-Assisted Learning Strategies (Fuchs et al., 2001) have a positive impact on learning. For example, a program described by Zimmerman et al. (1996) utilizes peers in a 5-week classroom intervention. The students are introduced to the concept of summaries, asked to summarize reading, and then taught to score classmates' summaries by using a teacher-provided model and grading criteria.

TABLE 9.1. Peer-Supported Reading Comprehension

1. Introduce the concepts of summaries, and assign the summarization of reading text.
2. Have classmates score one another's summaries, using a teacher-provided model summary of the passage(s) and grading criteria.
3. Check how well the students were able to follow the grading criteria and model.
4. Encourage the students to highlight ideas in their summaries during their reviews for weekly quizzes based on the readings.
5. Continue this process over a 5-week period, having students monitor the following:
   a. The amount of time they spent summarizing the material.
   b. The number of pages in the text material.
   c. The number of main ideas they included in their summaries.
   d. The number of ideas they highlighted during review.
   e. Their anticipated scores on the weekly quizzes.
   f. Their actual quiz scores.

Note. Adapted from Zimmerman, Bonner, and Kovach (1996). Copyright 1996 by the American Psychological Association. Adapted by permission.

The teacher then checks how well the students were able to follow the grading criteria and model, encourages students to use their summaries as they review for weekly quizzes, and then has students monitor this strategy and its effects on their grades over a 5-week intervention period. The steps involved in this process are delineated in Table 9.1.

Carefully designed homework assignments can also significantly improve reading skills. For example, when students and parents are asked to collaborate in drawing inferences about reading material, students' ability to draw inferences increase significantly (Bailey, Silvern, Brabham, & Ross, 2004). Providing parents with specific guidelines on how to help their children with reading homework, as well as assigning tasks requiring parental involvement, also improves student achievement. The reader is referred to Chapter 2 for strategies involving parents.

Preparation

Assessing Students' Reading Skills and Strategies

The assessment of reading while studying has two components. Students' *ability* to read the assigned materials must be established, and then their *reading strategies* must be appraised. Several methods can be used to determine whether a student can read assigned material, including standardized tests, curriculum-based assessment, cloze procedures, and assessing text readability level.

Most broad-based achievement measures—such as the Comprehensive Test of Basic Skills (CTB/McGraw-Hill, 1990); the California Achievement Tests (CTB/McGraw-Hill, 1993); the Woodcock–Johnson III (WJ III; Woodcock et al., 2001); and the Wechsler Individual Achievement Test—Second Edition (WIAT-II; Wechsler, 2001)—include reading components. Analysis of the scores generated by these tests can facilitate understanding of difficulties and strengths. However, often global standardized test scores are not useful for assessing reading study skills because their results are too general, they yield little information relative to the student's ability to handle specific material, and they do not lead to effective intervention planning.

More explicit information is obtained through the use of assessment tools targeted at reading, such as the Gray Diagnostic Reading Tests—Second Edition (GDRT-2; Bryant, Bryant, & Wiederholt, 2004); the Gray Oral Reading Tests—Fourth Edition (GORT-4; Wiederholt & Bryant, 2001); the Woodcock Reading Mastery Tests—Revised (Woodcock, 1998); and the Gates–

MacGinitie Reading Tests, Fourth Edition, Forms S and T (MacGinitie, MacGinitie, Maria, & Dreyer, 2000). These tools can result in effective intervention planning, but they address global reading skills, not those specific to students' assignments.

Reading skills relative to students' assignments can be determined by using *curriculum-based assessment.* With this method, the student is asked to read and answer comprehension questions. The student should be able to identify words with at least 90% accuracy and answer comprehension questions with at least 75% accuracy (Scott, Wolking, Stoutimore, & Harris, 1990). Although curriculum-based assessment in reading is usually conducted by having a student read aloud to an adult, students can be taught to monitor their word recognition by making a tally for each word they do not know when they read to themselves, and to ask themselves questions about the material. Again, they should not miss more than 10% of the words, and should be able to answer the majority of comprehension questions without difficulty.

Another method to assess comprehension of textbook material is to devise a *cloze procedure* by photocopying approximately 250 words from the text, leaving the first and last sentences complete, and blanking out every fifth word in the intervening sentences. The student should be able to guess at least 60% of the missing words when reading passages aloud (Jacobson, 1990).

Still another possible method to determine whether reading assignments are at an appropriate level is to *determine the readability level* of the text and compare this score with the student's reading level. Book publishers often calculate and make public the readability index of text books. Readability levels can also be calculated by typing a passage into a word-processing program and running the grammar checker (usually under Tools, along with the spell checker).

Reading strategies can be assessed through self-report, semistructured interviews, trace analysis, and student logs. One *self-report tool* with specific questions relative to reading is Metacognitive Awareness of Reading Strategies Inventory (MARSI; Mokhtari & Reichard, 2002), found in Worksheet 9.2. The MARSI contains a list of 30 reading strategies that have been found to be effective. In addition, Worksheet 9.1 is a checklist that students can use for self-appraisal. Tools in other chapters that can be used to assess general strategies include Worksheets 7.2, 8.1, 8.2, and 8.4.

In a *semistructured interview,* the student is asked to describe how he or she approaches a reading assignment. For example, a student might be asked, "Do you have any particular method for reading your English or history assignments? When you have difficulty, what methods do you use? Do you have any particular method for reading your science assignments? When you have difficulty reading science, what methods do you use?"

In *trace analysis*, the student shares materials already read with the consultant, along with his or her notes, highlights, outlines, and other manifestations of reading strategies. Often the student also orally describes the reading material; explains the pictures and graphs; reads a passage aloud; and finds information by using the index or table of contents, *thinking aloud* as he or she works.

Determining the Reason for Reading and Selecting an Appropriate Reading Style

Before starting to read, students should determine the reason(s) they are reading the material and select reading strategies accordingly. As described in Handout 9.1, Reading Chart, students can read to gain knowledge, gain specific information, find evidence, complete a task, find pleasure or leisure enjoyment, explore or review, and/or search for information. Students need to be helped to understand that reading speed should vary. When reading for pleasure, we may speed up when reading exciting novels, or slow down our speed at the end of a great book so that it won't end too soon. When reading to comprehend difficult textbooks or technical manuals, we slow down or may even vocalize (read aloud, move our lips, or whisper) or subvocalize (say each word silently in our heads) to gain a better understanding. When we look up a word in a dictionary, we rapidly scan for the correct alphabetical section, look at the guide words at the top of the page to determine whether the word can be found on that page, and adjust our search accordingly. Sometimes we scan a document to see whether it will meet our needs, then go back and skim it for usable information. Many times, slow, word-by-word reading is not the appropriate method. Students must be taught that varying their reading speed is an important skill, and must be given permission to skip words, passages, or sections that are not germane to the purpose of reading.

> A school psychologist discovered that **Carl** felt stupid because of his very slow work habits. Observing him work on an assignment, she realized that Carl read word by word through the entire chapter when trying to answer the homework questions. When he was told that he could read the question first and then try to find out where in the chapter a particular topic was covered by looking at headings, Carl was amazed that he could "skip" the chapter parts that did not answer questions he was trying to answer. "I always thought it was cheating if you didn't read it all," he declared.

Overviewing the Material

Prereading takes very little time but is a very important technique to use in increasing the ability to understand material. Prereading material gives students the big picture. It indicates what is coming and where to "put" that information based on prior knowledge. Also, prereading allows the students to decide whether further reading is warranted or whether another book should be chosen for the purpose at hand. After prereading, students can then use critical reading skills to carefully read the material for details.

Nonfiction is preread by reviewing nontextual cues (title, author, publication date, headings and subheadings, pictures, graphs, charts); reading the introduction, preface, and conclusion; and skimming the body. Students should look for the author's use of organizers such as numbers, lists, steps, bullets, or ordinal words ("first," "second," "next," "finally"); words that are boldfaced, in italics, or in different fonts, styles, or colors; and key concepts set off in the margins or listed as learning objectives. Fiction is preread by reading the covers, introduction, and author's biography; reviewing the first 10–25 pages to determine setting, character, and plot; and then starting from the beginning and reading carefully.

Skimming is the technique used to look up a specific word in the dictionary or a telephone number in the phone book. When we skim, we search for particular words or ideas by moving our eyes quickly down the page and do not read word by word. This useful strategy is similar to visually searching a crowded room for a friend: We quickly "skim" over all the faces until we spot the one for which we are searching. Skimming reading material is a time-saving technique that zeros in on the specific information being sought.

Scanning during the prereading process enables students to obtain a general impression of the material's value and whether it will be helpful and sufficient. Reading the first and last sentence of each paragraph is a scanning strategy that gives readers quick answers to questions they may ask about the relevance of a particular material, because often (though not always) the main ideas are embedded in the first or last sentences of the paragraphs. This cursory overview can save substantial time and effort for students conducting research as they choose appropriate sources. Secondary and postsecondary students particularly benefit from learning to scan, because they are faced with a large amount of material to read, as well as increasingly complex readings. Moreover, when reading a journal article, students can read the abstract, introduction, and conclusion, and then scan the headings. This helps them locate relevant material quickly and allows them to decide whether a more detailed reading will be necessary.

Obtaining Appropriate Supplemental Materials

After the assessment has been completed and the material overviewed, appropriate supplemental materials will need to be accessed if it has been determined that the assigned material is at the student's frustration level. One method is to help the student find *alternative written, audio, or video materials* on the same topic that are easier to understand.

Students can use this principle by reading *Cliffs Notes*, looking up topics in an encyclopedia, looking up material on the Internet, or reading material on the same subject that is at an easier level. Audio materials are readily available; computer software can "read" scanned passages aloud for those students in need of auditory material to supplement visual materials. For students with learning disabilities or visual impairment, audiotapes of many books and textbooks are available from Talking Books or Recording for the Blind and Dyslexic. Reading aloud is both beneficial and enjoyable to students of all ages. In addition, most students are better able to understand difficult reading material after having watched a film on the same topic.

Computer programs to increase reading comprehension, improve reading vocabulary, and increase reading speed have become more commonplace, and many can be tailored to particular content (e.g., social studies vocabulary can be inserted). Increasingly, textbook publishers are augmenting print with computer-assisted instruction materials that can be extremely useful to increase comprehension. Computer-assisted instruction uses software, CD-ROMs, or interactive video discs to guide and individualize instruction. These materials have been found to greatly increase knowledge of social studies (Higgins & Boone, 1990), algebra (Kime & Clark, 1998), word recognition and decoding (Wise & Olson, 1994), and biology (Jones, 1993).

Personal copies of textbooks enable students to read more effectively because they permit active interacting with the material by underlining important points and writing margin notes in reaction to the text. Many students use highlighters, but writing margin notes is preferable because it is more active.

Finally *"real" and interesting reading material* should be used. While basic reading skills should certainly be systematically taught to students with poor reading skills, keeping students exclusively in skill workbooks without the opportunity to read "real" stories, novels, and nonfiction robs them of chances to use their skills. Students cannot gain an understanding of plot, character development, or an author's viewpoint if their reading is limited to skill workbooks. Students will not generalize reading strategies if they think that reading is only sounding out words with little attention to comprehension, or that subjects like social studies or science have nothing to do with reading. Even weak readers can enjoy stories and chapter books, as well as other high-interest, low-difficulty materials.

Performance

Fostering Concentration

Reading takes concentration, time, and effort. One often must read a passage several times before adequate comprehension takes place. Students must be taught this explicitly.

> **Petra's** freshman English teacher, a novice professor, expressed shock upon finding out that students in his class had only read *Othello* once before the exam. His students were even more shocked to find out that he had expected them to read it at least three times!

Students also must be taught to pay attention as they read and to monitor their attentiveness. It is not uncommon for individuals to read on "automatic pilot" and suddenly realize that they have been turning the pages while "reading," but not actually paying attention to or understanding the words their eyes "saw."

To foster concentration, it can be helpful for students to determine how long they can concentrate on the particular material and plan breaks accordingly. Many students find that the methods to increase comprehension described below, such as taking notes, outlining, mapping, and writing down questions while reading, and so forth, also increase their ability to focus attention. Concentration is also increased by remembering to relate already familiar material to the subject being read about, predicting what will come next, visualizing the material by making a "mental movie," or constructing timelines to track described events.

Increasing Reading Comprehension

In order to comprehend reading material, it is necessary for readers to reconstruct the text and relate its information to previously learned material or experiences, using familiar words, analogies, metaphors, summaries, questions, or other devices to "make it their own." As Wittrock (1990) discusses, sometimes it is necessary, particularly with very poor readers, to help them understand that comprehension is as much a part of reading as is decoding. Such individuals have "never through reading known the joy of discovering a new understanding, the emotions of happiness or sorrow, or the fun of humor" (p. 172), and must be encouraged to attend to the meaning of words, sentences, paragraphs, and chapters by generating an interpretation, plot, or theme to unify the text into a whole. There are many techniques to help students reconstruct reading material and generate meaning, and thereby increase their ability to comprehend. These include finding the main ideas, checking for "clicks" and "clunks," questioning, rapid reviewing, imaging, thinking of examples, summarizing, keeping, reading journals, making graphic organizers, note taking, outlining, generating meaning, using computer-based learning environments, developing personal study guides, quizzing, and SQRW (survey-question-read-write).

- *Identifying the most important information and finding the main idea.* Skilled readers search for the most important information and attend to it. One method to do this is to identify the main idea of each paragraph or passage. A structured approach to this strategy is to follow four steps summarized by the acronym READ, plus a fifth step (Strichart & Mangrum, 2002, p. 193):

1. Read the paragraph, looking for words that are repeated.
2. Evaluate each sentence and underline the important words.
3. Analyze the important words to learn what they have in common.
4. Decide the paragraph's main idea.
5. Finally, find or write a sentence telling what the underlined words have in common.

- *Checking for "clicks" and "clunks."* As first described in Chapter 8, students of all levels can monitor their understanding every so often (perhaps at the end of each page) by checking for "clicks" (understanding) and "clunks" (nonunderstanding). When they encounter a "clunk," they should go back and reread to convert it into a "click."
- *Questioning.* Comprehension is improved when students ask themselves questions about the material as they read it, particularly if they question material at a deeper level. For example, they may ask themselves whether the material is true and supported by evidence from their own lives or other material they have read. Or they might pause and ask themselves, "What will come next?" Similarly, *predicting* what the author will address next or conclude increases comprehension.

• *Rapid reviewing.* Some students find that rapid reviewing improves both reading comprehension and memory. After reading a section, students write down everything they can remember without looking back at the text. If they can't remember at least 80% of the key points, they have read too much material before reviewing. They then reread the material and repeat the process until the key points can be recalled.

• *Imaging.* Developing visual images of reading material has been found to increase reading comprehension. In this strategy, a student might make a "mental movie" of a novel, or create a visual image of an arithmetic word problem.

• *Thinking of examples.* Thinking of examples and possible applications greatly increases comprehension. Often writers include examples and vignettes to foster this process (as we have done in this book). Other times, it is up to the readers to supply their own examples and applications.

• *Summarizing.* Reading comprehension can be greatly increased by teaching students to generate meaning from reading material using their background knowledge. This can be accomplished by having students read a short passage and then write a summary in their own words that combines information from more than one sentence.

• *Keeping reading journals.* Comprehension is augmented when students write reflective responses in their reading journals after reading material. It is augmented further when they revise their reflective responses after rereading or after discussing the material with others.

• *Using graphic organizers.* Additional tools that promote reading comprehension are graphic organizers. These organizers promote comprehension because they provide information in a visual modality, show relationships, and foster nonlinear thinking. Sometimes graphic organizers are provided by authors in the form of maps, charts, diagrams, and timelines. Skilled readers always attend to these materials. Alternatively, students can draw a picture, graph, or diagram that conveys the information in the material. Student-developed graphic organizers are particularly helpful because they provide students with the opportunity to "construct" meaning from a passage (Baxendell, 2003; Jones et al., 1988; Sebranek et al., 1998). The steps to take in developing a graphic organizer are outlined in Chapter 3, and various types of graphic representations and their uses are illustrated in Handout 3.1.

• *Taking notes.* Taking notes from reading material has been repeatedly shown to significantly increase learning, both because of the note-taking process itself and because it generates a product useful in reviewing for exams (Armel & Shrock, 1996). Survey, Question, Read, Write (SQRW; Strichart & Mangrum, 2002) is a method specific to reading. The student Surveys the title, introduction, heading, and conclusions of the reading assignment; develops Questions about the material, using "who, what, where, when, and why" to change headings and subheadings into questions; Reads the material for answers to the questions; and Writes down the answers to the questions. Additional information on general note-taking methods is included in Chapter 3.

Gerry was a very successful student, in comparison with his long-time friend **Harry**, who has been introduced at the beginning of this chapter. While Harry "read" by leafing through the text while watching TV, Gerry preread the chapter 4 days before the unit test by reading the titles, headings, subheadings, and captions under the pictures, graphs, maps, and tables. The next day he read the objectives at the beginning of the chapter, the questions at the end of the chapter, and then the entire chapter, even though the first half had been covered in class. When he didn't understand something, he backtracked until it was clear. Gerry took notes by making a vertical line down his paper and writing the headings and subheadings as questions on the left side, and answers using main ideas and supporting details from the text on the right. The day before the test, he quizzed himself on the questions and answers he had developed, and made sure he was also able to answer the questions provided by the textbook author at the end of the chapter. Not surprisingly, Gerry aced the exam while Harry failed it.

• *Outlining*. Outlining is one of the most effective recording techniques, because it succinctly summarizes a large volume of material into a hierarchical presentation with clear demarcation of the most important issues in headings. Outlining is frequently taught in the intermediate grades, but students' ability to outline should also be checked at the secondary level and taught and reinforced across curriculum lines. Computers can be used to assist with outlining, because most word-processing programs have an outline function that can be used to facilitate outlining readings into broader or more detailed outlines (Anderson-Inman et al., 1996). To use this function, students (1) create a chapter skeleton by typing headings and subheadings into an outlining program; (2) carefully read each paragraph and insert key words and main ideas into the outline; and (3) test their knowledge by expanding and contracting the outline to show or hide material. Some computer-based mapping programs convert outlines into graphics and vice versa, enabling students to synthesize scientific concepts and information.

• *Generating meaning*. Comprehension improves when students generate personal meaning from the text. Most often, this is accomplished by using prior knowledge and experiences to inform the reading. Meaning might also be generated by *hypothesizing about the meaning of the material* while reading, and testing those hypotheses as reading progresses; by drawing upon past experiences to make inferences about points not explicitly stated; or by attending to the most important points in the material and relating them to one another (Pressley & Afflerbach, 1995). It can also be accomplished by reacting to a passage from two different perspectives (Gajria & Salvia, 1992; Wittrock, 1990). For example, the reader of this chapter could first read it for information relative to working with a high school student with a reading problem, and then reread it for information to help deliver an in-service training session about reading to general education teachers.

• *Computer-Based Learning Environments (CBLE)*. Computer-based learning environments, such as Point&Query, AutoTutor, and iSTART, have been developed to increase reading comprehension in sciences and technology courses (Graesser, McNamara, & VanLehn, 2005). These programs augment material presented in texts with scaffolded questions that move beyond recall to metacognitive understanding, and these have the great advantage of giving a student an opportunity to ask 120 comprehension questions per hour—700 times the normal rate that an individual student is likely to ask questions in the classroom. The iSTART program (McNamara, Levenstein, & Boonthum, 2004), a Web-based program designed for use with advanced students, has been found to increase both reading comprehension and metacognitive processes.

Improving Vocabulary

Students need methods to deal with unfamiliar words they encounter when reading. Devine (1987) has recommended that when students encounter an unfamiliar word, they use an approach captured by the acronym SSCD: Sound (sound out the word to see if it is already in their listening vocabulary); Structure (analyze for familiar prefixes, suffixes, and roots); Context (guess at the meaning, using clues in the passage); and Dictionary (use the dictionary or glossary when still stumped).

The Vocabulary Worksheet, developed by Landsberger (2006), has students draw a graphic organizer to learn new vocabulary words. In a center box, a student enters a vocabulary word (e.g., "cow"). In a box above the word, the student enters the definition or brief description of the word (e.g., "a domestic mammal, the mature female of cattle of the genus *Bos*"). To the right, the student enters properties that identify the item ("usually 4–5 feet tall, raised on farms for milk or meat, may have horns, feeds on grass"), and to the left the student writes examples with distinguishing characteristics (e.g., "Guernsey, brown and white, from island of Guernsey, raised for milk; Angus, black, hornless, from Scotland, raised for meat").

Monitoring Reading Strategies

While reading, students need to constantly monitor their success and modify their strategies when they encounter difficulty. To monitor success, students can ask themselves the questions posed in Worksheet 9.1: (1) Does this strategy help me focus my attention on important information? (2) Does this strategy help me organize the information? (3) Does this strategy help me read with understanding? and (4) Does this strategy help me learn the information? If the answer to any question is "no," the student should select another strategy.

Appraisal

During the appraisal stage, students monitor their outcomes. It is not enough for teachers, consultants, and parents to simply identify students' difficulties in applying reading strategies to their studying and independent learning. Students must learn how to identify their difficulties themselves in order to become independent learners. Thus they must become proficient in assessing their own reading skills, selecting remediative strategies, and monitoring their success.

After completing a reading task, skilled readers take into consideration the newly-read information and revise their previously held knowledge and opinions accordingly. They use the tools they developed during the performance phase, such as notes and graphic organizers, to deeply process and learn important material. They reflect upon their reading by evaluating, interpreting, questioning, reviewing, and summarizing to determine whether they sufficiently understand the material; if not, they seek additional materials or obtain help (Pressley & Afflerbach, 1995).

Finally, they consider the strategies they used while reading, determine whether these were successful, and use that information to modify their approaches to future reading tasks (Dawson & Guare, 2004). As Zimmerman et al. (1996) indicate, "this may be daunting if they have habitually followed other practices for a long time" (p. 56). In order for them to effectively utilize their newfound strategies, it is important for them to monitor the success of these strategies. It is helpful for adults to encourage this monitoring, and to focus on the learning process as well as the learning outcomes.

Help Students Develop Their Personal Learning Guides (HILLs)

The reading strategies that students develop will need to be modified as they advance through their schooling: the strategies that are effective with sixth-grade social studies will not be effective with college-level chemistry. Therefore, students should be encouraged to keep both completed and blank copies of assessment and intervention sheets in their binders, so that they can continually reflect upon and readjust their reading strategies. Materials pertinent to this topic include the following:

Worksheet 9.1. Student Self-Regulated Reading Checklist
Worksheet 9.2. Metacognitive Awareness of Reading Strategies Inventory (MARSI)
Handout 9.1. Reading Purposes and Methods
Table 9.1. Peer-Supported Reading Comprehension

WORKSHEET 9.1.

Student Self-Regulated Reading Checklist

Student ______________________________ Date ________________

Before I read this material:

__ I overviewed the material by prereading or scanning.

I checked that I can read this material comfortably.

__ I could read at least 9 out of 10 words accurately in this reading material.

__ I added audio materials, films, or alternative reading material if the reading was too hard.

I knew the reason I was reading was:

__ to learn,

__ to gain specific information,

__ to find evidence,

__ to complete a task,

__ for pleasure or leisure,

__ to explore or review, and/or

__ to search for information.

While I read this material:

__ I used methods to increase my concentration.

__ I changed my reading speed according to the type of reading.

I improved my understanding by:

__ Attending to the most important information and finding the main ideas.

__ Checking for "clicks" and "clunks."

__ Questioning and predicting what will come next.

__ Rapid reviewing.

__ Imaging.

__ Thinking of examples.

__ Summarizing and paraphrasing.

__ Reading charts, graphs, and timelines in the text.

__ Keeping and revising a reading journal.

__ Drawing a graphic organizer.

__ Taking notes.

__ SQRW (Scan, Question, Read, Write).

__ Outlining.

__ Generating meaning (hypothesizing about meaning, relating points, making inferences).

__ Computer-based learning.

__ Another strategy: ______________________________

(contiinued)

Student Self-Regulated Reading Checklist *(page 2 of 2)*

I improved my vocabulary as I read, using:
__ SSCD: Sound, Structure, Context, Dictionary.
__ Vocabulary worksheet.
__ Another strategy ____

I checked how well my strategies worked by asking myself:
__ Does this strategy help me focus my attention on important information?
__ Does this strategy help me organize the information?
__ Does this strategy help me read with understanding?
__ Does this strategy help me learn the information?

After I finished reading:
__ I thought about what I had read, and reviewed notes and graphic organizers.
__ I determined that I understood the material or sought additional information.
__ I decided which reading strategies worked well and which ones needed changing in the future.

Notes:

WORKSHEET 9.2.

Metacognitive Awareness of Reading Strategies Inventory (MARSI)

A. Write your response to each statement (i.e., 1, 2, 3, 4, or 5) in each of the blanks.

   1 means "I **never or almost never** do this."
   2 means "I do this **only occasionally**."
   3 means "I **sometimes** do this" (about **50%** of the time).
   4 means "I **usually** do this."
   5 means "I **always or almost always** do this."

B. Add up the scores under each column. Place the result on the line under each column.

C. Divide the subscale score by the number of statements in each column to get the average for each subscale.

D. Calculate the average for the whole inventory by adding up the subscale scores and dividing by 30.

E. Compare your results to those shown below.

F. Discuss your results with your teacher or tutor.

1. I have a purpose in mind when I read. _____
2. I take notes while reading to help me understand what I'm reading. _____
3. I think about what I know to help me understand what I'm reading. _____
4. I preview the text to see what it's about before reading it. _____
5. When text becomes difficult, I read aloud to help me understand what I'm reading. _____
6. I write summaries to reflect on key ideas in the text. _____
7. I think about whether the content of the text fits my purpose. _____
8. I read slowly but carefully to be sure I understand what I am reading. _____
9. I discuss my reading with others to check my understanding. _____
10. I scan the text first by noting characteristics like length and organization. _____
11. I try to get back on track when I lose concentration. _____
12. I underline or circle information in the text to help me remember it [if allowed]. _____
13. I adjust my reading speed according to what I'm reading. _____
14. I decide what to read closely and what to ignore. _____
15. I use reference materials (dictionaries) to help understand what I'm reading. _____

(continued)

Metacognitive Awareness of Reading Strategies Inventory *(page 2 of 2)*

16. When text becomes difficult, I begin to pay closer attention to what I'm reading.		____	
17. I use tables, figures, and pictures in text to increase my understanding.	____		
18. I stop from time to time to think about what I'm reading.		____	
19. I use context clues to help me better understand what I'm reading.	____		
20. I paraphrase (restate in my own words) to better understand what I'm reading.			____
21. I try to picture or visualize information to help me remember what I'm reading.		____	
22. I use typographical aids like boldface type and italics to identify key information.	____		
23. I critically analyze and evaluate the information presented in the text.	____		
24. I go back and forth in the text to find relationships among ideas in it.			____
25. I check my understanding when I come across conflicting information.	____		
26. I try to guess what the text is about when reading.	____		
27. When the text becomes difficult, I reread to increase my understanding.		____	
28. I ask myself questions I'd like to have answered in the text.			____
29. I check to see if my guesses about the text are right or wrong.	____		
30. I try to guess the meaning of unknown words or phrases.		____	
Total	____	____	____

Average	Global Reading Strategies	(Divide total by 13)	____		
	Problem-Solving Strategies	(Divide total by 8)		____	
	Support Reading Strategies	(Divide total by 9)			____

HANDOUT 9.1.

Reading Purposes and Methods

Students should be taught that there are many ways to read. At different times they need to read silently, aloud, slowly, carefully, quickly, with comprehension, word by word, or skimming over the words. The list below illustrates that the type of reading we do and the reading methods we choose should depend on our purpose for reading. A successful reader varies his or her reading speed and reading methods according to the task.

Purpose (Why am I reading?)	Sample Question	Reading method (How should I read?)
Gain knowledge	How does the body digest food?	Preread text, do careful detailed reading, and reread
Gain specific information	What is the phone number of the store? Is my topic included in this book? How did the Cubs do?	Skim phone book Skim book's index/glossary Skim or scan newspaper
Find evidence, arguments, and examples	How can I persuade others to agree with me?	Identify relationships and use logic to synthesize facts
Complete a task	How do I set up my blackberry?	Follow directions carefully in sequential steps
Explore	What would happen if . . . ?	Scan material
Review	Do I know this information?	Skim/pose and answer questions/ verify correctness
Search	Which chapter covers this? How can I search large volumes of information?	Skim book's table of contents Scan quickly
	Examples	
Enjoy	Read a novel or joke book Read poetry and plays	Silently read at comfortable speed Read aloud, with emotion
Relax	Relieve boredom	Read at any speed that works
Improve health/ mind states	Improve mood Self-improvement Read a love letter	Read at a comfortable speed Read word by word, reread frequently

10

Empowering Students to Self-Regulate Writing

Although writing is primarily used to communicate with others, it usually is completed in solitude and, as such, maximally taxes the skills of even the most self-regulated learner.

OVERVIEW

Charles was sure he was incapable of learning how to write well. Even as a high school student, he could produce only a simple paragraph of two or three sentences after long hours of staring at a blank sheet of paper. When his parents hired a writing tutor to help him prepare for the SAT writing exam, she systematically helped Charles build his writing skills by first having him observe her write while thinking aloud, and then having him use the writing process himself in response to creative story starters and interesting topics. She taught him to use graphic organizers and helpful references such as a thesaurus, and to maintain constant awareness of his intended audience.

After 6 months, the tutor challenged Charles to submit an essay to a contest for a $500 gift certificate. The competition provided the incentive for Charles to refine his writing skills as he worked on word choice and using a powerful voice to describe "Why the Atrium Mall Is My Favorite Mall" in 100 words or less. Winning the second prize of a $100 gift certificate was so thrilling that Charles sought other opportunities to write. Eventually some of his science fiction appeared in a local publication, and he joined the school newspaper staff.

Students often become "stuck" when asked to write, because writing is very complex. It requires that the writer simultaneously plan and organize; remember multiple trains of thought; attend to the words being written; effectively use a production method such as handwriting or keyboarding; and remember details such as capitalization, grammar, punctuation, and spelling. Writing also results in "published" documents—that is, documents that are made public and thus open to others' reading, review, and criticism. Because of this complexity and publicity, writing assignments such as term papers are often prime sources of frustration, procrastination, and learning difficulties.

How can students learn to think of writing as an opportunity for communication, rather than as an onerous and overwhelming task? How can consultants empower students to obtain appropriate help from others while they move toward being independent writers? This chapter addresses strategies to improve study skills and independent learning in written language (including spelling) in both academics and personal life. Suggestions in this chapter are appropriate for students who have difficulty planning, organizing, and completing writing assignments, or who are confronting an unfamiliar or complex genre. For a concise listing of information in this chapter, the reader is referred to Worksheet 10.1, Writing Strategies Checklist.

Myriad writing skills are required in many common, everyday activities of varied importance. In our daily lives, we write emails, blogs, shopping lists, letters, To-Do lists, and information on calendars. In our academic and professional lives, we fill out applications; complete assignments; write answers to questions on tests; write research papers; and take notes during lectures, workshops, meetings, and training sessions. Through writing we can solve problems, brainstorm ideas, express opinions, teach, or express ourselves creatively—in ways that can move others long after we are gone. Every type of writing is undertaken to preserve our thoughts and to communicate, now or at a later time, with others or ourselves. Clearly, those who lack the skills necessary to write effectively are at a distinct disadvantage in school and in society.

Helping students understand this fact enables them appreciate the value of this form of communication and the importance of becoming skilled writers. Although writing is usually taught during classes in English and language arts, it is required throughout the academic curriculum. Science, social studies, and math teachers require that students write homework assignments, journal entries, short-answer or essay items on tests, and research reports. Students who have adequate self-regulatory study skills in writing are likely to be less resistant to completing almost all assignments, regardless of the subject area (Zimmerman et al., 1996). Thus the ability to communicate in writing is one of the most important outcomes of schooling. However, although writing is used to communicate, it is usually conducted in solitude. It can maximally tax the skills of even the most self-regulated independent learner.

Expert performance in writing, like expert performance in other areas such as athletics, chess, and music, is enhanced through guided instruction, repetition, and successive refinement (Ericsson, Krampe, & Tesch-Romer, 1993). As Zimmerman (1999) has described, to become independent writers, students must:

1. *Observe and recognize* success in another person's performance.
2. *Emulate and adopt* the model's pattern and process.
3. *Self-monitor* while learning new strategies until they are automatic.
4. *Self-regulate* in adapting to changed tasks and audiences.

Observing and recognizing success require attending to and perceiving differences between success and failure. *Observation* is facilitated by watching a model making and correcting errors. Providing *coping models*, where instructors intentionally make key mistakes in order to demonstrate correcting errors themselves, is more effective than providing *mastery models* where students see only flawless examples (Zimmerman, 2002).

When emulating and self-monitoring, students use the multistep *writing process* and employ a process of prewriting, drafting, revising, editing, and publishing. This process is enhanced by self-recording and monitoring goal approximation, and results in both improved writing skills and heightened feelings of self-efficacy (Zimmerman, 1999).

When self-regulating, students independently adapt their writing to changed tasks and audiences. They also become "experts" and shift their attention from discrete strategy implementation to attaining desired outcome goals, such as demonstrating knowledge, persuading an audience, or obtaining positive feedback from editors.

Although instruction in writing benefits all students, it is critical for most students with disabilities and for students whose native language is not English. These students have difficulty managing the complex skills required in writing, and for them, explicit strategy instruction using a structured, step-by-step method of writing is particularly important. Such a method has been found to increase the writing competence of even very young typically developing students (Saddler, Moran, Graham, & Harris, 2004), as well as students with learning disabilities (De La Paz & Graham, 1997)—particularly when it employs a self-regulated strategy development model that enables them to effectively plan, organize, write, and revise a written product (Chalk, Hagan-Burke, & Burke, 2005).

RESEARCH FOUNDATIONS

Writing, or "language by hand," draws on different neurological functions and processes than "language by ear" (aural), "language by eye" (reading), or "language by mouth" (oral) (Berninger, Abbott, Abbott, Graham, & Richards, 2002, p. 39). Thus, although writing appears to use the same tools (letters, phonemes, syntax, and semantics) as reading and spoken language, in fact it requires unique strategies and sources of expertise.

Writing problems can be manifested in short, incomplete, poorly organized papers that convey irrelevant information and contain grammatical and spelling errors. Difficulties with written assignments can stem from a variety of sources, such as deficiencies in working memory (McCutchen, 2000); difficulties with writing fluency as a result of deficiencies in handwriting or spelling (Berninger, Rutberg, & Abbott, 2006); insufficient motivation and self-efficacy (Bandura, 1997); inadequate planning (Graham, Harris, & Mason, 2005); or deficiencies in self-regulation (Zimmerman, 2002). To improve students' writing performance, interventions should promote a positive attitude toward writing by modifying assignments and engineering success; teach explicit strategies that focus on planning, revising, and fluid production; and adapt instructional methods, materials, and expectations for individual students (Graham & Harris, 2002; Troia & Graham, 2003).

The promotion of a positive attitude toward writing can be fostered by using a process-oriented approach to writing that includes frequent writing opportunities, mini-lessons in critical writing skills, a community of writers producing authentic written work, conferences with teachers in which students receive constructive and individualized feedback, and opportunities for students to share and publish their work (Calkins, 1986; Graves, 1983). Many classroom teachers use these principles when they institute a Writers' Workshop (Pritchard, 1987).

Some students need more specific instruction than is provided in Writers' Workshops to be able to produce high-quality writing, however. Explicit strategies taught to these students, even those with disabilities, enable them to become strategic, self-regulating, and proficient. One well-established method is Self-Regulated Strategy Development (SRSD), which can result in improved quality, increased knowledge about writing, and more positive self-efficacy as writers. SRSD has been found to be successful in helping students write, read, and complete assignments—whether they are general education students; students with learning disabilities (Harris & Graham, 1999; Sexton, Harris, & Graham, 1998); students with behavioral disorders (Mason, Harris, & Graham, 2002); general education, gifted and talented students (De La Paz, 2005); or minority students attending schools that serve low-income populations (Graham et al., 2005). SRSD also has been demonstrated to improve performance on high-stakes tests (Berninger et al., 2006; De La Paz, Owen, & Harris, 2000).

A critical component of the SRSD approach is a strong emphasis on planning. Successful writers spend a great deal of time involved in planning activities, such as goal setting, brainstorming, and organizing, before starting to write. Students with writing difficulties—particularly students with learning disabilities—often do not plan their writing at all (Troia & Graham, 2003).

Fortunately, students can be taught to employ planning strategies to significantly improve their writing skills. They need additional support to generalize the planning strategies to new settings, which can be in the form of guided peer support (Graham et al., 2005).

Writing fluency is reduced when students have significant spelling and handwriting difficulties; for this and other reasons, deficiencies in these areas impede success and self-efficacy as writers. Direct instruction in spelling positively influences students' writing (Berninger et al., 1998), because improved spelling augments writing fluency; increases students' motivation to communicate in writing, because they and others can read it; and improves grades, because often others "equate writing ability with both spelling and quality of text produced" (Berninger et al., 2006, p. 291). When students are taught the "regular irregularities" typical in English, both their spelling and writing significantly improve. Difficulties with handwriting have a similar impact on writing (Berninger et al., 1997). Like improved spelling, improved handwriting affects writing fluency, enables others to read students' work, and improves grades because illegible writing is reflected in lowered grades.

Despite vast individual differences in skills and interests, unfortunately often students are given identical instruction in writing (Troia & Graham, 2002). Teachers who assign individualized and extensive writing assignments can quickly become overwhelmed by the sheer volume of student papers to read and grade, as well as by the need to cover a great deal of content material and to teach large classes with students of widely diverse backgrounds, levels of motivation, and writing skills. All of these factors combine to result in sparse corrective feedback and insufficient time spent in writing instruction (Troia & Maddox, 2004). A number of strategies make it possible for teachers to adapt instructional methods, materials, and expectations for individual students without becoming completely overwhelmed. These include an integrated curriculum, supported literacy, peer collaboration, and the use of technology.

An *integrated curriculum* can be an effective method to improve writing skills, because it incorporates writing into the content areas. For example, social studies and language arts can be integrated to increase an understanding of history while improving writing skills (De La Paz, 2005). Even with high-risk students, an integrated curriculum that includes cooperative classroom processes, high-interest reading material, instruction in reading comprehension, integrated instruction, and a process-based approach to writing can be successful (Stevens, 2003).

Supported literacy engages students in integrated thematic units in which they read, discuss, and write about age-appropriate texts in general education classrooms. Using this approach, and participating in the full range of challenging reading and writing activities, enable students with disabilities to perform similarly to nondisabled students even in challenging assignments such as text interpretation (Cobb Morocco, Hindin, & Mata-Aguilar, 2001).

Peer collaboration has also been found to be an effective instructional modification in teaching writing, because constructive peer feedback greatly improves the writing product that is later corrected by teachers. It also provides social reinforcement. Well-designed collaborative writing experiences enable students with and without disabilities to use their knowledge in ways that exceed their independent competence (Englert, Berry, & Dunsmore, 2001), and peer collaboration is integrated into effective writing programs (De La Paz et al., 2000).

Finally, educators can increasingly turn to *technology* to provide support for student writing. Even second-grade students make better editing choices when they type their writing (Fletcher, 2001), and after only a short period of keyboard instruction, most students can type more quickly than they can write (Bahr & Nelson, 1996). Technology can support students as they plan, draft, edit, and publish writing assignments (Bahr & Nelson, 1996; Gillette, 2006), and the use of computers (along with teacher participation, extracurricular instruction, and personalized assistance) can increase student motivation (Daniels, 2004). Sophisticated software products—such as electronic clip-art sets, digital camera products, talking-overlay creators for alternative keyboards, talking-screen creators, and word prediction programs—can assist in creating the needed individualized, intense experiences for students with disabilities and enable them to express themselves in stories and written reports (Gillette, 2001). Students of low to moderate ability particularly benefit from Summary Street, a computer tutor that guides them through successive cycles of revising with automated feedback (Franzke, Kintsch, & Caccamise, 2005).

METHODS

Preparation

To become independent writers, students must recursively follow the self-regulation cycle described in Chapter 1: *preparation*, *performance*, and *appraisal*. Students can be coached through these steps in the classroom, small groups, or individual sessions. In addition, secondary and postsecondary students should be encouraged to take extra classes in writing and study skills, to explore the many software programs that exist to assist with the writing process, and to visit learning centers at universities for help with their writing skills.

Preparatory steps in writing include observing successful models; determining audience, genre, and style; enhancing motivation; collaboratively brainstorming; researching, gathering, and reviewing all needed information; developing a preliminary organizational plan, such as an outline or a graphic organizer; breaking down complex assignments into clear, distinct, and manageable parts; and obtaining a necessary level of writing fluency by assessing and improving basic skills. For most students, these strategies must first be taught explicitly by adults and then fostered in student-regulated application.

Observing Successful Models

Students usually have had many opportunities to observe others reading long before they try to read themselves. Many students' parents start reading to them when they are toddlers, if not before, and opportunities to hear stories read aloud abound in public libraries, in preschools, and on TV shows such as *Sesame Street*. Unfortunately, there are far fewer opportunities for children to observe others using the writing process, and still fewer opportunities for children to observe models demonstrating the *coping process* in which the model makes and corrects errors. Therefore, it is particularly important that consultants and teachers deliberately demonstrate and discuss the writing process for students. In addition to observing adults in their own environments employing the writing process, students can "observe" experts employing the writing process by reading biographical material in which professional writers describe their writing strategies, such as Annie Lamott (1995). This approach is particularly effective when the student has personally read and enjoyed the writer's work.

Observing continues to be essential through advanced levels of education because increasingly difficult writing genres are required. For example, intense mentoring opportunities can be particularly helpful, as when graduate assistants collaborate with their professors on research studies. This collaboration provides students with opportunities to observe the planning, writing, and rewriting involved in the complex process of publishing research, and prepares them for independent scholarship in the future.

Determining Audience, Genre, and Style

Clearly articulating the audience before beginning to write is helpful during the preparatory phase of the writing process because the audience determines the required organizational scheme, the appropriate writing style, and the depth and breadth of information needed. Being appropriately responsive to audiences requires that students foster the ability to "put yourself in their shoes," imagine being a member of the audience, and imagine the likely responses of others as they read the written material. These skills are developed when students receive constructive feedback from teachers, parents, and peer reviewers during the writing process. In advanced writing there is often more than one audience, and developing the ability to see these multiple perspectives can be challenging. For example, psycheducational reports are read by parents and students as well as educators, and effective authors of these reports take that into consideration as they select style and vocabulary (Harvey, 1997).

Enhancing Motivation

Motivation to write can be augmented by encouraging individual students to become proficient in multiple writing genres, particularly those in which they have a high interest. When offered many choices of genres and given constructive and specific feedback, students often blossom into enthusiastic and prolific writers. Handout 10.1, Writers Workshop Genre Ideas contains hundreds of ideas to use in stimulating student writing. To help them know how to write appropriately in various genres, students need to learn that each genre has its own structure, format, appearance, purpose, audience, and set of "rules," both formal and informal. For example, recipes are written very differently from research papers. Students should be encouraged to do both serious and fun writing as they experiment with various genres. An effective method to help them learn writing genres is conducting an ongoing Writers' Workshop, during which students write independently, revise work in progress, and share writing with others.

> **Anton** dreaded the thought of writing because he had been previously told that he could not write well, and he believed what he had been told. However, Anton's dread was reversed by his sixth-grade classroom's Writers' Workshop. The teacher gave students a list of 100 enticing types of writing genres from which to choose, so every week all students in the class were busy "doing their thing." Anton had always thought that writing only involved writing compositions, so he was thrilled to be allowed to write "fun stuff"—"wanted" posters, acrostics, concrete poems, a newspaper ad for his baseball card collection, and party invitations. Soon his "Writing in Progress" folder was packed with works in various genres. He looked forward to meeting with his teacher for their "conference" and sitting in the Author's Chair to share his work with classmates. He was also proud to be asked for his feedback from others as they worked to revise their efforts. He tried many new types of writing after watching others "publish" theirs, and he loved the freedom to choose which type of writing he would work on next. Anton soon thought of writing as a tool rather than a dreaded assignment.

Collaboratively Brainstorming

Often brainstorming and talking about a writing task during the preparation phase are of enormous help to students. Such brainstorming can be with a peer, family member, or teacher.

> **John,** a high school sophomore, did pretty well in school but hated to write. One day, when he was very frustrated trying to come up with a topic for a persuasive writing assignment, his father helped by encouraging John to talk about some of the things about which he felt strongly. As John spoke about the need to place stray animals in good homes to prevent their being euthanized, his father jotted down key words. They then referred to John's textbook's "persuasive writing checklist," which John used to develop his paper. Verbally expressing his strong feelings about animals primed the pump, and John became excited about the possibility of influencing classmates (his audience) to help save animals. Once motivated, John could list many reasons why he felt strongly about this topic, and his draft almost wrote itself.

Locating Information

In the prewriting stage of the writing process, students must locate information by using research materials such as books, maps, graphics, newspapers, dictionaries, libraries, the Internet, and other reference tools, in both electronic and print forms. It is also important to ensure that students know how to use the computer catalog in the library and then learn how to locate the material, either in the stacks or through interlibrary loan. Surprisingly large numbers of older students are not independent in using these essential resources, and even college students often require additional monitoring and support as they conduct library research. Regardless of the source, after obtaining information, the student needs to review it to determine its appropriateness and comprehend the information. The effective reading strategies to process large amounts of information that were discussed in Chapter 9, such as scanning, skimming, and processing reading materials, are essential at this stage.

Developing a Preliminary Organizational Plan

Before students begin to write, they will find it very helpful to develop a preliminary organizational plan with an outline or a graphic organizer. Handout 3.1 in Chapter 3 depicts many examples of graphic organizers that can be used in this manner. Computer outlining and word-processing programs can greatly facilitate the use of outlines, particularly for students with learning disabilities (Anderson-Inman et al., 1996). Regardless of the preliminary organizational strategy used, students should be encouraged to understand that the scheme developed in the prewriting process may be significantly altered in the final product.

Assessment

Assessing students' written language takes multiple steps. First, the student's basic writing and expository writing skills are assessed, followed by the ability to self-regulate the writing process.

ASSESSMENT OF WRITING SKILLS

As with reading, many standardized assessment tools address some aspects of writing skills. Most broad-based achievement measures, such as the Comprehensive Test of Basic Skills (CTB/McGraw-Hill, 1990) and the California Achievement Tests (CTB/McGraw-Hill, 1993), include spelling and language mechanics as components. Others, such as the SAT I (Educational Testing Service, 2004) and many state achievement tests, such as the Indiana ISTEP+ require and score writing samples. The scores generated by these tests can facilitate an understanding of areas of difficulty and needed instruction. For example, if a student's language mechanics on the California Achievement Tests are below the 5th percentile, these areas will cause difficulties when that student attempts to write. However, such scores are gross measures and do not lead to effective intervention planning.

At the individual level, the Test of Written Language—Third Edition (TOWL-3; Hammill & Larsen, 1996) requires a student to generate a writing sample that is then scored for contextual conventions, contextual language, and story construction. The TOWL-3 also includes subtests that measure spelling, vocabulary, style, logical sentences, and sentence combining. The results of this assessment can be helpful in describing a student's writing skills relative to a national normative sample. Although these scores can be helpful in determining areas of academic weakness, they are not necessarily aligned with curriculum frameworks and requirements.

A more specific and targeted assessment can be completed with *curriculum-based measurement*, wherein curriculum-based probes are administered, and valid and reliable indicators of performance are calculated and graphed. In writing, these indicators might include correct letter sequences, number of words spelled correctly, and correct word sequences.

Finally, with *curriculum-based assessment*, more complex aspects of writing can be assessed through the analysis of written language samples (Nelson & Van Meter, 2002). This is most effective when the assessor employs the grading rubric used by a student's teacher to conduct the analysis. Alternatively, Handout 10.2, Reviewer's Checklist and Handout 10.3, Writing Applications Guide could be used.

ASSESSMENT OF THE WRITING PROCESS

Assessment of a student's writing process is best assessed through combining curriculum-based assessment, interviewing, and trace methodology. To assess students' writing process using *curriculum-based assessment*, students are led through an analysis of their methods. During interviews, students are asked to describe how they deal with various aspects of writing assignments. In trace methodology, the consultant or teacher examines observable indicators of the student's writing strategies and process, including notes, outlines and story maps, drafts, and rewrites. When using any of these assessment approaches, the consultant, teacher, and student collaborate in considering the student's use of preparation, performance, and appraisal. A menu of interview questions is included in Worksheet 10.2, Writing Questions. In addition, Worksheet 10.1, Self-Appraisal of Writing Skills and Worksheet 10.3, Writing Strategies Checklist can be useful to summarize the results of the findings.

After considering the results of standardized tests, curriculum-based measurement, curriculum-based assessment, trace methodology, and interviews, the consultant, teacher, and student can determine curriculum-based strengths and needs. These are then used to establish goals, suggest interventions, evaluate change after intervention, and initiate the next round of planning.

Spelling, Handwriting, and Production Skills

As discussed previously, spelling and production methods such as handwriting and keyboarding affect writing fluency, which in turn affects the writing process. Therefore, it is important to provide supplemental instruction in these basic processes during the preparation phase of writing instruction, so that a lack of writing fluency is not a deterrent.

Further, although we may think of spelling as part of the elementary school curriculum, we are actually required to learn how to spell words throughout our lives; the words simply get longer and more complex, while less direct instruction is provided. Even for native English speakers this is an unfortunate problem, because English spelling is complex. Although some words can be spelled phonetically, many sounds can be spelled in multiple ways. To spell accurately, students must maintain precise visual images of words, so that they can determine when a word "looks right." Attaining English spelling skills can be particularly elusive for students with learning disabilities and for those whose native language is not English. Deficiencies in spelling often remain long after remedial efforts have improved reading skills for these students.

With the advent of word processors and spell checkers, students have ready access to spelling correction, and some individuals conclude that learning to spell is therefore archaic and unnecessary (Mooney & Cole, 2000). On the other hand, no one has uninterrupted access to word processors and spell checkers. A serious inability to spell can embarrass students in both their academic and personal lives. Strategies to improve spelling skills are enumerated in Handout 10.4, Steps to Spelling Mastery and can include the following:

- *Backchaining,* which involves making and using worksheets showing each spelling word arranged vertically with progressively missing letters. The student says the word and studies its spelling on the first line; he or she covers the correctly spelled word and fills in the missing letter(s). This latter step is repeated until the word is spelled without any visual cues (e.g., "heft, __eft, __ __ ft, __ __ __ t, __ __ __ __"). To save time and provide a learning experience, students themselves can be enlisted to generate their backchaining practice sheets as homework assignments and then fill in the missing letters in subsequent lessons.
- Looking for and highlighting *small words within larger words.* For example, a student might highlight prefixes and suffixes and memorize their meaning (e.g., "im=" means "not").
- Learning to *separate a word into syllables marked with vertical lines,* remembering that each syllable must have a vowel in it; then pronouncing each syllable as it is written.
- *Vocabulary worksheets* that require (1) each word spelled correctly, (2) its part(s) of speech, (3) definition(s), (4) student-made sentence(s) using each meaning of the word properly, (5) synonyms and antonyms, and (6) a picture representing each meaning of the word.
- Creating and reviewing *flashcards,* each with a word on one side and its definition on the back.
- Creating a *personal dictionary* of often-misspelled words. It can be particularly helpful to teach students to analyze these words to discover personal patterns of errors.
- Using the *multisensory (AVKO) method,* where students (1) hear the word being pronounced correctly (Auditory) while looking at the word (Visual); and (2) "write" the letters of the word with their an index finger (Kinesthetic) while pronouncing the sounds blended into the word (Oral) (McCabe, 1985).
- Using mnemonics for homophones. For example, to differentiate *vane, vein,* and *vain,* a student might think of weather*vanes* with the letters NE for northeast; of *veins* that carry blood and make people who hate the sight of blood shriek, "eeeeeee!" when they see it; running for the train was in *vain;* and a *vain* person says, "Ain't nobody better than me!"

HANDWRITING AND PRODUCTION SKILLS

In addition to spelling, writing fluency is affected by handwriting or other production skills. Many students benefit from direct instruction in keyboarding and word-processing skills (including cutting, pasting, and other revision mechanisms), as well as from using spelling and grammar checkers, electronic dictionaries, thesauruses, and encyclopedias. Furthermore, students must be taught to check for the accuracy of computer-generated corrections before accepting them. For instance, they must learn how to critically review suggestions generated by spelling and grammar checkers and determine which of the alternatives is correct.

Performance

With no appreciation of writing as a *process,* freshman **Alberto** incorrectly assumed that he could produce a completed piece of writing in one step. After he obtained a D on his first college essay, he signed up for tutoring. His tutor first gave Alberto a laminated card with the five stages of the writing process to keep, and then she taught him each stage during the next week. To help with *prewriting,* she modeled brainstorming a list of possible topics based on her experiences and interests, and showed him how one idea often sparks another. Then she had Alberto take about 3 minutes to brainstorm his own list of ideas, choose the best topic, and complete a "mind map" template of the main ideas and supporting details about his topic.

She then explained that as Alberto wrote his rough *draft* that evening, he should convert each main idea into a paragraph enriched with details and feelings, without regard for spelling and punctuation.

The next day, his tutor reviewed how to complete the next steps of the writing process: *revising* and *editing*. First, Alberto was asked to read his draft to another student, and then to revise and reorganize it based upon that feedback. Next, his tutor helped Alberto "manage his vocabulary" by incorporating rich action verbs and vivid adjectives and adverbs, to encourage readers to form their own images based on what he described. Finally, his tutor gave Alberto a thesaurus and a list of transition words to help him move smoothly from one idea to the next. After his revisions were completed, Alberto edited his draft for grammar, spelling, punctuation, capitalization, and paragraph structure by using a Writing Conventions Checklist, a computer spell checker, and a style manual. As he submitted his writing to his professor (the *publishing* stage of the writing process), Alberto knew that his essay was a solid piece of writing.

Because they generally read only the polished and final versions of written material, students often have no idea that even the most expert writers write and rewrite repeatedly. Expecting themselves to produce a polished and final version on the first try, and finding that to be impossible, can result in sheer aggravation or paralysis due to "writer's block." Teachers and consultants can counteract this paralysis by teaching students the writing process. As illustrated in the vignette above, the five steps of the writing process are (1) prewriting, (2) drafting, (3) revising, (4) editing, and (5) publishing. The components of these steps are listed in Worksheet 10.1.

The *prewriting* step has been discussed in the "Preparation" section of this chapter. When *drafting*, students organize the information and ideas that were developed in the prewriting process, and churn out a first draft without regard for spelling or grammar. They also select reporting techniques such as charts, graphs, models, maps, pictures, and photographs in addition to written narratives. Charts and graphs need not be limited to the subjects with which they are traditionally associated. For example, a map can be used in English to indicate dialect use, in addition to being used in history to indicate political divisions (Devine, 1987).

After the first draft is completed, the student requests that a reviewer (peer, parent, teacher, or consultant) provide feedback. Pertinent questions to consider are found in Handout 10.2. At this stage, the reviewers must be careful to avoid being overly critical or focusing on grammar and spelling. After receiving the reviewer's feedback, the student *revises*. Often the student will need to gather additional information to include in the revision. As they revise, students also consider the structure of their writing, making sure that every sentence is complete, that each paragraph focuses on a main idea, that paragraphs are arranged in a logical sequence, and that the reader is provided with transitions from one idea to the next. Students often need help thinking of transition words that increase the clarity and impact of their writing. A comprehensive list of possibilities is included in Handout 10.5, Transition Words.

During *editing*, students polish their writing; proofread for success or failure in answering the purpose of the assignment; ensure that they meet the needs of the audience; and check for legibility, neatness, spelling, capitalization, and punctuation errors. The acronym CAPS can help students remember essential elements to check before publication (Capitalization, Appearance, Punctuation, and Spelling). If a word-processing program is used, the student uses the spell checker and grammar checker, and then double-checks for inadvertent errors.

Finally, the work is *published*. In schools, particularly in the early grades, written assignments are often manually recopied in polished versions. For students with poor handwriting, however, teachers should consider accepting computer-prepared assignments at a relatively early age. When handwriting has been taught for several years and the student continues to be unsuccessful even with intense individualized instruction, printing or using computers should be allowed in the interest of improved communication. Regardless of the age at which the student turns to computer use, its word-processing capabilities greatly facilitate legibility and efficiency in written assignments.

> No one, not even **Raymond**, could read his extremely poor cursive handwriting. In desperation, his sixth-grade teachers suggested that he print. Raymond was thrilled with this liberating suggestion; his family members were happy that they could read his printed phone messages; and his teachers were shocked to discover the insightful thinking that he was finally able to convey.

Appraisal

During the appraisal phase of writing, the student reviews the writing experience; evaluates it for successes and difficulties; and reviews the experience by applying the questions "What did I do?", "How well did it work?", and "What do I need to change?" (Dawson & Guare, 2004). In addition, many of the assessment strategies discussed above, such as interview questions, trace methodology, and curriculum-based assessment, can be useful tools in the appraisal process. These subjective techniques are helpful to assess strengths and weaknesses in self-regulation, particularly when augmented by quantitative outcome measure data such as scores on spelling tests and grades on essays.

Sharing the rubrics that are used to evaluate writing with students, and having them use the rubrics to evaluate their own writing, can be a very valuable strategy. For example, Handout 10.3 was developed by Dr. Chickie-Wolfe (2005c) based on the rubric used in the Indiana high-stakes tests, ISTEP+ (Indiana State Department of Education, 2005). After having been introduced to this rubric, former students have reported that they continue to use it to appraise their writing. As students become independent, they can use tools such as Worksheets 10.1, 10.2, and 10.3 to assess their own work and modify future strategies.

Help Students Develop Their Personal Learning Guides (HILLs)

The writing strategies that students develop will need to be modified as they advance through their schooling; the strategies that are effective for a fifth-grade creative writing assignment will not be effective for writing a dissertation. Therefore, students should be encouraged to keep both completed and blank copies of assessment and intervention sheets in their Personal Learning Guides, so that they can continually reflect upon and readjust their writing strategies. Materials pertinent to this topic and appropriate for inclusion in the writing portion of the binder include the following:

Worksheet 10.1. Writing Strategies Checklist
Worksheet 10.2. Writing Questions
Worksheet 10.3. Self-Appraisal of Previous Writing Skills
Handout 10.1. Writers' Workshop Genre Ideas
Handout 10.2. Reviewer's Checklist
Handout 10.3. Writing Applications Guide
Handout 10.4. Steps to Spelling Mastery
Handout 10.5. Transition Words

WORKSHEET 10.1.

Writing Strategies Checklist

Student ______________________________ Date ________________

Before I wrote:

__ I observed or looked at a good example.

I knew the reason I was writing was:

__ to communicate quickly (email, shopping list),
__ to demonstrate what I know to a teacher (essay question, math exposition),
__ to express myself creatively, or
__ to provide new information to a larger audience (article, book).

I decided:

__ My audience is ____________________.
__ My style would be very casual, informal, formal, or professional.

I prepared by:

__ Collaboratively brainstorming ideas with someone (a study buddy or parent).
__ Researching, gathering, and reviewing all information needed.
__ Developing a preliminary organization plan (outline or graphic organizer).
__ Breaking down complex writing assignments into clear, distinct, and manageable parts.

While I wrote:

__ I wrote a very *rough first draft* based on my preliminary organization plan.
__ I obtained feedback that focused on content, not spelling or grammar.
__ I researched and reviewed additional information (if needed).
__ I incorporated reviewer comments and added details and further information (if needed).
__ I corrected for structure (complete sentences, each paragraph focused on a main idea, paragraphs arranged in a logical sequence, transitions from one idea to the next).
__ I revised my organizational plan (if needed).
__ I wrote my *second draft*, taking into consideration the structural corrections and new organizational plan.
__ I checked for mechanics (grammar, spelling, punctuation, capital letters; if I used a word-processing program, I ran grammar and spell checkers and then double-checked myself); if appropriate, I had another person check as well.
__ I incorporated corrections.
__ I reread from my audience's perspective(s), compared my work with the grading rubric (if available), and revised again for clarity.
__ I published the *final version*.

(contiinued)

Writing Strategies Checklist *(page 2 of 2)*

During the writing process, I monitored how well my strategies worked by asking myself:

__ Does this strategy help me avoid procrastinating?

__ Does this strategy help me organize the information?

__ Does this strategy help me convey information clearly?

After I finished writing:

__ I decided which writing strategies worked well and how I should change them in the future.

__ I determined that I communicated well with my audience.

Notes:

WORKSHEET 10.2.

Writing Questions

1. Where did the idea for the writing come from? Was it interesting? If not, how could you have selected a more interesting topic?

2. How did you research the topic? Where else might material have been found?

3. What organizers did you use before starting to write?

4. How long before the due date was the first draft completed?

5. Who reviewed the first draft? Were they helpful? If not, who might be more helpful?

6. How were spelling uncertainties or errors corrected?

7. Were charts, graphs, maps, or other reporting methods besides writing included? If so, do skills for any of these methods need improvement?

8. How legible was the final product? Do handwriting or keyboarding skills need improvement?

9. How might the steps taken for this assignment be improved upon for a future assignment?

WORKSHEET 10.3.

Self-Appraisal of Previous Writing Skills

Prewriting	Information sources I have used successfully: Writing genres I have mastered: Organizers (outlines, graphic organizers) I have used successfully:
Drafting	Was the rough draft completed?
Reviewing	Reviewers who gave me helpful feedback:
Revising	Was feedback incorporated? Was the draft revised for clarity, content, and transitions?
Editing	Which words do I often misspell? Which grammatical errors do I need to watch for?
Publishing	Were grades and comments on my writing positive? Were they helpful? Explain.
Appraising	Which writing strategies work well for me? Which writing strategies don't work well for me? What steps can I take to increase positive comments and use more successful strategies?

HANDOUT 10.1.

Writers' Workshop Genre Ideas

Poems: Concrete, Acrostic, Free Verse, Sonnet, Haiku, Lyric, Limerick, Couplet, Hyperbole, Onomatopoeia, Cinquain
Mysteries or ghost stories
Short stories
Short Chapter Books
Myths
Legends
Fables
Folktales
Letters: Friendly, Business, Love, To the Editor, Voice of the People, Complimentary, Complaint, Suggestion, Apology, to Santa Claus
Advertisements
Posters: Wanted (contemporary, based on political figures, historic, or illusive/abstract)
For Sale: Informational, Instructional, Entertaining, Lost: Animal, Person, or Memory
Lists: Grocery, Famous People, Famous Places, Wishes, Friends, Accomplishments, Dreams, Books read, Favorites like foods, trips, color, Boys' names, Girls' names, Nicknames, Humorous names, Synonyms, Antonyms, Associations, Fast-Food Places, Candy Bars, Things to Avoid, Diseases, Sounds, Musical Instruments, Songs, Things that are Heavy, etc.
Personal Narratives
Persuasive Essays
Historical Fiction
Technical Writing
Hieroglyphics
Invitations
Short Stories
Science Fiction
Expository Writing (non-fiction): Factual writing with citations of references
Research Papers
Reports
Fictional Writing
Holiday Writing: Stories, Famous Places, Costumes, Customs, Vocabulary Words, Foods
Greeting Cards
How-To Writing (step-by-step directions with illustrations)
Self-Help Writing (ideas that help others become better)
Picture Captions
Recipes
Calendars
Price Lists
Quotations
Chants
Cheers
Resumés
Rap
Job Applications
Newsletters
Proposals
Grants
Dictionaries: Often-misspelled words, Action Verbs, Descriptive Adjectives and Adverbs
Manuals
Magazine Articles
Newspaper Articles: Features, Police Blotter Summaries, Retractions, Headlines, Sports Stories
Boys' and Girls' names That Go Together (Example: Louis and Louise)
Formal First Names and Their Nicknames (Example: Michael and Mike)
Funny Names with Occupations (Example: An Optometrist named Dr. I. C. Spots)
Sarcastic Retorts

(continued)

Writers' Workshop Genre Ideas *(page 2 of 3)*

Alliterations
Similes
Metaphors
Jokes: Knock-knock, puns, funny personal experiences, "What do you get when you cross a . . . ?"
Weather Reports
Almanac Entries
Encyclopedia Entries
Diaries
Journals
Short Books
Children's Picture Books
Creative Writing
Idioms with literal illustrations
Adventure Stories
Animal Stories
True Life Stories
Romance stories or poems
Comic Books
Bills
Receipts
Inventories
Addresses
Phone numbers
Email addresses
Favorite websites
Family Trees
Abstracts
Summaries
Mind Maps
Venn Diagrams
Flow Charts
Catalogs
Flyers
TriFolds
Pamphlets
Notes: Thank you, Memos, Corrections, Congratulations, Informational
Announcements: Births, Engagements, Weddings, Mergers/Acquisitions, Name Changes, Graduations, Awards, Accomplishments
Study Guides
Outlines
Book Reports
Commercials
Product Labels: Medicine bottles, clothing, pillows, mattresses, cereal boxes, bottles, cans, packages, CDs, DVDs, Appliances, Smoke Alarms, Candy Bars
Book Covers: Front, Inside, Back
Book Dedications and Acknowledgements
Glossaries
Indexes
Appendices
Notices: Classroom, School, Public Auctions, Estate Sales, Garage Sale, End of Business Sales
Warnings
Nutritional Information
Marketing (designing and packaging a new product)
Languages (common words said in different languages and word origins)
Television Anchorpersons' scripts
Countries and Religions
States and Capitals

(continued)

Writers' Workshop Genre Ideas *(page 3 of 3)*

Websites
Blogs
Email messages
Chat Room Conversations
State Parks Information
Plays
Screenplays
Ideas for New Television Shows
Ideas for New Movies
Guides and Guidelines
Song Lyrics
Nursery Rhymes
Terror Alerts
Story Starters
Movie Reviews
Book Reviews
Food Critic (restaurant or school cafeteria food reviews)
Interviews
Interrogations
Infomercials
Television Shopping Product Ads
Credit Reports
Fictional Movie Credits
Toy Catalog Descriptions
Contemporary Breaking News Flashes (television, radio, newspaper, Internet)
Historical News Flashes (Town Criers, Caveman, Native American Indians, etc.)
Directions: How to Get to a Nearby Location, How to Make Something, How to Get Home from School, How to Solve a Problem, How to Resolve a Conflict, or How to Study
What If . . . ?
Can You Picture . . . ?
Travel Brochures
911 Dispatcher Responses
Lecture Notes
Student Excuses
Animal Commands
Directions for Playing a New Game
Longest Run-On Sentences
Funny But Confusing Sentences (Example: "Having three legs, the boy sat on the stool.")
Names of New or Improved Products and Their Uses
Words typed by only the right hand on the keyboard (Example: "jump")
Words typed by only the left hand on the keyboard (Example: "faster")
Lists of words that can be made from the letters of a long word
Travel Expense Accounts
A Family's Monthly Budget
Other ideas: Suggestions from Students with Teacher Approval (Because the list of possible writing genres is endless, student input should always be welcomed and encouraged.)

HANDOUT 10.2.

Reviewer's Checklist

When you are reviewing a first draft, check for the following:

Is there a clear main idea or thesis?

Does the writing meet the intention of the assignment?

Does each paragraph have a topic sentence or main idea?

Are there sufficient supporting details to support each main idea?

Is every sentence complete?

When you are reviewing a revised version, check for each of the points above. In addition, check the following:

Are there good transitions from one topic to another?

Is the writing clear?

Does the writing interest the reader?

Are there errors in spelling?

Are there errors in grammar?

Are there patterns to these errors?

HANDOUT 10.3.

Writing Applications Guide

S Style

O Organization

I Ideas

L Length

Style:

- S Supporting details
- N No rambling
- I In-depth information
- F Focused on topic
- F Fully explores topic

Organization:

- S Sequence
- L Logical progression
- O Order is clear
- B Beginning, middle, and end

Ideas:

- V Verbs are strong
- V Varied sentence patterns
- O Original
- W Word usage

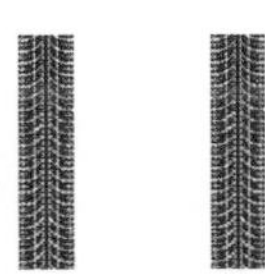

- S Sounds natural
- C Challenging vocabulary
- I Interesting
- D Details are rich
- D Descriptions are vivid

Length:

- L Lots of thinking and title
- G Great story

HANDOUT 10.4.

Steps to Spelling Mastery

1. Keep a list of words you would *like* to know how to spell.
2. Use *backchaining* (for example, "heft, __eft, __ __ ft, __ __ __ t, __ __ __ __").
3. Separate words into *syllables*, remembering that each syllable needs a vowel; then pronounce each syllable as it is written.
4. *Cover–copy–compare*.
5. Make *vocabulary worksheets* with each word, its part(s) of speech, definition(s), sentence(s) using the word, synonyms, antonyms, and picture(s).
6. Make and use *flashcards*, each with a word on one side and its definition on the back.
7. Use your ears, mouth, eyes, hand, and mind to learn:
   a. *Listen* carefully to (and possibly look up) the word's correct pronunciation.
   b. *Speak* it.
   c. Make a visual image of the correctly spelled word by looking at it carefully and then *picturing* it with your eyes closed.
   d. *Write* it several times, each time checking for correctness.
   e. *Remember* a sentence using the word correctly in context.
8. Make a *personal dictionary* of often-misspelled words, and analyze these to find patterns.
9. Carefully look at and *analyze* words for roots, prefixes, suffixes, and other patterns to link the current word with previously learned words.
10. Use *memory tricks* (for example, "excellent" and "cemetery" have only e's).
11. Routinely refer to a *misspeller's dictionary.*

HANDOUT 10.5.

Transition Words

Opinion

again	finally	in addition	moreover
also	first, second	in the first place	next
besides	further	lastly	similarly
equally important	furthermore	likewise	

Paragraph Concluders

in any case	for the preceding reasons	in other words	on the whole
in any event	in brief	in short	without a doubt
in the final analysis	in conclusion		

Connectors

after	as long as	due to	until
although	as soon as	even though	unless
and	because	if in order to	when
as	because of	since	whenever
as if	before	though	while

Detail Introducers

for example	for instance	as evidence

Cause and Effect

accordingly	consequently	hence	so that
as	due to	if . . . then	therefore
as a result	for	in effect	this results in
as a result of	for this reason	since	thus
because			

Compare and Contrast

although	for instance	in spite of	on the other hand
as if	furthermore	instead	otherwise
also	however	just as	provided that
and	compared to	likewise	similarly
another	even if	like	still
as opposed to	for example	nevertheless	too
besides	in addition	moreover	whereas
but	in a like manner	of course	while
by contrast	in the same way	on the contrary	yet
conversely			

(continued)

Transition Words *(page 2 of 2)*

Chronological Order

after that	before	in the end	since
afterward	earlier	in the meantime	then
at first	eventually	later	soon
at once	finally	meanwhile	subsequently
at the present	following	next	then
at the same time	in the beginning	now	thereafter

Spatial Order

above	beneath	into	to the side of
across	between	next to	toward
against	beyond	on	under
along	by	opposite	underneath
among	down	outside	up
around	facing	over	upon
at	in front of	throughout	within
behind	in the middle of	to	without
below	inside		

Order of Importance

above all	more important	of less importance	to begin with
best of all	most important	of major concern	worst of all
least important	of greater importance	of minor concern	

11

Empowering Students to Master Math, Science, and Technology

To meet the demands of our rapidly changing world, students need to have sophisticated skills in math, science, and technology. Many times these skills will need to be self-taught.

OVERVIEW

Ted always starts his adult-education computer classes by asking his students what they already know, so he can build on their knowledge and tie the new learning to previously learned information. He then gives a general overview of the topic, presents subsystems and shows how they interact, and provides multiple examples of applied problem solving. He gives his students choices of assignments to facilitate a high level of interest, and then watches them actually perform tasks at the computer to assess and monitor their skills. Students who catch on quickly are highly curious, enjoy hands-on learning, and have a desire to produce high-quality work. They are neither intimidated by technology nor handicapped by perfectionism. One day after class, a student stopped to ask for help with his new iPod; he had read the manual that came with it, but found it "confusing and useless." Ted smiled and confessed he didn't know iPod technology himself. "Just keep trying to apply the things you already understand, and you'll probably get it. Rarely does new technology involve totally new concepts—first relate back to technology you already understand, and then ask others questions. Let me know how it goes!"

Skills in math, science, and technology are important for school success and are highly correlated with adult employment and income (Rivera-Batiz, 1992). When high school students are not successful in math and science courses, they cannot take college-level courses in business, science, math, or technology, and are excluded from many future employment opportunities (Crosnoe, Lopez-Gonzalez, & Muller, 2004). Even in non-technology fields this knowledge is critical: A fundamental knowledge of computers is essential in today's world; math skills are required to manage personal finances; and science knowledge improves problem solving in both personal and professional lives.

Although everyone's level of math, science, and technology knowledge is of concern, it is of even greater concern for minority and economically disadvantaged students. Many of them enroll in fewer high school math and science classes than majority students do, and many are tracked into lower-level courses regardless of grade point average or scores on standardized tests (Kelly, 2004; Zuniga, Olson, & Winter, 2005), especially in academically rigorous schools (Crosnoe et al., 2004). Latino and African American university students indicate they feel that their high schools should have provided them with higher-quality instruction in math, science, critical thinking, and study skills; that they should have had greater access to college preparatory courses; and that their race and ethnicity had considerable impact on their high school experiences (Thompson & Joshua-Shearer, 2002).

This chapter addresses strategies specific to learning mathematics, science, and technology. It contains suggestions appropriate for students who are having difficulties in any of these areas throughout elementary, secondary, and postsecondary schooling. For a concise summary of concepts presented in this chapter, see Worksheet 11.1, Math, Science, and Technology Strategy Checklist.

RESEARCH FOUNDATIONS

Many students and adults are not skilled independent learners in math, science, or technology. Many study strategies discussed in previous chapters, ranging from time management to reading for comprehension, apply to the acquisition of math and science skills and knowledge. There are also some study strategies specific to these areas, but these strategies are so rarely taught that 50% of college-level math and engineering majors fail exams and courses, and an even greater number of students avoid these courses altogether. However, math, science, and technology study skills are fortunately quite teachable and can lead to significantly improved grades (Boelkins & Pfaff, 1998; Seon & King, 1997).

Over the past few decades a considerable change has occurred in the focus of math and science education. Whereas it previously emphasized memorizing isolated facts, procedures, concepts and skills, it now emphasizes gaining conceptual *understanding* and acquiring mathematical and scientific *dispositions*. The National Council of Teachers of Mathematics, the American Association for the Advancement of Science, and the National Research Council concur that to attain such understanding, students must constructively interact with material and "assume control and agency over their own learning and problem-solving activities" (De Corte, Verschaffel, & Op 't Eynde, 2000, p. 687). High achievers, low achievers, and students with disabilities all benefit from constructivist-oriented, hands-on instruction and activities because they gain more extensive and integrated knowledge, are more engaged metacognitively, and develop better information processing (McCarthy, 2005; Wu & Tsai, 2005).

Although the ability to self-regulate learning is essential for successful constructivist learning, traditional math and science curricula tend to be highly teacher-regulated. Teaching students to self-regulate in math and science appears to be more difficult than teaching the same processes in reading and writing—possibly because adults tend to view math skills as discrete, or because they do not have deep-level math knowledge and feelings of mathematical self-efficacy themselves (Ross, Hogaboam-Gray, & Rolheiser, 2002). Even for those teachers who have a strong commitment to constructivist approaches, it appears difficult to maintain productive dialogue about mathematical concepts in the classroom (Williams & Baxter, 1996) or to engage students in reciprocal learning (Resnick, 1988).

The conflict between the constructivist and traditional methods of education in math, science, and technology tends to make the diagnosis of learning difficulties in these areas problematic, because what is considered a disability from one perspective (such as fact fluency) is discounted by the other (Geary, 2004). Furthermore, compared to research in reading, research regarding the causes of difficulties/disabilities in math is much less extensive (Augustyniak, Murphy, & Phillips, 2005; Geary, 2005; Mazzocco, 2005), and research in learning difficulties/disabilities in science and technology is almost nonexistent.

Nonetheless, some factors that contribute to difficulties in these areas have been identified (Fuchs et al., 2005). Students can experience difficulties with math, science, and technology because of erroneous beliefs about themselves or the subject area; persistent frustration or anxiety; inadequate attention-monitoring strategies, poor working memory, or limited memory retrieval strategies; deficiencies in fundamental skills; inadequate visual–spatial skills; phonological processing deficiencies; reading comprehension deficiencies; inadequate problem-solving skills; an inability to generate and test hypotheses; deficiencies in written language; or poor test-taking strategies.

As in other areas of learning, students must experience guided instruction, repetition, and successive refinement of skills in order to become proficient in math, science, and technology. To develop self-regulatory, intentional approaches to learning, students must *observe and recognize* success in another person's performance; *emulate and adopt* the model's pattern and process; *self-monitor* while learning new strategies until these strategies become automatic; and *self-regulate* in adapting to changed tasks and audiences (Schunk & Zimmerman, 1994). After observing a model select strategies and correct errors until a solution is attained, students engage in guided practice while the instructor gives hints and immediate feedback. Supports are then gradually faded until the students discern and correct errors independently (Mathan & Koedinger, 2005).

Individuals who are successful in math, science, and technology are expert problem solvers. They use the same basic problem-solving strategies and skills, regardless of the type or size of the problem—whether it is adding two digits or determining the cure for a fatal disease. That is, they tap their knowledge base, determine the nature of the problem to be solved, generate an adequate representation of the problem, have a foundational knowledge of procedures and strategies to use in solving the problem, utilize metacognitive strategies to assess the problem parameters, select and apply appropriate strategies, monitor their strategy use during problem solving, and modify strategies when appropriate (Scheid, 1993; Schunk & Zimmerman, 1994).

METHODS

Effective instruction in math, science, and technology focuses on concepts and relationships as well as skills; provides students with problem-solving strategies; attends to students' beliefs, attitudes, and affect regarding math, science, and technology; goes beyond basic skills to a comprehensive curriculum; is sensitive and responsive to the students' skills and cognitive-developmental level; builds upon previous knowledge; includes questioning and listening to students; employs dyadic and small-group instruction; models problem solving, particularly by using coping models; employs manipulatives and hands-on learning; frequently assesses student knowledge and problem-solving strategies; and employs student self-evaluation. Teachers introduce and support constructive and goal-oriented learning that activates students' prior knowledge, and help them build conceptual frameworks that organize fragmented ideas into meaningful wholes (Coleman, 2005). They also embed instruction "in authentic contexts that are rich in resources and offer ample opportunities for interaction and collaboration" (De Corte et al., 2000, p. 691).

Once again, self-regulation and attention to *preparation, performance*, and *appraisal* differentiate skilled from unskilled learners in math, science, and technology (De Corte & Somers, 1982; De Corte et al., 2000; Krutetskii, 1976). During the *preparation* phase, skilled learners decide on a learning goal; connect the activity to "real life"; brainstorm ideas with a study buddy, teacher, or parent; gather and review all needed information; simplify the problem into clear, distinct, and manageable parts; read the problem carefully and ensure comprehension; think and plan before beginning to solve the problem; employ a concrete, hands-on approach to solve new types of problems; ensure that they have the fundamental knowledge needed to complete the required tasks; construct a diagram of the problem; check whether any general strategies are appropriate; relate the new problem to previously solved problems; design a hierarchical solution plan; and ensure that they understand relevant readings.

During the *performance* phase, students implement the solution plan. They estimate the answer and use that estimation to check results. They obtain help and additional information when needed, and constantly monitor progress by asking themselves: "What is my goal today? What am I doing? Why am I doing it? Am I staying focused? How will what I am doing help me? Did I reach my goal?"

During the *appraisal* phase, students check that all important information was used, that the solution fits with estimates and predictions, and that the solution makes sense. If not, they identify the source of the discrepancy and recycle through preparation and performance. After verifying the solution, self-regulating students determine how the solution might have been differently obtained, check the appropriateness of the original diagram, relate the problem to previously solved problems, and determine how a similar problem might be more effectively solved in the future. Finally, self-regulating students consider which strategies worked well (or not) and make notes about anything that should be changed in the future.

Preparation

Skilled learners in math, science, and technology take considerable time during the preparation phase of problem solving. In contrast, unskilled learners spend almost no time in preparation and tend to "dive in," using a trial-and-error approach. Schoenfeld (1992) found that students working on unfamiliar math problems spent 5% of their time reading the problem and 95% of the time exploring possible solutions. They demonstrated a total lack of cognitive and metacognitive self-regulatory strategies. In contrast, experts spent 5% of their time reading the problem, 70% of their time analyzing and planning, and only 25% exploring and verifying solutions. The experts continually reflected on their progress, and backtracked and returned to analyze in a recursive cycle when necessary.

Assessment

Assessing students' ability to learn math, science, and technology is multifaceted for several reasons. First, the assessment of knowledge in these fields is difficult, because they are highly complex; a student may be proficient in one area or subarea (such as the ability to logically process geometric proofs), yet have considerable difficulty with another (such as memorization of geometric formulas). And because these fields are so broad, no single instrument can adequately assess all domains and subdomains. Second, some areas fundamental to learning in these fields—including the ability to focus attention, use working memory effectively, and apply visual–spatial facility—are neither easily observed nor easily assessed. Moreover, the deep conceptual understanding and systematic, creative problem solving integral to success in math, science, and technology do not lend themselves to traditional test procedures.

However, psychologists can assess some psychological processes that underpin the ability to understand mathematical and scientific concepts. Methods to assess attention and working memory are addressed in Chapter 8. Nonverbal problem-solving and visual–spatial skills can be assessed with certain subtests of the Wechsler Intelligence Scale for Children—Fourth Edition (WISC-IV; Wechsler, 2003), such as Block Design and Matrix Reasoning.

Assessing whether or not students understand critical semantics in math and science problems can be accomplished by using *error analysis*, or giving students problems with errors and seeing whether they can detect them. For example, students might be given word problems that are not solvable because the problems are missing essential information (Van Haneghan, 1990).

As is the case for previous areas, most broad-based achievement measures include some assessment of math skills. For example, the Comprehensive Test of Basic Skills (CTB/McGraw-Hill, 1990); the California Achievement Tests (CTB/McGraw-Hill, 1993); the Woodcock–Johnson III (WJ III; Woodcock et al., 2001); and the Wechsler Individual Achievement Test—Second Edition (WIAT-II; Wechsler, 2001) yield scores that consultants can use to help teachers, students, and parents understand areas of difficulty and strength. However, often the results of these global standardized tests are not useful for assessing math and science skills, because they are too general, yield little information relative to a student's ability to handle specific material, and do not lead to effective intervention planning.

A few standardized tests focus exclusively on math skills; the Test of Mathematical Abilities—Second Edition (TOMA-2; Brown, Cronin, & McEntire, 1994) is one example. Furthermore, math, science, and technology skills can alternatively be assessed via *authentic, curriculum-based measures* that integrate learning goals. This process has been found to be more accurate than teacher judgments in most areas of students' mathematics functioning (Eckert, Dunn, & Codding, 2006). To assess math through curriculum-based measurement, the student is given 1 minute to solve a set of curriculum-based problems. Next, the number of digits computed correctly are counted, recorded, and graphed to indicate progress over time. A tool to facilitate this process is Monitoring Basic Skills Progress—Second Edition (Fuchs, Hamlett, & Fuchs, 1999).

Assessing the process of learning math, science, and technology can be accomplished through *think-aloud* and *trace methodology* focusing on the following (Schoenfeld, 1992):

1. What are you doing? (Can you precisely describe it?)
2. Why are you doing it? (How does it fit into your solution?)
3. How does what you are doing help you? (What will you do with the outcome?)

Often these processing answers and analyses can be written by students in their math journals to be shared with peers and/or teachers.

Performance

Fostering Positive Motivation and Beliefs

As described in Chapter 4, developing a positive goal orientation is essential for independent learning. Unfortunately, considerable confusion currently exists about the goals of math and science education. Although learning for understanding and acquiring a mathematical and scientific disposition have been defined as critical, there continues to be considerable interest in students' memorizing facts, as evidenced by frequent derisive media reports regarding math and science facts that "the average person" does not know. This conflict is confusing for students, teachers, and family members and is detrimental to student motivation. In our opinion, this is not an either–or situation: Students need to have some basic grounding in math and science facts in order to be able to succeed as conceptual thinkers, but they also need to have an understanding of concepts in order to avoid being locked into minutiae.

BELIEFS ABOUT THE SELF

Students have distinct self-concepts in different academic subjects by fifth grade (Marsh, 1986). Many students suffer from negative beliefs regarding their ability to succeed in math, science, and technology, which in turn affects their approach to problem solving in these domains (Ames & Archer, 1988). Students who like science and believe they can do well achieve at a higher level, regardless of demographic status (Von Secker, 2004). Beliefs regarding math and science self-efficacy are more closely linked to participation in math and science classes in high school than are math and science grades during fifth and sixth grades (Simpkins, Davis-Kean, & Eccles, 2006). Students' appraisals of adults' beliefs regarding the importance of (and students' competence in) math and science, as well as their perceptions of adult support, predicted the students' own self-perceived importance, competence, scholastic behavior, and performance in these courses. Even after controlling for maternal education, Latino students reported lower perceived competence than did white students (Bouchey & Harter, 2005).

BELIEFS ABOUT MATH, SCIENCE, AND TECHNOLOGY

Students often develop erroneous beliefs concerning math, science, and technology that have a negative impact on their performance in these fields. For example, students often believe that there is only one correct answer, that there is only one correct method to solve problems, that one should be able to arrive at that correct answer quickly, that expertise in math consists of being able to remember and follow absolute rules, and that mathematics has little to do with thinking or problem solving. These erroneous beliefs, which are detrimental to the ability to solve new and challenging problems, can be held by even high-achieving students (De Corte et al., 2000; Schoenfeld, 1988). Coleman (2002) found that even gifted students categorized math and much science homework as "busywork" that does not require actual thinking!

Most alarmingly, and quite detrimentally to motivation, students also tend to have the impression that math and science have little to do with real life. As a result, they do not apply common sense as they solve problems. For example, when asked to calculate how many 1-meter planks one can cut from four 2.5-meter planks, students often reply with "10" instead of "8"—correctly multiplying 4×2.5 to obtain 10, but not realizing that after two 1-meter planks are cut from a 2.5-meter plank, the remaining 0.5 meter from each plank becomes scrap and cannot be used toward another 1-meter plank (De Corte et al., 2000; Schoenfeld, 1992). Conversely, even strong real-life skills may not be generalized to academics. For example, Nunes, Schliemann, and Carraher (1993) found that young street vendors who used invented strategies to calculate sums quickly and accurately when dealing with their customers did not use these strategies in school. Instead, they used the formal strategies they had been taught by their teachers, and made many more errors in the academic setting than at work!

In order for students to be successful in math, science, and technology, they must understand (1) that they are capable of achieving success, and (2) that success in these areas is important in their lives. The first of these requires guided instruction and scaffolded, successful learning experiences. The second requires tying learning to real-life experiences. This gap between the subjects of math and science and the students' lives appears to be particularly difficult to bridge. The following strategies can be helpful:

- Have students generate math and science problems using real-life situations.
- Hold classroom discussions relating the application of every process studied to students' lives.
- Ask students to interview family members and other adults regarding the use of math, science, and technological subjects in their work and personal lives.

- Use whole-class project-based learning, using driving questions of paramount interest to students.
- Have students make up real and humorous story problems from situations they encounter every day in school, at home, and in their communities.

Fostering Positive Affect and Managing Negative Affect

Coping with negative emotions such as frustration and anxiety, and fostering positive emotions such as optimism, are also essential to success in math, science, and technology. To a certain extent, being able to foster optimism and a positive image of problem solving is dependent upon problem-solving success. Students who have sufficient skills and knowledge to anticipate eventual success are able to self-regulate both motivation and affect so that they can better focus their attention and respond to negative experiences without "falling into dysfunctional patterns of behavior" (De Corte et al., 2000, p. 699).

Learning to cope with and accept frustration is particularly important. Students tend to believe that they should not experience frustration, but in truth, everyone experiences frustration as they learn new concepts. McLeod, Metzger, and Craviotto (1989) found that both experts and novices experienced frustration when encountering difficulty solving a problem, but that their emotional reactions differed considerably. Novices quit or persisted with the same unsuccessful strategy, while experts *stayed calm* and flexibly revised their strategy.

> **Leslie** told everyone how much she hated math class; often in class she scowled and complained about how stupid it was. Her teacher was puzzled, because he knew that once she caught on to new concepts, her skills were very good. He decided to speak with Leslie about her persistent negative attitude toward math.
>
> "I hate it! I just don't get it," she began. "I get all tense the minute you start to talk, because I realize that I don't understand one thing that you are saying."
>
> "Well, that's the way it is supposed to be, Leslie," he said. "If I only taught you material you already knew, you would never make progress. You are not *supposed* to know what I'm talking about at the beginning of the lesson. The feelings you have are natural, and you should just let them happen. Everyone experiences feelings of confusion and uncertainty right at the beginning of learning something new, no matter what they are trying to learn. Don't interpret that to mean that you are not getting it. Give yourself permission to wait until the information has been presented and 'digested' a bit. Don't be so quick to judge yourself, and you'll see that math is not really a problem for you at all."

For many students, finding methods to deal with anxiety regarding math and science is essential. Factors contributing to anxiety for students in one statistics class included a lack of connection between the concepts and daily life experiences, a too-rapid pace of instruction, a demanding and unsupportive instructor's attitude, and easily transmitted math phobia (Pan & Tang, 2005). Students can be afraid of certain math or science concepts before they have even encountered them.

> **Elgis's** head went down on his desk when his teacher announced that they would be starting a unit on fractions. As she continued to explain the unit, Elgis gently tapped his forehead again and again on his desk, then began to shake his head from side to side. His classmates could hear him breathing deeply and moaning quietly. His teacher approached Elgis and asked what was happening. "This is going to be terrible!" he lamented. "I've heard my brother talk about fractions and how hard they are, and I hate this already. I'm going to fail!"

Obviously a great deal of encouragement and reassurance, as well as many successful learning experiences, are required when anxiety regarding math, science, or technology reaches this level. The following strategies are useful methods to encourage student self-regulation of emotions regarding math, science, and technology:

- Teach students to accept initial frustration when they first encounter a new concept.
- Use multidimensional instructional methods.
- Attend to students' anxiety, and teach them anxiety reduction strategies such as those described in Chapter 5.
- Encourage students to deliberately stay calm and regroup their problem-solving strategies when they encounter difficulty in solving a problem.

Fostering Time Management

Managing time well is critical to learning in math and science, because skilled performance requires both memorization and conceptual understanding—both of which take time. As might be anticipated from the review of the literature in Chapter 7, math and science skills are substantially improved by spaced learning. Studying and completing math and science problems daily are vastly superior to cramming before tests. Students can be encouraged to study a half hour daily the week before a test, rather than to cram for hours the night before a test; the chances are high that they will obtain significantly higher grades.

Fostering Cognitive Strategies

ATTENTION-FOCUSING STRATEGIES

The ability to focus attention is of fundamental importance and is critical to success in math achievement, because the ability to solve problems is linked to working memory (Fuchs et al., 2005). These can be fostered by *performance feedback*, particularly immediate feedback, and *goal setting*. Being able to self-select goals is important for some students (Codding, 2003).

Students' attentiveness can also be increased by *students' self-monitoring* of both attention and performance. The ACT–REACT program has been found to help chronically disengaged students take control of their learning. Students use a graphic organizer, a timing devise, individualized math assignments, and a self-monitoring sheet or booklet with prompts for (1) setting a daily goal (e.g., "My goal today is to solve 15 problems"); (2) cues to focus attention, such as pictures of a focused student and the question "Am I staying focused and working like this?"; and (3) evaluating goal attainment (e.g., "How many problems did I complete?"). Students check for their attending behaviors every 5 minutes and for performance (problem completion) every 30–45 minutes (Rock, 2005, p. 6).

When teachers employ *high-response strategies,* they increase student attention and involvement, particularly for urban, low-achieving learners. For example, teachers might modify the usual practice of calling on students who have raised their hands by using response cards, wherein each student is provided with a white laminated board on which he or she can write a response to every question (Lambert, Cartledge & Heward, 2006).

STRATEGIES TO INCREASE FACT FLUENCY

Students who have difficulty in math make counting errors. They continue to count long after other students have switched to direct retrieval of math facts in early elementary school; have erroneous long-term memory of addition facts; and have difficulty in the retrieval of math facts due to an inability to inhibit irrelevant associations (Geary, 2005). They may not remember which items have been previously counted because of deficiencies in their working memory.

Although there is no consensus that students need to master math facts (Geary, 2004; Latterell, 2005), a lack of fluency in computation of math facts is associated with lower math achievement. For example, controlling for computational fluency substantially reduces the well-known advantage that Chinese students have relative to American students in math achievement (Geary, Liu, & Chen, 1999). A lack of fluency probably results in an overtaxed working memory, leaving less memory available for problem solving (Fuchs et al., 2005; Geary, 2004).

Insofar as it is necessary to free up working memory for problem solving, it is helpful for students to learn basic math facts as thoroughly as possible. This can be fostered by:

- Nurturing students' understanding that moving from calculation to rote recall to instantaneous recall is desirable—not as an end to itself, but to *facilitate problem solving* in the future.
- Using the *Write–Say* method, wherein after receiving feedback that an answer is incorrect, the student reinforces the corrected answers by writing and saying them three to five times (Brosvic, Dihoff, & Epstein, 2006).
- Providing *immediate* (not delayed) *feedback*. This can increase accuracy from 20% to 80%, whether that feedback is auditory from an educator or visually through an Immediate Feedback Assessment Technique (IFAT) (involving a sheet similar to a lottery card, where the student uncovers an answer and knows immediately whether or not the answer is correct) (Brosvic et al., 2006).
- Providing performance feedback via weekly *curriculum-based measurement*, which indicates to students whether their fact fluency has improved over the previous week. This results in significantly improved fluency gains and decreased errors (Eckert, Rosenthal, et al., 2006) and is especially helpful when students maintain the graphs.
- Having students use the *Cover, Copy, and Compare* technique, in which they look carefully at an academic stimulus (such as a math fact), cover the stimulus, copy the stimulus from memory, and evaluate the response by comparing it to the original stimulus (Skinner, McLaughlin, & Logan, 1997).
- *Rigorously avoiding public humiliation* regarding a lack of fact fluency. Posting absolute grades (or times) is highly detrimental, because it increases the frustration and humiliation of students with relatively weak skills. Instead, focus should be placed on improved performance relative to a student's own previous performance.
- Using *computer programs and games* that reinforce the memorization of facts. For example, when using Math Flash software, students type answers to fact questions into a computer; when an answer is correct, the computer provides positive reinforcement by "clapping," saying the fact aloud, and awarding "points" and "prizes" (Fuchs, Hamlett, & Powell, 2003).

On the other hand, a lack of fact fluency can be quite resistant to intervention. It is actually possible to improve other math skills without change in this particular skill, just as it is possible for a student to become a skilled writer without being a skilled speller. For example, Fuchs et al. (2005) found that small-group tutoring did not improve fact fluency but did improve math computation and concepts/applications, thereby reducing the number of students eligible for identification as having learning disabilities in math.

MEMORY RETRIEVAL STRATEGIES

As described in Chapter 8, every student needs to determine the best method for him or her to memorize key technological, math, and science facts. In addition to rote memorization, most students need to tie these definitions, important ideas, key examples, and theorems to previously learned information or to visual images for correct application. For example, students often confuse the formulas for the area (πr^2) and circumference ($2\pi r$) of circles, because they contain many of the same elements. It is helpful to understand the basic concept that finding the area of a shape is length times height, so that radius squared is a logical element in the formula for the area of a circle.

In some situations, a mnemonic device is particularly helpful. For example, "Please Excuse My Dear Aunt Sally" gives the order of math operations: Parentheses, Exponents, Multiply or Divide, and Add or Subtract.

Fostering Appropriate Calculator Use

Calculators are essential tools in many high school math classes and are now an integral element in the calculation of complex problems. Therefore, adults should ensure that students are skilled in using scientific or graphing calculators. On the other hand, calculators should not be used at the expense of thinking. Students should estimate answers whenever they use calculators, to catch errors that might result in nonsensical answers.

Fostering Visual–Spatial Skills

If students have difficulty with visual–spatial skills, it can be manifested in math, science, and technology in a number of ways. Students may have difficulty copying math problems so that the columns are aligned; they may have trouble discriminating and generating geometric shapes; and they may have difficulty reading or drawing graphs, diagrams, and charts. For such students, it is helpful to:

- Use lined paper turned on its side or graph paper to align columns in math problems.
- Provide worksheets of problems rather than have the students copy them.
- Teach students to leave blank spaces between completed problems and to circle the number of each problem.
- Provide models of completed and similar diagrams and charts as examples.

Fostering Reading in Math, Science, and Technology

Because of difficult vocabulary, abstract concepts, and texts lacking in organizational features, reading for comprehension in math, science, and technology can be particularly challenging for students. Methods to increase reading comprehension are provided in Chapter 9, and Worksheet 9.1 can be used in science, math, and technology classes to help students realize that they need to use these strategies in all classes.

To foster learning math and science vocabulary, maintaining a personal dictionary can be particularly helpful. Memory games, such as using student-made flashcards, are also beneficial.

> **Miss Fox** uses the math, science, and social studies texts assigned to her fifth grade students to teach phonics, summarization skills, prereading, scanning, skimming, reading comprehension, identification of main ideas and supporting details, word origin, spelling, sequencing, and vocabulary. Since math and science use challenging words and symbols that have Greek and Latin roots, her students find this method of vocabulary building to be particularly enriching. In addition, when her students write in math journals, create their own math story problems, answer essay questions, prepare science lab reports, or conduct research for specialty projects, she ensures that they use the writing process described in Chapter 10.

Instead of teaching various subject areas as separate, fragmented topics, she recommends integrating several academic areas into each lesson. For example, reading and math skills can be practiced during science to connect concepts, improve overall understanding, and make learning relevant.

Fostering Problem Solving

Integral to academic success in both math and science is problem-solving ability. A strategy that helps students solve problems is *focusing on key information*. Students need to carefully read and reread each problem to make sure that they understand the exact process involved. It often helps to underline key words or to highlight each action word and sign (in equations, the operand or sign) in a different color; draw a picture or diagram of the problem; use manipulatives or other concrete objects, such as rulers, number lines, or Cuisenaire rods; make a table; guess and check; work backward; simplify the problem; look for unstated assumptions; build on previous knowledge; and check for reasonableness.

The ability to *generalize* problem-solving strategies—that is, to apply previous knowledge and previously successful skills and strategies to new problems—can be conceptualized as a "transfer challenge." It is facilitated when students are asked to group problems based on structural rather than superficial features, and when instruction is *schema-based* (Fuchs & Fuchs, 2005). Even students whose fundamental math skills are weak benefit from schema-based problem-solving instruction. Such instruction proceeds as follows:

1. Students are taught that *transferring* skills means to move them from one situation to a new situation, such as moving skills in single-digit addition to two-digit addition and then on to adding prices to obtain a total at the store.
2. Students learn that features of math problems can be transferred in four ways, but that the problems still require familiar solution strategies. The features can be (a) transferred into a different format that looks new, (b) transferred by using new vocabulary, (c) transferred by asking a new question, or (d) transferred by being incorporated into a bigger problem.
3. Illustrative examples are provided, followed by partially solved examples.
4. Students work in dyads to solve problems with transferred features.
5. Students complete homework, with the reminder to search for transferred features and utilize known problem-solving strategies.
6. After strong problem-solving strategies are well established, students monitor their own performance by setting goals and using self-appraisal (Fuchs & Fuchs, 2005).

Fostering Use of the Scientific Method

A primary goal of science education is to empower students to think scientifically. Students needs specific, scaffolded instruction in methods to set up an experiment in which all but one variable are held constant while one variable is systematically changed. This particular concept can be quite difficult for students to understand, as it requires formal operations thinking. To help them overcome this difficulty, students need to investigate topics within their experience and be provided with hands-on applications.

Project-based science promotes a constructivist approach to learning science. It powerfully promotes student interest and self-regulation in a number of creative ways. Students are engaged in and empowered to address compelling real-life questions, such as "Why should someone not drive a car after drinking alcohol?" or "How are diseases, particularly STDs, actually transmitted?" (Hug, Krajcik, & Marx, 2005; see http://know.umich.edu). Project-based science involves (1) identifying a driving question; (2) conducting investigations by collecting data, interpreting results, and reporting findings; (3) developing artifacts; (4) collaborating with peers, teachers, families, and community members; and (5) using exciting technological tools to support the process. It provides students with the opportunity to design, investigate, collect and interpret data, and report results that answer the questions "what," "how," "why," and "when" (Patrick & Middleton, 2002; Randi & Corno, 2000).

Fostering Writing in Math, Science, and Technology

When students keep *math journals* and explain how they approached a problem with words or diagrams, a deeper understanding of processes is fostered. Writing in journals also encourages higher-order thinking to justify the methods students chose, explain why they got the problem wrong, or show a different way to reach the same answer. In addition, journaling makes it easier for teachers to determine when students are confused or need further instruction. Even for students with learning disabilities, journals can be very helpful because they provide a structured, non-oral method to explain their thinking (Baxter, Woodward, & Olson, 2005). Students who have severe difficulty with written language can still keep math journals, because pictorial representations of problems and telegraphic explanations are acceptable.

When writing *science and laboratory reports,* students should use the same strategies they use for all other written material. Suggestions included in Chapter 10 are relevant, as are Worksheets 10.1 and 10.3, and Handouts 10.2, 10.4, and 10.5.

Addressing Conceptual Deficits

Students who are having difficulty with math often repeatedly make errors that indicate a lack of understanding basic concepts. For example, a typical error in subtraction is to subtract the larger number in the subtrahend from smaller number in the minuend, indicating a lack of understanding that the minuend is the number to be subtracted *from* (Scheid, 1993).

Scaffolding instruction enables students to acquire the knowledge and skills necessary for self-regulated learning. Such scaffolding includes establishing key concepts, procedures, and skills by providing modeling, hints, cuing questions, and open-ended questions. After this foundation, the teacher breaks down a problem into components, or provides a portion of the solution, so that students solve problems with just enough support to find success. The teacher then incrementally scaffolds autonomy by illustrating different approaches to the same problem, asking students to model problem solving, and transferring responsibility to students. Throughout, student learning is supported by creating a positive classroom climate, fostering intrinsic motivation, encouraging peer collaboration, and nurturing (Meyer & Turner, 2002).

When teachers encourage students to *review problems already completed and try new problems that were not assigned,* students make more effective progress because they are encouraged to be cognizant of their skill levels and to differentiate "routine," "review," and "challenging" problems (akin to reading at the "independent," "instructional," and "frustration" levels). Teachers can encourage this practice by daily assigning routine problems from the current lesson, harder problems from recent lessons, and some review problems. Such assignments give the students explicit guidance in working with easier problems first, obtaining corrective feedback, and asking questions before progressing to harder problems (Boelkins & Pfaff, 1998).

Teachers can also *assign problems of varying types* to foster understanding. Working on only one type of problem at a time can result in the rote application of procedures. In contrast, working on a mixture of problems enables students to move toward learning to apply ideas in varied contexts. It also promotes retention and helps prepare for tests.

Using *graphic organizers,* and focusing on *changing concepts accompanied by concrete examples,* result in significantly better acquisition of scientific concepts and more positive attitudes toward science as a subject (Uzuntiryaki & Geban, 2005). Items in Handout 3.1 can be used by both teachers and students to help students understand how concepts in math, science, and technology relate to one another.

Finally, even at the secondary level, *integrating the curriculum* across subject areas has been demonstrated to be highly effective (Feng, VanTassel-Baska, & Quek, 2005).

> **Ali**, a high school freshman, was fascinated with the weather. She watched the weather report several times a day and even kept track of which TV channel made the most accurate predictions. However, in school Ali was failing science and proclaimed that she hated it. Quite by accident, Ali's language arts teacher noticed her writing in a notebook that was filled with data about weather conditions in various cities. Curious, Ali's teacher asked about it. Once Ali started talking about the weather, her information was nonstop. When Ali's science teacher learned of her interest from the language arts teacher, this interest was tapped in both classes. Ali was challenged to write a research paper on any weather condition. Her report on tornadoes was so thorough that Ali's science teacher sent it to the meteorologist at the local news station along with a letter describing this student's incredible knowledge about weather conditions. Ali was invited to visit the TV station and "shadow" the meteorologist for a day. Her attitude toward and grades in science improved vastly as Ali realized that her love of weather might result in an exciting career.

Fostering Peer Collaboration

In conjunction with teacher-led instruction, promoting peer collaboration via dyadic and small-group work is an essential component of fostering self-regulated learning in math, science, and technology (Schunk & Zimmerman, 1994). Teachers should encourage students to participate in *math and science study groups* whose members foster comprehension by discussing and correcting each other's efforts. When students work together on a nightly basis, until every member of the group not only completes the homework correctly but also *understands* the concepts and processes, this can raise grades for all participants. This has been found to be an effective strategy for complex math and science curricula even at elite colleges (Derek Bok Center for Teaching and Learning, 1993; Treisman, 1992). In addition, *peer and cross-age tutoring* in science and math fosters achievement for both tutors and tutees, and improves their attitudes toward school, self-concepts, and sense of academic efficacy (Robinson, Schofield, & Steers-Wentzell, 2005).

Fostering Home–School Collaboration

As discussed in Chapter 2, some parents are hesitant to help their children with math and science homework because their own skills are weak, or because the children are learning to solve math or science problems differently than the parents were taught. However, because math homework is usually assigned daily, parents often monitor math homework completion and participate in intervention designed to increase completion and accuracy. In addition, concern about students' passing high-stakes math tests has generated interest in increasing parental involvement in students' acquisition of math skills. Several interventions can successfully address these concerns.

As discussed previously, *collaborative behavior management programs targeting math homework completion* can be very successful, even for students with learning disabilities or emotional and behavioral disorders. In one program, homework completion rose from an average of 2% to

89% after parents, students, and educators collaborated on a program designed to improve student self-regulation via self-evaluation, self-monitoring, self-recording, and self-reinforcement combined with parental monitoring and reinforcement (Cancio et al., 2004). The reader is referred to Chapter 6 for methods of implementing such programs.

Deliberately including family members in homework assignments is a highly effective method to increase home involvement in the educational process, and with clear and adequate instruction it can be used even when family members do not have a strong background in math or science. The vignette that opens Chapter 2, describing Clair and her father working on building a trebuchet and using the scientific method to test it, is an example of this approach.

When teachers *ensure that homework requires thought,* they increase the involvement of all students. Coleman (2002) found that with students in a residential school for gifted students, "homework that required thinking rekindled their interest in learning for its own sake" (p. 44). Disconcertingly, even these gifted students often completed homework in a rote, thoughtless manner—particularly homework that students described as "busywork," such as worksheets and groups of problems in math and science. According to these students, this homework was straightforward, concrete, factual, and quickly done, and they tended to complete it while watching TV or talking with friends. In contrast, reading; writing lab reports, papers, and essays; conducting research; and completing projects and presentations were described as requiring thinking. Clearly, thinking of homework as busywork, completing it when engaged in another activity, and completing it in a rote and careless manner do not result in meaningful learning. Without thought, work completion does not result in learning. Therefore, insofar as possible, teachers should strive to assign homework that requires deep mental processing.

Teaching parents to be skillful tutors can also be an effective intervention. Keller (2004) describes an inner-city school in which parents and siblings were taught specific methods to help children with math homework, raising the passing rate on a high-stakes test from less than 50% to 75% of the student population. In this program, fourth-grade students who had previously completed a practice high-stakes test attended a 2-hour workshop in which the corrected practice test and a list of "problem areas" were shared with family members. Students took a short practice test as the families watched; then family members described to the group what their children did well, and the successful students described their problem-solving strategies. Finally, the teachers gave suggestions to parents and siblings on how they might support students as they worked on math skills at home.

When family members are unable to help with math, science, and technology homework, it is important that students be connected with appropriate supports. These might include after-school support from teachers or tutoring.

> When the parent–teacher conference was underway, **Mark**'s father began by explaining that helping Mark with his math homework was a nightly disaster. It often ended with the father shaking his head and walking away in disgust as Mark slouched helplessly in frustration, more confused than when they began. Mark's mother admitted that she was poor in math herself, so she was unable to offer any help. The teacher suggested tutoring, which was available at no charge from high school National Honor Society members, and told them of a class on study skills being offered at the nearby college campus. The parents arranged these opportunities for their son, and after he participated in them, Mark's math grades improved—as did his relationship with his father. Also, several study strategies he learned to help him in math were easily transferred to other subjects.

While somewhat controversial, *online tutors* such as www.tutor.com provide an electronic "chat" connection and a white board to live tutors in English and Spanish in a number of subjects, including math through second-year algebra. Many libraries subscribe to this service. Apangea Smart Help (www.apangealearning.com) provides computer-driven programmed lessons in topics ranging from arithmetic to algebra, supplemented by a live tutor when difficulty is experienced. Each lesson is composed of basic instruction, a quiz, and a series of increasingly difficult word problems. Problems are broken down into discrete steps and the program allows students to access resource information such as glossaries and formulas. When students make errors, they are alerted, given hints, and connected to a live tutor if they continue to have difficulties. Fees are hourly, and the program has the advantage of permitting teachers to obtain information about the progress of their students (Fleisher, 2006).

Appraisal

Students' progress toward independent learning in math, science, and technology is facilitated when teachers *fade instructional support* rather than providing continuous written instructional support, because fading better prepares students to independently construct scientific explanations (McNeill, Lizotte, Krajcik, & Marx, 2006). In addition, *student self-assessment* is a strategy very conducive to self-regulated learning (De Corte et al., 2000). When students are taught to use four stages of math self-evaluation, their math skills can improve significantly, but this requires that they be taught these strategies over time. Ross et al. (2002) found that it was necessary for these lessons to occur over a 12-week period. In addition, they found that it was necessary to have a simultaneous weekly after-school in-service training session for teachers, during which the teachers participated in the four-stage self-evaluation process (Rolheiser, 1996), developed rubrics, shared successful experiences associated with the process, and collaboratively planned classroom activities. As with teaching students to self-monitor their behavior, teaching students to self-evaluate math, science, and technological proficiency is best accomplished by:

1. Making learning goals very explicit, and including students in the development of evaluation criteria.
2. Directly teaching students how to apply the evaluation criteria or rubric.
3. Having students self-evaluate, and then giving them feedback on their self-evaluations.
4. Helping students use their self-evaluation data to determine areas of strength and need, and develop plans for the future (Ross et al., 2002). When students self-assess, as in grading their own papers, increased student learning results (Saddler & Good, 2006).

Help Students Develop Their Personal Learning Guides (HILLs)

The strategies that students develop to learn math, science, and technology will need to be modified as they advance through their schooling; the strategies that are effective in learning the multiplication tables will not be effective with calculus. Therefore, students should be encouraged to keep both completed and blank copies of assessment and intervention sheets in their binders, so that they can continually reflect upon and readjust their skills in learning to understand math, science, and technology. Materials pertinent to this topic and appropriate for inclusion in the math, science, and technology portion of the Personal Learning Guide include Worksheet 11.1, as well as various worksheets and handouts from earlier chapters (see cross-references in this chapter's text).

WORKSHEET 11.1.

Math, Science, and Technology Strategies Checklist

Student ______________________________ Date ____________________

Before I began:

__ I decided on a learning goal and connected this activity to "real life."

__ I brainstormed ideas with someone (a study buddy, teacher, or parent).

__ I gathered and reviewed all needed information.

__ I simplified the problem into clear, distinct, and manageable parts.

__ I obtained the grading rubric.

__ I read the problem carefully and made sure I understood it.

__ I thought and planned before beginning to solve the problem.

__ I found a concrete, hands-on approach to solve new types of problems.

__ I made sure I knew how to do the required tasks.

__ I constructed a diagram of the problem.

__ I checked whether I could use general strategies or relate this problem to previous problems.

__ I designed a hierarchical solution plan.

__ I made sure I understood the reading.

While I worked:

__ I implemented the solution plan.

__ When I used a calculator, I also estimated the answer.

__ I obtained help when needed.

__ I checked for understanding.

__ I checked that I had memorized necessary information well enough to solve the problem.

During my work session, I monitored how well my strategies worked by asking myself:

__ What is my goal today?

__ What am I doing?

__ Why am I doing it?

__ Am I staying focused?

__ How will what I am doing help me?

__ Did I reach my goal?

(continued)

Math, Science, and Technology Strategies Checklist *(page 2 of 2)*

After I finished working:

__ I checked that all important information was used, that the solution fits with estimates and predictions, and that the solution makes sense.

__ If not, I identified the source of the discrepancy and recycled through preparation and performance tasks.

__ After my solution was checked, I determined how the solution might have been differently obtained, checked how appropriate my calculation or drawing was, related the problem to previously solved problems, and determined how a similar problem might be more effectively solved in the future.

Notes on what I did; what worked well, what I should change in the future:

12

Empowering Students to Successfully Take Tests and Improve Performance

Self-regulated learners consider tests and performances as opportunities.

OVERVIEW

Tom Lanning was a seventh grader who, faced with his first end-of-the-semester exams, had no idea how to approach them. A week before the exam, his mother sat down with him and helped him draw up a study plan and schedule. After he reviewed his class notes, textbooks, and graded unit tests and quizzes, she helped him develop lists of possible exam questions and answers. Tom's friend Joseph spent the night just before the exam at Tom's house, because his single-parent mother was out of town. Mrs. Lanning suggested that after the boys reviewed their book and class notes, that they should quiz each other, using Tom's questions and answers. Then the three of them played a version of the TV quiz show *Jeopardy*, with Mrs. Lanning calling out "answers" and the boys competing to be first to shout out correct "questions." Tom and Joseph both mastered the material and did well on the test.

Every student needs help in discovering the most efficient and effective ways for him or her to approach tests and performances such as oral presentations. Along with written assignments, tests and performances are the primary methods by which students' learning is demonstrated and assessed. The ability to "test well" and to clearly convey learned information is critical at every academic level, and test-taking strategies have long been a component of study skill training. Traditional approaches have focused on tests and performances at the classroom level. However, with the passage of the No Child Left Behind legislation, all but the most severely disabled students are required to take and pass state-regulated tests at several points throughout their elementary and high school years. The impact of these "high-stakes tests" is enormous and far-reaching for both students and educators (McColsky & McMunn, 2000). Students are required to obtain predetermined scores to progress from one grade to the next; to graduate from high school; and to be granted admission to college, or graduate, law, or medical school. Classroom and school averages on these tests have been used to grant merit-based pay to teachers and to determine whether administrators, entire schools, and even districts are severely penalized. Consequently, strong performance on such tests has become enormously important for educators, families, and students

(Moore, 1994). It is obviously more important than ever that students know methods to deal successfully with these challenges.

In addition to taking tests, students are often required to demonstrate knowledge and skill during performances such as music recitals, oral debates, athletic events, project presentations, and theater productions. Performances are similar to tests in that they lead to an evaluation of the student and generate many of the same benefits and possible detriments as do tests. Because of these similarities, many of the concepts, strategies, and methods that are relevant to taking tests are relevant to student performances. This chapter reviews methods that adults and students can use to help improve test taking and other measures of performance. A concise summary of this chapter's methods can be found in Worksheet 12.1, Test-Taking and Performance Checklist.

RESEARCH FOUNDATIONS

Tests and performances can have both positive and unintended negative consequences. Possible positive consequences for classroom tests and performances are motivation to review and learn materials, the incentive to integrate information, the opportunity to work with peers to master skills, the determination of areas in need of additional instruction, and the opportunity to demonstrate knowledge and skill. Negative consequences for classroom tests and performances can be confusion regarding learning outcomes, an overemphasis on grades to the detriment of learning, debilitating anxiety, feelings of low self-efficacy, excessive competition, and negative student–adult or parent–teacher relationships. Similarly, positive consequences of high-stakes testing can include increased expectations for student knowledge and skill development, support for low-performing students, standardization of curriculum across schools, attention to curriculum frameworks, and support for low-achieving schools (McColsky & McMunn, 2000). Negative consequences of high-stakes testing can include sacrificing learning for attempting to improve test scores via inappropriate instruction, unethical methods of test preparation, undue stress for educators and students, and the loss of community respect and support for schools.

Although it has always been recognized that students should prepare for classroom tests and exams, preparing students to take standardized tests is a newer phenomenon. Relatively recently, students have sought help to prepare for these tests. Preparing for SAT exams, for example, has become very common—whether in face-to-face tutorials or in online opportunities to take practice tests through test preparation services such as Kaplan, Princeton Review, Peterson's, or Number2.com (Loken, Radlinski, Crespi, Millet, & Cushing, 2004). These programs tend to emphasize familiarizing students with test format and vocabulary (Marzano & Kendall with Gaddy, 1999). Students can better convey the information they already know, produce more thoughtful responses, perform more strategically, and reduce their anxiety when they are familiar with test format, have practical informational skills, learn appropriate test-taking behaviors, are familiar with relevant reading strategies, and are aware of the influence of test results on their lives.

Therefore, it is important that students be appropriately prepared to take tests (Crocker, 2005). However, test preparation can be appropriate or inappropriate. Appropriate strategies include teaching the content related to the assessment measure, teaching test-taking skills, teaching toward test objectives when those objectives are in accord with curricular objectives, teaching students test vocabulary, and providing practice test sessions on the content domain. Inappropriate practices—which are more likely when educators perceive little value in testing (Moore, 1994) or are extremely fearful of the results—include limiting instruction to test question formats, limiting instruction to material on the test, using former test questions as instructional guides, or actually teaching test questions and providing the answers (Mehrens, 1991, as cited in Gulek, 2003). In addition, students often use inappropriate test preparation strategies when they study on their own. They delay preparing for even high-stakes tests until days before the test, neglect to cover the full content of the test and focus on quick and short-answer verbal items rather than items that require time such as reading and responding to questions on reading passages (Loken et al., 2004). Furthermore, test preparation can be particularly difficult for students with disabilities (Chaleff, 2000; Scruggs, Mastropieri, & Tolf-Veit, 1986).

METHODS

Strategies appropriate to use in helping students learn how to prepare for tests and performances address the factors depicted in Figure 12.1. The reader may notice that this figure is almost identical to Figure 1.1 in Chapter 1. This similarity is intentional, because all of the student variables that affect study skills in general coalesce to have a profound impact on successful test taking and performance.

Thus it is important that consultants and teachers focus on increasing motivation, reducing anxiety, improving time management, and helping students become assessment-literate (Gulek, 2003). Once these areas are mastered, students can learn to generalize these methods and self-monitor their implementation.

Preparation

Successful test takers and performers self-regulate motivation; manage negative and increase positive emotions; self-manage behavior; apply and appraise cognitive and metacognitive strategies; manage time; attend to physical functioning, such as nourishment and adequate rest; apply rele-

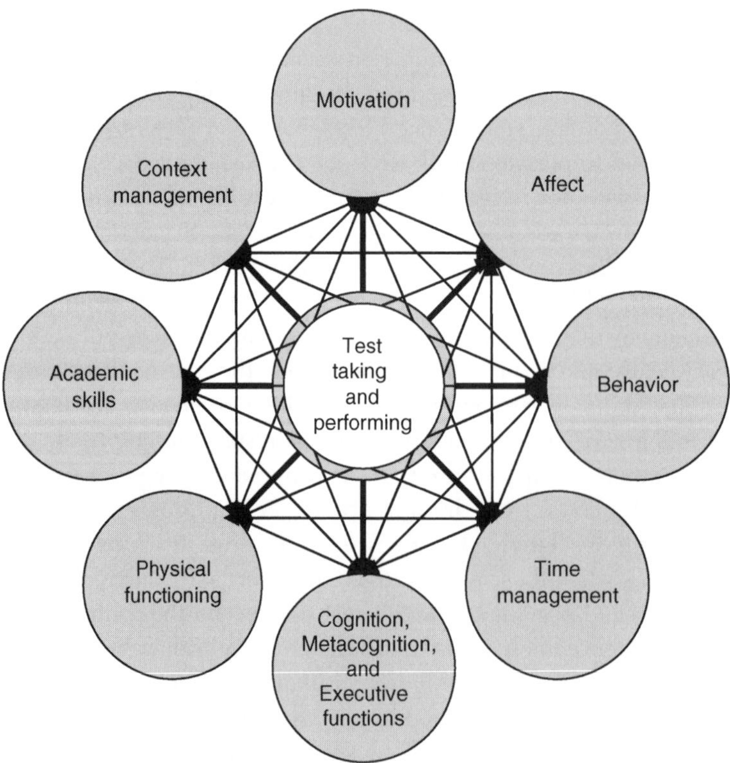

FIGURE 12.1. Student factors involved in test taking and performance.

vant reading, writing, and problem-solving strategies; turn to family, peers, and educators for appropriate support; and manage environmental variables. All of these factors have been addressed in previous chapters. This chapter will focus on a few elements that are critical to successful test taking and performance.

In addressing *motivation*, the most successful test takers and performers maintain positive goals, such as learning the material and doing *well* (as opposed to either not doing poorly or achieving perfection). In terms of test taking and performance, the most critical *affective* variable is anxiety control. The reader is referred to Chapter 5 for appropriate methods to deal with anxiety, such as obtaining sufficient sleep, moderating stimulant (caffeine) intake, and using relaxation strategies. Anxiety can be reduced after studying, but before the actual test or performance, through the use of relaxation and imagery (Mooney & Cole, 2000). Students can do the following:

1. Find a relaxing atmosphere, take deep breaths, and think of something relaxing.
2. After a few minutes of relaxing, allow learned information to "surface."
3. Visualize entering the exam confident, happy, and ready to do well.
4. Imagine the questions focusing on known and easily expressed information.
5. Visualize leaving the test happy, successful, and ready to celebrate.

In terms of *time management*, the most critical variables regarding test taking are preparing for tests in advance, avoiding procrastination, and spacing learning trials. As Zimmerman et al. (1996) explain, if students do not manage their time well, they do not have time to employ good study strategies. Chapter 7 presents multiple methods to manage time to facilitate successful test taking and performance.

Many *cognitive strategies* are obviously critical in preparing to take tests. In particular, students need help in selecting effective memory-enhancing methods to remember key information. Memory-enhancing strategies should be developed well in advance of tests, reviewed several times, and modified for each test or performance. The memory strategies described in Chapter 8 (including rehearsal, repetition, association, organization, verbal elaboration, and mnemonics) are clearly critical to good test-taking preparation, as is encouraging students to space learning over several sessions.

Reading study strategies are also critical in preparing for tests. One of the most effective methods is for students to develop personal study guides (i.e., student-developed test review sheets) by generating questions they believe might be used to assess their knowledge in the future. This technique is described in detail in Chapter 9; it is also helpful for students to use study guides provided by teachers or test publishers. In addition, many tests require written responses. Methods to facilitate students' writing skills are discussed in Chapter 10.

As illustrated in the vignette that opened this chapter, enlisting *family members and friends* to help prepare for tests and performances can be very beneficial. Such quizzing and reviewing provides the spaced and repeated trials essential for the overlearning that is necessary for successful test taking. Methods to enlist the support of family and friends in preparing for taking tests are discussed in Chapter 2.

Another important tool is collaborating with a study buddy or participating in a study group that requires that every member not only completes assignments, but understands and learns important information. Often working toward comprehension requires students to work collaboratively, discussing and correcting each other's understanding of concepts and procedures (Derek Bok Center for Teaching and Learning, 1993). Such collaborative learning can take place in the classroom or in study groups. As noted in Chapter 11, study groups whose members work together on a nightly basis, until every member of the group *understands* the concepts and processes, can raise grades for all participants (Treisman, 1992). Study partnerships are just as valuable for capable students as they are for those who experience school-related difficulties.

In their first class at law school, students were encouraged by their professor to find a study partner. Though **Dawn and Sandy** came from divergent cultural backgrounds, each was intelligent, competent, and competitive. Both students would probably have done well in law school on their own; in fact, many high-achieving students prefer to work alone. However, they discovered that they worked well together during that first class, and their partnership continued through law school and beyond. This partnership sparked a unique quest for excellence and led to a successful approach that resulted in significant accomplishments for each.

These partners first identified the ways each of them typically approached studying. They described learning styles, strengths, and weaknesses. With massive amounts of material to be read, analyzed, and remembered daily, they soon learned to rely on their combined strengths, each contributing a different piece toward the good of the partnership. For some classes, they divided the workload. Each read a group of cases, wrote outlines and briefs, and presented the synopses to the other for discussion and analysis. For classes that required presentations, such as trial advocacy, one person practiced presenting while the other recorded the time and looked for relevant points, logic, and concise arguments. They edited each other's work, benefited from repeating their conclusions aloud while teaching each other, and learned to trust each other's skills. They revisited ideas a week or so later for review, and thereby improved their long-term memory. This approach enabled them both to pass their bar exams on the first attempt.

Finally, many *classroom variables* can be modified to foster good preparation for test taking and performance. Clearly, classroom teachers can encourage all of the activities described above. In addition, teachers can orchestrate classroom practices to facilitate positive test-taking experiences. It is particularly helpful when teachers:

- Identify the key points they expect their students to learn.
- Involve as many senses as possible in presenting the lesson.
- Encourage students to process lecture information in some way (e.g., turn to a study buddy and state the most important thing the teacher just said).
- Provide opportunities for guided practice and rehearsal (through games, projects, models, experiments, etc.).
- Assess the students' preparedness for taking the test.
- Describe the format of the upcoming test (often a rubric showing the way the test will be graded is helpful, as are sample tests from previous years).
- Allow choices, if possible, in the way the students demonstrate their knowledge (e.g., paper-and-pencil products, oral presentations, or making a model and labeling the parts).
- Quiz and assess frequently.
- Emphasize the importance of the information, and indicate how learning the information will help the students in upcoming units.
- When possible, attend to test content and corrective feedback rather than grades.
- Provide ample time for students to complete tests.
- Encourage students to develop and answer possible test questions.

When students are required to write what they believe would be good test questions as they read, comprehension and memory improve. Moreover, this activity helps students identify and focus on the main ideas and supporting details of their assigned topic.

For the class test, **Mae's** graduate school professor asked each member to write five questions of at least two types (multiple-choice, short-answer, true–false, matching, or essays), along with the correct answers. The professor then edited the submitted questions, prepared a study guide using the student-generated questions, allowed students to work in groups to discuss and write correct answers to the questions, and then told the class that half of the exam would be composed of their questions. After the exam, Mae told her professor that she had never read assigned readings so thoroughly, and her usual text anxiety was significantly reduced.

Performance

In test taking and performing, as is the case for all other variables affecting studying, effective students cycle through *preparation*, *performance*, and *appraisal*. However, in the test-taking and performing situations, the student additionally cycles through preparation, performance, and appraisal *within the performance phase*. That is, while taking the actual test, students again prepare, perform, and appraise as depicted in Figure 12.2.

In preparing during the actual test or performance, students should:

- Deliberately regulate anxiety.
- Listen carefully to directions, and ask for clarification when necessary.
- Carefully review the directions and sample items, underlining key words.
- Scan the entire test to determine its scope.
- Jot down memorized information (such as dates, names, and formulas) as soon as possible,
- Set up and keep a schedule for the test session, and
- Outline the important points to be covered before responding to an essay question.

During the performance phase of taking a test or performance, students should:

- Read each question carefully.
- Attempt to answer every question, but move on when they are stumped. (In a multiple-choice test, if two answers can be eliminated, it is worth guessing.)
- Make sure that the question and answer numbers correspond.
- Write neatly.
- Address all aspects of the questions carefully, noting key words like "define," "compare and contrast," "explain," "describe," and "justify."

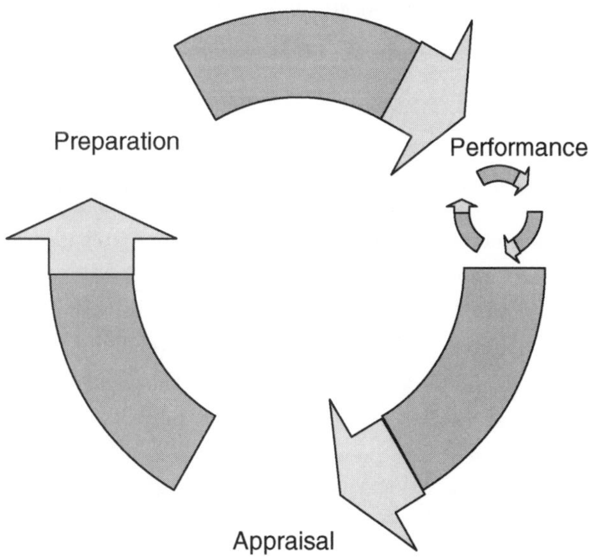

FIGURE 12.2. The self-regulation cycle in test taking and performance.

During the appraisal phase of test taking, students should:

- Recheck work for accuracy, completeness, and legibility.
- Proofread and correct answers.

Appraisal

After completing a test, exam, or performance, effective independent learners evaluate their performance and strategies to determine what worked and did not work. They also compare their anticipated performance with their actual performance. Adults can help students master this step by:

- Teaching students how to interpret their test scores, including confidence intervals.
- Helping students by placing test results within the context of other measures, such as portfolio assessments and "personal best" files.
- Helping students compare their performance with an ideal performance—for example, by listening to a tape or watching a video of their performance.
- Encouraging students to review feedback provided by others.
- Encouraging students to use positive affirmations, such as those found in Table 12.1.
- Using Worksheet 12.1 to appraise their strategies and revise their plans for future test and performance preparation.

Help Students Develop Their Personal Learning Guides (HILLs)

Students should be encouraged to keep both completed and blank copies of assessment and intervention sheets in their Personal Learning Guides, so that they can continually reflect upon and readjust their test-taking and performance strategies. Materials pertinent to this topic, and appropriate for inclusion in the test-taking and performance portion of the Personal Learning Guide binder, include:

Worksheet 12.1. Test-Taking and Performance Checklist
Table 12.1. Student Affirmations about Test Taking and Performances

TABLE 12.1. Student Affirmations about Test Taking and Performances

- I invest adequate time and effort in studying for my tests and preparing for performances.
- I am well prepared and confident of doing a good job.
- Relaxing before and during a test or performance helps me focus and do my personal best.
- I know about test-taking strategies, and I use them effectively during a test.
- Tests and performances are just one way of showing my knowledge about a topic.
- I have been successful in the past, and I will be successful today.
- I analyze my errors and profit from both oral and written feedback.
- I discuss my progress with my teachers and ask for suggestions on ways to improve.
- I am prepared, and I will do well!
- I relax . . . breathe . . . and stay focused.

WORKSHEET 12.1.

Test-Taking and Performance Checklist

Ahead of time:	
	I know ahead of time what material will be on the test, or required for my presentation/ performance.
	I make and use study guides.
	I find out the question formats and review examples.
	I know how the test/performance will be graded.
	I work with a study buddy or in a group.
	I check whether I have learned the material.
	I use studying strategies that I know work for me.
	I try to think of the test/performance as a learning tool and an opportunity to demonstrate knowledge.
	I picture myself doing well and feeling good afterward.
Just before the test/performance:	
	I control my anxiety by taking a break, walking, or exercising.
	I relax and practice positive visualization.
	I eat and drink properly, and get adequate sleep.
	I bring more than one writing implement and all needed materials.
	I moderate my use of caffeine.
At the beginning of the test/performance:	
	I listen to directions carefully and ask for clarification when something isn't clear.
	I jot down memorized information I think I will need as soon as possible (dates, formulas, etc.).
	I outline answers to essay questions (thesis statement, main ideas, supporting details).
	I have a plan to spend the most time on the questions that carry the most points.
	I read written directions twice, underline the key words, and ask for clarification.
During the test/performance:	
	I keep track of the time.
	If using a computer scoring sheet, I keep checking that I am on the correct number.
	I answer what I know well first, then go back to answer other questions.
	When taking a multiple-choice test, I eliminate answers I know are incorrect and then guess.
	I remain calm, project my voice, and use eye contact when making presentations.
	During a performance I remain focused and relaxed.

(continued)

Test-Taking and Performance Checklist *(page 2 of 2)*

Toward the end of the test/performance:	
	I check that my name is on all papers and that my answers are in the correct place.
	I read over written questions again and then reread my answers, checking that I have answered every part of every question.
	I check for legibility of written work.
After the test/performance:	
	I review my results and understand them.
	I consider my results in the context of all my learning.
Notes: What worked well? What did not work well? What should be changed next time?	

References

Abikoff, H., Courtney, M., Pelham, W. E., & Koplewicz, H. S. (1993). Teachers' rating of disruptive behavior: Influence of halo effects. *Journal of Abnormal Child Psychology, 21*, 519–534.

Achenbach, T. M., Rescorla, L., McConaughy, S. H., Pecora, P. J., Wetherbee, K. M., & Ruffle, T. M. (2003). *Achenbach System of Empirically Based Assessment.* Burlington: University of Vermont, Research Center for Children, Youth, & Families.

Alberto, P. A., & Troutman, A. C. (1995). *Applied behavior analysis for teachers* (4th ed.). Englewood Cliffs, NJ: Merrill.

Amatea, E. S., Daniels, H., Bringman, N., & Vandiver, F. (2004). Strengthening counselor–teacher–family connections. *Professional School Counselor, 8*, 47–56.

Ames, C. (1992). Classrooms: Goals, structures, and student motivation. *Journal of Educational Psychology, 84*, 261–271.

Ames, C., & Archer, J. (1988). Achievement goals in the classroom: Students' learning strategies and motivation processes. *Journal of Educational Psychology. 80*, 260–267.

Anderson, J., & Gunderson, L. (1997). Literacy learning from a multicultural perspective. *Reading Teacher, 50*, 514–516.

Anderson-Inman, L., Knox-Quinn, C., & Horney, M. A. (1996). Computer-based study strategies for students with learning disabilities: Individual differences associated with adoption level. *Journal of Learning Disabilities, 29*, 461–484.

Armel, D., & Shrock, S. A. (1996). The effects of required and optional computer-based note taking on achievement and instructional completion time. *Journal of Educational Computing Research, 14*, 329–344.

Arnedt, J. T., Owens, J., & Crouch, M. (2005). Neurobehavioral performance of residents after heavy night call vs. after alcohol ingestion. *Journal of the American Medical Association, 294*, 1025–1033.

Augustyniak, K., Murphy, J., & Phillips, D. K. (2005). Psychological perspectives in assessing mathematics learning needs. *Journal of Instructional Psychology, 32*, 277–286.

Austin, T. (1994). *Changing the view: Student-led parent conferences.* Portsmouth, NH: Heinemann.

Bachevalier, J., Malkova, L., & Beauregard, M. (1996). Multiple memory systems: A neuropsychological and developmental perspective. In G. R. Lyon & N. A. Krasnegor (Eds.), *Attention, memory, and executive function* (pp. 185–198). Baltimore: Brookes.

Baddeley, A. D. (1992). Working memory: The interface between memory and cognition. *Journal of Cognitive Neuroscience, 4*, 281–288.

Baddeley, A. D. (2003). Working memory: Looking back and looking forward. *Nature Reviews: Neuroscience, 4*, 829–839.

Bahr, C. M., & Nelson, N. W. (1996). The effects of text-based and graphics-based software tools on planning and organization of stories. *Journal of Learning Disabilities, 29*, 355–372.

Bailey, L. B., Silvern, S. B., Brabham, E., & Ross, M. (2004). The effects of interactive reading homework and parent involvement on children's inference responses. *Early Childhood Education Journal, 32*, 173–178.

Baker, L., & Brown, A. L. (1984). Metacognitive skills and reading. In R. Barr, M. L. Kamil, P. Mosenthal, & P. D. Pearson (Eds.), *Handbook of reading research* (Vol. 2, pp. 353–394). New York: Longman.

Baker, L., & Lombardi, B. R. (1985). Students' lecture notes and their relation to test performance. *Teaching of Psychology, 12*, 29–32.

Balli, S. J., Demo, D. H., & Wedman, J. F. (1998). Family involvement with children's homework: An intervention in the middle grades. *Family Relations, 47,* 149–157.

Bandura, A. (1986). *Social foundations of thought and action: A social cognition theory.* Englewood Cliffs, NJ: Prentice-Hall.

Bandura, A. (1997). *Self-efficacy: The exercise of control.* New York: Freeman.

Barber, B. L., Eccles, J. S., & Stone, M. R. (2001). Whatever happened to the jock, the brain, and the princess?: Young adult pathways linked to adolescent activity involvement and social identity. *Journal of Adolescent Research, 16,* 429–455.

Barkley, R. A. (1996). Critical issues in research on attention. In G. R. Lyon & N. A. Krasnegor (Eds.), *Attention, memory, and executive function* (pp. 45–56). Baltimore: Brookes.

Barton-Arwood, S. M., Wehby, J. H., & Falk, K. B. (2005). Reading instruction for elementary-age students with emotional and behavioral disorders: Academic and behavioral outcomes. *Exceptional Children, 72,* 7–27.

Bauer, S. R., Sapp, M., & Johnson, D. (1999). Group counseling strategies for rural at-risk high school students. *High School Journal, 83,* 41–51.

Baumeister, R. F., & Heatherton, T. F. (1996). Self-regulation failure. *Psychological Inquiry,* 7, 1–15.

Baumrind, D. (1991). The influence of parenting style on adolescent competence and substance use. *Journal of Early Adolescence, 11,* 56–95.

Baxendell, B. (2003). *Different types of graphic organizers and their uses.* Retrieved from www.wm.edu/ttac/articles/teaching/Graphic Organizers.pdf

Baxter, J. A., Woodward, J., & Olson, D. (2005). Writing in mathematics: An alternative form of communication for academically low-achieving students. *Learning Disabilities Research and Practice, 20,* 119–135.

Beck, A. T., & Steer, R. A. (1996). *Beck Anxiety Inventory.* San Antonio, TX: Psychological Corporation.

Beck, A. T., Steer, R. A., & Brown, G. K. (1996). *Beck Depression Inventory-II.* San Antonio, TX: Psychological Corporation.

Beghetto, R. A. (2001). Virtually in the middle: Alternative avenues for parental involvement in middle-level schools. *The Clearing House, 75,* 21–25.

Beidel, D. C., Turner, S. M., & Taylor-Ferreira, J. C. (1999). Teaching study skills and test-taking strategies to elementary school students. *Behavior Modification, 23,* 630–646.

Bembenutty, H. (1999). Sustaining motivation and academic goals: The role of academic delay of gratification. *Learning and Individual Differences, 11,* 233–258.

Bempechat, J. (2004). The motivational benefits of homework: A social-cognitive perspective. *Theory into Practice, 43,* 189–196.

Bempechat, J., Drago-Severson, E., & Boulay, B. A. (2002). Attributions for success and failure in mathematics: A comparative study of Catholic and public school students. *Catholic Education: A Journal of Inquiry and Practice,* 5, 357–372.

Benson, J. (1998). Test review of the Motivated Strategies for Learning Questionnaire. From J. C. Impara & B. S. Plake (Eds.), *The thirteenth mental measurement yearbook* [Electronic version]. Retrieved from the Buros Institute's *Test Reviews Online* website: http//www.unl.edu/buros

Benton, S. L., & Benton, S. (in press). Test review of the Behavior Rating Inventory of Executive Function Self-Report Version. From B. S. Plake & J. C. Impara (Eds.), *The fifteenth mental measurement yearbook* [Electronic version]. Retrieved from the Buros Institute's *Test Reviews Online* website: http//www.unl.edu/buros

Benton, S. L., & Benton, S. (2004). Review of the Behavior Rating Inventory of Executive Functioning Self-Report Version. In *Mental Measurement Yearbook Database.* Lincoln, NB: Buros Institute of Mental Measurements. Retrieved electronically 11/23/05.

Berndt, D. J., & Kaiser, C. F. (1996). *Multiscore Depression Inventory for Children (MDI-C).* Los Angeles: Western Psychological Services.

Berninger, V. W., Abbott, R. D., Abbott, S. P., Graham, S., & Richards, T. (2002). Writing and reading: Connections between language by hand and language by eye. *Journal of Learning Disabilities, 35,* 39–57.

Berninger, V. W., Rutberg, J. E., & Abbott, R. D. (2006). Tier 1 and Tier 2 early intervention for handwriting and composing. *Journal of School Psychology, 44,* 3–30.

Berninger, V. W., Vaughn, K., Abbott, R., Abbott, S., Brooks, A., & Rogan, L. (1997). Treatment of handwriting fluency problems in beginning writing. *Journal of Educational Psychology, 89,* 652–686.

Berninger, V. W., Vaughn, K., Abbott, R., Brooks, A., Abbott, S., & Reed, E. (1998). Early intervention for spelling problems: Teaching spelling units of varying size within a multiple connections framework. *Journal of Educational Psychology, 90,* 587–605.

Betz, N. E. (1978). Prevalence, distribution, and correlates of math anxiety in college students. *Journal of Counseling Psychology, 25,* 441–448.

Bjorklund, D. F., Miller, P. H., & Coyle, T. R. (1997). Instructing children to use memory strategies. *Developmental Review, 17,* 411–441.

Boekaerts, M., de Koning, E., & Vedder, P. (2006). Goal-directed behavior and contextual factors in the classroom. *Educational Psychologist, 41,* 33–51.

Boekaerts, M., & Niemivirta, M. (2000). Self-regulated

learning: Finding a balance between learning goals and ego-protective goals. In M. Boekaerts, P. R. Pintrich, & M. Zeidner (Eds.), *Handbook of self-regulation* (pp. 417–451). San Diego, CA: Academic Press.

Boelkins, M. R., & Pfaff, T. J. (1998). Teaching calculus students how to study. *PRIMUS: Problems, Resources, and Issues in Mathematics, 8*, 253–264.

Boller, K. (1996). Conceptualizing, describing, and measuring components of memory. In G. R. Lyon & N. A. Krasnegor (Eds.), *Attention, memory, and executive function* (pp. 221–231). Baltimore: Brookes.

Boone, G. L. (1999). Cognitive self-instruction to foster self-regulation in regular education students (study skills, metacognition, academic achievement). *Dissertation Abstracts International, 60*(5), 1444A.

Boothroyd, R. A. (1998). Test review of the Parent–Child Relationship Inventory. From J. C. Impara & B. S. Plake (Eds.), *The thirteenth mental measurement yearbook* [Electronic version]. Retrieved from the Buros Institute's *Test Reviews Online* website: http//www.unl.edu/buros

Borkowski, J. G., & Burke, J. E. (1996). Theories, models, and measurements of executive function. In G. R. Lyon & N. A. Krasnegor (Eds.), *Attention, memory, and executive function* (pp. 235–261). Baltimore: Brookes.

Bos, C. S., & Vaughn, S. (1994). *Strategies for teaching students with learning and behavior problems.* Boston: Allyn & Bacon.

Bouchey, H. A., & Harter, S. (2005). Reflected appraisals, academic self-perceptions, and math/science performance during early adolescence. *Journal of Educational Psychology, 97*, 673–686.

Bronfenbrenner, U. (1979). *The ecology of human development: Experiments by nature and design.* Cambridge, MA: Harvard University Press.

Bronstein, P., Duncan, P., Clauson, J., Abrams, C. L., Yannett, N., Ginsburg, G., et al. (1998). Preventing middle school adjustment problems for children from lower-income families: A program for Aware Parenting. *Journal of Applied Developmental Psychology, 19*, 129–152.

Brophy, J. (1986). *On motivating students.* East Lansing: Michigan State University Institute for Research on Teaching. (ERIC Document Reproduction Service No. ED276724)

Brosvic, G. M., Dihoff, R. E., & Epstein, M. L. (2006). Feedback facilitates the acquisition and retention of numerical fact series by elementary school students with mathematics learning disabilities. *Psychological Record, 56*, 35–54.

Brown, A. L. (1980). Metacognitive development and reading. In R. J. Spiro, B. B. Bruce, & W. F. Brewer (Eds.), *Theoretical issues in reading comprehension* (pp. 453–481). Hillsdale, NJ: Erlbaum.

Brown, A. L., Armbruster, B., & Baker, L. (1986). The role of metacognition in reading and studying. In J. Orasanu (Ed.), *Reading comprehension: From research to practice* (pp. 49–75). Hillsdale, NJ: Erlbaum.

Brown, M. B. (2004). Academic motivation: Strategies for parents. In A. S. Canter, L. Z. Paige, M. D. Roth, I. Romero, & S. Carroll (Eds.), *Helping children at home and school II: Handouts for families and educators* (pp. 52.1–52.3). Bethesda, MD: National Association of School Psychologists.

Brown, V. L., Cronin, M. E., & McEntire, E. (1994). *Test of Mathematical Abilities—Second Edition (TOMA-2).* Austin, TX: PRO-ED.

Bryan, T., Burstein, K., & Bryan, J. (2001). Students with learning disabilities: Homework problems and promising practices. *Educational Psychologist, 36*, 167–180.

Bryan, T., & Sullivan-Burstein, K. (1997). [Teacher vs. student estimates of homework difficulty]. Unpublished raw data.

Bryant, B. R., Wiederholt, J. L., & Bryant, D. P. (1991). *Gray Diagnostic Reading Tests—Second Edition (GDRT-2).* Austin, TX: PRO-ED.

Butcher, J. N., Williams, C. L., Graham, J. R., Kaemmer, B., Archer, R. P., Tellegen, A., et al. (1992). *Minnesota Multiphasic Personality Inventory—Adolescent (MMPI-A).* Minneapolis: University of Minnesota Press.

Butler, D. L., (1998) The strategic content learning approach to promoting self-regulated learning: A report of three studies. *Journal of Educational Psychology, 90*, 682–697.

Butterfield, E. C., & Albertson, L. R. (1995). On making cognitive theory more general and developmentally pertinent. In F. Weinert & W. Schneider (Eds.), *Research on memory development* (pp. 73–99). Hillsdale, NJ: Erlbaum.

Calkins, L. (1986). *The art of teaching writing.* Portsmouth, NH: Heinemann.

Cancio, E. J., West, R. P., & Young, R. (2004). Improving mathematics homework completion and accuracy of students with EBD through self-management and parent participation. *Journal of Emotional and Behavioral Disorders, 12*, 9–23.

Carlson, C. L., Booth, J. E., Shinn, M., & Canu, W. H. (2002). Parent-, teacher-, and self-rated motivational styles in ADHD subtypes. *Journal of Learning Disabilities, 35*, 104–113.

Carlson, L., Glover, J. A., & Zimmer, J. W. (1981). First letter mnemonics: DAM (Don't Aid Memory). *Journal of General Psychology, 104*, 287–292.

Carlton, M. (2004). Motivating learning in young children. In A. S. Canter, L. Z. Paige, M. D. Roth, I. Romero, & S. Carroll (Eds.), *Helping children at home and school II: Handouts for families and educators* (pp. 53.115–53.117). Bethesda, MD: National Association of School Psychologists.

Carns, A. W., & Carns, M. R. (1991). Teaching study skills, cognitive strategies, and metacognitive skills through self-diagnosed learning styles. *School Counselor, 38*, 341–346.

Cassidy, S. (2004). Learning styles: An overview of theories, models, and measures. *Educational Psychology, 24*, 419–444.

Center for Effective Collaboration and Practice. (1999). *Addressing student problem behavior: An IEP team's introduction to functional behavioral assessment and behavior intervention plans* (2nd ed.). Washington, DC: American Institutes for Research.

Chaleff, C. (2000). Helping our students meet the standards through test preparation classes. *American Annals of the Deaf, 145*, 33–40.

Chalk, J. C., Hagan-Burke, S., & Burke, M. D. (2005). The effects of self-regulated strategy development on the writing process for high school students with learning disabilities. *Learning Disability Quarterly, 28*, 75–87.

Chickie-Wolfe, L. A. (1995, October). *Student-engineered behavior change*. Paper presented at the International Conference on Behavior Disorders, Council for Children with Behavior Disorders, Dallas, TX.

Chickie-Wolfe, L. A. (2005a). *Cognitive nourishment: Life-changing affirmations for the savvy teacher.* Thousand Oaks, CA: Corwin Press.

Chickie-Wolfe, L. A. (2005b). *Writers' Workshop genre ideas*. Locally published manuscript, Eads Elementary School, Munster, IN.

Chickie-Wolfe, L. A. (2005c). *Writing applications guide.* Locally published manuscript, Eads Elementary School, Munster, IN.

Chickie-Wolfe, L. A., & Harvey, V. S. (2006a). *Studying is not the same as doing homework: Expanding study strategies and self-regulation with the Study Pie*. Unpublished manuscript.

Chickie-Wolfe, L. A., & Harvey, V. S. (2006b). *Using visualization and comparison to develop self-regulatory skills in elementary school students*. Unpublished manuscript.

Chiu, L., & Henry, L. L. (1990). Development and validation of the Mathematics Anxiety Scale for Children. *Measurement and Evaluation in Counseling and Development, 23*, 121–127.

Christenson, S. L. (2004). The family–school partnership: An opportunity to promote the learning competence of all students. *School Psychology Review, 33*, 83–104.

Christenson, S. L., & Anderson, A. R. (2002). Commentary: The centrality of the learning context for students' academic enabler skills. *School Psychology Review, 31*, 378–393.

Clark, R. M. (1990, Spring). Why disadvantaged students succeed: What happens outside of school is critical. *Public Welfare*, pp. 17–23.

Cleary, T. (2006). The development and validation of the Self-Regulation Strategy Inventory—Self-Report. *Journal of School Psychology, 44*, 307–322.

Cobb Morocco, C., Hindin, A., & Mata-Aguilar, C. (2001). Building a deep understanding of literature with middle-grade students with learning disabilities. *Learning Disability Quarterly, 24*, 47–58.

Codding, R. S. (2003). *Examining the efficacy of performance feedback and goal-setting interventions in children with AD/HD: A comparison of two methods of goal setting.* Unpublished doctoral dissertation, Syracuse University.

Coleman, L. J. (2002). A shock to study. *Journal of Secondary Gifted Education, 14*, 39–52.

Coleman, M. R. (2005). Academic strategies that work for gifted students with learning disabilities. *Teaching Exceptional Children, 38*, 28–32.

Conners, C. K., & MHS Staff. (2000). *Conners' Continuous Performance Test II.* North Tonawanda, NY: Multi-Health Systems.

Cooper, H., Lindsey, J. J., & Nye, B. (2000). Homework in the home: How student, family, and parenting style differences relate to the homework process. *Contemporary Educational Psychology, 25*, 464–487.

Cooper, H., Valentine, J. C., Nye, B., & Lindsey, J. J. (1999). Relationships between five after-school activities and academic achievement. *Journal of Educational Psychology, 91*, 369–378.

Cosden, M., Morrison, G., Gutierrez, L., & Brown, M. (2004). The effects of homework programs and after-school activities on school success. *Theory into Practice, 43*, 220–226.

Cowan, N. (1993). Activation, attention, and short-term memory. *Memory and Cognition, 21*, 162–167.

Cowan, N. (2005). Working memory capacity limits in a theoretical context. In C. Izawa & N. Ohta (Eds.), *Human learning and memory: Advances in theory and application. The 4th Tsukuba International Conference on Memory* (pp. 155–175). Mahwah, NJ: Erlbaum.

Creative Therapy Associates. (2005). *Feelings—How are you feeling today?* Retrieved from www.ctherapy.com/feelings_home.asp

Crocker, L. (2005). Teaching for the test: How and why test preparation is appropriate. In R. P. Phelps (Ed.), *Defending standardized testing* (pp. 159–174). Mahwah, NJ: Erlbaum.

Crosnoe, R., Lopez-Gonzalez, L., & Muller, C. (2004). Immigration from Mexico into the math/science pipeline in American education. *Social Science Quarterly, 85*, 1208–1226.

Csikszentmihalyi, M. (1990). *Flow: The psychology of optimal experience.* New York: Harper.

CTB/McGraw-Hill. (1990). *Comprehensive Test of Basic Skills*. Monterey, CA: Author.

CTB/McGraw-Hill. (1993). *California Achievement Tests*. Monterey, CA: Author.

Daniels, A. (2004). Composition instruction: Using technology to motivate students to write. *Information Technology in Childhood Education Annual, 16*, 157–177.

Dawson, P., & Guare, R. (2004). *Executive skills in children and adolescents: A practical guide to assessment and intervention.* New York: Guilford Press.

De Corte, E., & Somers, R. (1982). Estimating the outcome of a task as a heuristic strategy in arithmetic problem solving: A teaching experiment with sixth graders. *Human Learning: A Journal of Practical Research and Application, 1*, 105–121.

De Corte, E., Verschaffel, L., & Op 't Eynde, P. (2000). Self-regulation: A characteristic and goal of mathematics education. In M. Boekaerts, P. R. Pintrich, & M. Zeidner (Eds.), *Handbook of self-regulation* (pp. 687–726). San Diego, CA: Academic Press.

Deci, E., & Ryan, R. (1985). *Intrinsic motivation and self-determination in human behavior.* New York: Plenum Press.

De Groot, E. V. (2002). Learning through interviewing: Students and teachers talk about learning and schooling. *Educational Psychologist, 37*, 41–52.

De La Paz, S. (2005). Effects of historical reasoning instruction and writing strategy mastery in culturally and academically diverse middle school classrooms. *Journal of Educational Psychology, 97*, 139–156.

De La Paz, S., & Graham, S. (1997). Effects of dictation and advanced planning instruction on the composing of students with writing and learning problems. *Journal of Educational Psychology, 89*, 203–222.

De La Paz, S., Owen, B., & Harris, K. R. (2000). Riding Elvis' motorcycle: Using self-regulated strategy development to PLAN and WRITE for a state writing exam. *Learning Disabilities Research and Practice, 15*, 45–54.

Delgado-Gaitan, C. (1992). School matters in the Mexican-American home: Socializing children to education. *American Educational Research Journal, 29*, 495–513.

DeMarie, D., Miller, P. H., Ferron, J., & Cunningham, W. R. (2004). Path analysis tests of theoretical models of children's memory performance. *Journal of Cognition and Development, 5*, 461–492.

Denckla, M. B. (1996). A theory and model of executive function: A neuropsychological perspective. In G. R. Lyon & N. A. Krasnegor (Eds.), *Attention, memory, and executive function* (pp. 263–278). Baltimore: Brookes.

Derek Bok Center for Teaching and Learning. (1993). *Thinking together: Collaborative learning in science* [Videotape]. Cambridge, MA: Harvard University.

Desmedt, E., & Valcke, M. (2004). Mapping the learning styles "jungle": An overview of the literature based on citation analysis. *Educational Psychology, 24*, 445–464.

Devine, T. G. (1987). *Teaching study skills* (2nd ed.). Boston: Allyn & Bacon.

Diener, C., & Dweck, C. S. (1978). An analysis of learned helplessness: Continuous feedback in performance strategy and achievement cognitions following failure. *Journal of Personality and Social Psychology, 36*, 451–462.

DiPerna, J. C., & Elliott, S. N. (2000). *Academic Competence Evaluation Scales (ACES).* San Antonio, TX: Psychological Corporation.

Doll, B., Zucker, S., & Brehm, K. (2004). *Resilient classrooms: Creating healthy environments for learning.* New York: Guilford Press.

Drummond, K. V., & Stipek, D. (2004). Low-income parents' beliefs about their role in children's academic leaning. *Elementary School Journal, 104*, 197–213.

Duckworth, A. L., & Seligman, M. E. P. (2005). Self-discipline outdoes IQ in predicting academic performance of adolescents. *Psychological Science, 16*, 939–944.

Dunlap, G., Kern, L., dePerezel, M., Clarke, S., Williams, D., Childs, K., et al. (1993). Functional assessment of classroom variables for students with emotional/behavioral disorders. *Behavioral Disorders, 18*, 275–291.

Dunn, R., & Dunn, K. (1978). *Teaching students through their individual learning styles: A practical approach.* Reston, VA: Prentice-Hall.

Ebbinghaus, H. (1885). *Memory: A contribution to experimental psychology.* New York: Teachers College, Columbia University.

Eckert, T. L., Dunn, E. K., & Codding, R. S. (2006). Assessment of mathematics and reading performance: An examination of the correspondence between direct assessment of student performance and teacher report. *Psychology in the Schools, 43*, 247–265.

Eckert, T. L., Rosenthal, B. D., Ricci, L. J., Quintero, N. E., Benson, H. L., Vance, M. J., et al. (2006, March). *A classwide performance feedback intervention to improve children's mathematics skills.* Poster presented at the annual meeting of the National Association of School Psychologists, Los Angeles.

Educational Testing Service. (2004). *SAT I.* Princeton, NJ: Author.

Elliot, A. (1999). Approach and avoidance motivation and achievement goals. *Educational Psychologist, 34*, 169–189.

Englert, C. S., Berry, R., & Dunsmore, K. (2001). A case study of the apprenticeship process: Another perspective on the apprentice and the scaffolding metaphor. *Journal of Learning Disabilities, 34*, 152–171.

Epstein, J. L., & Van Voorhis, F. L. (2001). More than minutes: Teachers' roles in designing homework. *Educational Psychologist, 56*, 181–193.

Ericcson, K. A., & Charness, N. (1994). Expert performance: Its structure and acquisition. *American Psychologist, 49*, 725–747.

Ericsson, K. A., Delaney, P. F., & Weaver, G. (2004). Uncovering the structure of a memorist's superior "basic" memory capacity. *Cognitive Psychology, 49*, 191–237.

Ericsson, K. A., Krampe, R. T., & Tesch-Romer, C. (1993). The role of deliberate practice in the acquisition of expert performance. *Psychological Review, 100*, 363–406.

Ericsson, K. A., & Kintsch, W. (1995). Long-term working memory. *Psychological Review, 102*, 211–245.

Erikson, E. (1963). *Childhood and society* (2nd ed.). New York: Norton.

Esler, A. N., Godber, Y., & Christenson, S. L. (2002). Best practices in supporting home–school collaboration. In A. Thomas & J. Grimes (Eds.), *Best practices in school psychology IV* (pp. 389–411). Bethesda, MD: National Association of School Psychologists.

Eslinger, P. J. (1996). Conceptualizing, describing, and measuring components of executive function: A summary. In G. R. Lyon & N. A. Krasnegor (Eds.), *Attention, memory, and executive function* (pp. 366–395). Baltimore: Brookes.

Fantuzzo, J., McWayne, C., Perry, M. A., & Childs, S. (2004). Multiple dimensions of family involvement and their relations to behavioral and learning competencies for urban, low-income children. *School Psychology Review, 33*, 467–480.

Feng, A. X., VanTassel-Baska, J., & Quek, C. (2005). A longitudinal assessment of gifted students' learning using the integrated curriculum model (ICM). *Roeper Review, 27*, 78–83.

Ferrari, J. R., Johnson, J. L., & McKown, W. G. (1995). *Procrastination and task avoidance: Theory and research.* New York: Plenum Press.

Field, T., Diego, M., & Sanders, C. E. (2001). Exercise is positively related to adolescents' relationships and academics. *Adolescence, 36*, 105–110.

Fitzpatrick, C. (in press). Test review of the Behavior Rating Inventory of Executive Function. From B. S. Plake & J. C. Impara (Eds.), *The fifteenth mental measurement yearbook* [Electronic version]. Retrieved from the Buros Institute's *Test Reviews Online* website: http//www.unl.edu/buros

Flavell, J. H. (1979). Metacognition and cognitive monitoring: A new area of cognitive developmental inquiry. *American Psychologist, 34*, 906–911.

Fleisher, P. (2006). Help is on the way: Online tutoring services expand students' options. *Technology and Learning, 26*(9), 14–18.

Fletcher, D. C. (2001). Second graders decide when to use electronic editing tools. *Information Technology in Childhood Education Annual, 12*, 155–174.

Foley, R. M., & Epstein, M. H. (1992). Correlates of the academic achievement of adolescents with behavioral disorders. *Behavior Disorders, 18*, 9–17.

Forbes, E. E., & Dahl, R. E. (2005). Neural systems of positive affect: Relevance to understanding child and adolescent depression. *Development and Psychopathology, 17*, 827–850.

Franzke, M., Kintsch, E., & Caccamise, D. (2005). Summary Street®: Computer support for comprehension and writing. *Journal of Educational Computing Research, 33*, 53–80.

Friedland, J. G., Mandel, H. P., & Marcus, S. I. (1996). *Achievement Motivation Profile (AMP)*. Los Angeles: Western Psychological Services.

Fuchs, D., Fuchs, L. S., Thompson, A., Svenson, E., Yen, L., & Otaiba, S. A. (2001). Peer-assisted learning strategies in reading: Extensions for kindergarten, first grade, and high school. *Remedial and Special Education, 22*, 15–21.

Fuchs, L. S., Compton, D. L., Fuchs, D., Paulson, K., Bryant, J., D., & Hamlett, C. L. (2005). The prevention, identification, and cognitive determinants of math difficulty. *Journal of Educational Psychology, 97*, 493–513.

Fuchs, L. S., & Fuchs, D. (2005). Enhancing mathematical problem solving for students with disabilities. *Journal of Special Education, 39*, 45–57.

Fuchs, L. S., Fuchs, D., Hamlett, C. L., Phillips, N. B., Karns, K., & Dutka, S. (1997). Enhancing students' helping behavior during peer-mediated instruction with conceptual mathematical explanations. *Elementary School Journal, 97*, 223–249.

Fuchs, L. S., Hamlett, C. L., & Fuchs, D. (1999). *Monitoring Basic Skills Progress—Second Edition.* Nashville, TN: Vanderbilt University.

Fuchs, L. S., Hamlett, C. L., & Powell, S. R. (2003). *Math Flash* [Computer software]. (Available from L. S. Fuchs, 328 Peabody, Vanderbilt University, Nashville, TN 37203)

Gable, R. A., & Hendrickson, J. M. (2000). Strategies for maintaining positive behavior change stemming from functional behavioral assessment in schools. *Education and Treatment of Children, 23*, 286–298.

Gable, R. K. (1998). Test review of the Motivated Strategies for Learning Questionnaire. From J. C. Impara & B. S. Plake (Eds.), *The thirteenth mental measurement yearbook* [Electronic version]. Retrieved from the Buros Institute's *Test Reviews Online* website: http//www.unl.edu/buros

Gajria, M., & Salvia, J. (1992). The effects of summarization instruction on text comprehension of students with learning disabilities. *Exceptional Children, 58*, 508–516.

Gardner, H. (1993). *Frames of mind.* New York: Basic Books. (Original work published 1983)

Garhammer, M. (2002). Pace of life and enjoyment. *Journal of Happiness Studies, 3*, 217–256.

Garner, R. (1994). Metacognition and executive control. In R. B. Ruddell, M. R. Ruddell, & H. Singer (Eds.), *Theoretical models and processes of reading* (4th ed., pp. 715–732). Newark, DE: International Reading Association.

Garner, R., & Reis, R. (1981). Monitoring and resolving comprehension obstacles: An investigation of spontaneous lookbacks among upper-grade good and poor comprehenders. *Reading Research Quarterly*, 16, 569–582.

Geary, D. C. (2004). Mathematics and learning disabilities. *Journal of Learning Disabilities, 37*, 4–15.

Geary, D. C. (2005). Role of cognitive theory in the study of learning disability in mathematics. *Journal of Learning Disabilities, 38*, 305–307.

Geary, D. C., Liu, F., & Chen, G. (1999). Contributions of computational fluency to cross-national differences in arithmetical reasoning abilities. *Journal of Educational Psychology, 91*, 716–719.

Gerard, A. G. (1994). *Parent–Child Relationship Inventory (PCRI)*. Los Angeles: Western Psychological Services.

Gettinger, M., & Nicaise, M. (1997). Study skills. In G. G. Bear, K. M. Minke, & A. Thomas (Eds.), *Children's needs II: Development, problems, and alternatives* (pp. 407–418). Bethesda, MD: National Association of School Psychologists.

Gettinger, M., & Seibert, J. K. (2002). Contributions of study skills to academic competence. *School Psychology Review, 31*, 350–365.

Gillette, Y. (2001). Pictures to print: A software scaffold to written literacy. *Journal of Head Trauma Rehabilitation, 16*, 484–497.

Gillette, Y. (2006). Assistive technology and literacy partnerships. *Topics in Language Disorders, 26*, 70–84.

Gioia, G. A., Isquith, P. K., Guy, S. C., & Kenworthy, L. (2000). *Behavior Rating Inventory of Executive Function (BRIEF)*. Lutz, FL: Psychological Assessment Resources.

Glasser, W. (1990). *The quality school: Managing children without coercion*. New York: Harper.

Glasser, W. (1998). *Choice theory: A new psychology of personal freedom*. New York: HarperCollins.

Gleason, M. M., Archer, A. L., & Colvin, G. (2002). Interventions for improving study skills. In M. A. Shinn, H. M. Walker, & G. Stoner (Eds.), *Interventions for academic and behavior problems II: Preventative and remedial approaches* (pp. 651–680). Bethesda, MD: National Association of School Psychologists.

Goldberg, I. (1995). Implementing the consultant teacher model: Interfacing multiple linking relationships. *Journal of Educational and Psychological Consultation, 6*, 175–190.

Goleman, D. (1995). *Emotional intelligence*. New York: Bantam Books.

Gottfried, A. E. (1986). *Children's Academic Intrinsic Motivation Inventory (CAIMI)*. Odessa, FL: Psychological Assessment Resources.

Graesser, A. C., McNamara, D. S., & VanLehn, K. (2005). Scaffolding deep comprehension strategies through Point&Query, AutoTutor, and iSTART. *Educational Psychologist, 40*, 225–234.

Graham, S., & Harris, K. R. (1996). Addressing problems in attention, memory, and executive functioning. In G. R. Lyon & N. A. Krasnegor (Eds.), *Attention, memory, and executive function* (pp. 349–366). Baltimore: Brookes.

Graham, S., & Harris, K. R. (2002). Prevention and intervention for struggling writers. In M. Shinn, H. M. Walker, & G. Stoner (Eds.), *Interventions for academic and behavioral problems II: Prevention and remedial approaches* (pp. 589–610). Bethesda, MD: National Association of School Psychologists.

Graham, S., Harris, K. R., & Mason, L. (2005). Improving the writing performance, knowledge, and self-efficacy of struggling young writers: The effects of self-regulated strategy development. *Contemporary Educational Psychology, 30*, 207–241.

Grant, A. M. (2003). Towards a psychology of coaching: The impact of coaching on metacognition, mental health and goal attainment. *Dissertation Abstracts International, 63*(12), 6094B.

Graves, D. H. (1983). *Writing: Teachers and children at work*. Exeter, NH: Heinemann.

Gray, J. R. (2004). Integration of emotion and cognitive control. *Current Directions in Psychological Science, 13*, 46–48.

Gregor, A. (2005). Examination anxiety: Live with it, control it or make it work for you? *School Psychology International, 26*, 617–635.

Greiner, J. M., & Karoly, P. (1976). Effects of self-control training on study activity and academic performance. *Journal of Counseling Psychology, 23*, 495–502.

Gresham, F. M., & Elliott, S. N. (1990). *Social Skills Rating System (SSRS)*. Circle Pines, MN: American Guidance Service.

Grolnick, W. S., & Slowiaczek, M. L. (1994). Parents' involvement in children's schooling: A multidimensional conceptualization and motivational model. *Child Development, 65*, 237–252.

Gulek, C. (2003). Preparing for high-stakes testing. *Theory into Practice, 42*, 42–50.

Guy, S. C., Isquith, P. K., & Gioia, G. A. (2004). *Behavior Rating Inventory of Executive Function—Self-Report Version (BRIEF-SR)*. Lutz, FL: Psychological Assessment Resources.

Hadwin, A. F., & Winne, P. H. (2001). CoNoteS2: A software tool for promoting self-regulation. *Educational Research and Evaluation, 7*, 313–334.

Hale, J. E. (2001). *Learning while black: Creating edu-*

cational excellence for African American children. Baltimore: Johns Hopkins University Press.

Hallahan, D., Lloyd, J., Kauffman, J., & Looper, A. (1983). Academic problems. In R. Morris & T. Kratochwill (Eds.), *Practice of child therapy: A textbook of methods* (pp. 113–141). New York: Pergamon Press.

Halperin, J. M. (1996). Conceptualizing, describing, and measuring components of attention: A summary. In G. R. Lyon & N. A. Krasnegor (Eds.), *Attention, memory, and executive function* (pp. 119–136). Baltimore: Brookes.

Hambleton, R. K. (in press). Test review of the Academic Competence Evaluation Scales (ACES). From B. S. Plake & J. C. Impara (Eds.), *The sixteenth mental measurement yearbook* [Electronic version]. Retrieved from the Buros Institute's *Test Reviews Online* website: http//www.unl.edu/buros

Hammill, D. D., & Larsen, S. C. (1996). *Test of Written Language—Third Edition (TOWL-3).* Austin, TX: PRO-ED.

Harackiewicz, J. M., Barron, K. E., Pintrich, P. R., Elliot, A. J., & Thrash, T. M. (2002). Revision of achievement goal theory. *Journal of Educational Psychology, 94,* 638–645.

Harris, K. R. (1986). Self-monitoring of attentional behavior vs. self-monitoring of productivity: Effects on on-task behavior and academic response rate among learning disabled children. *Journal of Applied Behavior Analysis, 19,* 417–423.

Harris, K. R., Friedlander, B. D., Saddler, B., Frizzelle, R., & Graham, S. (2005). Self-monitoring of attention versus self-monitoring of academic performance: Effects among students with ADHD in the general education classroom. *Journal of Special Education, 39,* 145–156.

Harris, K. R., & Graham, S. (1999) Programmatic intervention research: Illustrations from the evolution of self-regulated strategy development. *Learning Disability Quarterly, 22,* 251–262.

Harvey, V. S. (1997). Improving readability of psychological reports. *Professional Psychology: Research and Practice, 28,* 271–274.

Harvey, V. S. (2002). Best practices in teaching study skills. In A. Thomas & J. Grimes (Eds.). *Best practices in school psychology IV* (pp. 831–845). Bethesda, MD: National Association of School Psychologists.

Hattie, J., Biggs, J., & Purdie, N. (1996). Effects of learning skills interventions on student learning: A meta-analysis. *Review of Educational Research, 66,* 9–136.

Hayes, S. C., Gifford, E. V., & Ruckstuhl, L. E. (1996). Relational frame theory and executive function: A behavioral approach. In G. R. Lyon & N. A. Krasnegor (Eds.), *Attention, memory, and executive function* (pp. 279–305). Baltimore: Brookes.

Heaton, R. K., Chelune, G. J., Talley, J. L., Kay, G. G., & Curtiss, G. (1993). *Wisconsin Card Sorting Test, Revised and Expanded (WCST).* Odessa, FL: Psychological Assessment Resources.

Hebert, T. P., & Furner, J. M. (1997). Helping high ability students overcome math anxiety through bibliotherapy. *Journal of Secondary Gifted Education, 8,* 164–179.

Henning-Stout, M. (1994). *Responsive assessment: A new way of thinking about learning.* San Francisco: Jossey-Bass.

Higgins, K., & Boone, R. (1990). Hypertext computer study guides and the social studies achievement of students with learning disabilities, remedial students, and regular education students. *Journal of Learning Disabilities, 23,* 529–540.

Hong, E., & Milgram, R. M. (2000). Homework motivation and preference: A learner centered homework approach. *Theory into Practice, 43,* 197–205.

Hoover-Dempsey, K. V., Battiato, A. C., Walker, J. M. T., Reed, R. P., Dejong, J. M., & Jones, K. M. (2001). Parent involvement in homework. *Educational Psychologist, 36,* 195–209.

Horn, S. E. (2004). Teacher facilitation of self-regulated reading in ninth grade English. *Dissertation Abstracts International, 64*(9), 3233A.

Hug, B., Krajcik, J. S., & Marx, R. W. (2005). Using innovative learning technologies to promote learning and engagement in an urban science classroom. *Urban Education, 40,* 446–472.

Hughes, C. A., & Lloyd, J. W. (1993). An analysis of self-management. *Journal of Behavioral Education, 3,* 405–425.

Hughes, C. A., Ruhl, K. L., Schumaker, J. B., & Deshler, D. D. (1989). Effects of instruction in an assignment completion strategy on the homework performance of students with learning disabilities in general education classes. *Learning Disabilities Research and Practice, 17,* 1–18.

Indiana State Department of Education. (2005). *ISTEP+ teacher's scoring guide.* Indianapolis: Author.

Ingraham, C. L. (2000). Consultation through a multicultural lens: Multicultural and cross-cultural consultation in schools. *School Psychology Review, 29,* 320–343.

Jackson, T., MacKenzie, J., & Hobfoll, S. E. (2000). Communal aspects of self-regulation. In M. Boekaerts, P. R. Pintrich, & M. Zeidner (Eds.), *Handbook of self-regulation* (pp. 275–299). San Diego, CA: Academic Press.

Jacobson, J. M. (1990). Group vs. individual completion of a cloze passage. *Journal of Reading, 33,* 244–250.

Johnson, M. H. (1999). Developmental neuroscience. In M. H. Bornstein & M. E. Lamb (Eds.), *Developmental psychology: An advanced textbook* (4th ed., pp. 199–230). Mahwah, NJ: Erlbaum.

Jones, A. P. (1993). Note-taking and reviewing matrix notes: Effects on learning achievement and instructional time with interactive videodisc instruction. *International Journal of Instructional Media, 20*, 11–19.

Jones, B. F., Pierce, J., & Hunter, B. (1988). Teaching students to construct graphic representations. *Educational Leadership, 46*(4), 20–26.

Juvonen, J., Nishina, A., & Graham, S. (2000). Peer harassment, psychological adjustment, and school functioning in early adolescence. *Journal of Educational Psychology, 92*, 349–359.

Kamphaus, R. W., & Reynolds, C. R. (1998). *BASC Monitor for ADHD*. Circle Pines, MN: American Guidance Service.

Kampworth, T. J. (2006). *Collaborative consultation in the schools: Effective practices for students with learning and behavior problems* (3rd ed.). Upper Saddle River, NJ: Pearson/Merrill/Prentice Hall.

Kanfer, F. H., & Gaelick-Buys, L. (1991). Self-management methods. In F. H. Kanfer & A. P. Goldstein (Eds.), *Helping people change: A textbook of methods* (4th ed., pp. 305–360). New York: Pergamon Press.

Keith, T. Z., Diamond-Hallam, C., & Fine, J. G. (2004). Longitudinal effects of in-school and out-of-school homework on high school grades. *School Psychology Quarterly, 19*, 187–211.

Keller, B. (2004). Teacher taps parents to help with test prep. *Education Week, 23*, 6–7.

Kelly, S. (2004). Do increased levels of parental involvement account for social class differences in track placement? *Social Science Research, 33*, 626–659.

Kelly, W. E. (2002). Harnessing the river of time: A theoretical framework of time use efficiency with suggestions for counselors. *Journal of Employment Counseling, 39*, 12–21.

Kime, L. A., & Clark, J. (1998). *Explorations in college algebra*. New York: Wiley.

Kinnunen, R., & Vauras, M. (1995). Comprehension monitoring and the level of comprehension in high- and low-achieving children's reading. *Learning and Instruction, 5*, 143–165.

Kitchens, A. (1995). *Defeating math anxiety*. Chicago: Irwin.

Klineberg, T., Fernell, E., Oleson, P. J., Johnson, M., Gustafson, P., & Dahlstrom, K. (2005). Computerized training of working memory in children with ADHD: A randomized, controlled trial. *Journal of the American Academy of Child and Adolescent Psychiatry, 44*, 177–186.

Koch, A., & Eckstein, S. G. (1995). Skills needed for reading comprehension of physics texts and their relation to problem-solving ability. *Journal of Research in Science Teaching, 32*, 613–628.

Kostka, M. J. (2000). The effects of error-detection practice on keyboard sight-reading achievement of undergraduate music majors. *Journal of Research in Music Education, 48*, 114–122.

Kovalik, S., with Olsen, K. (1994). *Integrated thematic instruction* (3rd ed.). Kent, WA: Books for Educators.

Kozloff, M. A. (2005). Fads in general education. In J. W. Jacobson, R. M. Foxx, & J. A. Mulick (Eds.), *Controversial therapies for developmental disabilities: Fad, fashion and science in professional practice* (pp. 159–173). Mahwah, NJ: Erlbaum.

Kramer-Schlosser, L. (1992). Teacher distance and student disengagement. *Journal of Teacher Education, 43*, 128–140.

Krutetskii, V. A. (1976). *The psychology of mathematical abilities in school children*. Chicago: University of Chicago Press.

Kuepper, J. E. (1990). Best practices in teaching study skills. In A. Thomas & J. Grimes (Eds.), *Best practices in school psychology II* (pp. 711–721). Washington, DC: National Association of School Psychologists.

Kuhn, D. (2000). Does memory development belong on an endangered topic list? *Child Development, 71*, 21–25.

Lachar, D., & Gruber, C. P. (1995). *Personality Inventory for Youth (PIY)*. Los Angeles: Western Psychological Services.

Lachar, D., & Gruber, C. P. (2001). *Personality Inventory for Children, Second Edition (PIC-2)*. Los Angeles: Western Psychological Services.

Lakein, A. (1973). *How to get control of your time and your life*. New York: Penguin.

Lambert, M. C., Cartledge, G., & Heward, W. L. (2006). Effects of response cards on disruptive behavior and academic responding during math lessons by fourth-grade urban students. *Journal of Positive Behavior Interventions, 8*, 88–99.

Lamott, A. (1995). *Bird by bird: Some instructions on writing and life*. New York: Anchor.

Landsberger, J. (2006). *Vocabulary building exercise*. Retrieved from www.studygs.net

Langer, M., & Neal, J. (1987). Strategies for learning: An adjunct study skills model. *Journal of Reading, 31*, 134–139.

Lareau, A. (1996). Assessing parent involvement in schooling: A critical analysis. In A. Booth & J. Dunn (Eds.), *Family–school links: How do they affect educational outcomes?* (pp. 57–64). Mahwah, NJ: Erlbaum.

Latterell, C. M. (2005). *Math wars: A guide for parents and teachers*. Westport, CT: Praeger.

Laurendeau-Bendavid, M. (1977). Culture, schooling, and cognitive development: A comparative study of children in French Canada and Rwanda. In P. R. Dasen (Ed.), *Piagetian psychology: Cross-cultural contributions* (pp. 123–168). New York: Gardner Press.

Lazarus, B. D. (1996). Flexible skeletons: Guided notes

for adolescence. *Teaching Exceptional Children, 28*, 36–40.

Leland-Jones, P. J. (1997). *Improving the acquisition of sixth grade social studies concepts through the implementation of a study skills unit.* Ft. Lauderdale, FL: Nova Southeastern University. (ERIC Documentation Reproduction Service No. ED424154)

Lerner, J. (1997). *Learning disabilities: Theories, diagnosis, and teaching strategies* (7th ed.). Boston: Houghton Mifflin.

Levin, J. R. (1993). Mnemonic strategies and classroom learning: A twenty-year report card. *Elementary School Journal, 94*, 235–244.

Levine, M. (2002). *A mind at a time*. New York: Simon & Schuster.

Levine, M. D., & Hooper, S. R. (2001). *Survey of Teenage Readiness and Neurodevelopmental Status (STRANDS).* Cambridge, MA: Educators Publishing Service.

Lin, X., Schwartz, D. L., & Hatano, G. (2005). Toward teachers' adaptive metacognition. *Educational Psychologist, 40*, 245–255.

Linnenbrink, E. A., & Pintrich, P. R. (2002). Achievement goal theory and affect: An asymmetrical bidirectional model. *Educational Psychologist, 37*, 69–78.

Lockl, K. (2002). The development of self-regulated learning in elementary school children: Association between task difficulty and allocation of study time. *Psychologie in Erziehung und Unterricht, 49*, 3–16.

Loken, E., Radlinski, F., Crespi, V., Millet, J., & Cushing, L. (2004). Online study behavior of 100,000 students preparing for the SAT, ACH, and GRE. *Journal of Educational Computing Research, 30*, 255–262.

Loo, R. (2004). Kolb's learning styles and learning preferences: Is there a linkage? *Educational Psychology, 24*, 99–108.

Lovelace, M. K. (2005). Meta-analysis of experimental research based on the Dunn and Dunn model. *Journal of Educational Research, 98*, 176–183.

Lundin, S. C. (2006). *Manifesto*. Retrieved from www.charthouse.com

Lundin, S. C., Paul, H., & Christensen, J. (2000). *Fish!: A remarkable way to boost morale and improve results*. New York: Hyperion.

Macan, T. H. (1996). Time management training: Effects on time behaviors, attitudes, and job performance. *Journal of Psychology, 130*, 229–236.

Macan, T. H., Shahani, C., Dipboye, R. L., & Phillips, A. P. (1990). College students' time management. *Journal of Educational Psychology, 82*, 760–768.

MacGinitie, W. H., MacGinitie, R. K., Maria, K., & Dreyer, L. G. (2000). *Gates–MacGinitie Reading Tests, Fourth Edition, Forms S and T.* Itasca, IL: Riverside.

Madaus, M., Kehle, T. H., Madaus, J., & Bray, M. A. (2003). Mystery motivator as an intervention to promote homework completion and accuracy. *School Psychology International, 24*, 369–377.

Malecki, C. K., & Elliott, S. N. (2002). Children's social behaviors as predictors of academic achievement. *School Psychology Quarterly, 17*, 1–23.

March, J. (1997). *Multidimensional Anxiety Scale for Children.* North Tonawanda, NY: Multi-Health Systems.

Marchant, G. J., & Paulson, S. E. (1998). Test review of the Parent-Child Relationship Inventory. From J. C. Impara & B. S. Plake (Eds.), *The thirteenth mental measurement yearbook* [Electronic version]. Retrieved from the Buros Institute's *Test Reviews Online* website: http//www.unl.edu/buros

Margolis, H., & McCabe, P. P. (2003). Self-efficacy: A key to improving the motivation of struggling learners. *Preventing School Failure, 47*, 162–175.

Markman, E. M. (1979). Realizing that you don't understand: Elementary school children's awareness of inconsistencies. *Child Development, 50*, 634–655.

Marsh, H. W. (1986). Verbal and math self-concepts: An internal–external frame of reference model. *American Educational Research Journal, 23*, 129–149.

Martin, D., & Potter, L. (1998). How teachers can help students get their learning styles met at school and at home. *Education Chula Vista, 118*, 549–555.

Martinez Pons, M. (in press). Test review of the Behavior Rating Inventory of Executive Functioning Self-Report Version. From B. S. Plake & J. C. Impara (Eds.), *The sixteenth mental measurement yearbook* [Electronic version]. Retrieved from the Buros Institute's *Test*

Marzano, R. J., & Kendall, J. S., with Gaddy, B. B. (1999). *Essential knowledge: The debate over what American students should know.* Aurora, CO: McREL Institute.

Maslow, A. H. (1970). *Motivation and personality* (2nd ed.). New York: Harper & Row.

Mason, L. H., Harris, K. R., & Graham, S. (2002). Every child has a story to tell: Self-regulated strategy development for story writing. *Education and Treatment of Children, 25*, 496–506.

Mathan, S. A., & Koedinger, K. R. (2005). Fostering the intelligent novice: Learning from errors with metacognitive tutoring. *Educational Psychologist, 40*, 257–265.

Mazzocco, M. M. (2005). Challenges in identifying target skills for math disability screening and intervention. *Journal of Learning Disabilities, 38*, 318–323.

McAdams, D. P., & Pals, J. L. (2006). A new Big Five: Fundamental principles for an integrative science of personality. *American Psychologist, 61*, 204–217.

McCabe, D. (1985). *AVKO sequential spelling*. Birch Run, MI: Educational Research Foundation.

McCarney, S. B., & Bauer, A. M. (1990). *Attention Deficit Disorders Evaluation Scale*. Columbia, MO: Hawthorne Educational Services.

McCarthy, C. B. (2005). Effects of thematic-based, hands-on science teaching versus a textbook approach for students with disabilities. *Journal of Research in Science Teaching, 42,* 245–263.

McColsky, S., & McMunn, N. (2000). Strategies for dealing with high-stakes state tests. *Phi Delta Kappan, 82,* 115–121.

McCrae, R. R., & Costa, P. T. (2003). *Personality in adulthood: A five-factor theory perspective* (2nd ed.). New York: Guilford Press.

McCutchen, D. (2000). Knowledge, processing, and working memory: Implications for a theory of writing. *Educational Psychologist, 35,* 13–23.

McIlvane, W. J., Dube, W. V., & Callahan, T. D. (1996). Attention: A behavior analytic perspective. In G. R. Lyon & N. A. Krasnegor (Eds.), *Attention, memory, and executive function* (pp. 97–117). Baltimore: Brookes.

McLeod, D. B., Metzger, W., & Craviotto, C. (1989). Comparing experts' and novices' affective reactions to mathematical problem solving: An exploratory study. In G. Vergnaud (Ed.), *Proceedings of the Thirteenth International Conference for the Psychology of Mathematics Education* (Vol. 2, pp. 296–303). Paris: Laboratoire de Psychologie du Développement et de l'Education de l'Enfant.

McNamara, D. S., Levenstein, I. B., & Boonthum, C. (2004). iSTART: Interactive Strategy Trainer for Active Reading and Thinking. *Behavioral Research Methods, Instruments, and Computers, 36,* 213–221.

McNeill, K. L., Lizotte, D. J., Krajcik, J., & Marx, R. W. (2006). Supporting students' construction of scientific explanations by fading scaffolds in instructional materials. *Journal of the Learning Sciences, 15,* 153–191.

Meece, J. L., & Miller, S. D. (1999). Changes in elementary school children's achievement goals for reading and writing: Results of a longitudinal and an intervention study. *Scientific Studies of Reading, 3,* 207–229.

Mehrens, W. A. (1991). *Defensible/indefensible instructional preparation of high stakes achievement tests: An exploratory trialogue*. Paper presented at the annual meeting of the American Educational Research Association, Chicago.

Meichenbaum, D. H. (1977). *Cognitive behavior modification: An integrative approach*. New York: Plenum Press.

Meichenbaum, D. H., & Goodman, J. (1971). Training impulsive children to talk to themselves: A means of developing self-control. *Journal of Abnormal Psychology, 77,* 115–126.

Meichenbaum, D. H., & Turk, D. C. (1987). *Increasing treatment adherence*. New York: Plenum.

Merrell, K. W. (2001). *Helping students overcome depression and anxiety: A practical guide*. New York: Guilford Press.

Metcalfe, J., & Mischel, W. (1999). A hot/cool system analysis of delay of gratification: Dynamics of willpower. *Psychological Review, 106,* 3–19.

Meyer, D. K., & Turner, J. C. (2002). Using instructional discourse analysis to study the scaffolding of student self-regulation. *Educational Psychologist, 37,* 17–25.

Milgram, N., & Toubiana, Y. (1999). Academic anxiety, academic procrastination, and parental involvement in students and their parents. *British Journal of Educational Psychology, 69,* 345–362.

Miller, S. D. (1990). Low- and high-achieving fourth graders' ability to understand basal worksheet directions. *Elementary School Journal, 90,* 485–495.

Miller, S. D. (2003). How high- and low-challenge tasks affect motivation and learning implications for struggling learners. *Reading and Writing Quarterly, 19,* 39–59.

Miller, S. D., & Meece, J. L. (1999). Third graders' motivational preferences for reading and writing tasks. *Elementary School Journal, 100,* 19–35.

Miller, S. D., & Yochum, N. (1991). Asking students about the nature of their reading difficulties. *Journal of Reading Behavior, 23,* 465–485.

Minuchin, S. (1974). *Families and family therapy*. Cambridge, MA: Harvard University Press.

Mirsky, A. F. (1996). Disorders of attention. In G. R. Lyon & N. A. Krasnegor (Eds.), *Attention, memory, and executive function* (pp. 70–96). Baltimore, MD: Brookes.

Mischel, W., & Shoda, Y. (1995). A cognitive–affective system theory of personality: Reconceptualizing situations, dispositions, dynamics, and invariance in personality structure. *Psychological Review, 102,* 246–268.

Mithaug, D. K., & Mithaug, D. E. (2003). Effects of teacher-directed versus student-directed instruction on self-management of young children with disabilities. *Journal of Applied Behavior Analysis, 36,* 133–136.

Mokhtari, K., & Reichard, C. (2002). Assessing students' metacognitive awareness of reading strategies. *Journal of Educational Psychology, 94,* 249–259.

Mooney, J., & Cole, D. (2000). *Learning outside the lines*. New York: Simon & Schuster.

Moore, W. P. (1994). The devaluation of standardized testing: One district's responses to mandated assessment. *Applied Measurement in Education, 7,* 343–367.

Moos, R. H., & Trickett, E. J. (1987). *Classroom Environment Scale, Second Edition (CES)*. Palo Alto, CA: Consulting Psychologists Press.

Murphy, S. (Ed.). (2005). *The sport psych handbook: A complete guide to today's best mental training techniques*. Champaign, IL: Human Kinetics.

Naglieri, J. A., & Das, J. P. (1997). *Das–Naglieri Cognitive Assessment System (CAS)*. Itasca, IL: Riverside.

National Middle School Association. (1995). *This we believe: Developmentally responsive middle-level schools*. Columbus, OH: Author.

Neimark, E. D. (1979). Status of formal operations research. *Human Development, 22*, 60–67.

Nelson, N. W., & Van Meter, A. M. (2002). Assessing curriculum-based reading and writing samples. *Topics in Language Disorders, 22*, 35–59.

Nichols, C. W. (1991). *Assessment of Core Goals (ACG)*. Palo Alto, CA: Mind Garden.

Northwest Regional Educational Laboratory. (1999). *Parent partners: Using parents to enhance education*. Portland, OR: Author.

Nunes, T., Schliemann, A. D., & Carraher, D. W. (1993). *Street mathematics and school mathematics*. Cambridge, UK: Cambridge University Press.

Oakhill, J., & Patel, S. (1991). Can imagery training help children who have comprehension problems? *Journal of Research in Reading, 14*, 106–115.

Ogbu, J. (1995). Cultural problems in minority education: Their interpretations and consequences. *Urban Review, 27*(3), 189–205.

Ogden, W. R. (2003). Reaching all the students: The feedback lecture. *Journal of Instructional Psychology, 30*, 22–27.

Olympia, D. E., Petterson, H., & Christiansen, E. (2005). Behavior contracting. In S. W. Lee (Ed.), *Encyclopedia of school psychology* (pp. 46–49). Thousand Oaks, CA: Sage.

Olympia, D. E., Sheridan, S. M., & Jenson, W. (1994). Homework: A natural means of home-school collaboration. *School Psychology Quarterly, 9*, 60–80.

Ortiz, S. O., & Flanagan, D. P. (2002). Best practices in working with culturally diverse children and families. In A. Thomas & J. Grimes (Eds.), *Best practices in school psychology IV* (pp. 337–351). Bethesda, MD: National Association of School Psychologists.

Owen, S. V. (2001). Test review of the Achievement Motivation Profile (AMP). From B. S. Plake & J. C. Impara (Eds.), *The fourteenth mental measurement yearbook* [Electronic version]. Retrieved from the Buros Institute's *Test Reviews Online* website: http//www.unl.edu/buros

Oyserman, D., Bybee, D., & Terry, K. (2004) Possible selves as roadmaps. *Journal of Research in Personality, 38*, 130–149.

Pan, W., & Tang, M. (2005). Students' perceptions on factors of statistics anxiety and instructional strategies. *Journal of Instructional Psychology, 32*, 205–214.

Paris, S. G., & Jacobs, J. E. (1984). The benefits of informed instruction for children's reading awareness and comprehension skills. *Child Development, 55*, 2083–2093.

Paris, S. G., Lipson, M. Y. & Wixson, K. K. (1983). Becoming a strategic reader. *Contemporary Educational Psychology, 8*, 293–316.

Paris, S. G., & Paris, A. H. (2001). Classroom applications of research on self-regulated learning. *Educational Psychologist, 36*, 89–101.

Paris, S. G., & Winograd, P. (1990). How metacognition can promote academic learning and instruction. In B. F. Jones & L. Idol (Eds.), *Dimensions of thinking and cognitive instruction* (pp. 15–51). Hillsdale, NJ: Erlbaum.

Patrick, H., & Middleton, M. J. (2002). Turning the kaleidoscope: What we see when self-regulated learning is viewed with a qualitative lens. *Educational Psychologist, 37*, 27–39.

Pauk, W. (2000). *How to study in college*. Boston: Houghton Mifflin.

Peeters, M. A. G., & Rutte, C. G. (2005). Time management behavior as a moderator for job demand–control interaction. *Journal of Occupational Health Psychology, 10*, 64–75.

Peklaj, C. (2002). Differences in students' self-regulated learning according to their achievement and sex. *Studia Psychologica, 44*, 29–43.

Pekrun, R., Goetz, T., Titz, W., & Perry, R. P. (2002). Academic emotions in students' self-regulated learning and achievement. *Educational Psychologist, 37*, 91–105.

Perry, N. E. (1998). Young children's self-regulated learning and contexts that support it. *Journal of Educational Psychology, 90*, 715–729.

Perry, N. E., Nordby, C. J., & VandeKamp, K. O. (2003). Promoting self-regulated reading and writing at home and school. *Elementary School Journal, 103*, 317–338.

Phillips, D. (1987). Socialization of perceived academic competence among highly competent children. *Child Development, 58*, 1308–1320.

Piaget, J., & Inhelder, B. (1969). *The psychology of the child.* New York: Basic Books.

Pianta, R. C. (1999). *Enhancing relationships between children and teachers*. Washington, DC: American Psychological Association.

Pickering, S., & Gathercole, S. (2001). *Working Memory Test Battery for Children (WMTB-C)*. London: Harcourt Assessment.

Pintrich, P. R. (2000a). Multiple goals, multiple pathways: The role of goal orientation in learning and achievement. *Journal of Educational Psychology, 92*, 544–555.

Pintrich, P. R. (2000b). The role of goal orientation in self-regulated learning. In M. Boekaerts, P. R. Pintrich, & M. Zeidner (Eds.), *Handbook of self-regulation* (pp. 451–502). San Diego, CA: Academic Press.

Pintrich, P. R., & Schunk, D. (2002). *Motivation in education: Theory, research, and application* (2nd ed.). Upper Saddle River, NJ: Prentice Hall.

Pintrich, P. R., Smith, D. A., Garcia, T., & McKeachie, W. J. (1991). *A manual for the use of the Motivated Strategies for Learning Questionnaire (MSLQ)*. Ann Arbor, MI: National Center for Research to Improve Postsecondary Teaching and Learning.

Poznanski, E. O., & Mokros, H. B. (1996). *Children's Depression Rating Scale, Revised (CDRS-R)*. Los Angeles: Western Psychological Services.

Pressley, M. (2000). What should comprehension instruction be the instruction of? In M. Kamil, P. Mosenthal, P. Pearson, & R. Barr (Eds.), *Handbook of reading research* (Vol. 3, pp. 545–561). Mahwah, NJ: Erlbaum.

Pressley, M., & Afflerbach, P. (1995). *Verbal reports of reading: The nature of constructively responsive reading.* Hillsdale, NJ: Erlbaum.

Pressley, M., Cariglia-Bull, T., & Deane, S. (1987). Short-term memory, verbal competence, and age as predictors of imagery instructional effectiveness. *Journal of Experimental Child Psychology, 43*, 194–211.

Pritchard, R. (1987). Effects on student writing of teacher training in the National Writing Project Model. *Written Communication, 4*, 51–67.

Puntambekar, S. (1995). Helping students learn "how to learn" from texts: Towards an ITS for developing metacognition. *Instructional Science, 23*, 163–182.

Puustinen, M., & Pulkkinen, L. (2001). Models of self-regulated learning: A review. *Scandinavian Journal of Educational Research, 45*, 269–286.

Quintana, C., Zhang, M., & Krajcik, J. (2005). A framework for supporting metacognitive aspects of online inquiry through software-based scaffolding. *Educational Psychologist, 30*, 235–244.

Rademacher, J. A., Schumaker, J. B., & Deshler, D. D. (1996). Development and validation of a classroom assignment routine for inclusive settings. *Learning Disability Quarterly, 19*, 163–177.

Randi, J., & Corno, L. (2000). Teacher innovations in self-regulated learning. In M. Boekaerts & P. R. Pintrich (Eds.), *Handbook of self-regulation* (pp. 651–685). San Diego, CA: Academic Press

Rauch, M., & Fillenworth, C. (1995). Motivating students to use newly learned study strategies. *Journal of Reading, 38*, 567–568.

Reed, J. H., Schallert, D. L., & Deithloff, L. F. (2002). Investigating the interface between self-regulation and involvement process. *Educational Psychologist, 37*, 53–57.

Reetz, L. J. (1991). Parental perceptions of homework. *Rural Educator, 12*(2), 14–19.

Reid, R., & Harris, K. R. (1989). Self-monitoring of performance. *LD Forum, 15*, 39–42.

Resnick, L. (1988). Teaching mathematics as an ill-structured discipline. In R. Charles & E. Silver (Eds.), *The teaching and assessing of math problem solving* (pp. 32–60). Hillsdale, NJ: Erlbaum.

Reynolds, C. R., & Bigler, E. D. (1994). *Test of Memory and Learning.* Austin, TX: PRO-ED.

Reynolds, C. R., & Kamphaus, R. W. (2004). *Behavior Assessment System for Children, Second Edition (BASC-2).* Circle Pines, MN: American Guidance Services.

Rhoades, M. M., & Kratochwill, T. R. (1998). Parent training and consultation: An analysis of a homework intervention program. *School Psychology Quarterly, 13*, 241–265.

Rhode, C., Morgan, D. P., & Young, K. R. (1983). Generalization and maintenance of treatment gains of behaviorally handicapped students from resource room to regular classroom using self-evaluation procedures. *Journal of Applied Behavior Analysis, 16*, 171–188.

Rivera-Batiz, F. L. (1992). Quantitative literacy and the likelihood of employment among young adults in the United States. *Journal of Human Resources, 27*, 313–328.

Robinson, D. R., Schofield, J. W., & Steers-Wentzell, K. L. (2005). Peer and cross-age tutoring in math: Outcomes and their design implications. *Educational Psychology Review, 17*, 327–362.

Rock, M. L. (2005). Use of strategic self-monitoring to enhance academic engagement, productivity, and accuracy of students with and without exceptionalities. *Journal of Positive Behavior Interventions, 7*, 3–17.

Rogers, C. (1951). *Client-centered therapy.* Boston: Houghton Mifflin.

Rohwer, W. D. (1984). An invitation to an educational psychology of studying. *Educational Psychologist, 19*, 1–14.

Rolheiser, C. (1996). *Self-evaluation: Helping students get better at it.* Toronto: Visutronx.

Rosenberg, M. S. (1989). The effects of daily homework assignments on the acquisition of basic skills by students with learning disabilities. *Journal of Learning Disabilities, 22*, 314–322.

Rosenfield, S. A. (1995). Instructional consultation: A model for delivery in schools. *Journal of Educational and Psychological Consultation, 6*, 297–316.

Ross, J. A., Hogaboam-Gray, A., & Rolheiser, C. (2002). Student self-evaluation in grade 5–6 mathematics: Effects on problem-solving achievement. *Educational Assessment, 8*, 43–59.

Sabers, J., & Bonner, S. (in press). Test review of the Academic Competence Evaluation Scales (ACES). From B. S. Plake & J. C. Impara (Eds.), *The sixteenth mental measurement yearbook* [Electronic version]. Retrieved from the Buros Institute's *Test Reviews Online* website: http//www.unl.edu/buros

Saddler, B., Moran, S., Graham, S., & Harris, K. R.

(2004). Preventing writing difficulties: The effects of planning strategy instruction on the writing performance of struggling writers. *Exceptionality, 12*, 3–17.

Saddler, P. M., & Good, E. (2006). The impact of self- and peer-grading on student learning. *Educational Assessment, 11*, 1–31.

Sainsbury, M. (2003). Thinking aloud: Children's interactions with text. *Reading: Literacy and Language*, 131–135.

Salend, S. J., & Gajria, M. (1995). Increasing the homework completion rates of students with mild disabilities. *Remedial and Special Education, 16*, 271–278.

Salend, S. J., & Schliff, J. (1989). An examination of the homework practices of teachers of students with learning disabilities. *Journal of Learning Disabilities, 22*, 621–623.

Santa Rita, E. D. (1997). *Counselor-mediated contracts in self-management for students in the New Start Program*. Bronx Community College, New York. (ERIC Document Reproduction Service No. ED416912)

Sayger, T. V., Horne, A. M., Walker, L. M., & Passmore, J. L. (1988). Social learning family therapy with aggressive children: Treatment outcome and maintenance. *Journal of Family Psychology, 1*, 261–285.

Scheid, K. (1993). *Helping students become strategic learners: Guidelines for teaching*. Cambridge, MA: Brookline Books.

Schmitt, M. C. (1988). Effects of an elaborated directed reading activity on the metacomprehension skills of third graders. *National Reading Conference Yearbook, 37*, 167–181.

Schneider, W., & Pressley, M. (1997). *Memory development between two and twenty* (2nd ed.). Mahwah, NJ: Erlbaum.

Schoenfeld, A. H. (1988). When good teaching leads to bad results: The disasters of well-taught mathematics courses. *Educational Psychologist, 23*, 145–166.

Schoenfeld, A. H. (1992). Learning to think mathematically: Problem solving, metacognition, and sense-making in mathematics. In D. A. Grouws (Ed.), *Handbook of research on mathematics learning and teaching* (pp. 334–370). New York: Macmillan.

Schraw, G. (in press). Test review of the Behavior Rating Inventory of Executive Function. From B. S. Plake & J. C. Impara (Eds.), *The fifteenth mental measurement yearbook* [Electronic version]. Retrieved from the Buros Institute's *Test Reviews Online* website: http//www.unl.edu/buros

Schuerger, J. M. (2001). *16PF Adolescent Personality Questionnaire (APQ)*. Champaign, IL: Institute for Personality and Ability Testing.

Schunk, D. H. (1987). Peer models and children's behavioral change. *Review of Educational Research, 57*, 149–174.

Schunk, D. H. (1999). Social–self interaction and achievement behavior. *Educational Psychologist, 34*, 219–227.

Schunk, D. H., & Ertmer, P. A. (2000). Self-regulation and academic learning: Self-efficacy enhancing interventions. In M. Boekaerts, P. R. Pintrich, & M. Zeidner (Eds.), *Handbook of self-regulation* (pp. 631–649). San Diego, CA: Academic Press.

Schunk, D. H., & Zimmerman, B. J. (1994). *Self-regulation of learning and performance: Issues and educational applications*. Hillsdale, NJ: Erlbaum.

Schutz, P. A., & Lanehart, S. L. (2002). Introduction: Emotions in education. *Educational Psychologist, 37*, 67–68.

Scott, J., Wolking, B., Stoutimore, J., & Harris, C. (1990). Challenging reading for students with mild handicaps. *Teaching Exceptional Children, 22*, 32–35.

Scruggs, T. E., Mastropieri, M. A., & Tolf-Veit, D. (1986). The effects of coaching on the standardized test performance of learning disabled and behaviorally disordered students. *Remedial and Special Education, 7*(5), 37–41.

Sebranek, P., Meyer, V., & Kemper, D. (1998). *Write source 2000*. Wilmington, MA: Great Source Educational Group.

Sedita, J. (2001). *Study skills: A Landmark School study guide*. Prides Crossing, MA: Landmark School.

Seipp, B. (1991). Anxiety and academic performance. *Anxiety Research, 4*, 27–41.

Seligman, M. (1991). *Learned optimism*. New York: Knopf.

Seon, Y., & King, R. (1997). *Study skills can make a major difference*. Paper presented at the 23rd annual conference of the American Mathematical Association of Two Year Colleges, Atlanta, GA. (ERIC Document Reproduction Service No. ED417791)

Sergent, J. (1996). A theory of attention: An information processing perspective. In G. R. Lyon & N. A. Krasnegor (Eds.), *Attention, memory, and executive function* (pp. 57–69). Baltimore: Brookes.

Sexton, M., Harris, K. R., & Graham, S. (1998). Self-regulated strategy development and the writing process: Effects on essay writing and attributions. *Exceptional Children, 64*, 295–311.

Shapiro, E. S. (1996). *Academic skills problems workbook*. New York: Guilford Press.

Shapiro, E. S., Durnan, S. L., Post, E. E., & Levinson, T. S. (2002). Self-monitoring procedures for children and adolescents. In M. R. Shinn, H. M. Walker, & G. Stoner (Eds.), *Interventions for academic and behavior problems II: Prevention and remedial approaches* (pp. 433–454). Bethesda, MD: National Association of School Psychologists.

Shapiro, S. L., & Schwartz, G. E. (2000). The role of intention in self-regulation: Toward intentional systemic mindfulness. In M. Boekaerts, P. R. Pintrich, & M. Zeidner (Eds.), *Handbook of self-regulation* (pp. 255–273). San Diego, CA: Academic Press.

Shenkman, H. (1986). A theoretical model for a total approach to independent learning from text. *Reading Psychology, 7,* 111–119.

Sheridan, S. M., Kratochwill, T. R., & Bergan, J. R. (1996). *Conjoint behavioral consultation: A procedural manual.* New York: Plenum Press.

Shernoff, D. J., Csikszentmihalyi, M., Schneider, B., & Shernoff, E. S. (2003). Student engagement in high school classrooms from the perspective of flow theory. *School Psychology Quarterly, 18,* 158–176.

Sheslow, D., & Adams, W. (2003). *Wide Range Assessment of Memory and Learning, Second Edition (WRAML2).* Lutz, FL: Psychological Assessment Resources.

Shiffman, S., & Hufford, M. R. (2001). Ecological momentary assessment. *Applied Clinical Trials, 10,* 42–47.

Shiffrin, R. M., & Atkinson, R. C. (1969). Storage and retrieval processes in long-term memory. *Psychological Review, 76*(2), 179–193.

Shumow, L. (1998). Promoting parental attunement to children's mathematical reasoning through parent education. *Journal of Applied Developmental Psychology, 19,* 109–127.

Shumow, L., & Miller, J. D. (2001). Parents' at-home and at-school academic involvement with young adolescents. *Journal of Early Adolescence, 21,* 68–91.

Sigel, I., McGillicuddy-DeLisi, A., & Goodnow, J. (1992). Introduction. In I. Sigel, A. McGillicuddy-DeLisi, & J. Goodnow (Eds.), *Parental belief systems: The psychological consequences for children* (2nd ed., pp. xiii–xv). Hillsdale, NJ: Erlbaum.

Simpkins, S. D., Davis-Kean, P. E., & Eccles, J. S. (2006). Math and science motivation: A longitudinal examination of the links between choices and beliefs. *Developmental Psychology, 42,* 70–83.

Skinner, B. F. (1953). *Science and human behavior.* New York: Macmillan.

Skinner, C. H., McLaughlin, T. F., & Logan, P. (1997). Cover, copy, and compare: A self-managed academic intervention. *Journal of Behavioral Education, 7,* 295–306.

Skinner, C. H., Skinner, A. L., & Sterling-Turner, H. E. (2002). Best practices in contingency management. In A. Thomas & J. Grimes (Eds.), *Best practices in school psychology IV* (pp. 817–830). Bethesda, MD: National Association of School Psychologists.

Skinner, C. H., Williams, R. L., & Neddenriep, C. E. (2004). Using independent group-oriented reinforcement to enhance academic performance in general education classrooms. *School Psychology Review, 33,* 384–387.

Slate, J. R., Jones, C. H., & Dawson, P. (1993). Academic skills of high school students as a function of grade, gender, and academic track. *High School Journal, 76*(4), 245–251.

Slonski-Fowler, K. E., & Truscott, S. D. (2004). General education teachers' perceptions of the preferral intervention team process. *Journal of Educational and Psychological Consultation, 15,* 1–39.

Smith, C. R. (1989). Test review of the Classroom Environment Scale, second edition (CES). From J. C. Conoley & J. J. Kramer (Eds.), *The tenth mental measurement yearbook* [Electronic version]. Retrieved from the Buros Institute's *Test Reviews Online* website: http://www.unl.edu/buros

Snow, C. E., Burns, M. S., & Griffin, P. (1998). *Preventing reading difficulties in young children.* Washington, DC: National Academy Press.

Snyder, C. R., Harris, C., & Anderson, J. R. (1991). The will and the ways: Development and validation of an individual-differences measure of hope. *Journal of Personality and Social Psychology, 60,* 570–585.

Solomon Scherzer, C. R. (in press). Review of the Parent Success Indicator. From B. S. Plake & J. C. Impara (Eds.), *The sixteenth mental measurement yearbook* [Electronic version]. Retrieved from the Buros Institute's *Test Reviews Online* website: http//www.unl.edu/buros

Son, L. K. (2004). Spacing one's study: Evidence for a metacognitive control strategy. *Journal of Experimental Psychology: Learning, Memory, and Cognition, 30,* 601–604.

Son, L. K. (2005). Metacognitive control. *The Journal of General Psychology, 132,* 347–363.

Son, L. K., & Metcalfe, J. (2000). Metacognitive and control strategies in study-time allocation. *Journal of Experimental Psychology: Learning, Memory, and Cognition, 26,* 204–221.

Stahl, S. A., & Erickson, L. G. (1986). Detection of inconsistencies by above and below average reflective and impulsive sixth graders. *Journal of Educational Research, 79,* 185–189.

Stanley, B., Slate, J. R., & Jones, C. H. (1999). Study behaviors of college preparatory and honors students in the ninth grade. *High School Journal, 82,* 165–171.

Steinberg, L., Lamborn, S. D., Dornbusch, S. M., & Darling, N. (1992). Impact of parenting practices on adolescent achievement: Authoritative parenting, school involvement, and encouragement to succeed. *Child Development, 63,* 1266–1281.

Stevens, R. J. (2003). Student team reading and writing: A cooperative learning approach to middle school literacy instruction. *Educational Research and Evaluation, 9,* 137–160.

Stevens, S. H. (1996). *The LD child and the ADHD child: Ways parents and professionals can help.* Winston-Salem, NC: Blair.

Stevenson, C. S., Whitmont, S., & Bornholt, L. (2002). A cognitive remediation programme for adults with attention deficit hyperactivity disorder. *Australian and New Zealand Journal of Psychiatry, 36*, 610–616.

Stipek, D. J. (2002). *Motivation to learn: Integrating theory and practice* (4th ed.). Boston: Allyn & Bacon.

Stipek, D. J., & Gralinski, J. H. (1991). Gender differences in children's achievement-related beliefs and emotional responses to success and failure in mathematics. *Journal of Educational Psychology, 83*, 361–371.

Stoiber, K. C., & Kratochwill, T. R. (2001). *Outcomes PME: Planning, Monitoring, Evaluating.* San Antonio, TX: Psychological Corporation.

Strage, A. A. (1998). Family context variables and the development of self-regulation in college students. *Adolescence, 33*, 17–31.

Strichart, S., & Mangrum, C. (2002). *Teaching learning strategies and study skills with students with learning disabilities, attention deficit disorders, or special needs*. Boston: Allyn & Bacon.

Strom, R. D., & Strom, S. K. (1998). *Parent Success Indicator (PSI).* Bensenville, IL: Scholastic Testing Service.

Stroudt, K. C., & Reynolds, C. R. (2006). *School Motivation and Learning Strategies Inventory (SMALSI).* Los Angeles: Western Psychological Services.

Swanson, P. N., & De La Paz, S. (1998). Teaching effective comprehension strategies to students with learning and reading disabilities. *Intervention in School and Clinic, 33*, 209–218.

Sweidel, G. B. (1996). Study strategy portfolio: A project to enhance study skills and time management. *Teaching of Psychology, 23*, 246–248.

Taylor, D. J., Lichstein, K. L., & Durrence, H. H. (2003). Insomnia as a health risk factor. *Behavioral Sleep Medicine, 1*, 227–247.

Tenny, J. L. (1992). Computer-supported study strategies for purple people. *Reading and Writing Quarterly: Overcoming Learning Difficulties, 8*, 359–377.

Thompson, G. L., & Joshua-Shearer, M. (2002). In retrospect: What college undergraduates say about their high school education. *High School Journal, 85*, 1–15.

Tindal, J. (1998). Test review of the Instructional Environment System—II: A System to Identify a Student's Instructional Needs (second edition). From J. C. Impara & B. S. Plake (Eds.), *The thirteenth mental measurement yearbook* [Electronic version]. Retrieved from the Buros Institute's *Test Reviews Online* website: http//www.unl.edu/buros

Tobias, S., Everson, H. T., & Laitusis, V. (1999). *Towards a performance based measure of metacognitive knowledge*. Paper presented at the annual meeting of the American Educational Research Association, Montréal.

Trammel, D. L., Schloss, P. J., Alper, S. (1994). Using self-recording, evaluation, and graphing to increase completion of homework assignments. *Journal of Learning Disabilities, 27*, 75–81.

Trautwein, U., & Köller, O. (2003). The relationship between homework and achievement—still much of a mystery. *Educational Psychology Review*, 15, 115–145.

Treisman, U. (1992). Studying students studying calculus: A look at the lives of minority mathematics students in college. *College Mathematics Journal, 23*, 362–372.

Troia, G. A., & Graham, S. (2002). The effectiveness of a highly explicit, teacher-directed strategy instruction routine: Changing the writing performance of students with learning disabilities. *Journal of Learning Disabilities, 35*, 290–305.

Troia, G. A., & Graham, S. (2003). Effective writing instruction across the grades: What every educational consultant should know. *Journal of Educational and Psychological Consultation, 14*, 75–89.

Troia, G. A., & Maddox, M. E. (2004). Writing instruction in middle schools: Special and general education teachers share their views and voice their concerns. *Exceptionality, 12*, 19–37.

Tuckman, B. W. (2003). The effect of learning and motivation strategies training on college students' achievement. *Journal of College Student Development, 44*, 430–437.

Turner, J. C. (1995). The influence of classroom contexts on young children's motivation for literacy. *Reading Research Quarterly, 30*, 410–441.

Urdan, T. (1997). Examining the relations among early adolescent students' goals and friends' orientation toward effort and achievement in school. *Contemporary Educational Psychology, 22*, 165–191.

Urdan, T., & Maehr, M. (1995). Beyond a two-goal theory of motivation and achievement. A case for social goals. *Review of Educational Research, 65*, 213–243.

Urdan, T., Midgely, C., & Anderman, E. M. (1998). Role of classroom goal structure in students' use of self-handicapping strategies. *American Educational Research Journal, 35*, 101–122.

U.S. Department of Education. (1997). *Parent involvement and participation*. Washington, DC: Author.

Uzuntiryaki, E., & Geban, Ö. (2005). Effect of conceptual change approach accompanied with concept mapping on understanding of solution concepts. *Instructional Science, 33*, 311–339.

Valencia, S. W., & Calfee, R. (1991). The development and use of literacy portfolios for students, classes, and teachers. *Applied Measurement in Education, 4*, 333–345.

van Ede, D. M., & Coetzee, C. H. (1996). The Metamemory, Memory Strategy, and Study Technique Inventory (MMSSTI): A factor analytic study. *South African Journal of Psychology, 26*, 89–96.

Van Eerde, W. (2003). Procrastination at work and time management training. *Journal of Psychology: Interdisciplinary and Applied, 137*, 421–434.

Van Haneghan, J. P. (1990). Third and fifth graders' use of multiple standards of evaluation to detect errors in word problems. *Journal of Educational Psychology, 82*, 352–358.

Von Secker, C. (2004). Science achievement in social contexts: Analysis from national assessment of educational progress. *Journal of Educational Research, 98*, 67–78.

Vygotsky, L. S. (1978). *Mind in society.* Cambridge, MA: Harvard University Press.

Wade, W., Trathen, W., & Schraw, G. (1990). An analysis of spontaneous study strategies. *Reading Research Quarterly, 25,* 147–166.

Wagner, R. K. (1996). From simple structure to complex function: Major trends in the development of theories, models, and measurement of memory. In G. R. Lyon & N. A. Krasnegor (Eds.), *Attention, memory, and executive function* (pp. 139–156). Baltimore: Brookes.

Walker, L. J. (2004). Overcoming the patterns of powerlessness that lead to procrastination. In H. C. Schouwenburg & C. H. Lay (Eds.), *Counseling the procrastinator in academic settings*, Washington, DC: American Psychological Association.

Warton, P. M. (2001). The forgotten voices in homework: Views of students. *Educational Psychologist, 36,* 155–165.

Watkins, A. F. (2002). Learning styles of African American children: A developmental consideration. *Journal of Black Psychology, 28*, 3–17.

Watson, T. S., & Steege, M. W. (2003). *Conducting school-based functional behavioral assessments: A practitioner's guide.* New York: Guilford Press.

Wechsler, D. (2001). *Wechsler Individual Achievement Test—Second Edition (WIAT-II)*. San Antonio, TX: Psychological Corporation.

Wechsler, D. (2003). *Wechsler Intelligence Scale for Children—Fourth Edition (WISC-IV).* San Antonio, TX: Psychological Corporation.

Weiner, B. (1994). Integrating social and personal theories of achievement striving. *Review of Educational Research, 64*, 557–569.

Weiner, R. K., Sheridan, S. M., & Jenson, W. R. (1998). The effects of conjoint behavioral consultation and a structured homework program on math completion and accuracy in junior high schools. *School Psychology Quarterly, 13*, 281–308.

Weinstein, C. E., & Mayer, R. F. (1985). The teaching of learning strategies. In M. C. Wittrock (Ed.), *Handbook of research on teaching* (3rd ed., pp. 315–329). New York: Macmillan.

Weinstein, C. E., & Palmer, D. R. (1990). *LASSI-HS: Learning and Study Strategies Inventory-High School Version*. Clearwater, FL: H & H.

Wentzel, K. R. (1993). Does being good make the grade?: Social behavior and academic competence in middle school. *Journal of Educational Psychology, 85*, 357–364.

Wentzel, K. R., & Asher, S. R. (1995). Academic lives of rejected, popular, and controversial children. *Child Development, 66*, 754–763.

Wentzel, K. R., & Watkins, D. E. (2002). Peer relationships and collaborative learning as contexts for academic enablers. *School Psychology Review, 31,* 366–377.

Wiederholt, J. L., & Bryant, B. R. (2001). *Gray Oral Reading Tests—Fourth Edition (GORT-4).* Austin, TX: PRO-ED.

Williams, R. T. (1998). Test review of the Learning and Study Strategies Inventory—High School Version. From J. C. Impara & B. S. Plake (Eds.), *The thirteenth mental measurement yearbook* [Electronic version]. Retrieved from the Buros Institute's *Test Reviews Online* website: http//www.unl.edu/buros

Williams, S., & Baxter, J. (1996). Dilemmas of discourse-oriented teaching in one middle school mathematics classroom. *Elementary School Journal, 97*, 21–38.

Winne, P. H., & Perry, N. E. (2000). Measuring self-regulated learning. In M. Boekaerts, P. R. Pintrich, & M. Zeidner (Eds.), *Handbook of self-regulation* (pp. 531–566). San Diego, CA: Academic Press.

Wise, W. B., & Olson, K. R. (1994). Computer speech and the remediation of reading and spelling problems. *Journal of Special Education Technology, 12*, 207–220.

Wittrock, M. C. (1990). Generative processes of comprehension. *Educational Psychologist, 24*, 345–376.

Woloshyn, V. E., Pressley, M., & Schneider, W. (1992). Elaborative-interrogation and prior-knowledge effects on learning of facts. *Journal of Educational Psychology, 84*, 115–124.

Wolters, C. A. (1998). Self-regulated learning and college students' regulation of motivation. *Journal of Educational Psychology, 90*, 224–235.

Wolters, C. A. (2002). Regulation of motivation. *Educational Psychologist, 38*, 189–205.

Wolters, C. A. (2003). Understanding procrastination from a self-regulated learning perspective. *Journal of Educational Psychology, 95*, 179–187.

Woodcock, R. W. (1998). *Woodcock Reading Mastery Tests—Revised.* Circle Pines, MN: American Guidance Service.

Woodcock, R. W., McGrew, K. S., & Mather, N. (2001). *Woodcock–Johnson III.* Itasca, IL: Riverside.

Woodcock, R. W., McGrew, K. S., & Mather, N. (2003). *Woodcock–Johnson III Diagnostic Supplement to the Tests of Cognitive Abilities.* Itasca, IL: Riverside.

Wu, Y., & Tsai, C. (2005). Development of elementary school students' cognitive structures and information processing strategies under long-term constructivist-oriented science instruction. *Science Education, 89,* 822–846.

Xu, J., & Corno, L. (1998). Case studies of families doing third grade homework. *Teachers College Record, 100,* 402–436.

Young, K. T. (1994). *Starting points: Meeting the needs of our youngest children.* New York: Carnegie Foundation.

Young, S. (in press). Test review of the Parent Success Indicator. From B. S. Plake & J. C. Impara (Eds.), *The sixteenth mental measurement yearbook* [Electronic version]. Retrieved from the Buros Institute's *Test Reviews Online* website: http// www.unl.edu/buros

Ysseldyke, J., & Christenson, S. (1993). *The Instructional Environment System–II: A System to Identify a Student's Instructional Needs (Second Edition).* Longmont, CO: Sopris West.

Zabrucky, K., & Ratner, H. H. (1992). Effects of passage type on comprehension monitoring and recall in good and poor readers. *Journal of Reading Behavior, 24,* 373–391.

Zeidner, M., Boekaerts, M., & Pintrich, P. (2000). Self-regulation: Directions and challenges for future research. In M. Boekaerts, P. R. Pintrich, & M. Zeidner (Eds.), *Handbook of self-regulation* (pp. 749–768). San Diego, CA: Academic Press.

Zentall, S. S., Harper, G. W., & Stormont-Spurgin, M. (1993). Children with hyperactivity and their organizational abilities. *Journal of Educational Research, 93,* 112–117.

Zhou, G., Zhang, L., & Fu, G. (2001). A study on the relationship between self-regulated learning strategy and academic achievement. *Psychological Science* (China), *24,* 612–619.

Zimmerman, B. J. (1998a). Academic studying and the development of personal skill: A self-regulatory perspective. *Educational Psychologist, 33,* 73–86.

Zimmerman, B. J. (1998b). Developing self-fulfilling cycles of academic regulation: An analysis of exemplary instruction models. In D. H. Schunk & B. J. Zimmerman (Eds.), *Self-regulated learning: From teaching to self-reflective practice* (pp. 1–18). New York: Guilford Press.

Zimmerman, B. J. (1999). Acquiring writing revision skill: Shifting from process to outcome self-regulatory goals. *Journal of Educational Psychology, 91,* 241–250.

Zimmerman, B. J. (2000a). Attaining self-regulation. In M. Boekaerts, P. R. Pintrich, & M. Zeidner (Eds.), *Handbook of self-regulation* (pp. 13–39). San Diego, CA: Academic Press.

Zimmerman, B. J. (2000b). The role of observation and emulation in the development of athletic self-regulation. *Journal of Educational Psychology, 92,* 811–817.

Zimmerman, B. J. (2002). Acquiring writing revision and self-regulatory skill through observation and emulation. *Journal of Educational Psychology, 94,* 660–668.

Zimmerman, B. J., Bonner, S., & Kovach, R. (1996). *Developing self-regulated learners: Beyond achievement to self-efficacy.* Washington, DC: American Psychological Association.

Zimmerman, B. J., & Martinez Pons, M. (1986). Development of a structured interview for assessing student use of self-regulated learning strategies. *American Educational Research Journal, 23,* 614–628.

Zimmerman, B. J., & Martinez Pons, M. (1990). Student differences in self-regulated learning: Relating grade, sex, and giftedness to self-efficacy and strategy use. *Journal of Educational Psychology, 82,* 51–59.

Zins, J. E., & Erchul, W. P. (2002). Best practices in school consultation. In A. Thomas & J. Grimes (Eds.), *Best practices in school psychology IV* (pp. 625–643). Bethesda, MD: National Association of School Psychologists.

Zuniga, K., Olson, J. K., & Winter, M. (2005). Science education for Latino/a students: Course placement and success in science. *Journal of Research in Science Teaching, 42,* 376–402.

Index

Page numbers followed by an *f, t, w,* or *h* indicate figures, tables, worksheets, or handouts.